STRATEGY FOR CHAOS

Cass Series: Strategy and History
Series Editors: Colin Gray and Williamson Murray
ISSN: 1473-6403

This new series will focus on the theory and practice of strategy. Following Clausewitz, strategy has been understood to mean the use made of force, and the threat of the use of force, for the ends of policy. This series is as interested in ideas as in historical cases of grand strategy and military strategy in action. All historical periods, near and past, and even future, are of interest. In addition to original monographs, the series will from time to time publish edited reprints of neglected classics as well as collections of essays.

1. *Military Logistics and Strategic Performance*, Thomas M. Kane

2. *Strategy for Chaos: Revolutions in Military Affairs and the Evidence of History*, Colin Gray

3. *The Myth of Inevitable US Defeat in Vietnam*, C. Dale Walton

4. *Astropolitik: Classical Geopolitics in the Space Age*, Everett C. Dolman

5. *Anglo-American Strategic Relations and the Far East, 1933–1939: Imperial Crossroads*, Greg Kennedy

STRATEGY FOR CHAOS

Revolutions in Military Affairs

and the

Evidence of History

COLIN S. GRAY

University of Reading

With a Foreword by

WILLIAMSON MURRAY

FRANK CASS

LONDON · PORTLAND, OR

First published in 2002
First published in paperback in Great Britain by
FRANK CASS PUBLISHERS
Crown House, 47 Chase Side, Southgate
London, N14 5BP

and in the United States of America by
FRANK CASS PUBLISHERS
c/o ISBS, 920 N.E. 58th Avenue, #300
Portland, Oregon, 97213-3786

Website www.frankcass.com

Transferred to Digital Printing 2005

Copyright © 2002 Colin S. Gray

Reprinted 2003

British Library Cataloguing in Publication Data

Gray, Colin S. (Colin Spencer), 1943–
Strategy for chaos: revolutions in military affairs and
the evidence of history. – (Cass series. Strategy and
history; no. 2)
1. Strategy – Philosophy 2. Strategy – History
I. Title
355.4'01

ISBN 0-7146-5186-9 (cloth)
ISBN 0-7146-8483-X
ISSN 1473-6403

Library of Congress Cataloging-in-Publication Data

Gray, Colin S.
Strategy for chaos: revolutions in military affairs and the evidence of history/Colin S.
Gray; with a foreword by Williamson Murray.
p. cm. – (Cass series – strategy and history, ISSN 1473-6403; 2)
Includes bibliographical references and index.
ISBN 0-7146-5186-9 (cloth) ISBN 0-7146-8483-X (paper)
1. Strategy. 2. Military art and science. 3. Military history, Modern–Case Studies. I.
Title. II. Series.
U162 G724 2002
355.4–dc21

2002067625

Typeset in 10½/12 Minion by Cambridge Photosetting Services

To Dr Finella Brito Babapulle, for her dedication and skill

Contents

Foreword

The gap between historians and political scientists in dealing with strategy, war and military institutions has, if anything, widened over the past several decades. On the one hand, historians, those few who remain interested in such issues – given the rush to political correctness throughout the discipline – remain mired in the peculiarities and details of their peculiar period. One might best sum up the prevailing attitudes in the historical profession in the following terms: 'Generalize or suggest larger patterns of behavior? My goodness, we certainly wouldn't want to do that, would we?' Thus, most works on military or strategic history focus on the specific with little willingness – or interest – to generalize, much less theorize, about the larger issues and patterns of war throughout the ages. And that is why Thucydides remains by far and away the greatest strategic and military historian of all time, despite the fact that he wrote his seminal work on the history of the Peloponnesian War over 2,400 years ago.

There have, of course, been a few historians, Michael Howard in particular, who have attempted to deal with the wider implications of historical research and what it might suggest to policy-makers as they grapple with the intractable intellectual and moral problems involved in the making of strategy. But, for the most part, military and strategic historians have remained a small, isolated group in a discipline more interested in fleeing from the real world than in addressing the larger questions, on which history might actually provide a dim light for the future. And they have been all too unwilling to engage in the great defense debates that swirl around Washington's Beltway or even within the larger defense community.

Political scientists, on the other hand, have been all too willing to theorize without coming to grips with the harsh complexities of historical research or of the alien world – at least to many of them – of real facts. The result has been theories that bear little relation either to history or to how human institutions work. Yet, as Clausewitz suggested in his seminal work *On War*, any theory of war must remain closely tied to the historical record – at least, as we can know it. Theories of war and strategy which remove themselves from the realities of the historical record not only become increasingly irrelevant, but can at times become positively dangerous.

There have been a few political scientists who have been willing to grapple with historical scholarship in its breadth and depth. In the United States, the late Michael Handel and Eliot Cohen have brought a sense of the complexities as well as the rigor of historical scholarship to their work. By remaining consistently honest to the historical record, they have been able to combine the strengths of history with that of theory to extend our understanding of the role of war and strategy – past, present, and future. The third of the political scientists who have managed to relate theory to the real historical world has been the author of this present volume, Colin Gray. But, unlike Handel and Cohen, Professor Gray has also been able to inform his work with the extensive experience he gained in the Washington political and policy-making arena. Like Handel and Cohen, Gray has found his *Weltanschauung* informed, molded, and guided by Clausewitz's universe of complexity, ambiguity, and uncertainty.

Professor Gray has addressed a myriad of subjects, ranging from his early work on nuclear strategy at the Hudson Institute to naval strategy, geopolitics, and grand strategy, to name just a few. In all of his previous efforts, Gray's mixture of history, theory, and deep understanding of how the world works has placed him firmly in the camp of the neo-Clausewitzians – those who recognize that the fundamental nature, if not the means, of the conduct of war and strategy has not and will not change; at least as long as human beings are involved in the processes. In this volume, Gray now turns his analytic power to the examination of one of the most important insights to emerge from the demise of the Soviet Union and the emergence of the United States as the world's sole superpower in the early 1990s: the idea that revolutions in military affairs (RMAs) have been occurring throughout the history of the rise of the West to world domination over the past 500 years, and that we are on the brink of another period of revolutionary change in the means with which men (and increasingly women) wage war.

The idea of the possibility of revolutionary change first appeared in the writings of Soviet military theorists and leaders in the early to mid-1980s, as they began to recognize that technological developments in the US military threatened to render obsolete the vast military forces – nuclear as well as conventional – on which they had lavished so much of their gross national product. The Soviets appear to have been sensitized both by their belief in revolutionary change and by the fact that they were watching the larger framework of the emerging technological improvements of the United States (ranging from stealth and precision to computers and command and control), while the Americans themselves were submerged in the technological details of bringing new technologies on line. The Soviets were also undoubtedly sensitized by being on the receiving end of the new American capabilities in places such as the Bekka Valley.

Andrew Marshall's Office of Net Assessment in the Pentagon was the first in the United States to pick up on the significance of the Soviet writings, and in the early 1990s suggested that a fundamental change was occurring in how wars would be fought in the future. From the first, Marshall and his analysts have argued that such a revolution was only beginning, that the human elements would be by far and away the most important elements in its development, and that it was by no means certain that the US military would be the realizers of the transformation. That, of course, has not prevented a whole host of experts, both inside and outside the US government, from proclaiming that *they* have seen the future and *they* have the prescription, whatever it might be. To a considerable extent, Marshall and his office have waged a noble and at times Quixotic effort to bring wisdom to the debate about RMAs against a tide of those enamored only with technology. Not surprisingly, the US military services jumped in to add their version of the future RMA, which almost invariably boiled down to weapons systems from the Air Force's F-22 to the Army's ill-fated (and astonishingly misnamed – in view of the only place in the world where it could fight) 'Crusader' artillery system.

Yet the persistence of the RMA concept over the past decade, in a town where concepts and their acronyms appear and disappear with startling speed, suggests that there is something to the idea of revolutionary military transformation. The great difficulty that confronts the layperson, and most strategic and defense planners are lay people, is that so little historical analysis has examined the historical phenomena of RMAs outside of the seventeenth century. Various pieces exist, but for the most part they lie, untapped, deep within an historical literature more interested in the specific course of events rather than with larger patterns. Thus, it is relatively easy for the high priests of the coming RMA within the military or irresponsible political scientists to rummage through history in search of any odd fact or event that lends support to their current arguments, theories or weapons system.

In this book, Professor Gray has finally provided the analyst or policy-makers with an understanding of history, strategy, and even the processes of policy-making. He has managed to create a larger framework for thinking about revolutions in military affairs (one which largely agrees with that of MacGregor Knox and myself). In doing so, he has brought the historical record to bear on both the specifics of the processes that have contributed to RMAs in the past, as well as the creation of a theoretical framework to shed light on how we need to think about future RMAs. The theory is as important as the specifics, for without a theory there is no means to think coherently about what the past suggests. Yet, if the past does not form the basis for creating the theory, then any theory about RMAs will do. To paraphrase the old aphorism, 'if you don't know where you've been, then any road will do'.

Moreover, Professor Gray has tied strategy into the picture of understanding how to think about RMAs. Without a strategic framework that actually relates to the problems of the world as it is, all the success in creating an RMA or multiple RMAs will inevitably be for nothing, as the fate of Germany between

1860 and 1945 underlined all too well. In the 1860s, guided by the brilliance of Otto von Bismarck's grand strategy, the Prussian military's RMA destroyed a European balance of power that had lasted for over 200 years. But in the twentieth century, in World War I and World War II, the Germans created strategic frameworks of such imbecility that their nation managed not once but twice to take on virtually the whole of the rest of the world. And within that strategic framework, the German military's brilliant virtuosity in creating a number of RMAs was bound to founder. The brutal result was catastrophic defeat and the division of Germany for nearly 50 years.

As another 'American Century' begins, there is a profound lesson in this for the US military. Without a serious addressing of what the past suggests about RMAs, there will be no basis for serious debate and dialogue about potential paths to the future. Then any path, any technology, any weapons system will do, at least until war and the enemy appear to disabuse us of our arrogance and ignorance. In the end, Colin Gray has done an immense service not only to the historical and political-science communities, but to those who make strategic and military policy in the Pentagon as well. For the former, he has framed the debate about RMAs for the foreseeable future. For the latter, he has provided a deeply serious work of scholarship to frame the thinking that must take place. Whether anyone will pay attention is another question.

Williamson Murray
Senior Fellow, Institute for Defense Analysis, Alexandria, VA
June 2002

Preface

Strategy for Chaos both symbolises and represents the high ambitions of the editors of this new series on 'Strategy and History'. This book employs the kind of theory meaningful to a social scientist trying to render historical data an evidential base to advance understanding cumulatively. To that end, the work treats its duty to theory building and to respect for historical data with equal gravity and, sometimes, scepticism. Social scientists and historians are wont to compete energetically to demonstrate to each other that they are to be trusted neither when playing at home in their supposedly professional field, nor, far less, when they play away on the road on the other field of dreams. The debate over revolutions in military affairs (RMAs), the Big American Defence Debate of the 1990s, amply rewards the collector of errors. Social-scientific errors are committed by historians, while historical howlers abound in briefings by social scientists and technocrats. Meanwhile, seriously misleading beliefs of a social scientific, technological, and historical kind are commonplace among officials and politicians whose professionalism centres around manipulation of a policy *process*. A polity requires such professionalism, as Germany demonstrated negatively and repeatedly, but it requires also that the professionals charged with the making of policy and strategy should be educated in relevant historical contexts.

The recent American RMA debate generated much more noise than illumination. Quite aside from the problem of contributors who have barely hidden service or industrial interests colouring their arguments, even scholars notably competent as theory-developing social scientists or as archival historians are apt to underperform when they wander off their usual patch. One of the purposes of this new book series is to encourage the publication of studies which make an honest and tolerably successful effort to achieve synergy between the two broad disciplines. As the text below comments at suitable junctures, historians and the history they discover characteristically reveal a pull to singularisation, towards seeing events as being unique both in themselves and in context. Social scientists and the theories they invent betray the reverse tendency: no less characteristically they reveal a rush, historians would say a premature rush, to find more general meaning in particular behaviours. Inevitably, social scientists tend to be relatively weak when they boldly go into the zone of historical case studies. For their part, historians typically are far better at writing narrative and analysing unique happenings than they are at genuinely comparative scholarship. An unsurprising result of these parallel *déformations professionelles* is that the literature of the RMA debate contains some conceptually intriguing social science, and quite solid beginnings in historical study, but the twain scarcely meet and hardly ever in the same piece of work. Whether or not *Strategy for Chaos* improves the score for joint endeavour readers must judge for themselves.

The story told in this book is the end product of the coming together – some might claim it is a multiple analytical pile-up – of three once quite distinctive streams of discontent on my part. I have been separately convinced that: (1) strategy continues to be misunderstood, a conviction reinforced by the enduring evidence of erroneous conceptual usage (in much the same way I have difficulty taking on trust people who mispronounce 'nuclear', though I am assured that this is just a quaint American regionalism); (2) ideas about RMAs have been overdeveloped overly rapidly in the white heat of once intense American debate that was driven more by official encouragement, fashion, resources for study, and an absence of alternative *big* topics, than by the march of emerging, if contending, understanding(s); and (3) *complexity–nonlinearity–* (and especially)*chaos* theory has been accepted unduly uncritically by some generally prudent scholars of several professional persuasions as helping to explain the very nature of war and strategy. With respect to the third item in this triad I was somewhat surprised to find that the scientific world was by no means bowled over by the claims of chaos theory. I was less surprised to discover that the scholar (Alan Beyerchen) and the service (the US Marine Corps) who led the way in public recognition of the importance of nonlinearity and even chaos, had really 'lost the plot' from the Clausewitzian canon, when that canon is read reasonably. I came to the working conclusion that although war is the realm of chance, as Clausewitz claims, it is akin to a game of cards wherein the cards are not dealt wholly at random (my amendment to the master). If war is truly chaotic, with the outcome effectively the random and frequently nonlinear product of a host of totally unpredictable and hugely complex relations, then strategy has to be moot. Indeed, Clausewitz's own definition of strategy, 'The use of engagements for the object of the war', could be contradicted by such a wholesale nonlinear understanding of war. Plainly, some modern scholars have been overenthusiastic in their hasty borrowing of exciting ideas from alien scientific realms. Strategy is not meteorology and one size in theory does not fit both.

Both seriatim and holistically, I have sought to pursue better understanding of (1) strategy in general; (2) RMAs in general; and even (3) three candidate historical RMAs. My scholarly purpose simply has been to advance the frontier of knowledge in these highly contested areas, while my public policy purpose has been to seek to make a modest contribution to the better education of those who need to make decisions on our behalf concerning the dawning of an alleged information-led RMA. The occasional forays below into the murkily fluid dynamics of chaos theory are designed to contribute to the deeper understanding of strategy which, I claim, must govern and assay RMA performance.

Strategy for Chaos had its origins in a long-standing fascination with strategic theory which is embedded in, and occasionally refuelled by, the 'issue of the day' in public policy debate. Readers may detect some complementarities between the argument below and my 1999 (*Modern Strategy*) and 1990 (*War, Peace, and Victory*) books, whose foci bore some close association to those here. It is one thing simply to read and think about a *big idea*, such as RMA, absorbing the contending views of rivals in debate; it is quite another to have to expose one's own opinion on the matter. For placing me under the obligation to stand up and be counted somewhere on the spectrum of opinion on RMA, I must thank and blame my friend Jan Breemer of the Naval Post-Graduate School, Monterey, CA, and, behind him, Andrew Marshall of the Office of Net Assessment in the Office of the Secretary of Defense. At Jan Breemer's almost brutal insistence I drafted a long conference paper in 1995 which, even when later lightly translated into a monograph published under the auspices of the British Army (*The American Revolution in Military Affairs* in the Occasional Paper series of the Strategic and Combat Studies Institute of the then-Staff College), succeeded probably too well in being painfully even-handed between truth and error.

Another good friend, and this time now a colleague also – as co-editor of this new book series – Williamson ('Wick') Murray, a scholar advocate not renowned for being charitable to error, probably has had the most profound impact upon the arguments below. As my footnotes and highly 'select' bibliography make clear, he has played little short of a towering role in the recent debate over military innovation, both as scholarly entrepreneur and as individual scholar. I am grateful to him for his ability to present sharply framed arguments, with which I typically, though not invariably, agree. He is a superb example of a scholar who can function in the role of historical conscience for us poor benighted social scientists who have been known to raid the historical data, real or rumoured, in search of anecdotes to illustrate our grand theories. I despair for his proper appreciation of the effectiveness of the British Expeditionary Force in the First World War, but no one can be perfect. His book (edited with MacGregor Knox), *The Dynamics of Military Revolution, 1300–2050* (2001), is the outstanding collection of historical case studies of RMAs we have long needed. On a more personal note, I must thank Wick for his careful critical review of the manuscript of this book. Given that the final choice on which advice to accept is, of course, mine alone, he is not responsible for my literary infelicities, historical errors, or unjust arguments. Similarly, I am very grateful to Dale Walton and James Kiras for their editorial assistance. When invited to slash and burn, they knew their duty. Because this is a book designed primarily to help advance strategic theory, with some regret, and at a late stage, I chose to drop an extensive chapter on the origins and history of the RMA debate of the 1990s. Along with the additional historical case studies that I might have included, this conscious omission was mandated by the need to keep the manuscript within a length tolerable to the publisher.

Although there is a sense in which this book is all about the information-led RMA which is currently unfolding, with some reluctance I elected to deny myself the pleasure of treating this moving story – precisely because it is a moving story – as a case study. I admit to the conviction that a historical case study should have a historical conclusion, or at least the simulacrum of such (as with the defeat of the USSR in the nuclear-shadowed Cold War). Since I believe that strategy and RMAs do not vary in their nature, structure, and dynamics from period to period, there is no particular merit in seeking contemporaneity for its own sake. What the 'Afghan model' of US warcraft means for the future of war is a subject we can leave to journalists and think-tank analysts. Joint warfare reached a new stage late in 2001, when special focus teamed with long-range air power dropping satellite-assisted JDAMs (Joint Direct Attack Munitions). Whether or not this new variant of close air support, a variant which appears to retire the need for large and heavy (US) ground forces – and even for large air fleets – is a model for future conflict, war, strategy, and RMAs have persisting structures. What is seen today, whether it is war in South Africa in 1900, or war in Europe in 1918, is not *the* mould of future war. Instead, a contemporary combat, no matter how revolutionary it may appear, is but one very partial guide to the direction taken by strategic affairs.

Finally, I must thank my wife and daughter, Valerie and TJ, for their unbounded love and sustenance during what has proved to be an unusually long and seriously fraught literary pregnancy and birth. These have been quite exceptionally difficult times for my family, for which no bald statement of thanks can even approach adequacy. But you know the truth of it.

Abbreviations

ABM	anti-ballistic missile
BEF	British Expeditionary Force
BMD	ballistic missile defence
C⁴ISR	command, control, communications, computers, intelligence, surveillance and reconnaissance
CBSO	Counter-Battery Staff Office
CJCS	Chairman of Joint Chiefs of Staff
CPSU	Communist Party of the Soviet Union
CSA	Confederate States of America
DGZ	designated ground zero
DoD	Department of Defense (US)
JCS	Joint Chiefs of Staff
JDAM	joint direct attack munitions
LMG	light machine gun
LNO	limited nuclear option
MAD	mutual assured destruction
MLR	main line of resistance
MOE	measures of effectiveness
MR	military revolution
MTR	military-technical revolution
OHL	*Oberste Heeresleitung* (Supreme Army Command)
OMG	operational manoeuvre group
ONA	Office of Net Assessment
OODA	observation, orientation, decision, action
QDR	Quadrennial Defense Review
RMA	revolution in military affairs
SAC	Strategic Air Command
SALT	Strategic Arms Limitation Talks
SDI(O)	Strategic Defence Initiative (Organisation)
TQM	total quality management
USAF	United States Air Force
WMD	weapons of mass destruction

1

High Concept

By a wide margin, the idea of a revolution in military affairs (RMA) was the concept-of-the-decade among Western strategic thinkers in the 1990s.[1] RMA is a classic case of what, by analogy, Hollywood means by 'high concept'. As such a concept, RMA was fashionable and therefore literally bankable. Almost any topic that could carry the RMA label found a ready sponsor. One should not be unduly cynical about this phenomenon. Theory is important for future practice, and theorists require patrons. The market for strategic ideas is not entirely one of unrestricted open competition. The academy does not rule on the salience of particular ideas. Rather, as Raymond Aron expressed it: 'Strategic thought draws its inspiration each century, or rather at each moment of history, from the problems which events themselves pose.'[2] Aron was almost correct, but it is more true to claim that strategic thought draws its inspiration at each moment of history from the problems and opportunities flagged by officials acting as opinion leaders. It is the 'spin' put on contemporary challenges by a Secretary of State John Foster Dulles, or a Secretary of Defense Robert S. McNamara, that generates great debates, in their cases about nuclear deterrence and strategic stability.[3]

Of the many high concepts in strategic studies that were the focus of more and less scholarly exposition from the 1940s through to the 1990s, RMA ranks at the more imperial end of the scale of grandiosity. Such ranking is not reduced by the fact that RMA transpired to be a hugely contestable concept. That said, notably expansive understanding of what the RMA debate is all about has been signalled by significant players in the realm of strategy. US Secretary of Defense William S. Cohen advised that: 'A Revolution in Military Affairs (RMA) occurs when a nation's military seizes an opportunity to transform its strategy, military doctrine, training, education, organisation, equipment, operations, and tactics to achieve decisive military results in fundamentally new ways.'[4] There are notable problems with this definition, but Secretary Cohen's words are worth quoting both for the clarity with which they announce the importance of an RMA and for the scope of the claims advanced. Cohen talks of transformation, of decisive military results, and about fundamentally new methods. We are in the realm of high concept, indeed.

RMA is almost the latest of the high concepts around which policy-oriented theory in strategic studies has swirled over the past half-century.[5] The intellectual and policy progenitors to RMA include containment in the 1940s, nuclear deterrence and then limited war in the 1950s, strategic stability and arms control in the 1960s, détente in the 1970s, ballistic missile defence (BMD), and competitive strategies in the 1980s. Asymmetric threats, strategy, and warfare succeeded RMA in the late 1990s and the 2000s. Although some among that distinctly mixed bag of ideas had the potential to open doors to wide and deep understanding of major strands in strategic history,[6] the RMA hypothesis of the 1990s had the possibility of functioning as super-theory. Behind the hypothesis that an RMA was under way in the 1990s was the necessarily overarching proposition that the course of strategic history has been shaped by an irregular succession of great discontinuities which we are calling *revolutions* in military affairs, but which sometimes are referred to as military transformations. The very concept itself postulates the central significance of such discontinuities. The RMA hypothesis rests upon a theory which purports to explain, at least with broad brush strokes, how, why, when, and by which agency strategic history advanced, if not prospered.

The various official and commercial patrons of RMA theory (and theories) in the 1990s undoubtedly were motivated largely by parochial – albeit legitimate – concerns of US defence policy and even simply by business opportunity. The theory which those patrons triggered, however, was soon to appear anything but parochial as to client and topic. For example, in 1994, one of the earlier and better of the contributions to the RMA debate provided a candidate historical context for the developments of the 1990s that allegedly could be traced through ten succeeding RMAs from the fourteenth century to the present day.[7] In the mid-1990s there was a modest scale of mobilisation among professional historians as they scampered to protect both their turf and the quality of scholarship (i.e. good history) from ruthless seizure and exploitation by strategic theorists more concerned to illustrate an argument than to write careful history.[8]

This book is about matters historical, strategic theoretical, and sociological, while most especially it is about the connections between all three. More specifically, the discussion explores the strategic history of the past two hundred years, the period which frames the three historical case studies examined (in Chapters 6–8). I am interested in probing how social science and history have collaborated, and can collaborate, to contribute to a better understanding of the course of events.[9] As strategic theory should be able to improve understanding of history, so a faithful approach to history should enable the social scientist to apply theory to good effect in the interpretation of the richness of historical experience. There needs to be a constant dialogue between the social scientist-strategic theorist and the historian.

To deconstruct the book's title, the complex subject of strategy and revolutions in military affairs necessarily always stands on the edge of the chaos that lurks in the sometimes nonlinear realm of the use of force for political purposes. With due thanks to Christopher J. Langton, I acknowledge readily writings on chaos and complexity theory as one of the propellants for this analysis.[10] Complexity, even chaos, theory, duly translated for human behaviour, is important to my story because it poses a potentially fatal threat to the integrity of some leading variants of the RMA hypothesis. That hypothesis, though vulnerable to assault when it appears either in simple technocratic form, or, of course, when it is caricatured, nonetheless has performed valuable service, in some cases if only for its illustration of strategic error. The RMA debate of the 1990s sparked scholarly reconsideration of the nature of strategy and strategic effectiveness which, though scarcely novel in its outcome, highlighted matters of great significance for security which people and organisations are wont to forget. Argument about an RMA in the 1990s, and more broadly about RMAs in strategic history, have had the unexpected, certainly the unintended, consequence of flushing out new or refurbished theory on the nature and working of strategy. Truly, serendipity rules. With its focus upon allegedly revolutionary discontinuities, the RMA postulate and RMA theory slid unwarily into a debate over whether the nature, or only the character, of strategy and war changes.[11]

STRATEGY, COMPLEX AND SOMETIMES NONLINEAR

This book broadly is about strategic effectiveness, and narrowly concerns the contribution of alleged RMAs to that effectiveness. The nature, structure, and functioning of strategy are vital to the argument, as indeed is judgement on the ever changing tactical character, or – following Clausewitz – grammar, of strategy.[12] Because RMAs must function to express strategy, it is only by understanding the nature and working of strategy that a grip can be secured upon the promise in an RMA. Similarly, judicious interpretation of the constituents and the effect of historical RMAs can rest only upon a mature comprehension of strategy.

It is necessary to register the definition of seven key terms: *strategy, strategic history, war, RMA, nonlinearity, chaos,* and *strategic effectiveness.* The following are the connections between these terms for the limited purposes of this text: RMAs operate through strategy – certainly through strategic effectiveness – in and as strategic history which is inherently prone to some nonlinearity and can be chaotic in its course and consequences.

By *strategy* I mean the use made of force and the threat of force for the ends of policy. Of the terms defined here, strategy comes closest to enjoying truly authoritative treatment. My verbal formula is only the lightest of adaptations from Carl von Clausewitz: 'Strategy [is] the use of engagements for the object of the war.'[13] The most essential quality of this definition is that it insists upon

3

the instrumentality of strategy. Strategy is neither the use of force itself, nor is it policy, rather it is the bridge that should unite the two.

By *strategic history* I mean the course of historical events most directly affected by the threat or use of force. There is no suggestion implicit in the concept that a high fence and moat can or should separate strategic from non-strategic affairs. I take a broad and inclusive view of my subject. While acknowledging wholeheartedly the merit in the approach to strategic phenomena known as 'war and society',[14] and while recognising the continuous two-way traffic between civilian and military realms, still it is desirable and necessary to distinguish the nature of the subject of strategy. While conceding that ultimately everything relates to everything else, that concession does not cancel the analytical merit in asserting the integrity of strategic history as a field of study.[15] There is no clear outer boundary line, rather is there a grey zone, demarcating the strategic from the extra-strategic, but at least we have a decision rule (relevance to the threat or use of force) to assist us in judging what is more, or less, pertinent to our enquiries. The merit in this use of 'strategic' illuminates by contrast the reasons why the largely vacuous, at least unduly inclusive, concept of 'security' is best eschewed.[16] I am not hostile to security studies, but I do not know exactly what they are or how I would proceed to find out.

By *war* I mean organised violence carried on by political units against each other for political motives. This is a modest expansion (with the addition of 'for political motives') of the workmanlike definition provided by Hedley Bull in his book, *The Anarchical Society*.[17] Given the admittedly historically restricted scope of this enquiry (*c.*1800–*c.*2000), the contestability of definitions of war is not of great significance. However, the hypothesis that a contemporary information-led RMA is under way does refer to an emerging political and strategic context wherein, according to some theorists, traditional institutions – including war and the state – lose much of the character that has been their trademark since the middle of the seventeenth century.[18]

By *RMA* I mean a radical change in the character or conduct of war, or, in Jeffrey R. Cooper's words, 'a discontinuous increase in military capability and effectiveness'.[19] Unlike strategy and war, definition of this concept requires careful policing more for what should be excluded than included. A decade of experience with RMA debate highlights the necessity for an open mind as to catalytic agent or agents. Above all else, it is vital not to require by definition that RMAs be triggered by new technology. A classic example of what to avoid is revealed in the still popular definition offered in 1994 by Andrew F. Krepinevich. This definition has the signal virtue of recognising much of the complexity of the process of the RMA, but still it has two fatal flaws.

> What is a military revolution? It is what occurs when the application of new technologies into a significant number of military systems combines

with innovative operational concepts and organisational adaptations in a way that fundamentally alters the character and conduct of conflict. It does so by producing a dramatic increase – often an order of magnitude or greater – in the combat potential and military effectiveness of armed forces.[20]

The first fatal flaw in Krepinevich's definition is his requirement that an RMA functions, inter alia, with the application of new technologies.[21] The second such flaw is his claim that an RMA produces a dramatic increase in combat potential and military effectiveness. This point is of a commonsense nature, and should be true. However, it suffers from the same generic weakness of circular logic as did Basil Liddell Hart's imperial concept of the indirect approach in strategy. What is the indirect approach? It is the approach that tends to deliver meaningful victory.[22] How can we locate this wonderful approach in strategic history? We find it in the records of strategic success. If strategy works well, it has to be a case of the indirect approach. Returning to the notion of RMAs, how do we find them? When there is a dramatic increase in combat potential and military effectiveness. But can such potential and effectiveness be the product of events or processes other than RMAs? Although RMAs might be triggered by change in several, or more, of strategy's dimensions, it cannot be sound to require such change to result in a 'dramatic increase in combat potential and military effectiveness'. What if a military machine is revolutionised, but fails to deliver? If great military success is attributed as a matter of course to RMAs, then the RMA concept is diluted into thorough inutility. A combination of evolutionary improvement and an inept foe can suffice to bring victory. RMA is not a necessary, let alone a sufficient, condition for victory.

By *nonlinearity* I refer to a condition structurally characteristic of, though not always dominant in, strategy and war that denies authority to the rules of proportionality and additivity.[23] In a nonlinear system, output can be disproportionate to input, while the whole is not simply the aggregation of its component parts. For example, culture, ethics, and geography are not just pieces of the puzzle that can be slotted together with other such pieces to comprise the whole edifice of strategy. The problem is that culture, ethics, and geography interpenetrate, even though these dimensions of strategy are notionally, and in one case physically, distinguishable. Strategic culture is both a context that yields meaning to stimuli and – inconveniently for ease of study by scholars – is within the human and organisational players in that context.[24] Similarly, physical geography, though objectively distinctive, helps shape culture and indeed all dimensions of strategy.[25] If this seems rather opaque, readers are requested to withhold judgement for the moment. The most essential qualities of nonlinearity for the argument in this book are, to repeat, the apparently 'chaotic' disproportion between modest (or immodest) input and immodest (or

5

modest) output, and consequently the frequently non-additive working of strategy and war. A system is said to be 'chaotic' when its performance is both nonlinear and sensitive to initial conditions.[26] Therefore, by *chaos* I mean a condition of such complexity (e.g. strategy's many dimensions, as explained in detail in Chapters 4 and 5) and nonlinearity in performance, that prediction of system performance becomes all but impossible.

Strategy has to be viewed in two complementary, though tension-fraught, perspectives. First, it is a whole phenomenon which needs to be approached as a unity. Both Clausewitz and T. E. Lawrence understood this point intuitively and analytically. The former warns strongly that 'it would be disastrous to try to develop our understanding of strategy by analysing these factors [moral, physical, mathematical, geographical, and statistical] in isolation, since they are usually interconnected in each military action in manifold and intricate ways'.[27] The latter appreciates 'the whole house of war in its structural aspect, which was strategy, in its arrangements, which were tactics, and in the sentiments of its inhabitants, which was psychology'.[28] Lawrence advises that these apparently distinctive matters are really better regarded as 'points of view from which to ponder the elements of war'. Second, strategy needs to be appreciated as a house with many rooms, a phenomenon with distinguishable, though interpenetrating, elements, factors, or dimensions. Strategy is not perennially essentially shaped, let alone driven, by – for example – technology, geography, culture, theory and doctrine, or even by people. There is no truly independent variable or variables that can be studied, or manipulated, to yield reliable predictive advice on how strategic effectiveness in the necessary amount can be guaranteed.

Strategic effectiveness is a less common concept and term than is military effectiveness. This comparative rarity reflects accurately enough the greater difficulty of strategic, over military, effectiveness. By *strategic effectiveness* I mean the net (i.e. with the adversary dimension factored in) effectiveness of grand strategic performance, which is to say of behaviour relevant to the threat or actual use of force. That effectiveness can be measured in regard to the advancement of political goals. Military effectiveness, even in the form of a series of crushing victories, need not equate to strategic effectiveness because strategy's political dimension may shape a contest that is all but beyond military help.[29]

Strategy (and war) is complex and sometimes nonlinear in both technical and commonsense meanings. Military genius in command, advantageous geography, a supremely just cause – each, and its obverse, can be important, but strategic performance, indeed the course of strategic history writ large and small, cannot be reduced to any one of these factors. Not only does strategy have several, or many – as preferred for understanding – dimensions, but those dimensions are not entirely discrete, save conceptually. The levels of analysis – which is to say policy, grand strategy, military strategy, tactics, and preparation of all kinds for war – are thoroughly interdependent. For example, tactical behaviour is pointless out of strategic context, but strategic behaviour has to be done tactically. Beyond that functional view, each of the many dimensions of strategy behaves dynamically in ever shifting relations with every other one, while the whole edifice interacts with its several political and social, inter alia, contexts.

Alan Beyerchen takes the high ground of proper understanding when he emphasises that 'the heart of the matter is that the system's variables [e.g. strategy or war's dimensions] cannot be effectively isolated from each other or from their context; linearisation is not possible, because dynamic interaction is one of the system's defining characteristics'.[30] Also he observes that 'Clausewitz understands that war has no distinct boundaries and that its parts are inter-connected.'[31] Clausewitz warned of the 'dreary analytical labyrinth [that] would result' from a misguided scholarly effort to examine in isolation every factor, or dimension, of strategy.

> Heaven protect the theorist from such an undertaking! For our part we shall continue to examine the picture as a whole, and take our analysis no further than is necessary in each case to elucidate the idea we wish to convey, which will always have its origins in the impressions made by the sum total of the phenomena of war, rather than in speculative study.[32]

To recognise the nonlinearity and complexity of strategy is important, even vital, but in and of itself such recognition has only modest value for comprehension. Scholars, let alone responsible officials, are not excused further duty towards strategic understanding or performance just because they have lifted the veil and gained significant insight into the chaotic world of strategic behaviour. Much about strategic performance is literally unknowable because persistently it pertains to nonlinear conditions that must, as suggested above, defy reliable detailed understanding. The same could be said for the biological sciences, for economic behaviour, and for meteorology. However, to fail to know everything does not equate to knowing nothing. Moreover, with reference to strategy, security communities do not require immaculate performance, only performance good enough 'on the night'. The course of war is governed by relative, not absolute, competencies. To win one needs only to be better over-all than the enemy; one is not performing against some absolute standard of strategic virtue. To recognise that the strategic realm is complex and sometimes chaotically nonlinear is indeed to secure insight. But is this recognition only of bounded, if important, insight, or is it enthronement of a governing principle? How chaotic is strategy? More to the point, perhaps, if chaos rules, how is strategy feasible at all? These questions are posed, explored, and answered in Chapter 4.

Strategy is difficult.[33] It is difficult to understand because it has many dimensions constantly in dynamic interaction (e.g. geography, technology,

7

administration, quality of political and military command, theory, and doctrine). Also, strategy is difficult to understand and do because it can appear insubstantial and therefore elusive. Where lies the realm of strategy? It is neither the terrain of military threat and action, that is tactics, nor is it the ground of policy and politics. Whereas security communities educate skill groups to perform as politicians and soldiers,[34] how do they train their strategic thinkers and doers? Remember that strategy is not fighting, nor is it policy. Strategy is the purposeful use of fights and threats of fights to advance the goals of policy. At least, in an ideal polity that is how matters should be arranged.

THE ARGUMENT

By the *argument* I mean the architecture of key assumptions, asserted logical connections, and by inference the substantive narrative trajectory of the enquiry. What is presented here is an extended hypothesis, not detailed conclusions – those must wait, of course, upon the outcome of the quarrying in later chapters. These points risk exposing more than perhaps is usual or even prudent at the outset of an analytical quest, but it would be foolishly disingenuous of me to pretend that this book is the, or even my, first assault upon its subjects. In a sense it is the very maturity of the transnational RMA debate that both licenses and enables this book to attempt comprehensive appraisal. Much remains to be explored in the pages below, but the duration of the debate and this author's exposure and modest contribution to it allow the argument here to be framed with some confidence.

The intellectual keystone in the arch of my argument was flagged in the preceding section. Namely, *the structural complexity and substantial nonlinearity of strategy is always likely to frustrate some or all of the promise in an RMA*. This judgement, or caveat, is embedded in the whole argument outlined below. Rephrased, the dimensions of strategy that a particular RMA fails, or is unable, to reach – geography, for example, or political and military leadership – in principle must threaten the integrity of its promise of relative strategic advantage. Similarly, to extend the point, the adversarial dimension of strategy and war is perennially liable to thwart the aspirations of RMA proponents, through the working of what Edward N. Luttwak has revealed so brilliantly as 'the paradoxical logic of conflict'.[35] The most potent fuel for friction in war is the behaviour of an enemy who seeks to thwart you and impose his will. Success today may not mean success tomorrow if its sources become formulaic in application in the face of an enemy willing and able to learn from his own, and others', mistakes. The idea of a 'winning formula' in strategy – understood narrowly as a plan of action – is an oxymoron. Any method that becomes a formula must invite and reward the development of countervailing methods. It is surprising how frequently this elementary logic is neglected.

Seven interdependent points comprise the train of logic which shapes, sustains, and advances this whole enquiry.

1. *The nature and functions of strategy and war are immutable.*[36] A week may be a long time in politics, while a month can seem an eternity, but approximately three millennia of variably accessible strategic history is scarcely any time at all biologically, psychologically, or even socially. This book is not substantially about the causes of war, conditions for peace, or indeed in any fundamental sense about the standing of the social institution of war. Those are intriguing topics which thus far have attracted a huge and hugely inconclusive body of scholarship; they are not, however, prime targets for assault here.[37] Nonetheless, root-and-branch consideration of the nature and functions of strategy and war cannot be eschewed entirely in this enquiry. The historical case studies examined in Chapters 6–8 explore the record of candidate RMAs which, in the assertions of many, either achieved, or promised or threatened to achieve, a thoroughgoing transformation not only of the character of strategy and war, but of their nature and functions. The First World War was, after all, hailed by the hopeful and naive as the 'war to end wars'; while the nuclear revolution was keyed eponymously to a supposed 'absolute weapon' which could have 'utility [only] in non-use'.[38] The purported contemporary information-led revolution promises in its pure cybercombat options 'war' without physical pain, force, or indeed violence as usually understood.[39] I am not impressed by claims registered on behalf of successive variants of transformational theory bearing upon the nature and functions of strategy and war.[40] However, I recognise that this first point in the logic-chain of my argument is only a working assumption, albeit one in which I repose confidence.

2. *The character of strategy and war is ever changing.* Although, as hypothesised under paragraph 1 above, strategy and war have not altered in structure or purposes for millennia, their character has shifted both continuously and occasionally perhaps discontinuously in seismic measure, as society, economy, technology, and political fashion have changed. Perhaps paradoxically, strategy is as eternal in its architecture and components, as it is kaleidoscopic from conflict to conflict, both between and within historical periods. The dimensions of strategy have been stable throughout history, as Chapter 5 explains, but the character of each dimension and its dynamic role in the 'whole house' of strategy and war, must vary from case to case. Strategic performance is the dynamic and sometimes nonlinear product of the same interacting and synergistically interpenetrating elements, but the tactical grammar of strategy's 'doing' is always unique. For example, physical and mental geography always matters,[41] but they do not always matter to the same degree and consequence.

3. *From time to time strategic history can appear to accelerate to such a degree that great discontinuities, nonlinear 'events', are discernible which we have come to label as RMAs (or transformations of war).* Whether or not it is misleading to identify periods of rapid change, or apparently rapid change, as revolutionary,

9

is at least as much a matter of intellectual taste and political convenience as it is of empirical evidence. RMAs are intellectual constructs; they are the inventions of scholars and other thinkers. Napoleon's *corps d'armée*, British and German indirect artillery fire (1917–18), and atomic bombs were as actually corporeal as the identification of each as key to an RMA is a case of socially constructed knowledge. Conceptually and empirically, RMA remains very much a contestable hypothesis of a term. Whether or not the apparent speeding up of the pace of strategic history that we have identified as the RMA phenomenon tends unhelpfully to overreach on the evidence, and as a consequence tends to mislead, or whether it is helpful as a tool to aid strategic understanding, is a question central to this enquiry. While the RMA debate can be treated as a fascinating episode in strategic intellectual history, that debate happens to relate directly to extremely high stakes in national and international security.[42]

4. *The nature, which is to say the structure, and the somewhat nonlinear dynamic working of strategy limit the reliable scope and scale of advantage that exploitation of an RMA can confer.* Because of its complexity, inter alia, strategy is rarely approached holistically. Usually it is just too difficult a task to think systematically about strategy's dimensions, let alone to consider how those dimensions behave dynamically as fuel for the unity in behaviour that is strategic performance as relative effectiveness. Even thoughtful and mature approaches to the RMA question, written by people who are historically aware, can stumble on shortfalls in the holism department. For example, earlier in this chapter I quoted former US Secretary of Defense William Cohen's praise of RMAs. But Cohen defended his claim that exploitation of an RMA enables a nation 'to achieve decisive military results in fundamentally new ways', by offering some ill-advised historical hostages to critical scrutiny. He tells us that

> History offers several such examples [of RMAs]: the revolutionary French Republic's levée en masse; the development of the blitzkrieg by the German Air Force and Army; and extensive, sustained open ocean maritime operations developed by the US Navy. In all of these examples, the underlying technologies which made these revolutions possible were readily available to many countries. But in each case, only one country transformed the essential elements of its armed forces in such a manner as to achieve a dominant and decisive advantage in warfare.[43]

Cohen arguably is right to point to the cases that he does as RMAs, but he appears unaware of the grim irony in his choice of examples. Of his three historical cases of RMAs which supposedly enabled their exploiters 'to achieve a dominant and decisive advantage in warfare', two of the parties he praises (revolutionary and Napoleonic France, and Nazi Germany) proceeded to lose their wars.[44] What happened was that the complexity and dynamism of strategy and war proved vastly more potent than did the RMAs, which, admittedly, yielded major relative advantage *for a while*. Had Secretary Cohen considered

10

the French and German RMAs at issue in their full historical context – especially with reference to the course of events in the medium term – he might have appreciated dire synergies between 'adversary', 'time', and 'geography', regarded as dimensions of strategy and war, which can prove lethal to the legacy value of today's RMA on the battlefield.[45] Intelligent, well-resourced, and amply motivated adversaries, given time – which they were – and blessed with a permissive geography (Russia and Britain), found good-enough solutions to the French and German ways of war under illustrative discussion here. The moral of this point could hardly be clearer. Reductionist approaches to strategy and war can founder upon a complexity that they ignore at their peril.

5. *Fungibility is a two-edged sword. As strategy's complexity may confound strategic hopes that rest upon a narrowly based RMA, so also that complexity can provide sources of strategic compensation for relative weakness.* The Confederate States of America (Confederacy) lacked depth in economic resources as well as numbers of combat-capable white male adults relative to the war-making assets of the United States. But, during the first two years, for what the Confederacy lacked in industrial power and in numerical strength it found more than adequate compensation in superior generalship, better combat skills, and higher morale. Those relative, though fragile, advantages were much assisted by an extensive national physical geography, ingenious industrial improvisation, and maritime blockade-running. By 1864 Confederate armies had trained their Yankee enemy in the ultimate school of battle itself. Union generalship was much improved, and, unsurprisingly, high morale ceased to be a Confederate strength as the tide of military success flowed strongly, if irregularly, in favour of the Union.[46] Every historical conflict can be examined for bilateral evidence of fragility among the interpenetrating dimensions of strategy. Whereas the story of 'why (and how) the Allies won' the Second World War is a tale of the successful search for sufficient overall strategic effectiveness through Allied strengths (e.g. total resources, strategy-making organisation, maritime geography) to compensate for Allied weaknesses (e.g. lack of unity of command, relatively poor tactical skills in many areas), so the story of 'why (and how) Germany lost' must be a tale of the failure of fungibility.[47] Germany's areas of relative weakness (e.g. competence of political command, the effect of ideology on the scale of mobilisable assets, systematic errors over intelligence, military-procurement malpractices) proved decisively disabling, notwithstanding the undoubted elements of relative strength which might have overcome the weaknesses. These examples illustrate the argument that strategy and war are phenomena whose dynamic structure is always characterised by a struggle on the part of each belligerent to find and exploit offsets for areas of relative disadvantage. The course and outcome of every conflict yields evidence of success and of failure in this endeavour.

6. *Cases of possible RMAs can be presented to illustrate my thesis. I will explain how and why those particular historical RMAs occurred and matured as they did.*

In addition, I will show what those cases tell us about the nature and character of war and strategy. For reasons of personal interest and expertise, I have chosen as case studies the alleged RMAs effected (i) in the wars of the French Revolution and (First Napoleonic) Empire; (ii) in the First World War; and (iii) by nuclear weapons.

7. *RMA theory can be neither correct nor incorrect; necessarily the theory is keyed to contestable definitions of the concept. A decade of debate about RMA has produced powerful arguments both in praise and in criticism. On balance, however, albeit largely serendipitously, the great RMA debate of the 1990s served the course of strategic enlightenment.* It is important to reject RMA argument of an existentialist kind. RMAs do not exist 'out there', as it were in strategic nature, just waiting to be discovered by the intrepid explorer-theorist. It is misleading to reason, as does Jeffrey R. Cooper in a 1994 *tour de force*, that

> Revolutions, moreover, possess a [sic] interim dynamic different from evolutionary development. Revolutions are a recognition that conditions have changed and represent a legitimation of innovation and change, and a call to push at the boundaries.[48]

The difference between innovation that is just innovation and innovation that becomes revolution is not as clear as Cooper suggests. A point that is closely parallel is that the difference between arms competition and arms race tends to be a distinction without significant difference. While, intuitively, one can believe with Cooper that RMAs have some objective existence, even that they can be made purposefully by military revolutionaries, the historical evidence tends to insist upon recognition of continuities which undermine faith in RMA theory.[49]

The great RMA debate has yielded only modest wisdom, let alone knowledge and understanding of so-called RMAs, partly because of the contestability of possible evidence. But that debate has flushed out old but abiding truths and arguments about strategy, technology, and war, long overdue for renewed public airing. Specifically, as the body of this book reveals, largely inadvertently the RMA debate

- triggered a renewal of attention to, and appreciation of, the structure and dynamic functioning of strategy and war;
- compelled rigorous examination of the role of technology as a contributor to military and strategic effectiveness;
- triggered newly explicit appreciation of the role and importance of purposeful compensation among the dimensions of strategy and war;
- highlighted the necessity for careful historical scholarship as *the* evidential base for useful theory.

These are not trivial accomplishments. In point of fact, they comprise the rationale for this enquiry.

The connected points stated above comprise the logical spinal column of the book; holistically approached, they are the argument.

HISTORY AND SOCIAL SCIENCE

Theorists are prone to take their ideas too seriously, while social scientists as theorists are apt to compound that peril by adding an unmerited devotion to their most favoured methodologies. Of course, ideas and methods matter. Indeed, it is because they matter so much that we need to be relaxed in our approach to them lest the comfort of their fit with the selected data-as-evidence takes second place to an ill-judged procrustean standard of professionalism in research.[50] As a strategic theorist and social scientist, and because this book is an exercise in the application of strategic ideas according to a clear notion of how social science proceeds, I will open with three caveats in the form of eloquent quotations from both sides of the Atlantic. From Britain, Alex Danchev warns that '[p]aradigms are not politics. They are merely the pets and playthings of political scientists.'[51] Next, consider the sceptical American voice of Ralph Peters:

> Anyone who doubts that we have entered a postrevolutionary order need only consider the popularity of seminars and publications devoted to the Revolution in Military affairs, or RMA – irrefutable indicators that any truly revolutionary activity is over. The drag-on debates about whether there has been or is an RMA, what it portends, and how it differs from the 'military–technical revolution' are frivolous and irrelevant. The endless symposiums, studies, and articles are popular because they promise a home to those intellectually dispossessed by the end of the Cold War.[52]

The third caveat, this time borrowed gratefully from British historian Jeremy Black, is scarcely less subversive of intellectual confidence in the RMA debate than are the other two. Black writes as a specialist on eighteenth-century warfare who is troubled by the way in which periods are labelled and distinguished. He argues persuasively that,

> If themes of change and continuity are to be addressed in studying 1560–1660 and 1792–1815, then it is crucially necessary to consider ancien régime warfare, as claims of change are often made for 1560–1660 and 1792–1815 in the context of misleading assumptions about the stagnation, indecisiveness, and conservatism of ancien régime warfare.[53]

Black is leading up to a punch-line: 'if the emphasis is rather on a more dynamic, fluid or plastic *ancien régime* or early modern period, then it is less

13

necessary to focus on change or the causes of change in the late-eighteenth-century.' Or, with generically the same argument, it is less necessary to focus on change in 1917–18 or in the 1990s. The RMA postulate has to imply preceding and postdating periods of contrasting relative stasis. That necessary implication of relative immobility, while serving usefully to highlight the antecedent and succeeding periods of change (RMAs), also is likely to bias research towards its over-registration. After all, if RMAs can be viewed as isolated peaks on the plain, truly as nonlinear events, then they all but invite extraordinary explanation. To expand upon Black's point, whatever the virtue of the value-charged labelling of eras, strategic historians and theorists readily may find themselves analytically captive to unduly organising concepts. Words as tools can become words as master. For example, habitual reference to a particular passage of strategic historical experience as '*the* Military Revolution', or '*the* Napoleonic revolution', prejudges much of what is in need of explanation and justification. In the RMA debate of the 1990s, both historians and social scientists were guilty of galloping to the sound of the guns of intellectual combat (not to mention financial support), without first examining carefully whether or not this or that scholarly battle was worth fighting.

Just as we speak in prose whether or not we do so with self-conscious purpose, so RMAs can be effected whether or not the revolutionaries know what, or how much, they are doing. It is unsound to claim either that '[i]nitiation of a revolution requires revolutionaries',[54] except in a necessary and tautological – though paradoxically still important[55] – sense, or that there needs to be '*recognition* of a revolution in the making'.[56] Indeed, RMA theory of all kinds necessarily is hostage to the sense in the use of the concept of revolution.[57] We are in a realm of social construction that must appeal to history for empirical support at the level only of plausibility, not certainty. As usually is the case when scholars ply their trade, simple, even commonsensical understanding of RMA in the very early 1990s soon evolved into a complex hierarchy of conceptual possibilities. The RMA concept evolved from offering one size to fit all potential historical episodes to being an adjustable tool. No less useful an analytical tool is Occam's razor. In the spirit of Occam, while recognising the merit in some differentiation among RMAs of distinguishable scale and pervasiveness, I elect to settle for simple RMA as the preferred term of art. Other acronyms in the RMA family are introduced, but – to marry Occam and Clausewitz[58] – the culminating point of victory in RMA theorising is soon passed. I think it unlikely that this text will contribute too seriously to the incidence of acronym deficiency syndrome.

This book and its central thread of argument has to be an exercise in applied history for the purposes of social science. Perennial difficulties with endeavours such as this are either for the social scientist to grasp enough of the pertinent history so as to be armed adequately to support theory or for the historian to risk affronting a professional aversion to bold transhistorical theorisation. The dangers for each skill group are real but distinctive. The bold social scientific theorist, if fortunate, may map the contours of facts well enough, while occasionally walking into a tree of error through lack of really local knowledge. With luck, or care perhaps, the trees encountered through such ignorance will not matter for the grand theory advanced. One should presume, however, that the trees so encountered do matter. When historians differ, the strategic theorist is reminded appropriately of the probable fragility of the evidential basis to the bold idea.[59]

The RMA debate of the 1990s had many contributors to its provenance. Moreover, judgements as to who, or what, influenced whom, and when, are as problematical as by and large they are unimportant. For every unique, though rarely incontestable, strategic moment for every postulated RMA leader, there must be preceding enabling conditions which cumulatively have to be both necessary *and sufficient*. Similarly, there will be a period subsequent to that magical strategic moment when the RMA in question matures to its culminating point of relative (strategic) advantage.[60] For example, did the nuclear RMA switch on with the first test in the desert of New Mexico on 16 July 1945? With the military demonstrations against Hiroshima and Nagasaki on 6 and 9 August? With the making of this RMA by the US Strategic Air Command (SAC) and by US war planners in the late 1940s?[61] Or was the magic moment only reached in the first half of the 1950s, with the mature accommodation of nuclear-armed forces in policy and strategy and the emergence of a condition of mutual nuclear deterrence?[62]

If there was a strategic moment for the information-keyed RMA of the 1990s, it was the largely unexpected and in essence, though not in detail, unarguable success achieved by the Instant Thunder air campaign against Iraq of 16 January–22 February 1991.[63] Alternative, earlier events which might be canvassed as the strategic moment include the destruction of the Israeli destroyer *Eilat* by an SS-N-2 (Styx) missile in October 1967, the destruction of the Paul Doumer and Thanh Hoa bridges in North Vietnam by TV-optical and laser guided bombs respectively on 27 April and 13 May 1972,[64] and the sinking of HMS *Sheffield* by an Argentinian Exocet air-to-sea missile on 4 May 1982. Each of these dramatic events was significant, but they are better viewed as harbingers, as straws in the wind, than as the true Bastille Day for an RMA allegedly misdated to the 1990s. As noted above, a problem endemic to an RMA perspective upon strategic history is its research preference for the dramatic, its bias towards clear periodisation – after all, a *revolution* should clearly register a change of state,[65] and its siren call to indulge teleology.

This last point means that adherence to an RMA perspective is likely to prejudice the scholar against crediting significant change prior to a selected 'strategic moment'. If one postulates a revolutionary period or episode, the inexorable consequence has to be the consignment of preceding events or behaviours to the category of only modest relative significance at most. By definition, the events and behaviours that precede the revolution must have failed to achieve nonlinear change. It follows that an RMA perspective of any persuasion has to yield a consistent bias to research. This bias is not necessarily fatal to sound scholarship, but after the manner of a car whose steering persistently pulls to left or right, the researcher/driver is unlikely permanently to turn in an entirely safe performance in navigation.

To be fair to RMA advocates, the problem of teleology is one that social scientists, and even some historians, notice as a peril to which the latter are especially vulnerable. The RMA concept all but invites exaggeration of the scale and scope of change introduced by the alleged revolutionary discontinuity. Surprisingly, perhaps, incontestable historical facts can prove even more seductive than speculative intellectual constructions (e.g. the hypothesised Napoleonic and nuclear revolutions in warfare). Historians have understandable difficulty avoiding the malpractice of explaining causes in terms of outcomes, forgetting that history's unique outcomes (say, war in August 1914) are not uniquely possible. Thus, studies of 1900–14, or 1933–39, often are decorated with a subtitle inadvertently revealing of an undue hindsight, 'the road to war'.[66] It is encouraging for a social scientist such as myself to find a historian sensitive to this *déformation professionelle*. For an excellent example, in his politically incorrect revisionist study of the American Civil War, Gary W. Gallagher claims:

> All too aware that the Confederacy failed in its bid for independence, many historians have worked backward from Appomattox to explain that failure. They argue that the Confederacy lacked sufficient will to win the war, never developed a strong collective national identity, and pursued a flawed military strategy that wasted precious manpower. Often lost is the fact that a majority of white southerners steadfastly supported their nascent republic, and that Confederate arms more than once almost persuaded the North that the price of subduing the rebellious states would be too high.[67]

He explains further:

> Preoccupation with fissures within the wartime South arises from an understandable tendency to work backward from the war's outcome in search of explanations for Confederate failure. Historians begin with the fact that the North triumphed.[68]

What makes the fashionable theory of a lack of national will in the Confederacy so compelling is, of course, the fact of defeat in April 1865 (strictly, only the surrender on 9 April by Robert E. Lee's Army of Northern Virginia, which was taken generally to mean the defeat of the Confederate States). When the course of strategic history is explained in terms of its outcomes, the role of contingency is apt to be an early victim of neglect. Those historians who succumb to the 'road to ...' syndrome need to remember that human affairs are notably, though certainly not wholly, nonlinear.

THE MAKING OF A GREAT DEBATE

My attitude towards RMA is that, as befits an intellectual construct, it is more or less useful rather than true or false. In point of fact, the RMA postulate can be useful even when it is not empirically persuasive. For example: the RMA postulate of a moment or a period witnessing a radical change of state – say the alleged early modern European and Napoleonic RMAs – promotes careful study of the process of change in the periods preceding, even long preceding, those purportedly revolutionary eras. The result is that proponents of the RMA idea unintentionally spur research into innovations in periods of supposedly (by RMA definition) non-revolutionary change.[69] As a consequence, we learn more about the warp and woof of the course of strategic history writ large, and arguably revolutionary and other episodes. Serendipity triumphs yet again.

Although unenamoured of the RMA concept per se, I am impressed by the use to which it can be put, both deliberately and – more often and more significantly – otherwise, to shine light in dark places. Although several scholars have ventured insightful comments about, and have ventured some modest accounting for, the RMA debate of the 1990s, no one yet has sought to overfly the whole terrain of the subject in time and space.[70] Whatever the quality of debate about RMA topics, the raising of the RMA flag mobilised a wide variety of perspectives and skills, enabled some long antecedent ideas and streams of analysis to play significantly in a contemporary debate, and generally triggered a nonlinear intellectual and even (probably) policy event. Whether or not the RMA idea is empirically sound, as well as being useful, it is perhaps ironic that there is no room for argument over the discontinuity in strategic discourse effected by the advent of RMA debate in the United States in the early to mid-1990s. While the reality of substantial and varied items of intellectual (and some material and policy) provenance is readily conceded, between 1991 and 1995 RMA moved from the wilderness of little recognition to the dizzy status of 'acronym of choice' in the US defence community and far beyond.[71] The apparent novelty, as well as the imperial reach of the concept, much assisted its ready acceptance. The US defence community, indeed the strategic studies community more generally, is not known for its historical literacy.[72] The notion of irregularly periodic discontinuities in modes of warfare, which is to say the idea behind RMA, may be ancient history, but it did not seem so to theorists, officials, and commentators in the United States in the 1990s.

The modern history of American strategic debate bears some resemblance to the fashion industry. Scholars and institutions succeed by being fairly bold market leaders. The industry of defence analysis prospers through its ability to attract funding for the study and exposition of new or, more usually, refurbished ideas.[73] Just as the world's fashion houses strive competitively in their seasonal collections or novelty that will sell, so the defence intellectual community in its many institutional forms competes for market share in respect, official access, and cold hard cash. As fashion houses need new designs, so defence analysts and strategic theorists need new, or at least new-sounding, ideas.

A debate can become an apparently great debate as much for structural sociological as for substantive reasons. No matter how merit-worthy the RMA idea, a country like Britain has too few active strategic theorists, too few publication outlets, and offers too little genuine dialogue between those inside and those outside government to catalyse or sustain a great debate. In the United States, in sharp contrast, even a poor idea can threaten to become a serious contender for fashionable status, largely because of the size of the community of debaters. An idea begins to look serious when dozens of publications and conferences honour it with careful attention. These slightly sceptical comments are not intended as pejorative judgement on RMA theory. They are intended, however, to help explain how it is that a big-sounding notion, a 'high concept', can achieve take-off so rapidly. The US defence community provides the critical mass of accessible public interest, money, and therefore numbers of players, from which great strategic debate can emerge like a comet appearing suddenly above the horizon.[74]

The relationship between threat perception and RMA dynamics is too complex for treatment at this early juncture. We shall return to it later, both in specific historical contexts with respect to the case studies, and in the concluding chapter. Suffice it to say for now that the real-world catalyst of the RMA debate, the Gulf War of 1991, was waged by the West with a military instrument forged in and for the conduct of the Cold War (and, ultimately, for a third world war). The subsequent decade of American RMA debate was a context unguided by plausibly dominant threats or, consequently, by any higher direction of defence worthy of the honourable label, 'strategy'.[75] If the nuclear revolution was made during the Second World War (as the Napoleonic and First World War revolutions also were made in conditions of extreme duress), most essentially in response to the scientists' fears about possible German weaponisation of atomic science, in contrast the 'threat set' for the information-led RMA is opaque, contestable, and in no small measure indeterminate.[76]

Actual strategic history, that is to say real strategic behaviour, serves as oxygen to strategic intellectual combat. If strategic behaviour is quiet, so strategic debate becomes ever more enervated as it exhausts its existing event-fuel. The wars of Yugoslavian succession, and especially NATO's war conducted against Serbia in 1999, had only minor significance in reanimating RMA debate. Notwithstanding the ultimate success achieved by NATO with its campaign of aerial coercion, the deeply contested course and conduct of that campaign served usefully to remind people that strategy is a difficult art to practise.[77]

Despite the additional oxygen to the RMA debate supplied by the extraordinary nastiness in the Balkans in 1999, the great RMA debate – as distinguished from the real-world activity to which the debate refers – was fired into life by the Gulf War of 1991, picked up velocity in 1991–94, peaked in 1995–97, and aged with predictable rapidity in 1998–99. There is a natural life-cycle to all great strategic debates, the course of that over RMA included.[78] The dust had barely settled over Kosovo when the US defence community embraced the conceptual successor to RMA, 'asymmetric threats'. The real-world evidence of global terrorism made manifest in New York City on 11 September 2001 only served to accelerate the popularity of the idea of 'asymmetry' in strategic affairs.

The idea of RMA as a grand theory of strategic history may be novel, but the concept of qualitative change in the terms and conditions of warfare has to be as old as perception of its apparent existential reality. Sharp changes in military practice away from traditional methods cannot help but elicit complaint, scepticism, variably enthusiastic endorsement – in short, debate. People did not need a formal theory of RMA in order to know that a favourable discontinuity in relative military advantage might be achieved through managed change. Some historians today believe that they can identify many past RMAs, all or any of which, if judged worthy of the revolutionary label, would have been effected without benefit of the clergy of grand theory. In addition to a common lore of strategic experience which bequeaths appreciation of the possibility, though not necessarily the desirability, of radical change, defence analysts in the 1980s and 1990s could find some explicit conceptual guidance in a century's worth of strategic theory.

For a leading example, would-be RMA theorists in the last two decades of the twentieth century could find inspiration in the title of Jean Colin's 1912 work, *The Transformations of War*.[79] If Commandant Colin's analytical tour de force is unduly antiquarian for modern taste, how about the leading initial theorists for the nuclear era? In 1946, three small books of exceptional merit collectively laid down a marker difficult to miss. In *The Revolution in Warfare*, Basil Liddell Hart advised – in words drafted prior to his knowledge of the atomic bomb – that 'While the far-reaching effects of a superiority in mechanical forces have not yet been fully grasped, this qualitative evolution in warfare is already being overtaken by developments of an automatic nature [referring particularly to the use of such more or less guided missiles as Germany's V-1s and V-2s] that foreshadow a revolution in warfare.'[80] Also in 1946, William Liscum Borden began his treatise, *There Will Be No Time: The Revolution in Strategy*, with the grim observation that 'Atomic energy is so revolutionary that its full impact upon strategy may not become evident until after another war, if there is such a war.'[81] Still in 1946, truly a vintage year for strategic fore-sight, Frederick S. Dunn wrote in *The Absolute Weapon: Atomic Power and World Order*, that 'to speak of it [the atomic bomb] as just another weapon was highly misleading. It was a revolutionary development which altered the basic character of war itself.'[82]

This discussion simply illustrates the point that the idea of revolutionary change in war, certainly in warfare, has long been commonplace. If anything, the revolutionary ascription has descended into cliché, as with overuse of reference to the 'nuclear revolution'. Bold and skilful theorists did not need to invent the idea of RMA; in its bare essentials, at least, it has been lying around forever.

METHOD AND TRAJECTORY

This text is organised to consider and answer a series of discrete, but closely connected, questions. Chapters 2 and 3 provide detailed discussion of the RMA concept, rival RMA theories, and the evolving state of play in RMA debate.

Chapter 2 presents critically the leading theories of RMA (and associated concepts), gathering them for systemic review under the rubric of contested and contestable 'patterns in history'. The discussion provides ample warning against the siren calls from rival intellectually and intuitively appealing 'wave theories' of historical transformation.

Chapter 3 develops the basic architecture for the study of RMA. A nine-phase RMA life-cycle is proposed, which should have a universal writ. The analysis identifies an end-to-end historical process of RMA, which is likely to lack clear breakpoints, or nonlinear events. Given the central significance of the concept of revolution to RMA, this chapter continues to expose the difficulties posed by historical data that generally are inherently ambiguous vis-à-vis their possible meaning as evidence for theory. Although history is vital for social science, rarely can it resolve the theoretical problems of social scientific theorists. We cannot simply have resort to 'the facts' in order to develop superior RMA theory.

Chapters 4 and 5 enrich, complicate, but give meaning to the brew, by developing a theory of strategy that explains RMA phenomena. The organising assumption is that RMA behaviour is, and has to be, strategic behaviour. Chapter 4 probes strategy's predictive nature and examines critically the merit in the fashionable argument that because strategy is somewhat nonlinear and certainly is the realm of chance par excellence, it is also literally chaotically unpredictable in its outcomes. I am not overimpressed by that claim. Chapter 5 proceeds to explain in general terms why and how RMA behaviour has to be strategic behaviour. The chapter then explains how strategy 'works' – which explains also how RMAs must 'work'.

Chapters 6–8 present and treat three historical studies by the method of focused comparison. While each case (Chapter 6 – Napoleonic; Chapter 7 – the First World War; Chapter 8 – nuclear) is wholly unique in characteristic detail, a common architecture of theory binds them as examples of RMA subject to a common logic of strategic behaviour. These chapters will show how three particular RMAs worked strategically.

Chapter 9 employs the evidence from the case studies in order to develop ideas about compensation among strategy's dimensions. The guiding ideas in Chapter 9 are that war (and other strategic contests) is a duel, and that each belligerent brings distinctive strengths and weaknesses to the struggle. RMA theory addresses the duel by promising a radically favourable discontinuity in military effectiveness. My general theory of strategy provides context, and discipline, for RMA practice. What does the nature and working of strategy mean for RMA behaviour? That is the question. Chapter 9 also completes the analytical journey by revisiting the tensions between the idea of strategy as purposeful direction and a plan of action, and strategy as a zone of complexity whose dynamic working is both technically and figuratively chaotic in course and outcome.[83] Strategy (and war) is technically 'chaotic', in that it does not unfold neatly in a linear fashion. It is figuratively chaotic or ever threatening to become so, because, in the words of Sir Archibald Wavell:

> War is a muddle; it is bound to be. There are so many incalculable accidents in the uncertain business – a turn of the weather that could not be fore-seen, a message gone astray, a leader struck down at the critical moment – that it is very rarely that even the best-laid plans go smoothly.[84]

However, as I shall argue, strategy is not a hopeless endeavour in purposeful accomplishment just because it can be ambushed by chance, or by risks that transpire to be all too real. Such characterisation is structurally unsound. Rather, strategy has to be carried out despite the fact that it exhibits some nonlinearity and can be chaotic. Risk, chance, and uncertainty are not variables external to strategy; instead they are endemic to it. Before readers succumb to undue pessimism, they should notice that the consequences of the role of risk upon strategic performance can be offset by two further systemic conditions. The nonlinearity of strategy and war does not translate reliably into net disadvantage. The apparent discontinuities and somewhat unpredictable synergies of strategy in action are as apt to yield discontinuous benefit as its reverse. The damage that strategy's complexity and occasionally chaotic working may wreak upon our designs, in principle at least, must apply no less punitively to our enemies. To be strategically successful one needs only to be better than the foe. One does not need to record anything close to a perfect score on some cosmic assay of absolute strategic excellence.

The trajectory of the text begins with conceptualisation and theory in consideration of RMAs and strategy, and proceeds via history to understanding of how, why, and to what result the RMA phenomenon works as strategic behaviour.

NOTES

1. In a landmark article, Williamson Murray claims that 'The term *revolution in military affairs* (RMA) is a buzzword inside the [Washington] Beltway and among academics interested in defense affairs. As Dennis Showalter noted at a recent conference, "RMA has replaced TQM [total quality management] as the acronym of choice" among members of the Armed Forces': 'Thinking About Revolutions in Military Affairs', *Joint Force Quarterly*, 16 (Summer 1997), p. 69 (emphasis in original).
2. Raymond Aron, 'The Evolution of Modern Strategic Thought', in Alastair Buchan (ed.), *Problems of Modern Strategy* (London: Chatto & Windus, 1970), p. 25.
3. On 12 January 1954, US Secretary of State John Foster Dulles triggered a public debate on nuclear deterrence (and limited war) when he revealed in a speech that 'The basic decision [taken by the Eisenhower administration in 1953] was to depend primarily upon a great capacity to retaliate, instantly, by means and at places of our choosing.' Secretary of Defense Robert S. McNamara similarly triggered a lively public debate when on 18 September 1967 he propounded a theory of strategic stability keyed to a particular (action–reaction) theory of arms race dynamics. These speeches are reprinted in Philip Bobbitt, Lawrence Freedman, and Gregory F. Treverton (eds), *US Nuclear Strategy: A Reader* (New York: New York University Press, 1989), pp. 122–30 (Dulles), and 267–82 (McNamara). The contents of these speeches are considered in context in Colin S. Gray, *Strategic Studies and Public Policy: The American Experience* (Lexington: University Press of Kentucky, 1982), chs 3, 4, 7, 8, 9, and in Lawrence Freedman, *The Evolution of Nuclear Strategy*, 2nd edn (New York: St Martin's Press, 1989), chs 6, 16.
4. William S. Cohen (Secretary of Defense), *Annual Report to the President and the Congress* (Washington, DC: US Government Printing Office, 1999), p. 122.
5. See the elaboration of this point in Colin S. Gray, *The American Revolution in Military Affairs: An Interim Assessment*, Occasional Paper 28 (Camberley: Strategic and Combat Studies Institute, Joint Services Command and Staff College, 1997), esp. pp. 1–12.
6. 'Strategic history' is defined and discussed below in this chapter.
7. Andrew F. Krepinevich, 'Cavalry to Computer: The Pattern of Military Revolutions', *The National Interest*, 37 (Fall 1994), pp. 30–42. Krepinevich's list of military revolutions proved popular and has been reported or even reprinted frequently; for example, in Michael O'Hanlon, 'Can High Technology Bring US Troops Home?', *Foreign Policy*, 113 (Winter 1998–99), pp. 76–7. Krepinevich's candidate military revolutions are: (1) an *infantry revolution* of the first half of the Hundred Years War, and (2) an *artillery revolution* of the second half; (3) a *revolution of sail and shot*, (4) a *fortress revolution*, and (5) an infantry *gunpowder revolution*, all of the sixteenth century; (6) a *Napoleonic revolution*; (7) a *land warfare revolution* of the mid-nineteenth century, and (8) a *naval revolution* which unfolded from the 1840s until the First World War; (9) *interwar revolutions in mechanisation, aviation, and information*; and (10) a *nuclear revolution*. For an alternative, though overlapping, list of possible RMAs, see Murray, 'Thinking About Revolutions in Military Affairs', p. 70.
8. MacGregor Knox and Williamson Murray (eds), *The Dynamics of Military Revolution, 1300–2050* (Cambridge: Cambridge University Press, 2001), is by far the most substantial and sophisticated contribution by historians to date. In his 'Thinking About Revolutions

in Military Affairs', Murray provides useful commentary on the use and abuse of history by those debating RMA. Never one to pull a punch, he writes: 'One suspects that much of this enthusiasm [for RMA], *which rests upon only the slightest knowledge of the historical record*, may distort as much as it helps in thinking about military change and innovation' (p. 69, emphasis added). Murray's article is outstanding, but he is a professional historian with turf to protect – which is not to deny that it needs protecting from raiders (such as myself!) from the social and physical sciences. Historians' contributions to the great RMA debate with reference to eras preceding those featured as case studies in this book include the following: Andrew Ayton and J. L. Price (eds), *The Medieval Military Revolution: State, Society and Military Change in Medieval and Early Modern Europe* (London: Tauris Academic Studies, 1995); Bert S. Hall, *Weapons and Warfare in Renaissance Europe: Gunpowder, Technology, and Tactics* (Baltimore: Johns Hopkins University Press, 1997); David Eltis, *The Military Revolution in Sixteenth-century Europe* (London: Tauris Academic Studies, 1995); Geoffrey Parker, *The Military Revolution: Military Innovation and the Rise of the West, 1500–1800* (Cambridge: Cambridge University Press, 1988); James Scott Wheeler, *The Making of a World Power: War and the Military Revolution in Seventeenth-century England* (Phoenix Mill: Sutton Publishing, 1999); Russell F. Weigley, *The Age of Battles: The Quest for Decisive Warfare from Breitenfeld to Waterloo* (Bloomington, IN: Indiana University Press, 1991), pts 1–2; Clifford J. Rogers (ed.), *The Military Revolution Debate: Readings on the Military Transformation of Early Modern Europe* (Boulder, CO: Westview Press, 1995); Brian M. Downing, *The Military Revolution and Political Change: Origins of Democracy and Autocracy in Early Modern Europe* (Princeton, NJ: Princeton University Press, 1992); Michael Duffy (ed.), *The Military Revolution and the State, 1500–1800*, Exeter Studies in History 1 (Exeter: University of Exeter, 1980); Jeremy Black, *A Military Revolution? Military Change and European Society, 1550–1800* (London: Macmillan, 1991); idem, 'Eighteenth-century Warfare Reconsidered', *War in History*, 1, 2 (July 1994), pp. 215–32.

9. Colin S. Gray, 'Fuller's Folly: Technology, Strategic Effectiveness, and the Quest for Dominant Weapons', in A. J. Bacevich and Brian R. Sullivan (eds), *The Limits of Technology in Modern War* (forthcoming), is a pioneering venture to apply a social-scientific perspective to interpret the findings of a number of first-rate historical case studies. Unfortunately, the editors of this important and all but complete manuscript, appear to have failed to bring the project to closure.

10. Christopher J. Langton's contribution to chaos theory, and especially his attraction to the concept of 'the edge of chaos', is detailed in M. Mitchell Waldrop, *Complexity: The Emerging Science at the Edge of Order and Chaos* (London: Penguin, 1994), ch. 6, 'Life at the Edge of Chaos', esp. pp. 230–1. On the possible relevance of chaos theory to strategic subjects, see Stephen R. Mann, 'Chaos Theory and Strategic Thought', *Parameters*, 22, 3 (Autumn 1992), pp. 54–68; Alan Beyerchen, 'Clausewitz, Nonlinearity, and the Unpredictability of War', *International Security*, 17, 3 (Winter 1992/93), pp. 59–90; Roger Beaumont, *War, Chaos, and History* (Westport, CT: Praeger Publishers, 1994); David Nicholls and Todor D. Tagarev, 'What Does Chaos Theory Mean for Warfare?' *Airpower Journal*, 8, 3 (Fall 1994), pp. 48–57; Glenn A. James, *Chaos Theory: The Essentials for Military Application*, Newport Papers 10 (Newport, RI: Center for Naval Warfare Studies, Naval War College, October 1996); and Barry D. Watts, *Clausewitzian Friction and Future War*, McNair Paper 52 (Washington, DC: Institute for National Strategic Studies, National Defense University, October 1996). For an accessible introduction to chaos theory itself, see James Gleick, *Chaos: Making a New Science* (London: Penguin, 1988); David Ruelle, *Chance and Chaos* (London: Penguin, 1993); Stephen L. Kellert, *In the Wake of Chaos: Unpredictable Order in Dynamical Systems* (Chicago: University of Chicago Press, 1993); and Peter Coveney and Roger Highfield, *Frontiers of Complexity. The Search for Order in a Chaotic World* (London: Faber & Faber, 1995).

11. Colin S. Gray, 'RMAs and the Dimensions of Strategy', *Joint Force Quarterly*, 17 (Autumn/Winter 1997/98), pp. 50–4, and idem, *Modern Strategy* (Oxford: Oxford University Press, 1999), ch. 1, comprise earlier forays into the territory explored at length in this text.

12. Carl von Clausewitz, *On War*, trans. Michael Howard and Peter Paret (Princeton, NJ: Princeton University Press, 1976 [1832]), p. 605.

13. Ibid., p. 128.

14. For a superior brief discussion of the issues intertwined in 'war and society', see Geoffrey Best's 'Editor's preface' in J. R. Hale, *War and Society in Renaissance Europe, 1450–1620* (London: Fontana, 1985), pp. 7–10.

15. I applaud Clark G. Reynolds for his efforts to encourage 'strategic history', and acknowledge my debt to his writings. See his *Command of the Sea: The History and Strategy of Maritime Empires: Vol. One: To 1815*, 2 vols (Malabar, FL: Robert E. Krieger Publishing, 1983), pp. 9–12. I am grateful to Reynolds for drawing attention to Corelli Barnett as the originator of the term 'strategic history' in a letter to the *Times Literary Supplement* on 20 November 1969 (p. 1338): Clark G. Reynolds, *History and the Sea: Essays on Maritime Strategies* (Columbia: University of South Carolina Press, 1989), pp. 108–9, 126–7n.

16. Richard K. Betts is to the point when he advises that 'security studies ... is potentially boundless': 'Should Strategic Studies Continue?' *World Politics*, 50, 1 (October 1997), p. 9.

17. Hedley Bull, *The Anarchical Society: A Study of Order in World Politics* (New York: Columbia University Press, 1977), p. 184.

18. Radical views of contemporary changes in the state and in war inspire Martin van Creveld, *The Transformation of War* (New York: Free Press, 1991); idem, *The Rise and Decline of the State* (Cambridge: Cambridge University Press, 1999); and John Keegan, *A History of Warfare* (London: Hutchinson, 1993); idem, *War and Our World* (London: Hutchinson, 1998).

19. Jeffrey R. Cooper, *Another View of the Revolution in Military Affairs* (Carlisle Barracks, PA: Strategic Studies Institute, US Army War College, 15 July 1996), p. 21.

20. Krepinevich, 'Cavalry to Computer', p. 30.

21. To be fair, Krepinevich is careful to emphasise that 'while advances in technology typically underwrite a military revolution, they alone do not constitute the revolution' (ibid.).

22. If anything, I understate the evidential difficulty with Liddell Hart. He writes that '[d]uring this survey one impression became increasingly strong – that, throughout the ages, effective results in war have rarely been attained unless the approach has had such indirectness as to ensure the opponent's unreadiness to meet it.' B. H. Liddell Hart, *Strategy: The Indirect Approach* (London: Faber & Faber, 1967), p. 25.

23. Beyerchen, 'Clausewitz, Nonlinearity, and the Unpredictability of War', pp. 61–6, is particularly enlightening.

24. Gray, *Modern Strategy*, ch. 5.

25. Colin S. Gray, 'Inescapable Geography', in Gray and Geoffrey Sloan (eds), *Geopolitics, Geography, and Strategy* (London: Frank Cass, 1999), pp. 161–77.

26. Beyerchen, 'Clausewitz, Nonlinearity, and the Unpredictability of War', p. 65.

27. Clausewitz, *On War*, p. 183.

28. T. E. Lawrence, *Seven Pillars of Wisdom: A Triumph* (New York: Anchor, 1991 [1926]), pp. 191–2.

29. A prime example would be the barrenness of Napoleon's military success in Spain in 1808. See David G. Chandler, *The Campaigns of Napoleon* (London: Weidenfeld & Nicolson, 1967), ch. 61, 'Incomplete Achievement'; and David Gates, *The Spanish Ulcer: A History of the Peninsular War* (New York: W. W. Norton, 1986), pt 2. The classic extended treatment of military effectiveness is Allan R. Millett and Williamson Murray (eds), *Military Effectiveness*, 3 vols (Boston, MA: Allen & Unwin, 1988).

30. Beyerchen, 'Clausewitz, Nonlinearity, and the Unpredictability of War', p. 66.
31. Ibid., p. 90.
32. Clausewitz, On War, p. 183.
33. David Jablonsky, 'Why Is Strategy Difficult?' in Gary L. Guertner (ed.), The Search for Strategy: Politics and Strategic Vision (Westport, CT: Greenwood Press, 1993), pp. 3–45; and Colin S. Gray, 'Why Strategy is Difficult', Joint Force Quarterly, 22 (Summer 1999), pp. 6–12.
34. This is not to deny that whereas politicians benefit from on-the-job training all the time, only rarely are soldiers able to practise their trade of war.
35. Edward N. Luttwak, Strategy: The Logic of War and Peace (Cambridge, MA: Harvard University Press, 1987). Another excellent work of theory that places interaction between adversaries at the core of its understanding of strategy is André Beaufre, An Introduction to Strategy, trans. R. H. Barry (London: Faber & Faber, 1965), esp. p. 22. Although I treat the adversary as one of strategy's many dimensions (see Chapter 5), the view is eminently defensible that the adversary is better treated as a super-dimension implicit in the very meaning of strategy (and war). Clausewitz advises that the object of war is 'to impose our will on the enemy', and that it 'is not the action of a living force upon a lifeless mass (total nonresistance would be no war at all), but always the collision of two living forces': On War, pp. 75, 77.
36. In a valuable brief exposition, to my knowledge unique in the now vast RMA literature, Cooper makes explicit two distinctive meanings attributable to the nature of war. He explains usefully that in his monograph 'the term nature of war will be defined by the entities that engage in the conflict and the objectives over which they fight while conduct of warfare will refer to the modalities of the conflict, that is, how the war is fought … I do recognise that others use nature of war to refer to the immutable characteristics such as combat, leadership, valor, and blood': Another View, p. 42, n16 (emphasis in original). I do not share Cooper's preferred definition, being much closer to the view of the 'others' that he cites. Nonetheless, his definition is clear and useful. Most commentators simply refer confusingly to war's nature, character, and conduct, as if these terms are fully interchangeable.
37. The enormous literature that has accumulated since the 1920s on the causes of war(s) is no less enormously underimpressive. We need less industry, less morally committed endeavour, and rather more careful thought and well-researched history. The lack of dominant theory after 80 years of intensive scholarly effort should be allowed to suggest to us that there just might be fundamental problems of conceptualisation and researchability which impede progress.
38. Bernard Brodie (ed.), The Absolute Weapon: Atomic Power and World Order (New York: Harcourt, Brace, 1946); idem, War and Politics (New York: Macmillan, 1973), ch. 9, 'On Nuclear Weapons: Utility in Nonuse'.
39. See Roger C. Molander, Andrew S. Riddle, and Peter A. Wilson, Strategic Information Warfare: A New Face of War, MR-661-OSD (Santa Monica, CA: RAND, 1996); Lawrence Freedman, The Revolution in Strategic Affairs, Adelphi Paper 318 (London: International Institute for Strategic Studies, 1998); and James Adams, The Next World War (London: Hutchinson, 1998). John Arquilla and David Ronfeldt (eds), In Athena's Camp: Preparing for Conflict in the Information Age, MR-880-OSD/RC (Santa Monica, CA: RAND, 1997), is an exceptional collection of essays and studies, with unusually pertinent editorial commentaries. Zalmay Khalizad and John White (eds), Strategic Appraisal: The Changing Role of Information in Warfare (Santa Monica, CA: RAND, 1999), is generally less impressive, but still useful.
40. I assault transformational theory brutally (intemperately, in the words of one of my critics) in 'Clausewitz Rules, OK? The Future is the Past – with GPS', Review of International Studies, 25, Special Issue (December 1999), pp. 161–82.

41. For example, there are 'the Balkans' of physical geographical reality, as well as of somewhat socially constructed geopolitical reality, and there are 'the Balkans' of the imagination.
42. Whether or not there is one, or several, RMA(s) currently under way can appear to be an issue of interest to the kind of people who, in an earlier time, would have enjoyed expert debate about the number of angels that could dance on the head of a pin. Although strategic debate attracts some scholars who descend into a barren scholasticism, the RMA debate is inherently important. After all, RMA is – certainly can be – a grand theory of change in strategic history. Beneath the often fine distinctions and obscure and obscuring terminology lurk the issues of war and peace, victory and defeat, security and insecurity. At a more mundane, though vitally instrumental, level of analysis, RMA debate is about budgets, military doctrine, and force structure, and therefore organisational well-being.
43. Cohen, *Annual Report* (1999), p. 122.
44. This point is well made in Steven Metz and James Kievit, *Strategy and the Revolution in Military Affairs: From Theory to Policy* (Carlisle, PA: Strategic Studies Institute, US Army War College, 27 June 1995), pp. 17–18.
45. For the Napoleonic case, the emerging problems even for France as the RMA leader are suitably flagged in Robert M. Epstein, *Napoleon's Last Victory and the Emergence of Modern War* (Lawrence: University Press of Kansas, 1994). The German RMA met its comeuppance primarily in the east, as is well explained in David M. Glantz and Jonathan House, *When Titans Clashed: How the Red Army Stopped Hitler* (Lawrence: University Press of Kansas, 1995).
46. See Herman Hattaway and Archer Jones, *How the North Won: A Military History of the Civil War* (Urbana: University of Illinois Press, 1983); Richard E. Beringer and others, *Why the South Lost the Civil War* (Athens: University of Georgia Press, 1986); Gabor S. Boritt (ed.), *Why the Confederacy Lost* (New York: Oxford University Press, 1992); and Gary W. Gallagher, *The Confederate War* (Cambridge, MA: Harvard University Press, 1997).
47. Richard Overy, *Why the Allies Won* (London: Jonathan Cape, 1995), is particularly thought-provoking. There is unusual merit also in John Ellis, *Brute Force: Allied Strategy and Tactics in the Second World War* (New York: Viking, 1990), and Gerhard L. Weinberg, *A World at Arms: A Global History of World War II* (Cambridge: Cambridge University Press, 1994).
48. Cooper, *Another View of the Revolution in Military Affairs*, p. 21.
49. My argument may appear to verge perilously upon the postmodern, but actually it is the reverse of that which postmodern 'critical theory' would endorse. I am concerned lest RMA theory should proceed as an intellectual construction even though the empirical evidence of strategic history does not clearly support it. On the critical theory most relevant here, see Keith Krause and Michael C. Williams (eds), *Critical Security Studies: Concepts and Cases* (London: UCL Press, 1997), and Richard Wyn Jones, *Security, Strategy, and Critical Theory* (Boulder, CO: Lynne Rienner Publishers, 1999).
50. For example, see my debate with Alastair Iain Johnston about research on strategic culture: Colin S. Gray, 'Strategic Culture as Context: The First Generation of Theory Strikes Back', *Review of International Studies*, 25, 1 (January 1999), pp. 49–69; Alastair Iain Johnston, 'Thinking about Strategic Culture', *International Security*, 19, 4 (Spring 1995), pp. 32–64; idem, *Cultural Realism: Strategic Culture and Grand Strategy in Chinese History* (Princeton, NJ: Princeton University Press, 1995); idem, 'Strategic Culture Revisited: A Reply to Colin Gray', *Review of International Studies*, 25, 3 (July 1999), pp. 519–23. My central charge against Johnston is that, inadvertently, he elevates feasibility in research over the nature of the proper scope of the evidence. I contend that we humans, as encultured actors, are an integral part of our cultural context and

that culture is not strictly something 'out there' which can influence us. Whether or not I am persuasive in that particular case is of no significance here. The point, rather, simply is to provide illustration of the phenomenon of methodology riding roughshod over potential evidence.

51. Alex Danchev, 'On Specialness', *International Affairs*, 72, 4 (October 1996), p. 746.
52. Ralph Peters, *Fighting for the Future: Will America Triumph?* (Mechanicsberg, PA: Stackpole Books, 1999), pp. 18–19.
53. Jeremy Black, 'A Military Revolution? A 1660–1792 Perspective', in *The Military Revolution Debate*, p. 96.
54. Metz and Kievit, *Strategy and the Revolution in Military Affairs*, p. 15.
55. By definition, a revolution requires authors who functionally are revolutionaries. However, there is no strict necessity for those revolutionaries to intend to effect revolution. In the discussion of the life-cycle of RMA in Chapter 3, I recognise the need for human-agent authors as revolutionaries, but that analysis does not postulate a need for self-consciously revolutionary strategic behaviour. Such self-consciousness certainly is possible, and indeed was characteristic of some RMA ideas and activity in the 1990s. It is less certain that the candidate RMAs of the 1790s–1800s, 1917–18, or 1945 and after – to cite the case studies treated in Chapters 6–8 below – were crafted and executed with explicitly strategically revolutionary intent.
56. Cooper, *Another View of the Revolution in Military Affairs*, p. 23 (emphasis in original). I am sceptical of the need for such recognition, notwithstanding the judgement advanced by Peter Paret that 'A critical element in the revolution in war [that occurred at the end of the eighteenth century] was the ability of soldiers and governments to come to recognise the changes that were now possible, and then to act upon their recognition': *Understanding War: Essays on Clausewitz and the History of Military Power* (Princeton, NJ: Princeton University Press, 1992), p. 74. Paret's readers have to digest the claim I have just quoted in the context of this preceding point: 'By contrast [to political revolutions], the revolution in war that occurred at the end of the eighteenth century was not consciously structured ... Political change and the social changes associated with it – for instance, conscription and broader access to officer ranks – infused technical and tactical innovation with a revolutionary impulse.' These are murky waters for theory.
57. There is exceptional merit in Jeremy Shapiro, 'Information and War: Is It a Revolution?' in Khalilzad and White, *Strategic Appraisal*, pp. 113–53.
58. Clausewitz, *On War*, p. 566.
59. I acknowledge that history and historical evidence are subjects contested among historians. Richard J. Evans speaks for my approach to history when he writes: 'History is an empirical discipline, and it is concerned with the content of knowledge rather than its nature': *In Defence of History* (London: Granta Books, 1997), p. 149. Without downplaying the need for imagination and interpretation, Evans is decidedly unfriendly to postmodern constructivism: 'The truth about patterns and linkages of facts in history is in the end discovered not invented, found not made' (p. 252). He proceeds to conclude: 'I remain optimistic that objective historical knowledge is both desirable and attainable.' But, as we shall see, it is exceedingly unlikely that 'objective historical knowledge' will settle arguments about RMA theory. Readers who wish to know what the more cogent constructivists have to offer should attempt Alexander Wendt, *Social Theory and International Politics* (Cambridge: Cambridge University Press, 1999).
60. Metz and Kievit, *Strategy and the Revolution in Military Affairs*, p. 17.
61. See Harry R. Borowski, *A Hollow Threat: Strategic Air Power and Containment before Korea* (Westport, CT: Greenwood Press, 1982); and Steven T. Ross, *American War Plans, 1945–1950* (London: Frank Cass, 1996).

62. Robert Jervis argues that 'it is mutual second-strike capability and not nuclear weapons per se that has generated the new situation': *The Meaning of the Nuclear Revolution: Statecraft and the Prospect of Armageddon* (Ithaca, NY: Cornell University Press, 1989), p. 9.

63. See Richard P. Hallion, *Storm Over Iraq: Air Power and the Gulf War* (Washington, DC: Smithsonian Institution Press, 1992); and Eliot A. Cohen (director), *Gulf War Air Power Survey*, 5 vols and summary (Washington, DC: US Government Printing Office, 1993).

64. A. J. C. Lavalle (ed.), *The Tale of Two Bridges and the Battle for the Skies Over North Vietnam* (Maxwell AFB, AL: Air University Press, 1976).

65. 'Revolution involves more than change, and certainly more than simply change of an incremental variety. It represents a moment of transformation': Freedman, *Revolution in Strategic Affairs*, p. 7 (emphasis in original).

66. Consider Herbert Feis, *The Road to Pearl Harbor: The Coming of the War Between the United States and Japan* (Princeton, NJ: Princeton University Press, 1950); Samuel R. Williamson, Jr, *The Politics of Grand Strategy: Britain and France Prepare for War, 1904–1914* (Cambridge, MA: Harvard University Press, 1969); and Robert Boyce and Esmonde M. Robertson (eds), *Paths to War: New Essays on the Origins of the Second World War* (London: Macmillan, 1989). There is an element of unhistorical hindsight-foresight about each of the titles to these three excellent books with which I am uncomfortable.

67. Gary W. Gallagher, *The Confederate War* (Cambridge, MA: Harvard University Press, 1997), p. 3.

68. Ibid., p. 18.

69. For example: Hew Strachan, 'The British Army's Legacy from the Revolutionary and Napoleonic Wars', in Alan J. Guy (ed.), *The Road to Waterloo: The British Army and the Struggle Against Revolutionary and Napoleonic France* (Stroud: Alan Sutton, 1990), pp. 197–205; Black, *A Military Revolution?*; idem, 'Revolutionary and Napoleonic Warfare', in Black (ed.), *European Warfare, 1453–1815* (London: Macmillan, 1999), pp. 224–46; and Andrew Ayton and J. L. Price, 'Introduction: The Military Revolution from a Medieval Perspective', in Ayton and Price, *The Medieval Military Revolution*, pp. 1–22.

70. The roles of scholarly intellectual historian and advocate-theorist are not easily reconciled. Few people either have recognised that the RMA debate is now effectively concluded, or have been motivated to review the entire episode. There are extant no histories of the RMA debate of the 1990s, disinterested or partial. Commentators on RMA to date have been concerned to make their mark in that debate, rather than to tell the story. Freedman, *Revolution in Strategic Affairs*, does not aspire to tell the story, save insofar as the story helps explain the positions of several schools of thought. Nonetheless, he provides more background than is usual in the RMA literature.

71. Murray, 'Thinking About Revolutions in Military Affairs', p .69.

72. Williamson Murray notes that 'the collapse of serious historical studies from our leading universities and colleges in favor of deconstruction and gender studies is of considerable worry': 'Military Culture Does Matter', *Strategic Review*, 27, 2 (Spring 1999), p. 39. It is probably no consolation to recall that a generation ago Bernard Brodie expressed functionally the same concern as that just quoted from Murray. In 1973 Brodie advised that 'where the great strategic writers and teachers of the past, with the sole and understandable exception of Douhet, based the development of their art almost entirely on a broad and perceptive reading of history – in the case of Clausewitz and Jomini mostly recent history but exceptionally rich for their needs – the present generation of ' "civilian strategists" ["primarily Alain Enthoven, Malcolm Hoag, Henry Rowen, and Albert Wohlstetter", all trained as economists] are with markedly few exceptions singularly devoid of history': *War and Politics*, p. 475.

73. I consider myself a strategic theorist. Certainly, I have written strategic theory for more than 30 years. In addition, for many years, I have taught the history of strategic thought from earliest times until the present day. I do not believe that there are any new ideas about strategy. The reason why this personal belief is likely to be true is central to the argument of this book. Because the nature and purposes of strategy and war are unchanging, it is improbable that that eternal structure could be addressed by new ideas. This is not to deny that ideas can be forgotten and lost, or corrupted. Moreover, upon those ill-educated in strategic history virtually any strategic idea is likely to burst as a revelation with its contemporary advocate hailed as a genius.

74. I comment on this phenomenon in *American Revolution in Military Affairs*, pp. 5–14, and in 'The Revolution in Military Affairs', in Brian Bond and Mungo Melvin (eds), *The Nature of Future Conflict: Implications for Force Development*, Occasional Paper 36 (Camberley: Strategic and Combat Studies Institute, Joint Services Command and Staff College, September 1998), pp. 59–60.

75. I mean to claim only that largely as a consequence of the demise of the Soviet threat, means–ends planning worthy of the name 'strategy' was missing in the United States in the 1990s. This is not to deny the fact of an impressive quantity of activity and the conduct of several impressively extensive reviews. A so-called 'bottom-up' defence review was conducted in 1993 and duly summarised in Les Aspin (Secretary of Defense), *Annual Report to the President and the Congress* (Washington, DC: US Government Printing Office, January 1994), pp. 11–27; the outcome of the congressionally mandated 'Quadrennial Defense Review' (QDR) was explained in William S. Cohen (Secretary of Defense), *Annual Report to the President and the Congress* (Washington, DC: US Government Printing Office, 1998), pp. 5–10; while the 'Quadrennial Defense Review' was second-guessed by an extra-official study group (with official sanction) in the National Defense Panel, *Transforming Defense: National Security in the 21st Century, Report* (Washington, DC: Department of Defense, December 1997). In addition, a master document claiming to explain the *National Security Strategy of the United States* is issued regularly under the President's signature, while annually a document entitled the *National Military Strategy of the United States of America* appears over the signature of the Chairman of the Joint Chiefs of Staff (CJCS). The JCS also perpetrated '"Joint Vision 2010": America's Military – Preparing for Tomorrow', *Joint Force Quarterly,* 12 (Summer 1996), pp. 34–49, which was succeeded by a *Joint Vision 2020* (Washington, DC: US Government Printing Office, June 2000). If quality of strategic thought matched its quantity, the United States would be well defended indeed. The QDR of 2001 was somewhat overtaken by the advent of the Bush administration – which threatened to impose a truly radical 'military transformation' (i.e. RMA) – and by the need to allow prime-time focus to countering global terrorism (after 11 September 2001): Department of Defense, *Quadrennial Defense Review, Report* (Washington, DC: Department of Defense, 30 September 2001).

76. A point made strongly in Metz and Kievit, *Strategy and the Revolution in Military Affairs*, pp. 29–32, and in Brian R. Sullivan, 'The Future Nature of Conflict: A Critique of "The American Revolution in Military Affairs" in the Era of Jointery', *Defense Analysis*, 14, 2 (August 1998), esp. pp. 91–92.

77. Not only is precision in aerial bombardment difficult to achieve in the friction-prone real world of war, but even when it can be done it is no easy matter to guess how much damage (to what?) needs to be inflicted for coercion to succeed, which is the realm of strategic judgement. The coercive, or – in the jargon of yesteryear – the compellent, employment of air power in the Balkans in the 1990s sparked a modest flurry of conceptual activity. See Lawrence Freedman (ed.), *Strategic Coercion: Concepts and Cases* (Oxford: Oxford University Press, 1998); and Stephen J. Cimbala, *Coercive Military Strategy* (College Station: Texas A & M University Press, 1998). Intellectual

parentage of coercion as a strategic concept includes, preeminently, Thomas C. Schelling, *Arms and Influence* (New Haven, CT: Yale University Press, 1996); while James Cable, *Gunboat Diplomacy, 1919–1991* (London: Macmillan, 1994), deserves an honourable mention. A more recent work by Cable lends additional momentum to the theme of coercion: *The Political Influence of Naval Force in History* (London: Macmillan, 1998).

78. In my *American Revolution in Military Affairs*, p. 5, I ventured the extended proposition that the standard historical pattern in defence debate was as follows: (1) a triggering event in the real world; (2) prophetic statements of the desirable (thesis); (3) conceptual elaboration; which trips (4a) sceptical commentary (antithesis) and trails off into (4b) conceptual overelaboration; (5) critical filtering of sense from nonsense (synthesis); leading to (6) the hunt for the next big idea to discuss. At this time of writing, the US defence community is transitioning rapidly from RMA to 'asymmetric warfare'.

79. J. Colin, *The Transformations of War*, trans. L. H. R. Pope-Hennessy (London: Hugh Rees, 1912), esp. ch. 5.

80. B. H. Liddell Hart, *The Revolution in Warfare* (London: Faber & Faber, 1946), p. 29.

81. William Liscum Borden, *There Will Be No Time: The Revolution in Strategy* (New York: Macmillan, 1946), p. 1.

82. Frederick S. Dunn, 'The Common Problem', in Brodie, *The Absolute Weapon*, p. 4.

83. In the best book on strategy written in the twentieth century, J. C. Wylie tells us that strategy is a 'plan of action designed in order to achieve some end; a purpose together with a system of measures for its accomplishment': *Military Strategy: A General Theory of Power Control*, ed. John B. Hattendorf (Annapolis, MD: Naval Institute Press, 1989 [1967]), p. 14. Compare that perspective with Beyerchen's approach to, and interpretation of, Clausewitz in 'Clausewitz, Nonlinearity, and the Unpredictability of War'. Both Wylie and Beyerchen are correct; there is no question of choosing between them. In his editorial 'Introduction', Hattendorf reveals that Rear Admiral Wylie, US Navy, once famously demolished the pretentious language of a glib army budget spokesman who kept referring to 'a calculated risk' (pp. xxvii–xxviii).

84. General Sir Archibald Wavell, *Speaking Generally: Broadcasts, Orders and Addresses in Time of War (1939–43)* (London: Macmillan, 1946), p. 52.

2

RMA Anatomy: Patterns in History?

Anyone can manufacture definitions and coin terms with intriguing acronyms. Nothing as simple as the RMA idea per se, however, has been at stake in the debate. All debaters could, and by and large did, agree that *if the RMA concept is empirically plausible, and if contemporary trends appear to fit the concept well enough*, then the 1990s registered a radical change in the character or conduct of war, which is to say that the 1990s registered an RMA. The two qualifying 'ifs' are significant caveats. The debate in the 1990s included some, though probably insufficient, argument about the empirical plausibility of the RMA idea itself, the identity and character of the RMA(s) that might be under way, and also the prospective strategic significance of such an RMA. These three topics, though clearly interdependent, nonetheless are distinguishable.

This chapter poses and discusses the question 'what is an RMA?' Interesting though it is to pursue this enquiry, certainly a cast of thousands believed so in the 1990s, readers are warned that an RMA focus to debate is inherently limited and fragile. This book is designed principally to explore what RMA debate tells us about strategy, war, and the course of strategic history, rather than about RMA itself. Because RMA is merely an intellectual construct, albeit an appealingly imperial one with great explanatory potential, it is not wise to accord it effectively iconic significance.

WARNING LABEL

There is much to say in praise as well as in criticism both of the RMA hypothesis itself and of the use to which the hypothesis has been put to date. It is useful to flag here some of the more significant grounds for reservation over the merit in the RMA idea. These caveats may be regarded as an effort at intellectual vaccination against the potential to mislead of an RMA literature and debate that often – to risk the reification – took its subject and itself too seriously, and which was always on the threshold of loss of perspective. The warning label which these critical comments convey are preemptive cautionary counterpoints to the RMA anatomy as dissected in the balance of this chapter and to the discussion of RMA dynamics in Chapter 3. The issuing of clear warning at this stage largely obviates what otherwise would be a constant need to inject sceptical cautionary notes.

First, and hugely foremost, the RMA hypothesis bears what may be an empirically unsound bias in favour of discontinuity in strategic history. To observe that the discontinuity integral to the meaning of *revolution* in military affairs is simply a concentrated expression of the chaotically nonlinear nature of strategy and war would be no more than a half-truth, and a perilously misleading half-truth at that. As noted in Chapter 1, there is real value in borrowing complexity theory and the ideas of nonlinearity and chaos from the natural and mathematical sciences, but that value is rapidly lost if the borrowing is indiscriminate and excessive.[1] Strategic theorists can learn a lesson from the errors of those among their close associates in the fields of international relations theory and history who have borrowed and stolen not wisely but too well from literary 'critical theory', and other expressions of the postmodern ethos.[2] Both literary critical theory and complexity/chaos theory serve up at least two major kinds of hazards for the unduly credulous strategist. On the one hand, they are both contested bodies of ideas in their own scholarly realm-of-origin. On the other hand, both bodies of theory, especially in the simple (even often simplistic) forms in which they appear in strategic speculation, though potentially sources of important insight, have a distinctly ragged fit with the robust phenomenon of human nastiness that is the domain of strategy.

Even when the ideas of complexity and chaotic nonlinearity appear well adaptable to strategic experience, the central elevation of discontinuity, in RMA or military transformation, can be allowed inappropriately to prejudge enquiry as to what changed and what did not. Furthermore, such enthronement of discontinuity discourages careful consideration of the historical significance of preceding and succeeding periods. This argument should not be read as a bid to inflict lethal damage upon the RMA construct. All intellectual research tools come at a price. RMA is not unique in the fact that it carries some dangerous baggage. The transaction costs of employing the RMA idea include a constant need to make provision for the appreciation of continuities in strategic phenomena, because the RMA concept yields powerful oversteer in the opposite direction.

Second, no matter how carefully we speculate about RMA and apply theory to interpret strategic behaviour, there must always be an essential indeterminacy about the subject. I am acutely aware that by so organising this study as to deploy three hypothesised RMAs as case studies (in Chapters 6–8), I may appear summarily to dismiss important philosophical and empirical doubts. Whether or not the selected cases of RMA truly are such, the strategic behaviour that each encompasses assuredly occurred and is well worthy of investigation for our purposes. French Revolutionary and Napoleonic warfare happened and was important, whether or not one approves of the idea of a 'Napoleonic RMA'. A label is only a label; the contents of the can are unaffected by their tagging.

My second caveat is intended to warn readers against the nominalist fallacy. If we have a name for it, and if that name passes into common currency, then 'it' assumes some quality of reality. Virtually all discussion of RMA, including this one, encourages acceptance not only of the concept itself, but also of particular *hypothesised* historical RMAs to which frequent reference is made. There is an almost insidious commonsense plausibility about the RMA hypothesis which can disarm potential sceptics, especially when the acronym is widely favoured in everyday usage. Andrew W. Marshall, the godfather of the American RMA debate in the 1990s, was eminently plausible when he told the Senate Armed Services Committee on 5 May 1995 that

> The term 'revolution' is not meant to insist that the change will be rapid – indeed past revolutions have unfolded over a period of decades – but only that the change will be *profound,* that the new methods of warfare will be far more powerful than the old.[3]

Marshall is not, indeed cannot be, demonstrably correct, but he is certainly persuasive. However, grounds for scepticism lurk both about his recognition that 'revolution', to be such, need not happen speedily, and in his citing of the necessary truth that revolutionary change has to be *profound*. The trouble is that a distinctly non-speedy process of profound change might plausibly simply be regarded as the course of history much as usual. Is all profound change revolutionary? If we relax the temporal requirement for revolution, then surely change can hardly help but be profound?

A final quibble is the thought that 'new methods of warfare' may be judged revolutionary with reference to an absolute standard of unilateral effort, but how can that be a sensible approach for such a systemically bilateral (-plus) activity as war? Net assessment is inescapable, as Marshall, above all people, knows.[4] Investment in an RMA cannot itself guarantee that 'the new methods of warfare will be far more powerful than the old'. Strategic effect, which is, or should be, Marshall's meaning of power, can only be assessed in adversarial relation to the effect generated by the enemy. The complexity systemic to the nature of strategy and war limits the potency practicable for an RMA. The temporary outcomes possible through the dynamic, including nonlinear chaotic, character of strategy and war, are always likely to be governed and reduced by the enduring complex structure of the subject. This is an expression only of probability, not certainty, and is always liable to particular exceptions. A focus on, say, German, or whomever's, RMA leadership, has major potential to mislead theorists into neglecting both the complex structure of strategy, and the central persisting importance of conflict's adversarial essence.[5]

Third, RMA is one of those mega-concepts which in the word processors of careful scholars can be a valuable tool of strategic analysis, but which in the word processors of others can encourage misleading reductionism. As acronymic shorthand, RMA is difficult to better. However, the convenience of the hyper-terse economy of RMA usage encourages a neglect born of familiarity. This 'acronym of choice' in the 1990s,[6] because of its popularity, fuelled an existential assumption born of the nominalist fallacy, and oversimple analyses born of reification. Thus far, RMA has been deployed here in the spirit of a collective noun, referring generically to possible or actual radical changes in the character of warfare. But the price paid for apparently sharp-edged clarity in communication includes the possible encouragement of a grossly oversimplified view of the phenomena at issue. In general usage RMA is a compound term, a house with several rooms.

This third caveat is the point that all but universal reference to '*the* RMA debate', or to '*the* RMA', though harmless as informal communication among experts, can convey to those less expert the idea of a single kind of event and process. Observers of RMA debate could fail to notice that an important stake in the debate is decision on just what it is that is worth debating as RMA experience. By partial analogy, strategic commentators have to remember that in goodly measure limited war – and all wars are more or less limited – is waged both according to, and in violent contention over, particular limits. Careless contemporary references to 'the RMA' after a decade of intense debate illustrate the power of a handy acronym to fuel unrecognised reductionism.

Fourth, notwithstanding the popularity of social conservatism in the United States, and the lingering bitter aftertaste of a half-century of conflict with the heirs of the Bolshevik revolution (actually coup) of 1917, the idea of revolution remains a positive one for most Americans.[7] RMA, especially when explicitly nationally branded as 'the American RMA', enters the lists of US public debate with overwhelmingly positive cultural vibrations.[8] RMA sounds new, forward-looking, hi-tech, ruthlessly pragmatic, and, overall, hugely American. Inevitably, particular strategic cultures – consciously to risk oversimplification[9] – from seventh-century Byzantium to the United States today, favour ideas and methods which both fit their mix of strengths and weaknesses and have historical cultural resonance for them.[10] RMA today is as American as were machine tools in the 1840s,[11] the 'fleet train' in the 1940s,[12] and the global positioning system (GPS) in the 1980s.[13] RMA reflects an often admirable American preference for tackling big challenges in a suitably root-and-branch way, depending critically upon practical technologies.[14] RMA seems to offer a near-perfect expression of the preferred American way in warfare, offering technological compensation for weaknesses elsewhere (e.g. social unwillingness to take casualties and political nervousness of American boots on the ground).[15]

Fifth, although it would probably be a mistake to dismiss RMA debate simply as the concept *du jour* throughout the 1990s for the strategic literati who always need some unifying idea and issue to which they can rally for profitable debate, fashion did inflate its apparent significance. RMA had an unusually long service life as a topic 'with legs'; indeed, it remains nominally alive (as 'military transformation') as an issue area even today. When a defence community as large and well funded as the American adopts a concept or issue, the consequences are certain to be flattering to that subject. One reason, of no small importance, why so many people wrote about RMA in the 1990s was, simply, because RMA was the topic of the day. Whatever some impossibly objective judgement about inherent worth might advise, a principal merit of RMA in the 1990s was that many people wanted to read about it. I am in no position to criticise such activity, and no such criticism is intended here. The point is rather that it can be difficult to find the diamonds when so much rock has been shifted. A lively public debate is inherently likely to benefit under-standing. Analytical diamonds are reluctantly surrendered by a resisting terrain. But, to cite the famous distinction employed by Roberta Wohlstetter in her classic study of the intelligence context for Pearl Harbor 1941, there is a problem finding the true 'signals' amidst all the 'noise'.[16]

A decade of fashionable RMA debate has yielded a plethora of studies and commentaries which, necessarily, can be plotted for quality on a bell-shaped curve. In a strategic debating community as well populated as the American, the fashionable status of the RMA concept guaranteed production of a quantity of contributions that obscured quality. The potential for fashionable debates to mislead is truly formidable. Notwithstanding the powerful critiques to which leading RMA notions have been exposed, there is a distinct possibility that in the real world of American (inter alia) strategic practice, fashion may deliver imprudent efforts at implementation.

The five caveats about RMA aired immediately above are only caveats. The RMA hypothesis does not enjoy pole position here because the author believes it to be the golden key that opens the door for understanding the process of change in strategic history. Admittedly, though, even its theoretical applicability in such a heroic explanatory role is intriguing and exciting. RMA merits its prominent billing rather because it can be a useful enabler as a tool to prise open the complex edifice of strategy, for appreciation of strategy's structure and functioning. It follows that the proper focus for scepticism about RMA is not on the question, 'is RMA true?' (i.e. 'are there real live RMAs out there waiting to be captured?'), but rather, 'is the RMA hypothesis useful to improve strategic understanding?'

ANATOMY OF SPECIES

Much as zoologists discover that on close inspection a supposedly uniform species in fact comprises anatomically distinctive sub-species, so fieldwork by

35

RMA hunters in the rough terrain of strategic history has located distinguish-able classes of candidate-RMAs. There is no terminology officially sanctioned as correct, not even by Andrew W. Marshall, but research and debate in the 1990s did yield two persuasive distinctions and a range of plausible working hypotheses: between major and minor revolutions, and between revolutions that have technological innovation as their most potent catalyst and those that do not.[17] At a similarly superior level of generality and quality of insight, Williamson Murray argues that 'these revolutions [major, truly systemic changes, e.g. the French, industrial, and information revolutions] do not replace but rather overlay each other'.[18]

Given that RMA theory is difficult to test empirically, a fact that many people forget typically is true also for the non-laboratory physical sciences (e.g. geology, astronomy), our guide has to be an historically empathetic plausibility. Several alternative anatomies of candidate RMA phenomena contend for approval. Four distinguishable RMA anatomies have particular merit for their insight in explanation. None is, or can be, true, except in the sense in which each of the three first volumes of Lawrence Durrell's *Alexandria Quartet* is 'true'. Each of the four anatomies, though not presented as analytically of equal value – I acknowledge partiality – provides a different perspective on the same strategic behaviour.

Lest there be any misunderstanding over intellectual provenance, each of the four models, or paradigms, of RMA outlined below is inspired by a particular scholar or scholars. The judgements presented here are my own, but I am working with the intellectual products of the labours of many people over many years. So, what is the anatomy of RMA?

Great social waves of change
Alvin and Heidi Toffler offer us three great 'waves' in history. The three waves are in turn propelled by new kinds of productive activity, which function as the latest and most potent sources of wealth creation and allegedly find unique military expression in characteristic styles of warfare.[19] The Tofflers identify first-, second-, and now third-'wave' warfare, respectively with the rise of agriculture, then industry, and most recently with knowledge (or its close associate, information).[20] Notwithstanding the heavily Marxist underpinnings to their technologically and economically deterministic grand theory, the Tofflers and some of their followers have made an important contribution to RMA scholarship.[21]

The Tofflers' social-wave theory is elegant in its simplicity, for all its grandiosity, reductionism, and casual dating. Also, the theory stakes a massive claim about prime cause and (in this case, military) consequences which is highly plausible, significant, and, in more modest guise, is even endorsed by careful professional historians – reluctant though they might be to admit it. Many though the qualifications may be, there is certainly a broad-brush validity to the Tofflers' claims that the conditions for, and character of, warfare were revolutionised by the invention of agriculture, of industrial mass production, and, *ab extensio* – possibly today – of a knowledge-dependent economy.

To take just the modern case of so-called 'second-wave' warfare, there has to be some major, if not strictly all-case, validity to the hypothesis that societies and their polities prepare for war, and try to wage it, according to their fairly distinctive characters.[22] To find only three great social waves of revolutionary change is probably to be unduly demanding by way of criteria for revolution. However, it is scarcely more arbitrary, or less persuasive, than are theories which detect whole squads and platoons of RMAs. It is a principal virtue of the Tofflers' three-wave theory that it recognises, indeed risks over-recognising, the importance of context. As Andrew Latham notes, '[m]ilitary forces, of course, do not exist in a vacuum. Rather, they are products of complex historical processes that include social, political, material and cultural dimensions.'[23]

Ceteris paribus, security communities will wage war in ways, which is to say with styles, shaped by their more or less distinctive military and strategic cultures. Those cultures express traditional preferences deriving from the historical experience, geostrategic situation, and ideology of the society in question. 'National' strategic/military culture(s) and style are moderated by distinctive geostrategic contexts (e.g. maritime or continental, to risk over-simplification).[24] But they are also driven by the economic fuel identified in Toffleresque social-wave theory. For example, in 1914–18 Britain was not at practical strategic liberty to wage its traditionally preferred style of warfare, at least not if it was to deny Germany victory in the war and therefore hegemony in Europe.[25] In the age of '[t]he rise and decline of industrialised total warfare',[26] Britain was obliged to wage second-wave, industrialised mass warfare against Germany, a second-wave foe if ever there was one. Similarly, quaintly atavistic ideas revived in the 1930s of a British limited continental liability were shown by the events of 1939–45 to belong to a bygone age, prior to the era of total war.[27]

The proposition that military revolutions must ride on the backs of revolutionary social, economic, political, and technological change yields a healthy antidote to a persisting source of error in American-authored theory and analysis. Antidote is needed to a characteristically American tendency to treat strategic affairs in isolation from politics and society.[28] The great (American) RMA debate of the 1990s was unusually apolitical as such debates go, and therefore it appeared hazardously astrategic.[29] American theorists and other commentators debated the RMA thesis of the possibility of radical change in military tools and methods. But they did not debate the purpose that urgent prosecution of such an RMA would serve.[30] The critics who found fault with those RMA theorists who proceeded naked of historically particular strategic purpose, were not entirely on solid ground. The absence of anything worth calling a national security strategy – the US condition in the 1990s, notwithstanding the appearance of official publications which bore that elevated title[31] – had to constrain efforts to implement an RMA. But that absence is not necessarily an error. The basic rationales for the information-led RMA debated in the 1990s were, first, that opportunity beckons and, second, that the world remains a dangerous place. In other words, a relatively unimpressive current threat-set simply is the way things are (or were, in the 1990s). Probably inadvertently, some RMA critics imply that a United States in pursuit of RMA advantage requires the kind of plausible commanding strategy that can come only from identification of definite foes. Such a view is unsound. At least, it is unsound if intended literally.

The real error in much of the technology-keyed RMA theory of the 1990s did not lie in its failure to name particular enemies. Instead, the contextual error was the one addressed as the principal theme of this book: the context that matters most is the complex structure and sometimes nonlinear functioning of war and strategy upon which, and through which, RMA must operate. We should not criticise RMA proponents of various persuasions for neglecting to tailor their military–revolutionary vision explicitly to a rising China, a reviving Russia, regional rogues by name, or specific non-state but robustly 'networked' political or criminal menaces (e.g. an Osama Bin Laden). Of course an RMA will yield greater strategic return if it is anchored to a threat-set that is accurately predicted. Indeed it is possible that most of the RMA debate of the 1990s focused upon what time will reveal to be the wrong foes.[32] However, it would be absurd to require particular threat identification as a condition for progress in RMA. If politically definite threats are not evident beyond argument, it is unwise in the extreme for strategic theorists to predict them to the point of invention as a matter of convenience.

To consider the RMA debate overall is to face the need to venture into the realm of judgement about the character, some would say the nature, of future war. Such broad-gauged analysis must also address the point that defence planning needs guidance as to probable and possible threats, even when that guidance can only cite highly contingent menaces. The three-wave grand theory of the Tofflers, and other generically similar notions, suggest powerfully that truly infrequently a seismic shift in the context(s) and character of warfare leaves security communities with no practical option other than to ride the wave as best they are able. The Industrial Revolution of the nineteenth century changed modes of war systemically.[33] It is a broad proposition of many theorists of RMA that a knowledge, or information ('third-wave'), revolution is reshaping the terms and condition of conflict. Allegedly, this is a fact of today and tomorrow akin to the fact of industrialisation in the nineteenth century, and is no more avoidable in its implications.[34] Polities can try to ignore this information revolution, but the consequence for them assuredly would be revalidation of Joseph Stalin's famous aphorism: 'those who are left behind are beaten'. However, although plainly it is sensible to notice that this is significantly an information age, and while it is no less sensible to reason, *après* the Tofflers, that therefore this has to be an information age for warfare, the nagging question, 'so what?', lurks in the wings. The concept of information-age warfare, beyond being a tautologically necessary truth, may carry much less strategic meaning than some RMA theorists would have us believe. It is probably worth mentioning as a final sceptical note that it is far from certain that the Tofflers' third-wave hypothesis is well founded economically. While ours is obviously in some respects an information age, the idea that 'information' is the key to wealth creation is highly contestable.

Revolution in the revolution

If RMA is judged an idea useful both to help explain strategic history and also to provide focus for current defence policy and planning, and if one seeks a powerfully seamless architecture of theory, then one need look no further than to Williamson Murray's seminal article, 'Thinking About Revolutions in Military Affairs'. Murray draws a vital distinction between military revolutions (MRs), of which he finds only four in modern times, and RMAs, which are numerous indeed. In two strictly illustrative listings, he suggests respectively 21 and 23 RMAs since the fourteenth century.[35] Andrew F. Krepinevich suggested ten RMAs in an influential article in 1994.[36]

The two caveat 'ifs' with which this sub-section begins should not be dismissed as rhetorical flourishes or as merely token qualifiers. The reason why it is essential to preface this discussion with those caveats is precisely because Murray's treatment of the RMA postulate is so plausible, useful, and even seductive. To be accurate, and strictly fair, he is more reporting on, and tidying up, the RMA debate than he is leading a charge for RMA theory of any persuasion. Additionally, in a series of strongly worded articles on military culture, Murray has explained beyond the possibility of honest misunderstanding that he is under-impressed by the advertised military and strategic promise in the more technological variants of the contemporary RMA story.[37] Those readers not familiar with the full Murray canon on RMA, but who have read only his article in *Joint Force Quarterly* on 'Thinking About Revolutions in Military Affairs' or the introductory chapter to his co-edited book on *The Dynamics of Military Revolution*, could be at risk of capture by an unduly powerful framework for the interpretation of strategic history.

Taking Murray's theoretical architecture as the core for understanding, and adding at the margins to that core from the writings of the Tofflers, Jeffrey R. Cooper, Steven Metz, Brian R. Sullivan, and Jeremy Shapiro, one has ample material for a working theory of waves of change in strategic history[38] – if, on balance, it is judged sensible to seek such a megatheory. For those attracted to a complex, RMA-keyed theory of strategic-historical change, the ideas of the authors just cited comprise a superior mixed breed. By way of the tersest of presentations of Murray's theory: (1) very occasionally history records a

39

process of systemically radical change which registers on strategic history's Richter Scale as the seismic shock of a military revolution; (2) the earthquake that is the true military revolution (MR) is anteceded by pre-shock precursor, and by expressive direct and post-shock RMAs and (3) RMAs can be led by many possible factors, one of which is technological change – technologically driven RMAs are known as military–technical revolutions (MTRs).

Murray's nuanced presentation of the RMA concept in the context of occasional MRs appeals strongly to an intuitive grasp of how history moves, while empirically it is persuasive enough. Moreover, Murray's view is compatible with Toffleresque wave theory, with Metz's preference for a simple distinction between major and minor RMAs, with Sullivan's insistence upon an RMA/MTR divide, and also with Shapiro's thesis that there are characteristic strategists' and historians' views of military revolutions (see the discussion below). The thesis is that military revolutions are the product of such deep and broad forces, and have such all-pervading consequences and implications that they are beyond control by a cabal of enlightened, future-oriented, strategic thinkers and defence planners (or by anyone else). Cause and effect are not always unambiguously distinguishable, but the military instrument is more probably the child than the parent of broad and powerful social, economic, and political factors, interdependent though military matters and their context must be. This discussion skates dangerously close to the essentially contestable and unresolvable issue area of the relative importance of war, indeed of military concerns writ large, in history.[39] The analysis here deals with this immense topic only insofar as it must with reference to particular RMAs. I harbour no additional ambition in this already ambitious enquiry to shed new light on the significance of *strategic* topics for the general course of history. If serendipity strikes, so be it.

Scholars have to be careful not to be seduced by conceptual classification schemes that can obscure as well as clarify. The central proposition advanced by Murray and others – that strategic history's discontinuities appear in larger and smaller kinds – is inherently, as well as empirically, plausible. Notwithstanding their grandiosity in conception, the Tofflers' 'threepeating' social-wave theory is at least uniform. Each great 'wave' is propelled by radical change in the leading method of wealth production (even though it is not proven that 'information' will qualify), which is to say by the leading idea of what is most valuable, and each has characteristic broad consequences for the conduct of warfare. By way of contrast, classification of MRs, or unusually great RMAs, by professional historians offers troubling complications, though the difficulty may be largely semantic. At least the Tofflers clearly separate cause (first-, second-, or third-wave context) and consequences (first-, second-, or third-wave warfare). What are we to make of the following argument by Murray?

There appear to be two distinct historical phenomena involved in radical innovation and change. The first can be called military revolutions. *These were by far the more important, for they fundamentally changed the nature of warfare in the West.* There appear to have been four (two occurring at the same time): creation of the modern, effective nation-state based on organised and disciplined military power in the 17th century; the French Revolution and the industrial revolution beginning at the same time during the period 1789–1815, and World War I, 1914–18. We might compare them with earthquakes. *They brought with them such systemic changes in the political, social, and cultural arenas as to be largely uncontrollable, unpredictable, and above all unforeseeable* ... Such 'military revolutions' recast the nature of society and the state as well as of military organisations.[40]

There is confusion, certainly some likelihood of the promotion of confusion, here. Murray usefully distinguishes greater changes (MRs) from lesser (RMAs), but is it helpful to equate context with hypothesised content? There may or may not have been a series of military developments in the sixteenth and seventeenth centuries that in long retrospect warrant classification as 'the military revolution of early modern Europe'. But it has to be unhelpful to claim that the '17th century creation of the modern state' was the military revolution. Similarly, there is no doubting the historicity of the French and Industrial revolutions, and of the First World War, but were they the military revolutions in question? The Roberts–Parker debate, inter alia, among early-modern historians bequeathed to RMA theory writ large a somewhat casual titling of MRs which might have prejudicial consequences.[41] Was the modern state more the cause, or more the beneficiary, of a great change in warfare? Or was it both? The French and Industrial Revolutions certainly had radical consequences for warfare, but surely these were not themselves MRs, any more than was the First World War per se.

Murray's generally excellent analysis is not always as sensitive to the needs of theory-building as social scientists, at least this social scientist, would like. This is a less than systemic criticism of Murray, since much of his historical argument is strongly convincing. However, the point does relate to a central theme of this book. Specifically, the relations between historians and social scientists can be strained both when the former venture into theory-building, as does Murray on RMA, and when the latter voyage into historical analysis. Murray's analysis is outstanding for its success in 'getting the big things right enough'; certainly it appears so to this theorist. Nonetheless, several items in his essay merit critical attention, including points made in the quotation above to which I have added emphasis.

First, it is unfortunate that as an influential scholarly opinion-leader Murray should encourage the fallacious belief that military revolutions 'fundamentally changed the nature of warfare in the West'. Of course, one scholar's nature of warfare is another's character of warfare, but still it is implausible to claim that the French, Industrial, or First World War military revolutions effected as fundamental a change as is alleged. If the conduct of war alters from a typically limited military effort for limited political objectives to a far more ferocious and large-scale exercise, it is still war that one is discussing. War is war, whether it is waged by great armies or by small armies, and whether it is directed to secure heroically expansive or only modest political objectives.[42]

Second, Murray says of his four modern military revolutions that 'They brought with them such systemic changes in the political and social arenas as to be largely uncontrollable, unpredictable, and above all unforeseeable.' Excellent ideas are brought together in that sentence, but there is a vagueness, even opacity, about the words 'brought with them'. Did, indeed in what sense could, a postulated Napoleonic MR, for example, bring along the French and Industrial Revolutions? The meaning of Murray's phrasing is as inexact and puzzling as it is potentially significant. After all, what is under discussion is nothing less than the relationship between military revolution and its (inter alia) social, political, and economic contexts. This non-trivial matter of military event or process and its contexts pertains directly to cause and effect in military innovation.

The imposition of a pattern upon the course of (strategic) history is a perilous venture. Murray's hypothesised short list of four MRs in modern times does not include a nuclear revolution – an omission he corrects in *The Dynamics of Military Revolution*.[43] He cites the possibility of a fifth MR, but that candidate new entry is the child of information technology, not of the weaponisation of atomic physics. This is a case where a scholar was wrong (he did admit as much) but principally for the right reason. On Murray's initial understanding of what makes for true military revolutions, it is easy to see why the creation of the modern state, the French and Industrial Revolutions, and the First World War, made the élite grade, but the nuclear discovery (and its consequences) did not. The nuclear revolution, if such it was, manifestly did not have a seismic impact upon the social, political, and economic contexts of strategy. Moreover, as Murray notes, that alleged revolution has been utterly invisible in actual explosive deeds in warfare since 1945 in the eponymous 'nuclear era'.[44] So, how might Murray have been wrong? Arguably, because at the core of the nuclear fact, and for the first time in strategic history, there is a weapon which really might alter the nature of war – a point he conceded for great powers, but apparently found relatively unimpressive.[45] Nuclear war might, but only might, have an outcome thoroughly incompatible with the basic integrity of the logic chain integral to the meaning of strategy. Large-scale nuclear use could drop the bridge that is strategy; the bridge between political purpose and military capability.[46] Special respect is due a weapon that can trump all other weapons, that in effect could knock over the game table thereby cancelling the value of all other pieces on the board and all points scored to date.

Nuclear weapons have altered probably for ever the relationship between *grande guerre* and high policy. The facts that those weapons have not revolutionised politics domestically and have not changed much in the 'game of nations', should not mislead us. Murray was not persuasive when he sought to demote nuclear weapons simply to the category of 'possible RMA'. He attached their singularity quite strictly to the claim that their revolution, uniquely among the 21 RMAs on his illustrative list, has been solely technological in character (albeit, as he notes, 'almost entirely political' in impact 'except for their first use against the Japanese'). Murray is exceptionally persuasive, however, when he emphasises the historically modest role of technology in RMAs. He writes:

> The list [of 21 'possible RMAs'] suggests a number of points. First, given the enthusiasm for describing the coming RMA as technological, the historical record suggests that technological change represents a relatively small part of the equation.[47]

So modest is the role of technology as occasional leading-edge element that there are grounds for scepticism over the merit in the concept of a military–*technical* revolution (MTR). First, all strategic behaviour must have a technological dimension: the threat or use of force – a distinguishing characteristic for strategic activity – requires weapons as tools of the trade. More generally viewed, all strategic behaviour occurs in a particular technological context. Second, as Murray notes tellingly, the historical candidates for technology-led RMAs, let alone MRs, are exceedingly rare. Third, even when technology is in the front rank pushing, or more likely pulling, for radical change, it can function as a catalyst for major enhancement of military power only when it is assisted by ideas, organisation, and numbers (mass).[48] Appreciation of the complexity of strategy and war should depress enthusiasm for the idea of MTR.

Understanding of 'the Murray version', or – to be just – simply 'the Murray reading' of RMA studies, is assisted by recognition of the sense in Jeremy Shapiro's insistence upon the distinction between a historian's and a strategist's view of RMA. Shapiro's 'historian's view' is closer to Murray's explanation of MR than it is to RMA. Shapiro advises that:

> There are two radically different, though perhaps complementary, ways to view a military revolution. Historians typically take a long view and see a military revolution as an observable breaking point between two recognisably different types of warfare. This view of military revolutions tends to downplay the role of human agency in the making of a revolution. Such revolutions stem from exogenous forces which were bound,

sooner or later, to spark a fundamental shift in the methods of war. Technological, demographic, or social changes in this sense 'push' the revolution into being.[49]

The Tofflers' three waves fit this bill suitably, as would Murray's four-(later five-) item short list of great military revolutions in modern history (the invention of the state, the French Revolution, the Industrial Revolution, the First World War, and nuclear). Shapiro proceeds to explain 'the strategist's view'.

> The strategist is more concerned with the problems of the here and now and, as a result, sees a revolution as consisting of essentially clever, new solutions to previously insoluble geostrategic problems. These solutions usually, but not necessarily, use new technologies. In any case, the impetus is not some new exogenous technological or social reality but rather a particular nation's strategic problems.[50]

Shapiro's 'strategist's view' fits quite closely Murray's understanding of RMA as contrasted with MR. Moreover, Shapiro effects a useful and largely plausible reconciliation.

> These views of military revolutions do not strictly contradict each other. They can be reconciled by an understanding that sees the short-run motor of the strategist's revolution determining the path if not the ultimate outcome of the historian's revolution. However, in their details, these two views see very different revolutions and very different implications of any military revolution. *The strategist's revolution is made; the historian's happens.*[51]

This is a perceptive addendum to the theorising by Murray and others about distinctions between MR, RMA, and MTR. Shapiro adds further lustre to his name when he thickens Murray's claim for the unpredictability of MRs.

> The current proposed information-based revolution in military affairs has been the most self-conscious military revolution in history, yet most commentators have largely passed over the question of whether they see themselves as creating a strategist's revolution or predicting a historian's. While both types of revolution have analytical validity in retrospect, the utility of the historian's viewpoint to inform the current debate is very limited. While contemporaries can and must *create* military revolutions in the strategic sense, their ability to *predict* military revolutions in the historic sense is virtually non-existent ... These revolutions only seem clear in retrospect.[52]

Readers are at liberty to shop as they see fit for the concept or concepts they prefer among MR, RMA, and MTR (as well as alleged 'revolutions' in strategic affairs and security affairs). If taken too seriously, these ideas threaten to confuse, and to confound commonsense, more than they help to enlighten. The paragraphs immediately below provide a respectful, yet critical, restatement of the somewhat competing, though largely complementary, RMA concepts just discussed.

The character of war is always changing, but from time to time the pace of change accelerates, or appears to do so, with the result that there is a change of state in warfare. War must still be war, but it is waged in a noticeably different manner.

The conduct of war and other strategic behaviour has to express characteristics distinctive to their social context, broadly understood. Rather like the history of global weather, which has cycles within cycles within cycles, and so forth, all modified by apparent contingency, war and strategy have a history of change that lends itself to highly contestable explanation by complex cyclical theory.

War and strategy can be revolutionised as their social context is transformed by the invention of agriculture, industrial mass production, and *just possibly* by the emergence of knowledge-based enterprise. But war and strategy also can be revolutionised by occasional great upheavals in the political and social worlds which owe little if anything to radical change in the means and methods of wealth creation. The hypothesised military revolutions that attended (created, defended) the emergence of the modern state, the French Revolution and (First) Empire, and the First World War, were none of them unarguably the product of Toffleresque social wave forces, but they certainly recorded radical changes.[53]

In addition to the rare, exceptionally systemic, upheaval in military affairs, many aspects of military affairs frequently record change in their limited, but important, realms that might be termed revolutionary. Candidate RMAs of modest scope and dimension can pertain directly to fortification, naval architecture, medical provision, land and air transportation, amphibious operations, and so forth. These many hypothesised RMAs may be likened to foothills or low mountains in relation to towering peaks. Evidence of a succession of near simultaneous, probably synergistically interacting, RMAs may signal the emergence or possibility of a much greater convulsion, a true military revolution which transcends in its features the sum of its (inter alia) multiple-RMA parts.

Although the US defence community is culturally prone to exaggerate the relative significance of technology for strategy and war, we need to be alert to the error of making a vigorous effort to demote technology by way of analytical (over)compensation.[54] Occasionally, there is a discontinuity in military affairs in which the cutting edge for change truly is, or certainly includes, technological innovation. Of course, there are always dimensions other than the technological in play. Technology needs translation into weapons, and weapons have to function in person–machine systems, properly organised, acquired in critical mass, suitably tactically trained, and employed for advantageous operational effect. Nonetheless, technology counts. It always must count for something, because all strategic behaviour occurs, and is planned to occur, in a particular technological context. It may be useful to identify some episodes of change as constituting military–technical revolutions (MTRs). The adoption of the six-foot longbow by English armies at the beginning of the fourteenth century, the adoption of gunpowder artillery between the 1340s and the 1440s, the exploitation of railways for military logistics, the maturing of militarily practical aircraft, the weaponisation of the discoveries of atomic fission and fusion, and the military exploitation of the computer, could all be described as MTRs.

It may be fun to do battle with competing acronyms, but it is not always enlightening. Scholars need to address more the empirical, if contestable, referents that can be gleaned from strategic history, than they do their most favoured categories of analysis. For example, the contemporary emergence of a (US) style in warfare dependent on exploitation of information technologies has been hailed variously as third-wave warfare, an MR, an RMA, and merely as an MTR (viewed either as a variant of, or as a lower form of change possibly independent of, RMA).[55]

Not all in the great RMA debate is scholastic trivialisation. Whatever one elects to call the evidence of military change seen today, it matters profoundly whether what appears to be on offer is simply a *plat*, or *plats, du jour*, which we can purchase or not more or less as our taste dictates, or whether what is on offer are but variants of a whole diet truly mandatory for our security health. As Murray and Knox note, periodically if irregularly, the whole context for strategic behaviour alters so radically that the only practicable choice lies between on the one hand versions of adoption and adaptation, and on the other obsolescence leading to marginalisation and probably eventual defeat.[56] Modern state structures, industrial methods, and information systems are none of them in the 'optional' column for polities and societies. Some revolutions can be ignored or evaded, but others cannot. This fundamental point underlines much of the debate, which otherwise can appear trivial, over MRs, RMAs, and MTRs.

Action and reaction
Intersecting the ideas on MR, RMA, and MTR addressed above is an earlier perspective upon RMA, first aired in 1991 by mediaeval historian Clifford J. Rogers, which sees a long causal chain of action and reaction.[57] It is tempting to consign Rogers' theorisation to the bin of early efforts at RMA understanding subsequently overtaken by more refined notions. To propose such dismissal would not be without merit. However, it would risk missing what a professional historian finds convincing to help explain his particular period

of expertise (the fourteenth and fifteenth centuries), and it could discourage effort to explore causation in strategic behaviour.

In search of better understanding of the dynamics of historical change, Rogers borrowed the concept of 'punctuated equilibrium' from the biological sciences.

> In 1972, Stephen Jay Gould and Niles Eldredge proposed a new model for the evolutionary formation of species, which they dubbed 'punctuated equilibrium'. They argued that evolution proceeded by short bursts of rapid change interspersed with long periods of near stasis rather than constant, slow alteration.[58]

Critics of Gould and Eldredge argued compellingly that the model should allow a greater role to incremental change, but the basic idea, of evolution proceeding with plateaux of largely business-as-usual interrupted by spikes of creativity (strategic moments, perhaps), was accepted.

> This newer conception of punctuated equilibrium evolution, combining both incremental and 'revolutionary' change, seems to describe the process of military innovation extraordinarily well. After a long period of near-stasis, infantry began to evolve very rapidly around the beginning of the fourteenth century. Cannon appeared at about that time, evolved incrementally for a century, then in a burst of rapid advancement revolutionised war in Europe. Artillery fortifications began to develop at about the same time as artillery reached its height; evolved gradually over the course of a century; then in their turn effected a military revolution. *A similar process of punctuated equilibrium evolution in military technology continues even today.*[59]

Rogers summarises his theory thus: 'I will argue that Western military dominance derived from a *series* of sequential military revolutions, each an attempt to reverse a disequilibrium introduced by the previous one, rather than from a single "Military Revolution".'[60] It is understandable and probably laudable for historians to be uncomfortable with single conceptions so grand that they reduce drastically the rich complexity of history. Rogers writes critically of Roberts, Parker, and others who are tolerably content with the hypothesis of a single great early-modern Military Revolution.

> By attempting to subsume the innovations of five centuries into a single phenomenon, we may be imposing an artificial teleological unity on to a series of inherently distinct, separate developments. And, in doing so, we may be clouding our understanding of a critically important area of history, an area which fully deserves to be studied through the clearest possible lens.[61]

While I believe Rogers overreaches with his use of 'punctuated equilibrium evolution' theory, he underreaches in the final sentence quoted. All areas of history are important, none inherently more or less than others, and a single lens, no matter how clear, cannot in this case cope with the traffic of required understanding.

In recent decades the essentially simple, but potentially theoretically powerful, idea which attracted Rogers has attracted other theorists. To summarise, Rogers suggests that strategic history reveals a process of innovation (RMAs) wherein and whereby disequilibrium among military elements is produced by short bursts of radical change. Those short creative bursts lead to periods of relative advantage for, say, infantry, or gunpowder siege artillery. The disequilibrium thus effected motivates a (ultimately successful) hunt for offsetting methods, and/or weapons, of war. Even for Rogers' mediaeval zone of special expertise, let alone for the 1990s (note the historical reach claimed in the italicised words quoted), his logically compelling idea is unduly simple.

In 'Thinking About Revolutions in Military Affairs', Murray suggests persuasively that Rogers' (inter alia) hypothesis of a neat series of sequentially discrete RMAs imposes an undue orderliness upon strategic history.[62] One should add to Murray's reservations the objection that the necessarily competitive context for strategic behaviour cannot be assumed to follow a strategically logical and tidy path of action and reaction. Rogers appears unaware of the fact that while early-modern, and then mediaeval and modern, historians were merrily debating 'the Roberts thesis' and 'the Parker variant' on *The Military Revolution*, physical and social scientists were energetically debating the dynamics of competitive armament, in a phrase, 'arms-race theory'. Contemporary defence professionals discovered, or at least thought they had discovered (there were, and remain, problems of evidence on causality), that even the most apparently self-evident of action–reaction chains often are not what they appear to be.[63]

Security communities, mediaeval and modern, certainly develop new military means and methods which might counter the forces and techniques of the contemporary foe or of the foe expected tomorrow. However, the dynamics of innovation rarely reduce neatly to an orderly sequence of action and reaction. Innovation can proceed not so much, *à la* Rogers, 'to reverse a particular disequilibrium', but rather to exploit new possibilities for a strategically generic reason (e.g. it is desirable to be militarily more effective), to give practical expression to new military ideas, and even to serve domestic institutional interests. For example, American theorists in the 1960s invented a logically compelling theory of arms-race dynamics organised by the hypothesis of a tight linkage between arms-competitive actions and reactions borrowed simple-mindedly from the physical sciences: to every action there must be an equal and opposite reaction. This arms-race theory was deployed politically to claim that ballistic missile defence (BMD) would be strategically destabilising, a mortal sin in the Cold War universe of strategists. Allegedly, BMD *to protect people* would deprive the adversary of its hostages (if the BMD were tolerably militarily credible, that is, a logical consequence which must drive it to augment offensive nuclear forces so as to preserve the stability of deterrence).[64] It should follow logically that if an offence–defence action–reaction mechanism drives the 'arms race', then measures of arms control which stultify or forbid the defence must remove much of the policy motivation behind the build-up and modernisation of strategic nuclear offensive forces.

The problem with action–reaction theory as applied to the arms competition of the Cold War is that it is not true, at least it is not true enough. The ABM Treaty of 1972 broke the defence link in the offence–defence spiral in futility that supposedly drove the arms competition, but the offence expanded and modernised regardless.[65] In the immortal words of Charles E. Callwell: 'Theory cannot be accepted as conclusive when practice points the other way.'[66] The difficulty with Rogers' action–reaction theory of RMA is not that it has no merit. Of necessity there is an adversarial dimension to strategy and war. Rather, the difficulty is that Rogers and those theorists of more modern strategic affairs who favour a simple logic of RMA action and eventually offsetting RMA reaction, unwisely discount the salience both of historical contingency and of astrategic motivation.

For a telling case in point, a study by John France of the 300 years of 'Western warfare in the age of the crusades' appears at first sight to offer some limited support to Rogers' use of the theory of 'punctuated equilibrium evolution'. France informs us that '[t]here was no linear development [between 1000 and 1300] but, rather, a series of impulses produced changes that were not always sustained, and in the end much depended on powerful personalities.'[67] The idea of a 'series of impulses' could be interpreted as tolerably congruent with Rogers' use of the concept of punctuated equilibrium. Closer inspection, however, discourages such a view.

France is careful to bracket his registering of a 'series of impulses' with caveats claiming 'no linear development' and the fact that the changes in question 'were not always sustained'. The experience of Western mediaeval warfare as described by France thus on closer inspection does not fit easily with Rogers' model. Instead of the orderly linear realm of 'a *series* of sequential revolutions, each an attempt to reverse a disequilibrium introduced by the previous one', France describes instead the world of war of a high middle ages wherein

> the nobility were the dominant force, and there could be no academy of war – no career structure of merit – which might challenge their position. This explains the conservatism of armies and the erratic nature of change in Western warfare.[68]

Earlier, he writes:

> There was no forum in which to develop weapons. Warfare was episodic and there were no permanent staffs to form intellectual centres: the

'Twelfth-century Renaissance' bred no academies of war, for war already had its elite, who felt no need to give way to any new forces. By the end of the twelfth century, powerful monarchies were acquiring arsenals and these must have stereotyped arms and armour to a degree. But there was no marriage of thought and technology, so that advance remained piece-meal and by individual experiment. In these circumstances, new ideas would have been diffused only slowly and unevenly.[69]

Considered in conjunction, Rogers' model of the pattern of military inno-vation in early-modern Europe (and beyond), and France's near-rejection of any pattern for the high middle ages, suggest two points potentially important for our analysis. On the one hand, it is not wholly self-evident that the social context of Western warfare was so different in its essentials as between the periods 1000–1300 and 1300–1453 (or c. 1540), as to explain convincingly the contrast between the two views of military innovation. On the other hand, if we elect to trust in the period expertise of these scholars (i.e. not when they venture, as does Rogers, into open-ended extrapolation of his thesis), the possibility emerges that although strategy and war are structurally timeless, the architecture and dynamics of military innovation are not.

The possible period specificity of dominant explanations of RMA or its absence parallels the argument in David Kaiser's work on the causes of war. He allows that although war may be war in all periods, there will tend to be a similarity in war causality among polities in the same period.[70] France writes that 'It is a truth barely worth labouring that an army will reflect closely the nature of the society that produces it.'[71] That important, if commonplace, thought can be heavily amended for our purpose so as to read: 'An RMA will reflect closely in its origins, dynamics, course, and consequences the society (domestic and international) that produces it.'

While the concept of RMA may be usefully applicable to all historical strate-gic experience, we need to be alert to the strong probability that contextual differences among periods are likely to be reflected in different patterns in military innovation. It may be that any transhistorical grand theory of inno-vation, purporting to identify and explain a regular pattern in RMA, MR, or MTR, must be fundamentally flawed. The point is not that there is no such radical change, far from it. Rather, the argument is that any favoured theory which discerns a pattern in RMA occurrence (e.g. of punctuated equilibrium evolution, as in Rogers' studies) characteristic of a particular era, and can explain plausibly the reasons for that pattern, has to be suspect when it 'plays abroad' in 'away fixtures' in different periods. This caveat on RMA grand theory does not extend to the basic structure of the life-cycle of RMA. Chapter 3 provides a theory of that life-cycle which can accommodate all potential RMA behaviour in all periods. A timeless structure is consistent with shifting patterns in occurrence and scale of activity.

Business as usual

In the interest of encouraging a healthy scepticism, it is useful to conclude this analysis of the anatomy of RMA with an existentially challenging view. Borrowing from Commandant Jean Colin, British soldier and historian Cyril Falls began his study *A Hundred Years of War* with a chapter on 'The Transformations of War'.[72] Falls succeeds admirably in balancing recognition of change with issuing a warning against exaggeration of its importance. This chapter by Falls should be compulsory reading for those breathless discoverers of RMA who are, alas, all too often historically challenged in their under- standing.[73] Falls provides the most persuasive generic corrective to RMA thinking known to this author. He is not in any sense reactionary. In fact he is not even particularly conservative, while his professional credentials must accord him an unusual measure of respect a priori. *A Hundred Years of War* was completed in 1953. Falls was a staff officer in, and an official historian of, the First World War, and subsequently worked as a journalist and as a scholar.[74] In short, Cyril Falls (1888–1971) witnessed, and in most respects experienced, the great changes in warfare of the twentieth century. If the First World War produced a military revolution, or if the atomic bomb marked a turning point in strategic history, then Captain, later Professor, Cyril Falls was a man in a position to be suitably impressed.

Falls chose to emphasise the empty half of the glass of military change that is half full. He did so, moreover, with an analysis whose long Olympian perspective does not require the suppression of theoretically inconvenient facts.

> It will be seen therefore that the century to be covered [1850–1950] began with great innovations [e.g. rifling of breech-loading firearms, railways, electric telegraph]. And it kept up the process. The submarine, the internal combustion engine, the aircraft, wireless telegraphy and telephony, the tank, and finally the atomic bomb, complete a remarkable development.

Having flagged his full recognition of technical change in the conduct of war, Falls then proceeds to state a powerful caveat.

> Yet if there be one warning rather than any other which ought to be given at the beginning of our study, it is that the student should not believe everything moves only when he sees the process at a glance, and stands still when he does not see it moving. It is his eyes which are at fault. They see movement of a pattern and in circumstances which are familiar to them; they fail to detect it when those are unfamiliar. The more scholarly the enquirer becomes, the more conscious is he of endless change.[75]

Williamson Murray notes what amounts to a variant upon Falls' argument when he writes that once Clifford J. Rogers had implanted the idea that 'there was not one military revolution but a series that reached from the middle ages to the present day ...[n]ot surprisingly there has been a rush to examine virtually everything from the strategy of Edward III to *Blitzkrieg* operations in the light of what we call *revolutions in military affairs*.[76] I suspect that had the idea of business as usual, or near continuous innovation, rather than RMA, been the intellectual flavour of the time in the early 1990s, that is what careful scholarship most probably would have unearthed. To adapt the sanguine biblical aphorism of 'seek and ye shall find': 'know what you seek, and you are likely to find it'. Some words by Cyril Falls may help balance RMA theory.

> Observers constantly describe the warfare of their own age as marking a revolutionary breach in the normal progress of methods of warfare. Their selection of their own age ought to put readers and listeners on their guard. Careful examination shows that, historically speaking, the transformations of war are not commonly violent. The invention of gunpowder was one of the most violent; the construction of a heavier-than-air flying machine was a second; the exploitation of atomic energy may be expected to be another. Gunpowder and aircraft, however, proved less revolutionary – using the word in its true sense as connoting both complete and violent change – than contemporaries expected. Atomic energy has not, as these lines are written [1953], been tested in this respect.

Falls' punchlines could hardly appear more challenging to much of the radical transformational spirit of some of the RMA theory of the 1990s.

> It is a fallacy, due to ignorance of technical and tactical military history, to suppose that methods of warfare have not made continuous and, on the whole, fairly even progress ... It is also true that there have been periods in which progress has been slower than in others, at least in some respects ... These are exceptions, and in any case it is not to be expected that science in war, any more than in other activities, should be perfectly regular in its development. The irregularities are minor when the whole process is surveyed.[77]

This is as bold an analysis in denial of the RMA hypothesis, as that hypothesis, and its variants, is bold in its imperial claim to explain the patterns in the process of change in strategic history. Falls is, indeed can be, neither right nor wrong in his broad-brush characterisation. However, he was at least as competent a military historian as are those who signed on to serve in one or other of the competing legions of RMA theorists in the 1990s. Moreover, Falls' first-hand experience of 'the birth of the modern style of warfare' for three years on the Western Front from 1915 to 1918,[78] and his intimate, if somewhat less perilous long subsequent involvement in strategic matters, translate as formidable credentials as a base from which to theorise.

Falls' judgements are not quite as damning of the RMA thesis as a swift reading might mislead one to credit. He denies neither that change, even 'major transformations of war',[79] occurs, nor that the pace of change can vary. Most RMA theorists should be tolerably comfortable with this interesting summary by Falls of his views.

> The point which it is desired to make is that movement [i.e. innovation] goes on all the time and that since the sixteenth century it would be hard to find any period of fifty years at the end of which an army, with contemporary weapons and tactics, could not with ease have utterly destroyed an army with those of the start of the half-century. This is almost equally true of naval fleets, and recently at least as true. In air warfare the transformations which render obsolete equipment and tactics take place every six years at the longest.[80]

As noted above, Falls' perspective does not exclude recognition of the phenomenon of 'transformations of war', indeed quite the contrary. It does, however, accord more weight and significance to the irregularly paced processes of innovatory business as usual between historical episodes of RMA. By analogy, the outbreak of what became the Great War of 1914–18 can be explained in temporally complementary fashion with reference to: (1) crisis moves at the very end of July and in the first days of August 1914; (2) the events of the whole summer of 1914; (3) the policies and strategies of the relevant great and lesser powers in the decade leading up to 1914; (4) the structure of European balance-of-power politics, and the attendant ethos and assumptions,[81] from the 1870s to 1914; and (5) 'waves of great wars' in modern European history (1494–1529, 1618–48, 1672–1713, 1791–1815, and 1914–45).[82]

A QUESTION OF CONTINUITY

Scholars can employ their imagination to read the same data in different ways, none of which is correct or incorrect. This is why my 'anatomy of species' provides distinctive, yet generally complementary, lenses on the subject. The point of this discussion has been to enrich understanding of the processes of change in strategic history. Most emphatically, the purpose has not been to test more and less fashionable concepts and select a winner. Each school of thought on RMA contributes to strategic understanding not so much because it aids historical interpretation, but more because it helps expose the structure and dynamics of strategy and war.

Figure 2.1 illustrates notionally the patterns of change in the four perspectives on RMA anatomy presented above. Given the subjectivity in assessment of the incidence of allegedly revolutionary occurrences, the simple social-wave graphic alone is intended to match precisely the speculations of particular theorists.

Each graph plots a claimed pattern of relative significance of military change over time.

Figure 2:1: Patterns of Change

1. *Toffler three-wave theory*

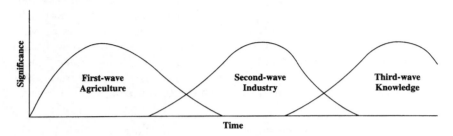

- The first wave lasted nearly 7,000 years, the second 250 years, the third is now nearly 50 years old.

2. *Revolution in the revolution: MR, RMA, MTR theory*

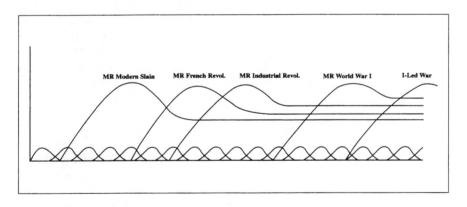

- The five MRs layer upon, rather than totally succeed, each other.
- The foothills are pre-shock, direct, and after-shock RMAs (to the 'earthquakes' of the five MRs).
- Some RMAs will be MTRs.
- Some theorists distinguish RMAs from MTRs.
- Strategic history is not as regular as the patterning here might suggest to the unwary.

3. *Punctuated equilibrium, action–reaction*

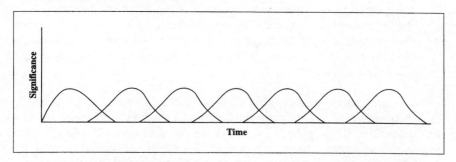

- Each RMA is negated fairly neatly in sequence by a succeeding and offsetting RMA.
- The periods between RMAs witness some significant evolution in means and methods for military effectiveness.

4. *Business as usual, continuous innovation*

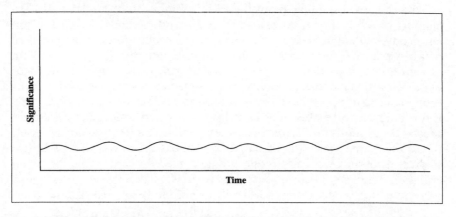

- Periodic transformations of war occur, but they stand out from a normal condition of generally steady innovation, not from periods of near-stasis.

So rich and intuitively appealing is the literature on RMA theory that fundamental questioning of the sense in its founding premise risks dismissal as a scholarly profanity. That founding premise appears with admirable directness in the first sentence of an interesting extended definition offered by Michael J. Vickers.

> *Military revolutions are major discontinuities in military affairs.* They are brought about by changes in militarily relevant technologies, concepts of operations, methods of organisation, and/or resources available. Relatively abruptly – most typically over two to three decades – they

55

transform the conduct of war and make possible order-of-magnitude (or greater) gains in military effectiveness. They sharpen the advantage held by the strategic/operational offense and create enormous intertemporal differentials of capability between military regimes. A hierarchy of change links these revolutions with broader social, economic, and scientific transformations.[83]

One cannot ask very usefully whether or not Vickers' exciting and exceptionally clear description is true. But one can and must enquire whether or not the description is misleading. By analogy, one can ask of troops who are impressive on parade: 'very pretty, but will they fight?' Vickers merits praise not only for the clarity of his definition and description of RMA, but also for the ruthlessness of his summary dismissal of a confusion of competing RMA concepts (if I may thus coin the collective noun for RMA notions): 'The "revolution in military affairs" should be considered interchangeable with military revolution or military–technical revolution.'[84]

What is most troubling about the RMA premise is not its claim that the conduct of war can be transformed in means and methods. So much is but an incontestable statement of the obvious. The problem lies in the potential of RMA theory to de-emphasise elements of continuity, as contrasted with discontinuity. In particular, there is a noteworthy possibility that the focus upon revolutionary change and its most immediate agents will incline RMA proponents to neglect those elements of continuity that are necessary enablers if revolution is to be effected.[85] Both historically and conceptually there are substantial grounds for disquiet over the popularity of RMA theory of recent years. The fourth 'anatomy of species' presented above was that of British soldier–historian Cyril Falls: recall that he argued for transformation by an evolution in military affairs. His writings serve as a sobering, yet non-atavistic, corrective to the outpouring of RMA theory in the 1990s. Falls advises that

> each new invention, each new tactic, takes its place in the armoury of warfare, meets new currents of opposition, fails here, triumphs there, adds to itself in this direction, lets a part of itself drop in that, and finally becomes so changed as to be almost unrecognisable. Yet it does not disappear altogether, and sometimes, a century, three centuries afterwards, circumstances become favourable to its re-establishment in a form astonishingly similar to the original.[86]

Falls also offers a basic judgement on what it is, actually who it is, that enables strategy to be done, no matter which style of warfare prevails. 'But we must never forget that it is the unknown fighting man who garners the fruits of strategy. Dogmatism which leaves out of account the human factor is worthless.'[87] The cutting-edge literature in the mid-1990s which explained and advocated 'the American RMA', was notably quiet in its treatment of the human factor.[88]

The discussion has considered different claimed anatomies of the historical pattern of RMA. The analysis proceeds next, in Chapter 3, to make sufficient sense of RMA theory – with relevant caveats – as to equip us to proceed into the realms of strategy and then of historical cases. In the trajectory of this book, as in the real world of strategic behaviour, the time has come dramatically to reduce, if not wholly banish, confusion, and identify an RMA theory that assists, rather than detracts from, strategic understanding.

NOTES

1. Since chaos theory invites excessive claims for its explanatory domain even among the ranks of professional scientists, it is scarcely surprising that its terms-of-art, or specialised jargon, have notable potential to mislead unwary social scientists. For example, Peter Coveney and Roger Highfield warn that 'In everyday language chaos is synonymous with randomness, making people contrast it with ordered behaviour, and thus think of some kind of precarious balance between opposites. But its scientific usage is quite different; there, as we have pointed out, the term masks the fact that chaotic dynamics is actually exquisitely organised': *Frontiers of Complexity: The Search for Order in a Chaotic World* (London: Faber & Faber, 1995), p. 277. Alan Beyerchen's brilliant article, 'Clausewitz, Nonlinearity, and the Unpredictability of War', *International Security*, 17, 3 (Winter 1992/93), pp. 59–90, both exaggerates war's nonlinearity and, most especially, inevitably has had the effect of encouraging such exaggeration by others. Complexity, chaos, and nonlinearity are important and valid ideas that are applicable to, indeed are inherent in the structure and dynamics of, strategy and war, but their relevance should not be overstated, as I fear is the case in these otherwise strongly praiseworthy articles: Williamson Murray, 'Clausewitz Out, Computer In: Military Culture and Technological Hubris', *The National Interest*, 48 (Summer 1997), p. 61; Mackubin Thomas Owens, 'Technology, the RMA, and Future War', *Strategic Review*, 26, 2 (Spring 1998), esp. pp. 65–7; and Paul K. Van Riper and F. G. Hoffman, 'Pursuing the Real Revolution in Military Affairs: Exploiting Knowledge-Based Warfare', *National Security Studies Quarterly*, 4, 3 (Summer 1998), pp. 4–6. My point is not that these authors and their leading source of inspiration (Beyerchen on Clausewitz) are wrong. They are not. Rather, the problem is that inadvertently they abuse the good idea of nonlinearity by neglecting the fact that much, perhaps most, strategic behaviour in peace and war is significantly linear.

2. See Horace L. Fairlamb, *Critical Conditions: Postmodernity and the Question of Foundations* (Cambridge: Cambridge University Press, 1994), for a root-and-branch review of the basics of critical theory; Keith Jenkins (ed.), *The Postmodern History Reader* (London: Routledge, 1997), for new history – if history it is – with a vengeance. Critical theory for historians is dismissed plausibly, if probably too gently, in Richard J. Evans, *In Defence of History* (London: Granta Books, 1997); while strategic studies is offered a 'critical' future in Keith Krause and Michael C. Williams (eds), *Critical Security Studies: Concepts and Cases* (London: UCL Press, 1997), and Richard Gwyn Jones, *Security, Strategy, and Critical Theory* (Boulder, CO: Lynne Rienner Publishers, 1999). I appreciate that assertion is not argument and that my belief that critical theory is largely folly is only my belief. As at the time of writing, no 'mainstream' scholar of strategy has made the effort to publish a comprehensive refutation of 'critical' security theory. The overwhelming reason – certainly for this author – is that 'critical' theory has been judged

unworthy of the time and effort needed for its refutation. This explanation, though true, is not a happy one. Since some serious scholars have 'gone critical' over the past decade or so – Ken Booth, for example (see his contributions to Krause and Williams, *Critical Security Studies*, pp. 83–119 and (with Peter Vale) 329–58) – the time is overdue for direct engagement in debate between traditional views and 'critical' critiques.

3. Andrew W. Marshall, Prepared Statement before the Senate Armed Services Committee, Subcommittee on Acquisition and Technology, 5 May 1995, p. 2 (emphasis added).

4. See George E. Pickett, James G. Roche, and Barry D. Watts, 'Net Assessment: A Historical Review', in Andrew W. Marshall, J. J. Martin, and Henry S. Rowen (eds), *On Not Confusing Ourselves: Essays on National Security Strategy in Honor of Albert and Roberta Wohlstetter* (Boulder, CO: Westview Press, 1991), pp. 58–85. Carl von Clausewitz advises that 'War is nothing but a duel on a larger scale. Countless duels go to make up war, but a picture of it as a whole can be formed by imagining a pair of wrestlers. Each tries through physical force to compel the other to do his will': *On War*, trans. Michael Howard and Peter Paret (Princeton, NJ: Princeton University Press, 1976 [1832]), p. 75.

5. Edward N. Luttwak, *Strategy: The Logic of War and Peace* (Cambridge, MA: Harvard University Press, 1987), is a classic statement of the paradoxical logic of conflict which has strategy's adversarial quality as its centerpiece. André Beaufre, *An Introduction to Strategy*, trans. R. H. Barry (London: Faber & Faber, 1965), declares that strategy 'is therefore the art of the dialectic of force, or, more precisely, *the art of the dialectic of two opposing wills using force to resolve their dispute*' (p. 22, emphasis in original).

6. Williamson Murray, 'Thinking about Revolutions in Military Affairs', *Joint Force Quarterly*, 16 (Summer 1997), p. 69.

7. S. P. MacKenzie identifies as a problem for sound scholarship 'the almost a priori assumption that revolutions have generated new ways of war and above all a new and more effective type of soldier. Universal and fervent belief in a revolutionary cause, to put it in very simple terms, is assumed to translate into military innovation and greater effectiveness on the battlefield: or, to simplify even more, right equals might': *Revolutionary Armies in the Modern Era: A Revisionist Approach* (London: Routledge, 1997), p. 1.

8. For example, William A. Owens, 'The American Revolution in Military Affairs', *Joint Force Quarterly*, 10 (Winter 1995–96), pp. 37–8. The fact that Owens was Vice Chairman of the JCS when he signed this article to press renders it substantially authoritative as a national proprietary claim.

9. Shu Guang Zhang, *Deterrence and Strategic Culture: Chinese–American Confrontations, 1949–1958* (Ithaca, NY: Cornell University Press, 1992); Colin S. Gray, *Modern Strategy* (Oxford: Oxford University Press, 1999), ch. 5; Alastair Iain Johnston, 'Strategic Cultures Revisited: Reply to Colin Gray', *Review of International Studies*, 25, 3 (July 1999), pp. 519–23; and Keith Krause, 'Cross-Cultural Dimensions of Multilateral Non-Proliferation and Arms Control Dialogues: An Overview', in Krause (ed.), *Culture and Security: Multilateralism, Arms Control and Security Building* (London: Frank Cass, 1999), pp. 1–22.

10. Pending the appearance of Edward N. Luttwak's long-promised study of Byzantine strategy, see Walter Emil Kaegi, Jr, *Some Thoughts on Byzantine Military Strategy* (Brookline, MA: Hellenic College Press, 1983); and John Haldon, *Warfare, State and Society in the Byzantine World, 565–1204* (London: UCL Press, 1999), esp. ch. 2. For the contemporary United States of America, see Edward N. Luttwak, 'Toward Post-Heroic Warfare', *Foreign Affairs*, 74, 3 (May/June 1995), pp. 109–21; and idem, 'A Post-Heroic Military Policy', *Foreign Affairs*, 75, 4 (July/August 1996), pp. 33–44; in the light of Russell F. Weigley, *The American Way of War: A History of United States Military Strategy and Policy* (New York: Macmillan, 1973); and Colin S. Gray, 'Strategy in the Nuclear Age: The United States, 1945–1991', in Williamson Murray, MacGregor Knox,

and Alvin Bernstein (eds), *The Making of Strategy: Rulers, States, and War* (Cambridge: Cambridge University Press, 1994), esp. pp. 589–98.

11. Merritt Roe Smith, 'Army Ordnance and the "American System" of Manufacturing, 1815–1861', in Smith (ed.), *Military Enterprise and Technological Change: Perspectives on the American Experience* (Cambridge, MA: MIT Press, 1987), pp. 39–86.

12. The 'fleet train' that enabled the US Navy to operate in seas remote from its infrastructure of land bases was the innovatory response of a service that was denied by politicians fortified bases in the western Pacific. See Edward S. Miller, *War Plan Orange: The US Strategy to Defeat Japan* (Annapolis, MD: Naval Institute Press, 1991), pp. 75–6, 345–6; and Thomas M. Kane, *Military Logistics and Strategic Performance* (London: Frank Cass, 2001), ch. 3. The navy was thus saved from itself. A great naval base in the western Pacific would have been indefensible in 1941–42.

13. See Peter Anson and Dennis Cummings, 'The First Space War: The Contribution of Satellites to the Gulf War', in Alan D. Campen (ed.), *The First Information War: The Story of Communications, Computers and Intelligence Systems in the Persian Gulf War* (Fairfax, VA: AFCEA International Press, October 1992), pp. 126–8; and Benjamin S. Lambeth, 'Air Power, Space Power, and Geography', in Colin S. Gray and Geoffrey Sloan (eds), *Geopolitics, Geography and Strategy* (London: Frank Cass, 1999), p. 74.

14. Owens' grand concept of a 'system-of-systems' finds ambitious naval interpretation in Arthur K. Cebrowski and John J. Garstka's idea for 'Network-Centric Warfare: Its Origins and Future', US Naval Institute *Proceedings*, 124, 1 (January 1998), pp. 28–35. For a yet broader examination of the network concept, see John Arquilla and David Ronfeldt, *The Advent of Netwar*, MR-789-OSD (Santa Monica, CA: National Defense Research Institute, RAND, 1996).

15. See Edward N. Luttwak, 'From Vietnam to *Desert Fox*: Civil–Military Relations in Modern Democracies', *Survival*, 41, 1 (Spring 1999), pp. 99–111.

16. Roberta Wohlstetter, *Pearl Harbor: Warning and Decision* (Stanford, CA: Stanford University Press, 1962).

17. These distinctions are made clearly in Steven Metz and James Kievit, *Strategy and the Revolution in Military Affairs: From Theory to Policy* (Carlisle, PA: Strategic Studies Institute, US Army War College, 27 June 1995), p. 10 (major and minor RMAs), and Murray, 'Thinking About Revolutions in Military Affairs', p. 70 (technology-led RMAs and others).

18. Murray, 'Thinking About Revolutions in Military Affairs', p. 71.

19. Alvin Toffler and Heidi Toffler, *War and Anti-War: Survival at the Dawn of the 21st Century* (Boston, MA: Little, Brown, 1993).

20. Van Riper and Hoffman praise the Tofflers for their emphasis on knowledge rather than mere information: 'Pursuing the Real Revolution in Military Affairs', pp. 2, 3, 7.

21. For example, Andrew Latham, 'Re-imagining Warfare: The "Revolution in Military Affairs"', in Craig A. Snyder (ed.), *Contemporary Security and Strategy* (London: Macmillan, 1999), pp. 210–35, is distinctly Toffleresque. The title is unpromisingly postmodern, and a Toffleresque/Marxist pedigree is not an unmixed blessing, but the analysis is sharp and insightful.

22. This, the Tofflers' central hypothesis, is compatible with the argument advanced by some strategic theorists that national strategic culture shapes a national style in strategy. Colin S. Gray, *Nuclear Strategy and National Style* (Lanham, MD: Hamilton Press, 1986), ch. 2; Krause, *Culture and Security*. Controversy over the evidentiary base, and most appropriate research methodology, for the study of strategic culture, should not be permitted to obscure the dominant plausibility of the central culturalist hypothesis.

23. Latham, 'Re-imagining Warfare', p. 212.

24. I recognise that not all nations 'have' states, just as I acknowledge that the political and security communities we recognise today as states are, in some features of their statehood,

expressions of a modern invention which already is showing signs of severe wear around the edges. See Emanuel Adler and Michael Barnett (eds), *Security Communities* (Cambridge: Cambridge University Press, 1998); and Martin van Creveld, *The Rise and Decline of the State* (Cambridge: Cambridge University Press, 1999). In common with Michael Howard, 'When are Wars Decisive?' *Survival*, 41, 1 (Spring 1999), pp. 126–35, I believe that strategic affairs pertain to all security communities in all periods, regardless of whether or not (modern) states are involved: Gray, *Modern Strategy*. A comprehensively different view animates John Keegan, *A History of Warfare* (London: Hutchinson, 1993).

25. On that British style of warfare, see David French, *The British Way in Warfare: 1688–2000* (London: Unwin Hyman, 1990); and Hew Strachan, 'The British Way in Warfare', in David Chandler and Ian Beckett (eds), *The Oxford Illustrated History of the British Army* (Oxford: Oxford University Press, 1994), pp. 417–34. Michael Howard, *The Continental Commitment: The Dilemma of British Defence Policy in the Era of the Two World Wars* (London: Temple Smith, 1972), is characteristically well argued, but is likely to be judged unduly continentalist by the balance of future historiography. A leading historian of the maritime persuasion, Andrew D. Lambert, laments the fact that a 'shift of arms' to the waging of total war 'forced her to participate in very un-British operations to sustain her allies'. It is not very helpful for Lambert to observe that 'Had the Entente used its armies wisely in 1914 there would have been no need for a massive British Army.' As he himself notes, '[i]n 1914 unrealistic offensives launched by the French and Russians deprived the Triple Entente of two million soldiers': review of Chandler and Beckett (see above, this note) in *The Journal of Strategic Studies*, 19, 2 (June 1996), p. 284. Niall Ferguson, *The Pity of War* (London: Allen Lane, 1998), is entirely sceptical of the need for Britain to participate in the Great War.

26. Latham, 'Re-imagining Warfare', p. 213.

27. B. H. Liddell Hart, *The British Way in Warfare* (London: Faber & Faber, 1932), ch. 1. The best treatment remains Brian Bond, *British Military Policy between the Two World Wars* (Oxford: Clarendon Press, 1980). There is, inevitably, a (tiny) school of thought among British historians critical of Britain's decision to go to war in 1939, and especially critical of Winston Churchill's determination to fight on in 1940 after the fall of France. For the argument of the leading critic see John Charmley, *Chamberlain and the Lost Peace* (London: Macmillan, 1989); idem, *Churchill: The End of Glory* (London: Hodder & Stoughton, 1993); and idem, *Churchill's Grand Alliance: The Anglo-American Special Relationship, 1940–57* (London: Hodder & Stoughton, 1995). The most persuasive response to Charmley (and others) is, first, to agree with his argument that the conduct of the Second World War, even participation in its ultimately victorious conduct, proved ruinous to Britain economically and as an imperial power. But, second, the point must be made that Britain had no prudent choice but to continue to resist, because Hitler was not a 'normally' grasping would-be hegemonic statesman into whose concept of a new international order Britain could fit with security. The necessity for an open-ended British commitment to war in 1940 is wonderfully explained, by powerful analogy, in Paul W. Schroeder, 'Napoleon's Foreign Policy: A Criminal Enterprise', *The Journal of Military History*, 54, 2 (April 1990), pp. 147–61.

28. Hedley Bull, 'Strategic Studies and Its Critics', *World Politics*, 20, 4 (July 1968), pp. 593–605; Colin S. Gray, *Strategic Studies: A Critical Assessment* (Westport, CT: Greenwood Press, 1982), ch. 4. The RAND style of defence analysis by rational choice, characterised by the methods and ethos of economic theory, could not cope with such qualitative factors as culture or strength of political motivation. Strategic analysis thus deprived reduces to a calculable science innocent of human beings, political stakes, or most of what generates friction. For example, see Glenn A. Kent, Randall J. DeValk, and David E. Thaler, *A Calculus of First-Strike Stability (A Criterion for Evaluating Strategic Forces)*, N-2526-AF (Santa Monica, CA: RAND, June 1988), a study that offers arbitrary

quantitative values, no hint of strategy, and no breath of real political context. Much of the root of the problem can be seen or inferred from the classic text, E. S. Quade (ed.), *Analysis for Military Decisions* (Chicago, IL: Rand McNally, 1964), a book advertised as 'the RAND lectures on system analysis'. My strictures are neither critical of quantitative methods per se nor dismissive of 'military science'. There is a 'grammar' of war (and strategy) that needs to be understood by those who would employ a military instrument: Clausewitz, *On War*, p. 605. Richard K. Betts, 'Should Strategic Studies Survive?' *World Politics*, 50, 1 (October 1997), esp. pp. 22–6, advances persuasively the important and unfashionable argument that 'military science' is a 'missing discipline'.

29. Metz and Kievit, *Strategy and the Revolution in Military Affairs*; and Brian R. Sullivan, 'The Future Nature of Conflict: A Critique of "The American Revolution in Military Affairs" in the Era of Jointery', *Defense Analysis*, 14, 2 (August 1998), pp. 91–100, emphasise this criticism.

30. It is only slightly unfair to comment that Joseph S. Nye, Jr, and William A. Owens, 'America's Information Edge', *Foreign Affairs*, 75, 2 (March/April 1996), pp. 20–36; and William J. Perry, 'Defense in an Age of Hope', *Foreign Affairs*, 75, 6 (November/December 1996), pp. 64–79, suggest so militarily potent an 'RMAed America' that strategic capability will be in the driving seat navigating for foreign policy ambition. While part of the problem was the difficulty of designing foreign policy for a post-Soviet 1990s, another assuredly was a Clinton administration bereft of people skilled in foreign policy navigation.

31. For example, William Clinton, *A National Security Strategy for a New Century* (Washington, DC: The White House, May 1997).

32. Metz and Kievit, *Strategy and the Revolution in Military Affairs*, esp. pp. 18–26.

33. Bernard Brodie, *Sea Power in the Machine Age* (Princeton, NJ: Princeton University Press, 1941); William McElwee, *The Art of War: Waterloo to Mons* (London: Weidenfeld & Nicolson, 1974), ch. 4; Dennis Showalter, *Railroads and Rifles: Soldiers, Technology and the Unification of Germany* (Hamden, CT: Archon Books, 1975); William H. McNeill, *The Pursuit of Power: Technology, Armed Force, and Society since AD 1000* (Chicago, IL: University of Chicago Press, 1982), chs 6–8; Edward Hagerman, *The American Civil War and the Origins of Modern Warfare: Ideas, Organization, and Field Command* (Bloomington: Indiana University Press, 1988); Martin van Creveld, *Technology and War: From 2000 BC to the Present* (New York: Free Press, 1989), pt 3; Philip Howes, *The Catalytic Wars: A Study of the Development of Warfare, 1860–1870* (London: Minerva Press, 1998); Manfred F. Boemke, Roger Chickering, and Stig Förster (eds), *Anticipating Total War: The German and American Experiences, 1871–1914* (Cambridge: Cambridge University Press, 1999).

34. See Colin S. Gray, *The American Revolution in Military Affairs: An Interim Assessment*, Occasional Paper 28 (Camberley: Strategic and Combat Studies Institute, Joint Services Command and Staff College, 1997), pp. 25–7, for another statement of this claim.

35. Murray, 'Thinking About Revolutions in Military Affairs', pp. 70, 73. For his second thoughts on the listing see Murray and MacGregor Knox, 'Thinking About Revolutions in Warfare?', in Knox and Murray (eds), *The Dynamics of Military Revolution, 1300–2050* (Cambridge: Cambridge University Press, 2001), p. 13.

36. Andrew F. Krepinevich, 'Cavalry to Computer: The Pattern of Military Revolutions', *The National Interest*, 37 (Fall 1994), pp. 30–42.

37. Murray, 'Clausewitz Out, Computer In' and 'Does Military Culture Matter?', *Orbis*, 43, 1 (Winter 1999), pp. 27–42; 'Military Culture Does Matter', *Strategic Review*, 27, 2 (Spring 1999), pp. 32–40.

38. Toffler and Toffler, *War and Anti-War*; Jeffrey R. Cooper, *Another View of the Revolution in Military Affairs* (Carlisle Barracks, PA: Strategic Studies Institute, US Army War College, 15 July 1994); Metz and Kievit, *Strategy and the Revolution in Military Affairs*;

Steven Metz, 'The Revolution in Military Affairs: Vision and Alternatives at Century's End', unpub. paper (Carlisle Barracks, PA: Strategic Studies Institute, US Army War College, September 1999); Sullivan, 'Future Nature of Conflict'; and Jeremy Shapiro, 'Information and War: Is It a Revolution?', in Zalmay M. Khalilzad and John P. White (eds), *Strategic Appraisal: The Changing Role of Information in Warfare*, MR-1016-AF (Santa Monica, CA: RAND, 1999), pp. 113–53. Shapiro's essay, though sceptical of much of RMA theory, manages to separate babies from bathwater.

39. Those in search of inspiration on this subject could do worse than consult McNeill, *Pursuit of Power*; Martin van Creveld, *The Transformation of War* (New York: Free Press, 1991); Keegan, *History of Warfare*; idem, *War and Our World* (London: Hutchinson, 1998); and Jeremy Black, *War and the World: Military Power and the Fate of Continents, 1450–2000* (New Haven, CT: Yale University Press, 1998).

40. Murray, 'Thinking About Revolutions in Military Affairs', pp. 70–1 (emphasis added).

41. Professional historians provided the American policy-oriented community with the powerful concept of temporally bounded military revolutions. This was an idea just waiting for its strategic moment to be exploited. In 1956 Professor Michael Roberts of the University of Belfast wrote a seminal article (deriving from an inaugural lecture in 1955), hypothesising that a military revolution was effected by Maurice of Nassau and Gustavus Adolphus of Sweden in particular and could be dated generously to 1560–1660 ('The Military Revolution, 1560–1660', in Clifford J. Rogers (ed.), *The Military Revolution Debate: Readings on the Military Transformation of Early Modern Europe* (Boulder, CO: Westview Press, 1995), pp. 13–35). This alleged revolution was keyed to what amounted to the invention of the early modern style of warfare. Roberts argued that those leaders achieved a dramatic improvement in tactical effectiveness by (inter alia) drilling pike-protected infantry with gunpowder hand weapons to fight with extreme discipline in linear formation. These military developments were purportedly vital to the process of modern-state building, a thesis explored extensively in Brian M. Downing, *The Military Revolution and Political Change: Origins of Democracy and Autocracy in Early Modern Europe* (Princeton, NJ: Princeton University Press, 1992). The 'Roberts thesis' was challenged powerfully by Geoffrey Parker, initially in an article first published in 1976, a challenge that he repeated over the course of the next decade. Geoffrey Parker, 'The "Military Revolution, 1560–1660" – A Myth?', in Rogers, *Military Revolution Debate*, pp. 37–54. In the same book Parker answers his critics: 'In Defense of The Military Revolution', pp. 337–65. Geoffrey Parker, *The Military Revolution: Military Innovation and the Rise of the West, 1500–1800* (Cambridge: Cambridge University Press, 1988), is another landmark publication. Parker did not dispute the postulate of a single great early modern military revolution; rather he believed that Roberts, preeminently an expert on Sweden, was unduly in thrall to the brief period of Swedish success at the beginning of the Thirty Years War (1618–48). Parker, in essence an expert on the Spanish Habsburgs, suggested that the date for the commencement of the early modern military revolution should be wound back to 1530. See Geoffrey Parker: *The Army of Flanders and the Spanish Road: The Logistics of Spanish Victory and Defeat in the Low Countries' Wars* (Cambridge: Cambridge University Press, 1972); *Phillip II* (London: Cardinal, 1988); *The Dutch Revolt*, rev. edn (London: Penguin, 1985); *The Grand Strategy of Phillip II* (New Haven, CT: Yale University Press, 1998). He argued that the revolution needs to be identified with efforts to overcome the revolutionary developments of gunpowder-artillery-proof fortifications, especially the so-called *trace italienne*, and with Spanish military prowess in general. The Roberts–Parker debate was riveting stuff for the edification and amusement of professional historians. Clifford J. Rogers, 'The Military Revolution in History and Historiography', in Rogers, *Military Revolution Debate*, pp. 1–10; David Eltis, *The Military Revolution in Sixteenth-Century Europe* (London: Tauris Academic Studies,

1995), ch. 2; Michael Prestwich, *Armies and Warfare in the Middle Ages: The English Experience* (New Haven, CT: Yale University Press, 1996), ch. 14; and James Scott Wheeler, *The Making of a World Power: War and the Military Revolution in Seventeenth-Century England* (Stroud: Sutton Publishing, 1999), are helpful overviews of the debate among professional historians. Predictably perhaps, this historians' debate had at least two consequences important for our subject. First, the two decades of unchallenged sway enjoyed by the 'Roberts thesis', and then the additional decade and more of emergence and dissemination of the 'Parker variation' (a telling phrase borrowed gratefully from Jeremy Black, *A Military Revolution? Military Change and European Society, 1550–1800* (London: Macmillan, 1991), pp. 4–7) locked many people rather uncritically into belief in the Military Revolution as existential historical reality. Not all historians were so persuaded, of course. For an excellent example of dissent, David A. Parrott wrote in 1985: 'Thus on counts of both tactics and strategy, I have reservations about the concept of a "military revolution" in the period 1500–1660': 'Strategy and tactics in the Thirty Years War', in Rogers, *Military Revolution Debate*, p. 245. This is the common problem of the Nominalist Fallacy. If something has a name, constantly is discussed, and is not fundamentally challenged, the audience, even those licensed as experts, are apt to accord 'it' a birth certificate and citizenship in the column of 'real items'. Second, no less inevitably, sparks from the ongoing Roberts–Parker debate eventually set fire to the imaginations of historians other than specialists on early-modern Sweden and Spain. If Roberts and then Parker could make a splash professionally, and if they could stake out well-respected claims for the relatively superior importance of *their* particular piece of historical turf, then so could others. Jeremy Black has divulged how it can be open season for RMA-spotting. Those consumers of historians' scholarship who look for a definite and usable (for possible policy relevance) history, might be dismayed by this among Black's judgements: 'Thus, on both land and sea, and in both qualitative and quantitative terms, there were major changes in the period after 1660. Whether they deserve description in terms of a revolution is of course subjective: *there are no agreed-upon criteria by which military change, especially qualitative developments, can be measured or, more significantly, revolution discerned*' ('A Military Revolution? A 1660–1792 Perspective', in Rogers, *Military Revolution Debate*, p. 98, emphasis added). Black is correct. His preferences for 1470–1530 and 1660–1720 as revolutionary eras in warfare neatly bracket the Roberts–Parker chronologies of, respectively, 1560–1660, and 1530–1660. It is not difficult to cast doubt on the RMA concept. An artillery revolution frequently is dated to 1420–40 (or 1453, with the fall of Constantinople to the Turks; see e.g. Clifford J. Rogers, 'The Military Revolutions of the Hundred Years War', in Rogers, *Military Revolution Debate*, p. 6. Mediaeval military historians discern infantry revolutions (involving combined arms action by bowmen, pikemen, and dismounted men-at-arms) as early as 1302–15 and certainly embracing most decades of the Hundred Years War (1337–1453); and Black, inter alia, argues for substantial continuity in innovation throughout the eighteenth century (see his *Military Revolution?*; 'Military Revolution?'; 'Eighteenth-century Warfare Reconsidered', *War in History*, 1, 2 (July 1994), pp. 215–32; and 'Revolutionary and Napoleonic Warfare', in Black (ed.), *European Warfare, 1453–1815* (London: Macmillan, 1999), pp. 224–46). If every period witnesses cumulatively revolutionary (evolutionary?) change in the character of warfare, can any period be said to be revolutionary?

42. Such at least is my view. Gray, *Modern Strategy*, provides explanation and argument.
43. Murray and Knox, 'Thinking About Revolutions in Warfare', pp. 6, 11.
44. On nuclear eponymy see Colin S. Gray, *The Second Nuclear Age* (Boulder, CO: Lynne Rienner Publishers, 1999).
45. In 1997, Murray admitted nuclear weapons to a long list of 'possible RMAs', but he did not then admit them to MR status. He wrote: 'In fact there is only one example on the

list of possible RMAs that is entirely technological: nuclear weapons. But even here there is some ambiguity since the impact of nuclear weapons has been almost entirely political except for their first use against the Japanese. Outside of great-power competition, nuclear weapons have *not* changed the nature of warfare': 'Thinking About Revolutions in Military Affairs', p. 70 (emphasis in original).

46. See Robert Jervis, *The Meaning of the Nuclear Revolution: Statecraft and the Prospect of Armageddon* (Ithaca, NY: Cornell University Press, 1989), ch. 1.

47. Murray, 'Thinking About Revolutions in Military Affairs', p. 70.

48. Ibid., 'The record further suggests that the crucial element in most RMAs is conceptual in nature'. See also Krepinevich, 'Cavalry to Computer', p. 30.

49. Shapiro, 'Information and War', p. 136.

50. Ibid., p. 137.

51. Ibid. (emphasis added).

52. Ibid., p. 138 (emphasis in original).

53. For just one example, the Industrial Revolution, see Trevor Wilson and Robin Prior, 'Conflict, Technology, and the Impact of Industrialisation: The Great War, 1914–18', *Journal of Strategic Studies*, 24, 3 (September 2001), pp. 128–57.

54. As possibly in Stephen Biddle, 'Victory Misunderstood: What the Gulf War Tells Us about the Future of Conflict', *International Security*, 21, 2 (Fall 1996), pp. 139–79, with its emphasis upon tactical skill. I also may be guilty of an undue unfriendliness to technology in my *Weapons for Strategic Effect: How Important is Technology?* Occasional Paper 21 (Maxwell AFB, AL: Center for Strategy and Technology, Air War College, January 2001).

55. See particularly Sullivan, 'Future Nature of Conflict'.

56. Murray and Knox, 'Thinking About Revolutions in Warfare', p. 7.

57. Clifford J. Rogers, 'The Military Revolutions of the Hundred Years War', in Rogers, *The Military Revolution Debate*, pp. 55–93.

58. Ibid., p. 77.

59. Ibid. (emphasis added).

60. Ibid., p. 57 (emphasis in original).

61. Ibid., p. 77.

62. Murray, 'Thinking About Revolutions in Military Affairs', p. 70.

63. Samuel P. Huntington, 'Arms Races: Prerequisites and Results', in C. J. Friedrich and S. E. Harris (eds), *Public Policy, 1958* (Cambridge, MA: Harvard University Press, 1958), pp. 40–86; Colin S. Gray, 'The Arms Race Phenomenon', *World Politics*, 24, 1 (October 1971), pp. 39–79; idem, 'Arms Races and Other Pathetic Fallacies: A Case for Deconstruction', *Review of International Studies*, 22, 3 (July 1996), pp. 323–35; Patrick Glynn, *Closing Pandora's Box: Arms Races, Arms Control, and the History of the Cold War* (New York: Basic Books, 1992); Grant T. Hammond, *Plowshares into Swords: Arms Races in International Politics, 1840–1991* (Columbia: University of South Carolina Press, 1993); Barry Buzan and Eric Herring, *The Arms Dynamic in World Politics* (Boulder, CO: Lynne Rienner Publishers, 1998).

64. The theory of arms race dynamics driven by an action–reaction mechanism was blessed by Secretary of Defense Robert S. McNamara in a speech delivered on 18 September 1967: 'San Francisco Speech', in Philip Bobbitt, Lawrence Freedman, and Gregory F. Treverton (eds), *US Nuclear Strategy: A Reader* (New York: New York University Press, 1989), pp. 267–82. McNamara states that '[w]e do not want a nuclear-arms race with the Soviet Union – primarily because the action–reaction phenomenon makes it foolish and futile' (pp. 274–5). Action–reaction theory is explained further in George W. Rathjens, 'The Dynamics of the Arms Race', *Scientific American*, 220, 4 (April 1969), pp. 15–25, and Paul Warnke, 'Apes On A Treadmill', *Foreign Policy*, 18 (Spring 1975) pp. 12–29.

65. Relying on highly credible testimony from Colonel General Nikolai Detinov, an engineer general officer with protracted first-hand knowledge of Soviet policy-making throughout

the period in question, William E. Odom adds nails to the coffin of an action–reaction dynamic driven by a conservatively estimated anxiety lest BMD deprive offensive forces of deterrent value. 'The US proposal for an ABM treaty ... came as a pleasant surprise. By ending the US ABM program, it would free the Soviets from engaging in simultaneous competition in both strategic offensive and defensive systems and permit Soviet ICBM programs to move ahead on schedule. Thus the ABM treaty appeared to have allowed a considerably larger number of offensive nuclear weapons in the Soviet arsenal than there would have been without it. According to Detinov, the logic of US views on the winnability of a nuclear war [i.e. that such a war could not be won] and how to achieve strategic "stability" played no role at all in the Soviet acceptance of the ABM treaty': *The Collapse of the Soviet Military* (New Haven, CT: Yale University Press, 1998), p. 71. The views of Detinov, to which Odom rightly allows great weight, are supported amply by the testimonial evidence presented in John G. Hines, *Soviet Intentions, 1965–1985, Vol. I, An Analytical Comparison of US–Soviet Assessments During the Cold War*, and *Vol. II, Soviet Post-Cold War Testimonial Evidence* (McLean, VA: BDM Federal, 22 September 1995). Alternative theories of arms race dynamics are scrutinised sceptically in Colin S. Gray, *The Soviet–American Arms Race* (Farnborough: Saxon House, 1976). Although there is considerable scope for creative theorising about the dynamics of the Soviet–American arms competition, we do know *for certain* that the theory of strategic stability which identified fear of BMD as the principal engine of offensive-force modernisation and augmentation was wrong. Of course, the Soviet defence community was motivated to negate whatever might emerge by way of US BMD deployments. However, behind that sincere motive was a preeminent concern to be able to wage nuclear war effectively for relative strategic advantage, not to preserve a condition of mutual assured destruction. The USSR never accepted the vulnerability of Soviet society as a desideratum beneficial for a cooperative regime of strategic stability. That enlightened prospect was a conceit of the American arms control community, born of wishful thinking.

66. C. E. Callwell, *Small Wars: A Tactical Textbook for Imperial Soldiers* (3rd edn, London: Greenhill Books, 1990 [1906]), p. 270.

67. John France, *Western Warfare in the Age of the Crusades, 1000–1300* (Ithaca, NY: Cornell University Press, 1999), p. 34.

68. Ibid., p. 232.

69. Ibid., p. 34. Incentives for, and impediments to, the transcultural diffusion of military ideas in the middle ages are discussed briefly in David Nicolle, 'Medieval Warfare: The Unfriendly Interface', *Journal of Military History*, 63, 3 (July 1999), pp. 579–600.

70. 'I argue ... that the sources and consequences of European international conflict differ radically from one era to another, and that they can be understood only in the context of contemporary European domestic and international politics': David Kaiser, *Politics and War: European Conflict from Philip II to Hitler* (Cambridge, MA: Harvard University Press, 1990), p. 1.

71. France, *Western Warfare in the Age of the Crusades*, p. 1.

72. Cyril Falls, *A Hundred Years of War* (London: Gerald Duckworth, 1953). For the inspiration, see J. Colin, *The Transformations of War*, trans. L. H. R. Pope-Hennessy (London: Hugh Rees, 1912).

73. Recall the parallel charge levelled by Bernard Brodie against the more social scientific of his former colleagues at RAND: *War and Politics* (New York: Macmillan, 1973), p. 475.

74. Cyril Falls as military historian is considered in the context of his professional life and his times in Hew Strachan, ' "The Real War": Liddell Hart, Cruttwell and Falls', in Brian Bond (ed.), *The First World War and British Military History* (Oxford: Clarendon Press, 1991), pp. 61–7. In addition to *A Hundred Years of War*, divisional, battle, and campaign

histories of the First World War, a biography of Marshal Foch, and a history of the Second World War, Falls wrote: *War Books: An Annotated Bibliography of Books about the Great War* (London: Greenhill Books, 1989 [1930]), and *The Great War, 1914–1918* (New York: Perigee Books, 1959). Writing in 1991, Strachan allows that Falls' '*War Books* ... makes judgements which stand up well today and which are remarkable for their wisdom so close to the event [i.e. 1930]': '"Real War"', p. 63. John Keegan, *The First World War* (London: Hutchinson, 1998), finds Falls' *Great War*, 'incisive and compact' (p. 480). In addition to *A Hundred Years of War*, Falls wrote several other popular general books on war which offer a rich vein of strategic and tactical wisdom. See Cyril Falls: *The Nature of Modern Warfare* (London: Methuen, 1941); *Ordeal by Battle* (London: Methuen, 1943); and *The Art of War* (London: Oxford University Press, 1961).

75. Falls, *Hundred Years of War*, pp. 12–13.
76. Murray, 'Thinking About Revolutions in Military Affairs', p. 70 (emphasis in original).
77. Falls, *Hundred Years of War*, p. 13 (emphasis added).
78. Jonathan Bailey, *The First World War and the Birth of the Modern Style of Warfare*, Occasional Paper 22 (Camberley: Strategic and Combat Studies Institute, Staff College, 1996).
79. Falls, *Hundred Years of War*, p. 11.
80. Ibid., pp. 15–16.
81. See James Joll, *1914: The Unspoken Assumptions* (London: Weidenfeld & Nicolson, 1968).
82. See Torbjorn L. Knutsen, *The Rise and Fall of World Orders* (Manchester: Manchester University Press, 1999), esp. p. 6. On cycles in history, see K. R. Dark, *The Waves of Time: Long-term Change and International Relations* (London: Pinter, 1998). The most obvious parent of the thesis that modern warfare on the grandest of scales has appeared in waves was the diplomatic historian, R. B. Mowat. See his *History of European Diplomacy, 1815 to 1914: The European States-System* (London: Edward Arnold, 1928), esp. p. 1.
83. Michael J. Vickers, 'The Revolution in Military Affairs and Military Capabilities', in Robert L. Pfaltzgraff, Jr and Richard H. Shultz, Jr (eds), *War in the Information Age: New Challenges for US Security Policy* (Washington, DC: Brassey's, 1997), p. 30 (emphasis added). I am grateful to Steven Metz of the US Army War College for drawing my attention to Vickers' work.
84. Ibid., p. 45 n1.
85. RMA theorists should be troubled when they find historians doubting that the changes in armament and technique in early-modern Europe 'amounted to a "military revolution"'. The historian just quoted proceeds to explain: 'For one thing, it is in many ways the continuity in the nature and practice of early-modern warfare when compared to that of the Middle Ages which is striking, rather than the differences': Frank Tallett, *War and Society in Early-Modern Europe, 1495–1715* (London: Routledge, 1997), pp. 65–6.
86. Falls, *Nature of Modern Warfare*, pp. 37–8.
87. Ibid., p. 101.
88. The charge pervades Van Riper and Hoffman, 'Pursuing the Real RMA'. The debate is joined and re-joined in James R. Blaker, 'Revolution(s) in Military Affairs: Why the Critique?' and F. G. Hoffman, 'Why the Critique? An Author's Response', *National Security Studies Quarterly*, 5, 1 (Winter 1999), pp. 83–9, 89–91.

3

RMA Dynamics

Social scientists can appear cavalier, easily satisfied at least, in their approach
to the empirical evidence for theory that they claim to locate in strategic history.
Protagonists in the RMA debate of the 1990s, for example, proceeded undis-
mayed by the fragility of pertinent empirical research. What is striking about
the RMA literature is the prevalence of didactic certainties, even though the
possible historical evidence is either inherently ambiguous or simply missing.[1]
Busy defence professionals lacked time and the patience to wait for the slow
emergence of a more reliable base of historical knowledge of RMA phenomena.[2]
So speedily did the great RMA debate achieve its velocity change (or 'delta-v')
to ascend into the orbit of live activity in the years 1991–94 that few people took
the trouble to engage, perhaps indulge, in fundamental enquiry. Now that the
debate has so lost momentum that natural orbital decay has brought the idea,
much reduced in splendour, back to earth, we can take the time to appreciate
just how flimsy are the intellectual and empirical underpinnings of speculation
about RMA.

This is not necessarily to criticise the RMA concept, or to deny its utility.
If I did not believe that RMA theory can aid strategic understanding this book
would not be worth writing. Rather it is the point that truly grand conceptions
for the interpretation of processes of change in strategic history, and vastly
ambitious schemes for the reordering of defence policy and strategy, have been
labelled and debated under the umbrella of an RMA theory that does not
come close to meriting the authority often imputed to it. It is true that the
RMA hypothesis provided more than adequate fuel for a great, albeit largely
American, debate (another World Series with most of the world absent).
However, much of the scale of that greatness is explained more by the sheer
size of the US defence debating community, and by the scale of the financial
and strategic stakes, than by the readiness of the RMA concept and its adjuncts
for policy prime-time.

In defence of the somewhat hard words just written, I submit that a decade
of extensive and intensive debate among scholars and policy-oriented strategic
commentators has failed to answer satisfactorily four basic questions about
RMA phenomena. Of course, good work has been done, and some poor ideas

have been revealed to be such. For example, an important measure of consensus has been achieved on the question of the relative significance of technology in military and strategic innovation. Similarly, today there is widespread assent to the idea that RMAs come necessarily neither as uniform, nor as discretely sequential, episodes in strategic history. Nonetheless, to date there is a notable absence of scholarly bedrock upon which theorists and policy-makers can build with high confidence.[3] Four basic questions remain almost embarrassingly open to speculative answer.

1. What is the (historical) evidence for RMA theory?
2. Why do RMAs happen?
3. How do RMAs 'work'?
4. What difference do RMAs make to the course of strategic history?

There is a sense in which posing these questions invites a charge of disingenuousness. After all, questions 2, 3, and 4 would be literally nonsensical were the answer to question one strongly negative. My reply in anticipation of the charge is that I do not regard RMAs, and cognate concepts, as strategic historical phenomena to be hunted down and brought into captivity. RMA is better viewed as a potentially valuable perspective upon strategic history that has reality as an organising idea in the minds of commentators and historians. The empirical story that provides the existential referents for RMA theory is interesting, but cannot be inherently conclusive. Propositions important to the reach and grip of the theory can be tested for plausibility of fit with historical data. Ultimately, however, there will be a residual zone of judgement and preference. Questions 1, 2, and 3 are considered in this chapter. Treatment of question 4, on the strategic historical consequences of RMAs, I defer to later chapters.

Williamson Murray is informative, yet probably misleading, when he writes:

> historians have done relatively little work on RMAs. Michael Roberts introduced the idea of a single military revolution in his inaugural lecture at Queens University Belfast in 1955. Thereafter until 1991, interest in the military revolution was focused on the 16th and 17th centuries; early modern historians argued among themselves about whether there was such a revolution and, if so, when it occurred and what form it took. That debate continues. Since the mid-18th century, however, military historians have concentrated on other issues such as innovation, effectiveness, adaptation, organizational behavior, or – the bread and butter of the profession – battle histories. *Modern historians quite simply have not been very interested in military revolutions ... The crucial point is that the historical record is not yet in; and until there is detailed research on the subject [RMAs] most commentaries may be distortive.*[4]

Murray is right in pointing to the paucity of focused historical study of RMA. Inadvertently he may mislead, however, when he suggests – certainly he implies – that a better grasp of the historical record should combat 'distortive' commentaries. There is everything to be said in favour of careful historical scholarship. The problem with RMA theory, though, is that it cannot be forged for truth according to some Rankean notion of a final solution by weight of detailed and *correct* scholarship.[5] Ever more rigorous and finely nuanced study of 1916–18 will not reveal beyond challenge whether or not those years of the Great War produced a true military revolution, one or several RMAs, or simply an unsurprising wartime acceleration in innovation. To employ and analyse the concept of RMA is, in a sense, akin to theology. No matter how plausible the reasoning, and no matter how suggestively illustrative the apparent facts, in the last resort there is no evading the necessity to choose between making, or not making, a leap of faith. Regardless of how competently and industriously Murray's historians quarry away, there is no final boulder to be moved beneath which will be the definitive proof that 1916–18 did or did not witness an MR, RMA, or any other acronym of choice. In principle, at least, with the aid of forensic science historians can answer the question, 'was Napoleon murdered?'[6] No less in principle, historians cannot truly answer the question, 'was Napoleon's conduct of war an RMA?' The former question intrinsically is a matter of fact; the latter is, and can only be, a matter of interpretation.

It follows that scholars are well advised to finesse this first fundamental and empirical question. The finesse is necessary because empirical enquiry must fail to answer a question that ultimately is not capable of empirical resolution. Alas, the impossible is impossible. Strange to record, perhaps, the intrinsically empirically mysterious identity of historical RMAs is not a matter of great significance. It merely alerts us to unprofitable lines of investigation which should be avoided. Conceptual reformulation is the proper response to the existential challenge in question 1.

If we rework the empirical question for feasibility and utility, the result should approximate the following: 'Which episodes of military innovation most plausibly have had the greatest significance for the course of strategic history?' With the language thus deflated, and the ambition for theoretical outreach suitably punctured, most potentially lethal problems for theory conveniently vanish. Chapters 6–8 treat three major episodes in military innovation which, by near universal scholarly assent, merit admission to the RMA hall of fame. Whether or not the three cases truly are RMAs is a matter to which the Scottish verdict-plus applies: RMA status is both not proven and *not provable*.

The events or episodes commonly now called RMAs (as well as MRs or MTRs) undoubtedly, indeed by definition, are cases of strategic behaviour in which radical change occurred or which promoted such change. Our interest lies in what those cases can tell us about the complex working of strategy and war, not in exact labelling. A bid for such labelling would be a futile endeavour, no matter how carefully conducted. The choice of cases for analysis is discussed at the beginning of Chapter 6.

PROVENANCE

If, for the sake of argument, Napoleonic warfare, warfare in (late) 1917–18, and nuclear threat and (mercifully hypothetical) nuclear warfare are postulated to be RMAs, MRs, or MTRs according to intellectual taste, where did they come from? Why did they occur? These episodes of innovation in the conduct of war are each described and analysed in some detail below. Because of the many inconsistencies in conceptual labelling even by scholars, a firm ruling on usage is required. Since nearly everyone agrees that my historical cases assuredly are RMAs – if RMA theory is deemed useful, that is – while most would accord them the status of super-RMAs (or MRs), I elect to refer to them all simply as RMAs. This decision does not elide recognition that some RMAs are more significant than others, which is to say, major as opposed to minor.[7] Furthermore, this drastic conceptual conflation will not be allowed to obscure the probability that the categories of 'major RMAs' (or MRs), as contrasted with 'minor RMAs' and MTRs, will have distinctively deeper origins, more complex dynamics, and profounder consequences.

Much as *security*, in contrast to *strategic*, studies has frontiers that are unhelpfully porous and uncertain for focus in analysis and theory,[8] so the idea of MR, in contrast to RMA, is apt to confuse context with subject. For example, without seeking to downplay the importance of political contextual factors, among others, my subject is the conduct of war by Napoleon and his enemies, or by the belligerent great powers in 1914–18. MR theory, as with Toffleresque social-wave speculation, gambles dangerously with dice too heavily loaded towards predetermined outcomes more likely to trivialise than elucidate their topics.

If industrial- or information-age societies necessarily conduct war according to their distinctive natures, what room remains for choice and contingency? So broad can be the brush-strokes applied to describe and explain major RMAs (or MRs), that historical understanding of who prospered strategically, and why, is not much assisted. The methodological issue here is very much the one flagged tellingly by Jeremy Shapiro with the distinction he draws between the historian's and the strategist's viewpoints.[9] An, if not the, historian's approach to the Napoleonic RMA can examine the rise and consequences of the whole alleged phenomenon at issue. A strategist, in contrast, is more likely to empathise with the historical figures and institutions which had to behave in real-time in the face of uncertainty in response to evolving circumstances. The realm of the strategist is the realm of possible RMA, not of MR.

Plainly, there are problems of evidence which bedevil efforts to fit episodes in historical strategic behaviour neatly into conceptual categories (MR, RMA, and so forth). As a consequence, it is sensible to focus on the reality of that behaviour with respect to the persisting dimensions of strategy and war. For example, articulation of a large body of soldiers into several *corps d'armée* is just that, no matter how one labels it on the scale of innovation.

As precursor pointers to later detailed analysis, the paragraphs immediately below pose and provide terse interim answers to four vital questions bearing directly upon RMA provenance.

1. Do RMAs occur plausibly as a direct result of perception of strategic challenge? *Après* Arnold J. Toynbee, are we talking of 'challenge and response',[10] if not quite of mechanistic action and reaction?
2. Is adoption of RMA discretionary? Perhaps adaptation to RMA is mandatory, while would-be faithful adoption is not.
3. Characteristically, how sharp a break with past practice is an RMA? Is there typically an astonishingly magical 'strategic moment' when a manifestly new style of war is unveiled?
4. Are RMAs made by prophets as much as by executors? Do RMAs emerge from the fertile brains and pens of strategic visionaries in long periods of peace (punctuated only by minor scuffles), or are they more often the desperately improvised practice of military executives in time of war?

These questions by no means exhaust the range of the possible on RMA provenance, but they do point research and analysis in particularly useful directions.

First, are RMAs the consequence of perception of strategic challenge? This question suggests such challenge as a possible necessary, though probably not wholly sufficient, cause of RMA. We have to beware of the existential trap. Even if plausible challenge–response nexuses are locatable for RMAs, how should we handle cases when RMA does not occur? Challenge–response theory is unlikely to advance understanding very far or convincingly. Such theory could not explain RMA-as-response without, of necessity, locating a potent strategic challenge. Similarly, within its own logic it could not handle cases of apparent non-response, at least ineffective response, in face of strategic challenge.

Of the cases examined in Chapters 6–8 one – the Napoleonic – was not plausibly driven by strategic challenge.[11] Although one can locate an extensive provenance for the preferred Napoleonic way in warfare that is both quite distant – stemming from the 1760s, if not before – and very recent – the revolutionary period of 1792–95 – *la patrie* was not significantly *in danger* during Napoleon's heyday as 'master of the battlefield' (say, from 1800 to 1807).[12] The Napoleonic RMA was the immediate product of one person's insatiable ambition,[13] of a French military system that throve on war and more war, and on apparent opportunity. The hugely heralded information- (or knowledge-)led RMA beckons seductively a lone US superpower which until very recently perceived and articulated no clear strategic challenge.[14] Of course

71

there are dangers abroad. Purportedly 'rogue' polities, post-modern terrorists, and aspiring-returnee superstates, all litter the landscape of possible twenty-first centuries.[15] But the fact remains that today the leader among the menaces just cited, global terrorism, does not provide much horsepower to push or pull either a major, or even a minor, RMA into physical reality. Indeed, today it is unclear how 'the American I-led RMA' which appears to beckon relates to the emerging threat environment. The future of warfare may derive more from the military–strategic context than from the military–technical.

The two among my RMA cases that seem to fit a pattern of challenge and strategic response are the First World War and the nuclear revolution. In 1915–16 the leading belligerents participating in the great unpleasantness recognised that they had to solve the problem of how, in contemporary conditions, to achieve tactical break-in for operational breakthrough and (strategic) breakout-for-victory. Strategic plans and the operational grand designs to effect them were strictly moot in the face of repeated and apparently systemically preordained tactical failure. The modern style of combined-arms warfare was invented in 1916–17 in theory, and executed by painful experiment in 1917–18 in direct response to the challenge of tactical, and hence operational and strategic, ineffectiveness. By way of some contrast, the nuclear revolution was pursued initially as a response not to demonstrated tactical failure, but rather as an offset to the expected strategic consequences of a possible German atomic bomb.[16] The military application of German research in atomic physics could challenge the verdict achieved by all other kinds and quantities of arms.

Second, are polities at liberty to opt in or out of participation in an RMA? The RMAs selected for examination in this book are so clearly in the major (perhaps MR), as contrasted with a minor, category, that their identity may prejudice commentary on general RMA theory. However, one should not confuse adoption with adaptation. The historical record shows that military effectiveness for strategic success does not strictly require adoption of the RMA *du jour*. Among other considerations, distinctive polities with characteristic social and military systems and military cultures generally are unable simply to adopt an RMA as a standard package (as if they could buy it from a catalogue).[17] For a tactical analogy, the wearing of green berets does not, in and of itself, create special forces' warriors.[18] Whether the country leading an RMA on balance is wise or foolish in its would-be revolutionary behaviour, any choice of change in style of warfare so radical as to merit the RMA label cannot be ignored by opponents. The question of interest is not whether foes choose to adopt the RMA leader's mode of war, but how they elect to adapt to it. The choices in adaptation include attempts at emulation and efforts at asymmetric negation.[19] Blithely to ignore an RMA is to risk suffering the fate of the Prussian Army in 1806 and the French Army under General Nivelle in 1917. Sir Arthur Wellesley did not ignore the Napoleonic way in war, but he was not obliged by circumstances either to adopt it or to adapt systematically to it. An excellence in the ability to execute traditional tactical forms sufficed for the Iron Duke.[20] His example, however, is the exception not the rule.

Each of my historical cases of (major) RMA either delivers or at least promises such military effectiveness that the principal foes of the RMA leader of the day are not free to ignore the new style of warfare. Every opponent will find its own feasible mix of adoption and adaptation. As a general rule, however, an attitude of superior disregard is not a reasonable choice. Napoleon's continental adversaries were obliged to adopt and to adapt, lest they be overrun *again*. Similarly, the great attritional battles of Verdun and the Somme in 1916 demonstrated that there were better and worse, which is to say correct and incorrect, ways of waging modern war.[21] A belligerent that failed to identify and execute the superior methods of war was likely to lose. Of course, one might lose anyway, given that the enemy also was learning how to wage modern war. Despite the ecological and moral issues arguably distinctive to nuclear weaponry, the rising but still second-class superpower of the 1940s and 1950s, the USSR, judged emulative adoption a necessary, but not sufficient, feature of its response to nuclear peril.[22] As for information-led warfare in the twenty-first century, debate already is well joined over the range of possibilities for asymmetric responses to that style of warfare.[23] The United States' foes may well pay tribute to the putative military potency of the information-led RMA by seeking offsets in the creation of cyber-havoc, or the terror of weapons of mass destruction, inter alia.

Third, do RMAs occur after the fashion of a Russian spring which bursts suddenly into life, or rather of an English spring which emerges all but imperceptibly out of winter in a smooth and lengthy development? The thesis of discontinuity is both persuasive yet fraught with the possibility that it may induce misunderstanding. On the one hand, there is no doubt that the Napoleonic way of war, the 'modern style of warfare' of 1917–18, and nuclear warfare, are each more (nuclear) or less (Napoleonic, First World War) radically different from the styles in war most popular only a few months or years previously. On the other hand, that apparent repeated nonlinearity in principle duly admitted, each of these major RMAs necessarily had extensive antecedents. The point is made superbly in an eloquent judgement written by Spenser Wilkinson in 1914.

> The year 1796 [when Napoleon assumed his first major command, the Army of Italy] is thus the beginning of an era, the necessary starting-point for the historical study of modern war. But in the processes of life and growth there is no beginning; what we call a beginning marks equally the end of one development and the start of another. If the exploits of the Army of Italy are the explanation of the subsequent history of Europe, their own explanation must be sought in the years that came before.

Napoleon and his soldiers were the outcome of the efforts, the controversies and the experiments of a whole generation of predecessors.[24]

Focusing on the novel elements of alleged RMAs has the potential to blind scholars and military practitioners to the vital significance of the perpetual military virtues. For an especially persuasive example, Williamson Murray develops the argument that the human factor, a constant, is always the most important determinant of military success. That factor, Murray reasons, plays in war most fundamentally through its obedience, or not, to a tactical battle-space discipline that flows from military culture.[25] His argument is not startling, but it is not much in evidence in the literature of RMA advocacy.

Fourth and finally, are RMAs more imagined by visionaries than done by executive agents? To postulate so stark an opposition between advance theory and practice is to overdraw for the sake of analytical clarity. As a working hypothesis, I suggest that in the practical world of strategy theory tends to follow, and in its turn modify, practice.

Of my three cases of major RMAs, only Napoleon's arguably was preceded by intellectually significant speculation and prophecy. Intellectual significance is not necessarily political significance. The 'nation in arms', the sine qua non for Napoleonic warfare, clearly was envisioned well before 1793.[26] But that prophecy was irrelevant to the actual emergence of such a nation, while France as that nation could plausibly threaten to impose a European hegemony only when commanded by Napoleon Bonaparte. He was educated, in part, by the military–strategic prophets of the ancien régime, but even more by what his own industry and intuition advised him was possible in the circumstances in which he found himself.[27] Napoleon made the Napoleonic RMA, but the French Revolution made Napoleon. Good ideas at the wrong time or in the wrong brain remain simply good ideas. The postulated information-led RMA is a similar story. As the French Revolution gave a young Corsican professional artilleryman his opportunity, so the end of the Cold War provided a permissive context for a non-, anti-, and even allegedly post-, nuclear RMA keyed to information technologies.[28] Bourcet and Guibert, Toffler and Ogarkovi: both the RMAs just cited had prophets who heralded a new dawn in military effectiveness.

Important though ideas assuredly are, and always have been, executive action is apt to be more important still. If the Napoleonic RMA was more carried out by Napoleon as opportunity knocked, albeit a Napoleon well educated by masters of theory, than it was implemented according to some blueprint for success,[29] then a parallel judgement applies to the nuclear RMA. It is probably fair to claim that the nuclear RMA was more made by General Curtis LeMay and US President Dwight D. Eisenhower[30] than it was envisioned, no matter how perceptively and prudently, by – say – a Bernard Brodie or an Albert Wohlstetter.[31] It may be important to note that all three of our major RMAs were implemented *in wartime*. Notwithstanding his substantial prescience, neither Ivan Bloch nor anyone else prior to 1915 had a comprehensive vision of a modern style of combined-arms warfare.[32] Similarly, nuclear strategy was implemented, at least in peacetime routines in readiness for war, before it was treated wholly pervasively by the realm of theory (if ever it was).[33]

Practice expresses actual or perceived necessity. That practice may be inspired or modified by strategic ideas, but typically it will perform or attempt what opportunity and available talent suggests to be feasible.

RMA LIFE-CYCLE

Without prejudice to the outcome of contention over the merit in RMA theory or the identities of historical RMAs (if any), it is useful to suggest a standardised process in 'the making of RMAs'. Of course, each candidate historical RMA must be richly distinctive in its detail. Nonetheless, RMAs of all kinds, of any magnitude, and in any period, are likely to share a common structure with fairly common structural–functional dynamics. As with the dimensions of strategy and war, which remain constant through all of strategic history,[34] so RMAs similarly can be understood according to a single template. Far from being an exercise in reductionism, this framework for enquiry accommodates as much richly distinctive period detail as research and analysis suggests is evidence. So, why and how do RMAs work? I suggest that the RMA process fruitfully can be understood as a nine-step process. The steps may overlap, while assuredly they have different periodicities, both among themselves in one RMA and from RMA to RMA.

My nine-step theory of the RMA life-cycle may appear to challenge the desideratum of Occam's razor, but it is necessary for this number of steps to be identified if the process of innovation is to be rescued from undue opacity. The paragraphs below explain that RMAs emerge from periods of *preparation* (step 1), that functionally, at least, they express *recognition of challenge* (step 2), if only the challenge of opportunity to explore and exploit. The theory specifies the importance of RMA *parentage* (step 3) in the context of an *enabling spark* (step 4) being struck which produces a *strategic moment* (step 5) of clear first actualisation of a new style in warfare. *Institutional agency* (step 6) is necessary to effect the *instrument* (step 7) of new military capabilities which carry the RMA forward. The new style of war is in a phase of *execution and evolving maturity* (step 8), beyond which lies a period of *feedback and adjustment* (step 9) as real enemies and no less real friction of all other kinds provide practical education 'in (and from) the field'.

1. *Preparation* (generally unplanned). RMAs occur following more or less lengthy periods of reform, or at least of change. If an RMA is by common-sense definition a nonlinearity, still it erupts and can be recognised as a radical discontinuity only in contrast to linear antecedent behaviour. An RMA may

well not have been a gleam in many, if any, eyes long in advance, but extensive preparatory work must be a necessary – albeit not sufficient – condition for the nonlinear event. Serendipity may rule. Many makers of revolution, RMAs and others, did not intend to make revolution, certainly not the revolution that occurred. The claims that step 1 for RMA is considerable preparation does not imply RMA-purposeful preparation. Each of the cases of RMA examined in Chapters 6–8 required (unplanned) preparatory behaviour that can easily be traced back 30–50 years.

2. *Recognition of challenge.* RMAs occur, in an important sense are made to occur (see below), for reasons judged important by their 'parents'. Brian R. Sullivan is not quite plausible when he asserts that 'an RMA is the military manifestation of a prior and radical political–strategic reorientation', but he is insightful.[35] RMAs, like wars, can be effected for a wide variety of reasons, and those reasons can be more or less strategic as well as more or less persuasive to relevant domestic audiences. The challenge to which some people will claim that a preferred RMA is the answer may well reside only in the realm of 'being all that we can be'. In other words, an RMA may be pursued by way of exploiting a perceived opportunity, rather than countering a particular strategic menace. The core point of step 2 is simply that there has to be a reason to implement an RMA. Some lawful authority needs to decide that there is a challenge, a threat, or an opportunity, in need of RMA solution. The executive agents of RMA may not define their role and mission in quite those terms, but functionally they have to register some challenge and identify RMA as the, or at least as an, answer.

3. *Parentage.* An RMA requires revolutionaries. This third step in the RMA process can overlap with the second and indeed with the fourth, fifth, and sixth steps. Individuals on their own authority, or with the authority of significant institutions (official or other) have to make, in the sense of conceive and nurture, the revolution. My point here in step 3 is no more than the claim that RMA requires conception and nurture by particular human agents, even if they do not intend to effect revolution. The agents of the RMA in newly republican France in 1792–94 were trying only to save a *patrie en danger*. It so happened that the consequences of French strategic behaviour in the first half of the 1790s lit the powder in the touch-hole for an RMA. However, the relevant politicians and soldiers of 1792–96 were desperate patriots as well as ruthless self-seeking opportunists, not RMA theorists or even self-conscious RMA executives.

Exactly how parents bring their RMA proposals to practical effect at the sharp end of strategy is a matter for the steps which succeed this one. Much as some great military and naval commanders are allowed the running room to demonstrate greatness by de facto teaming with a Potent Protective Political Patron (we might represent this idea as the P4 factor), so RMA parents, even if not themselves politically powerful, at least need the P4 factor to work for them. It might be recalled that the birth of the nuclear RMA as a real military programme, as contrasted with what transpired to be broad preparatory effort in atomic physics, lay in the relationship between Dr Vannevar Bush and President Franklin Delano Roosevelt.[36] For another case, the information-led RMA of the 1990s had Andrew W. Marshall as intellectual parent and patron, but its executive authors – the revolutionaries of the deed as well as of the word – comprised the team of Secretary of Defense William J. Perry and Vice-Chairman of the Joint Chiefs of Staff William A. Owens.[37] Revolutionaries for RMA need the political clout, or the patronage of those with political clout, in order to deliver the revolution.

4. *Enabling spark.* Writing about architecture, Le Corbusier advises that 'The advent of a new period only occurs after long and quiet preparatory work.'[38] We should add, however, that preparation, planned and unplanned, may come to nought. Moreover, even preparation and explicit recognition of challenge may not suffice to ignite an RMA. History is replete with apparently good enough armies that would have performed well had only commanders of suitable stature been available to lead them, or vice versa. Sometimes the hour produces the person. But then again, sometimes it does not.[39] The hour of need may not require a charismatic leader, but only powerful patrons (the P4 factor, cited above) who can enable would-be military revolutionaries to behave in an effectively revolutionary manner.[40] If an RMA has to be constructed by self-consciously revolutionary effort, rather than merely executed as change so linear in its cumulative evolution that the concept of revolution could scarcely apply, then some vital, enabling spark is needed. The nature and precise identity of that spark will be as variable as RMAs differ. With respect to the major RMAs considered in this book, the most plausible enabling spark, or leading-edge factors, were: Napoleon Bonaparte himself, for the Napoleonic RMA; the perfection of indirect artillery fire for the RMA of 1917–18; and the invention of the atomic bomb for the nuclear RMA.

5. *Strategic moment.* It may seem odd, if not downright peculiar, to identify as a vital step the postulate of a 'strategic moment' of first actualisation of an RMA vision, ahead of the itemisation of the institutional agency and military-instrument building that implement the revolution. My logic is strategic and political, rather than strictly historical. I wish to emphasise the fact, certainly the possibility, that RMAs, no matter how slow the preparatory period, can and usually do appear as a flash in the sky of strategic consciousness. There is, if you will, and to risk hyperbole, a 'strategic moment', a moment when new possibilities are signalled to those willing to receive such a message.

There are several reasons why we should be comfortable with the postulate of a strategic moment. Because our analytical framework encompasses the idea of a process of innovation over time, the potential for damage that might be wrought by the idea of all but magic moments is sharply reduced. Similarly, the potential of the concept of strategic moments to invest the *revolution* in

RMA with undue gravitas, must be greatly reduced by the extensive doubts already expressed about the overall validity of the idea of great strategic historical discontinuities. I contend that RMAs typically contain a 'strategic moment' which reveals, as in a flash, enticing and exciting new strategic possibilities. These moments may be the first full-up synergistic expression in unified action of trends which come together and achieve critical mass. In such cases, the moments could belong squarely within my step 8, 'execution and evolving maturity'. In addition, however, there are strong candidate strategic moments that are, and function as, the herald of more extensive possibilities, really as strategically revealing precursor events. Such moments are not themselves the main event, but they hint persuasively at what might be feasible.

Thomas J. Welch, a close associate of Andrew W. Marshall in the Office of Net Assessment (ONA), has explained what he calls a culminating event, and I term a strategic moment.

> A final feature of a definition of an RMA is a 'culminating event', a battle that employs the new systems, operational concepts, and organizations and that clearly demonstrates a dramatic change in the conduct of warfare. Examples might be France in 1940, or the Battle of Midway. In this sense, we [in ONA] do not see the 1990–91 Gulf War as the culmination of an RMA but rather as analogous to the Battle of Cambrai in World War I, where the innovative combination of airplanes, tanks, and radios hinted at what was to come later.[41]

As with the RMA concept itself, the notion of a strategic moment, or 'culminating event', is not empirically demonstrable. Scholars can choose whether to select as such moments events that truly are akin to brief and intriguing flashes of light, or events that show RMA behaviour at its most mature. I propose both to bear this distinction in mind and to allow each particular historical case to suggest its own pattern. For example, two leading candidates for the strategic moment(s) of the Napoleonic RMA are General Bonaparte's first Italian campaign in 1796 and the Emperor Napoleon's destruction of most of the continental armies of the Third Coalition in 1805 (the Ulm and Austerlitz campaigns). The 1796 (and its second phase in 1797) campaign was small in scale relative to the campaigns of the Empire, but most aspects of the Napoleonic way in warfare, including some of its warts, were amply demonstrated.[42] The year 1805 showed the Emperor and his new Grande Armée at their peak.

In the case of the RMA of the First World War, it is plausible to agree with Welch (and Marshall) that Cambrai (20 November–3 December 1917) was the strategic moment, though General Oskar von Hutier's assault against Riga (1 September 1917) merits consideration also. It is scarcely less plausible, however, to cite the opening of the attack by the Australian Corps against Hamel (4 July 1918), the Second Battle of the Marne (18 July 1918), or the first day of the Amiens offensive (8 August 1918, 'the black day of the German Army' in Erich Ludendorff's melodramatic words), or even the breaking of the Hindenburg Line by General Rawlinson's Fourth Army (beginning on 29 September 1918).[43] The Amiens and 'Hindenburg Line' operations were for the Allied variant of the RMA of 1917–18 what the Ulm manoeuvre and then Austerlitz had been for the Napoleonic revolution.

The case of Germany in 1918 is particularly instructive for the approach to RMA theory adopted in this book. It is a plausible hypothesis that there was a tolerable equivalence of expertise in the contemporary art of war in 1918 among the German, British, and French Armies at all levels. When an RMA is tested in the field, it is tested upon, and in some senses against, the enduring structure and dynamics of strategy and war. Strategic theorists must never forget that when they pontificate about, say, the German version of the RMA of 1917–18, they are talking about the behaviour of real people in an actual, and deeply muddy, historical context. RMA theory, to be useful, has to be ready to accommodate the reality of half-starved soldiers, too few in number, abused by indifferent operational and strategic guidance, and beset by material and morale problems of a galloping severity. One might object, not unfairly, that I have just outlined an extreme example. My response would be to say both that war is by definition an extreme activity and that every theory, in common with every practice, of RMA, must be able to cope with exogenous elements. Any theory of RMA which requires execution in battle only by entirely healthy troops, operating on level and unobstructed terrain of modest dimensions in clement weather, needs to be labelled with a strategic hazard warning.

The strategic moment for the nuclear RMA has to be the attack on Hiroshima on 6 August 1945.

6. *Institutional agency.* RMAs need agencies and agents for implementation. Those agencies must include appropriate military organisations with suitable military cultures, (probably) innovative operational concepts, and hard training in the practice of those concepts in the field.[44] In addition, new technologies may, but only may, play a vital role. No RMA can be implemented in the absence of military organisations competent or better at fighting in the new manner. Just as strategy has to be carried out through tactics, so RMA has to be executed by the agency of potent military forces. To be thus potent, those forces require suitable organisation (be it in a phalanx, in legions, by corps, in groups of all-arms panzer divisions, or in strategic rocket armies). Also they require the operational concepts which serve as the firm but flexible foundation for a doctrine of war which the troops practise in conditions as close to those of war itself as is practicable. New weapon technologies may play a critical role in the particular RMA brew in question. In that event, there must be a period for assimilation both of tactical competence in the effective handling and maintenance of the advanced weapons, and for understanding how the new or improved weapons should function in the conduct of war.

7. *Instrument*. Through the agency of organisation, concepts, doctrines, and training (and possibly new technologies also), the military instrument of an RMA is forged. Clausewitz and Jomini, not to mention all strategic experience, alert us to the enabling significance of sheer mass, numbers, or brute arithmetic.[45] No matter how elegant the organisational forms, how cunning the operational concepts, how savagely realistic the training, or how absolutely potent the military technology (from longbow to h-bomb and beyond, to misquote Bernard and Fawn Brodie),[46] numbers count. They do not usually count the most, but there is a sense in which they are always critical. Whatever the RMA at issue, it must be expressed in action in a sufficiency of man-machine (weapon and support) systems. Not only do RMAs have to be conceived and forged; their military instruments also have to be procured. The world's first integrated air defence system, invented by Britain in the late 1930s, had to be bought in the form of the mass of vital interdependent components necessary for tactical and operational effectiveness in war.[47] In its procurement aspect, the minor RMA – and minor miracle – of the military instrument of British air defence in 1940, was *numbers* of radar towers, trained operators, communication relays, RAF control rooms and their staffs and communication equipment, fighter aircraft with reliable radios, pilots, ground crews, and so on and so on back through training and industrial infrastructures to the policy that set it all in motion. Regardless of its nominal potency, the military instrument of any RMA has to have the size appropriate for execution of those novel operational concepts in the particular contexts of unique historical missions. In 1941–42, Germany's Östheer suffered from a weakness in quantity for its assigned task of the conquest of the USSR. In 1812, a similar condition eventually had doomed the great French adventure in Russia.[48]

8. *Execution and evolving maturity*. The life-cycle of an RMA captured in these nine steps includes periods of execution and evolving maturity, and then of modification in the light of opponents' behaviour. An RMA's shock effect for the destabilisation of the foe – in Sun Tzu's terms, the creation of disharmony[49] – must diminish rapidly with exposure.[50] Elephants and tanks – though hypothetically perhaps not nuclear weapons – are less effective after several close encounters with them are survived. Scholars and commentators can give the impression that they believe that trial by RMA is identical to trial by war. Alas, perhaps, some godlike reified Strategic History does not distribute medals to the security communities that carry through the cleverest, the most eloquently explained (or entertainingly 'briefed'), the most plausible, or the most startlingly unorthodox of RMAs. Instead, strategic history shows RMAs – conceptual and empirical caveats suppressed for the moment – to be instruments of policy, in common with the military capabilities which they fashion and refashion. The only test that really counts for an RMA in the pragmatic world of strategy is the examination by consequences. Armed with the classic question, 'so what?', we want to know what happened to those who led, and

to those who responded to, a process of RMA. We must hasten to add that the ultimate strategic failures of such RMA leaders as Napoleonic France, and (arguably) Wilhelmine and Nazi Germany, is not necessarily proof of the basic inefficacy of their designs for military revolution. Such failure may point, however, to some limitations in the reach or grip of the RMA at issue. Moreover, such failure is certain to indicate that the French, or German, actual conduct of war – shaped by a particular RMA (or RMAs) – was fatally ineffective in the last resort, which is trial by combat (this is the resort that history records in the 'win/loss' column). Step 8, 'execution and emerging maturity', refers simply to the military, then strategic, effectiveness secured by RMA implementation. As with each of these steps, 'execution' merges into the succeeding step, the adjustment phase.

9. *Feedback and adjustment.* This step does not imply any mechanistic process of action and reaction. There is no presumption here that as a foe responds to the evidence of an enemy's RMA in action, the RMA leader adjusts so as to negate the response. Step 9 is logically compelling and practicably empirical as a subject for research. The unremarkable claim in this step is that enemies not overwhelmed by violent first exposure to an RMA will have time, motive, and sometimes the ability, to learn how to frustrate the enemy's novel way in warfare. If 'no plan of operations extends with certainty beyond the first encounter with the enemy's main strength',[51] so no RMA survives intact the counteracting behaviour of an alert, intelligent, and competent foe. As a matter of research, we can examine how Napoleon's enemies sought to defeat his new way of war, his eponymous RMA. Similarly we can, and we will, investigate the ways in which opponents answered the artillery-led and nuclear RMAs of 1917–18 and 1945–plus. It may be unnecessary to add that this step 9 always has the potential to fuel a complete renewal of the RMA cycle. Readers are excused if they find this process non-trivially dialectical.

The nine steps just specified as constituting the RMA life-cycle are no more than an analytical tool. The argument is not that RMAs have nine steps from conception to death. Instead, the claim is that the RMA process usefully can be considered as having these steps. The number of steps may be conflated or expanded as preferred, but the content of any conceptual toolkit for understanding RMAs should contain these steps, however they are organised and whatever they are called.[52]

CLARIFYING CONFUSION

Much as Stewart Granger could ride away in the closing shot of *The Prisoner of Zenda*, or Alan Ladd could head for the horizon to conclude *Shane*, so this lengthy foray into the badlands of RMA theory can conclude with that useful closing line from many a Hollywood movie, 'our work here is done'. My argument has made about as much as it can, and probably more than it should, of the possibilities in RMA theory. The point now is reached where the trajectory of enquiry has to turn to matters of a kind more reliable than rival baskets of RMA speculation. Nonetheless, it is essential to identify, and try to improve on, the conceptual tools on offer to help clarify the intellectual confusion.

The chapters here concluded on RMA anatomy and dynamics fulfil the functions of familiarising readers with the significant conceptual features of the subject, flagging necessary caveats, separating useful from less useful questions, and specifying a way forward so that theory and historical data might work synergistically.

I have expressed serious reservations about RMA theory. Above all else, we should be concerned lest a concept which by any plausible definition files claims for sharp strategic discontinuity (RMA), should prejudice historical research and then bias policy analysis also. To convene conferences to discuss Atlantis is to dignify Atlantean hypotheses. Similarly, a debate about RMA has no small potential to encourage confusion between interesting concept and empirical reality.

Chapters 2 and 3 find the RMA concept – and adjunct concepts (e.g. MR, MTR) – both intriguing and useful, though, of necessity, not 'true'. There are grounds for concern lest some audiences for RMA ideas may believe in a positivistic doctrine of RMA keyed to a fallacious notion of RMAs in history. The relationship between theory in social science and historical evidence begs for more careful treatment than it often receives in public debate.

Although the RMA hypothesis is on balance useful, I seek to alert readers to the fact that a decade of intensive and extensive work on the subject has left answers even to the most basic of questions hugely incomplete. When we ask, 'what is the evidence for RMAs?', 'why do RMAs happen?', 'how do RMAs work?', and 'what are the consequences of RMAs?', the answers from a large literature remain confusing and unsatisfactory. This chapter has tried to clarify the confusion, recognise those issues that are literally unanswerable, yet make constructive suggestions to advance understanding. The discussion of the hypothesis and life-cycle of RMA, with a grand total of nine steps from 'preparation' (step 1) all the way to 'feedback and adjustment' (step 9), provides a template sufficiently flexible as to be applicable to the analysis of any postulated historical RMAs. Chapters 6–8 employ this nine-step approach to the RMA life-cycle in order to facilitate focused comparisons of historical data (which might prove to be evidence).

Before RMA theory meets hypothesised RMA cases, however, the persisting nature and working of strategy needs explanation. A sound theory of strategy and war must derive from an understanding of strategic experience that transcends belligerents, time, place, and technology. Only such a theory can be trusted to guide us through the thickets of rival RMA ideas, and might enable us make some general sense of the rich particularisms of detailed historical scholarship. Inspiration for this endeavour is provided by none other than the unduly unfashionable Baron Antoine Henri de Jomini.

> The new inventions of the last twenty years seem to threaten a great revolution in army organization, armament, and tactics. Strategy alone will remain unaltered, with its principles the same as under the Scipios and Caesars, Frederick and Napoleon, since they are independent of the nature of the arms and the organisation of the troops.[53]

NOTES

1. General Dennis J. Reimer, then Chief of Staff of the US Army, both informs us unequivocally that 'We are presently experiencing a revolution in military affairs', and states as fact that 'In the past two hundred years, six revolutions in military affairs have radically affected the conduct and character of war': 'Forward', in Robert L. Pfaltzgraff, Jr and Richard H. Shulz, Jr (eds), *War in the Information Age: New Challenges for US Security Policy* (Washington, DC: Brassey's, 1997), p. ix. The confidence in the claims is quite startling.

2. The RMA debate of the 1990s was significantly dissimilar to the great debate of the 1950s about strategy for the nuclear age. In the 1950s, all major debaters agreed that their subject lacked much of a historical hinterland. That neglect of historical perspective, discounting of distinctive cultures, and general under-appreciation of the continuities in strategic history, was unwise and unfortunate. Nonetheless, the knowing denial of history's relevance liberated the social scientific defence rationalists at RAND to proceed competently with their nuclear abstractions. In contrast, the RMA debate of the 1990s, the next great debate with a strategic domain comparable to the stakes in the nuclear case, was tied inalienably to historical argument. Whereas a Thomas Schelling and an Albert Wohlstetter had been inventing strategic reasoning and consequent recommendations for defence planning, out of a mixture of whole logical cloth and emerging military–technical data, RMA theorists assert that the military possibilities emerging now are but the latest in a series of historical RMAs. Regardless of whose views of RMA are judged most plausible, the principal scholarly authority for the entire debate is inescapably historical, as are its policy outcomes. If a growing body of respected historical scholarship were to cast significant doubt on the RMA premise, the foundation necessarily would crumble away beneath much of the theory concerning a contemporary information-led revolution. The nuclear revolution is considered in some detail in Chapter 8. For theorists of nuclear strategy, see Bernard Brodie, *War and Politics* (New York: Macmillan, 1973), chs. 9–10; Colin S. Gray, *Strategic Studies and Public Policy: The American Experience* (Lexington: University Press of Kentucky, 1982); Fred Kaplan, *The Wizards of Armageddon* (New York: Simon & Schuster, 1983); Lawrence Freedman, 'The First Two Generations of Nuclear Strategists', in Peter Paret (ed.), *Makers of Modern Strategy: From Machiavelli to the Nuclear Age* (Princeton, NJ: Princeton University Press, 1986), pp. 735–78; and John Baylis and John Garnett (eds), *Makers of Nuclear Strategy* (New York: St. Martin's Press, 1991). Andrew F. Krepinevich, 'Cavalry to Computer: The Pattern of Military Revolutions', *The National Interest*, 37 (Fall 1994), pp. 30–42, was particularly important both because the author wrote with the authority of a scholar close to Andrew W. Marshall and his Office of Net Assessment (wherein Krepinevich

worked for a while), and because he stated a powerful claim for the historical existentiality of RMA. It should be noted, however, that Krepinevich was careful to write only that '*there appear to have been* as many as ten military revolutions since the fourteenth century' (p. 31, emphasis added). As we have seen with General Reimer's claim as quoted, not all subsequent commentators would choose to qualify their historical claims (or, perhaps, even recognise the need for such qualification).

3. Which is why MacGregor Knox and William Murray (eds), *The Dynamics of Military Revolution, 1300–2050* (Cambridge: Cambridge University Press, 2001), is so important.
4. Williamson Murray, 'Thinking About Revolutions in Military Affairs', *Joint Force Quarterly*, 16 (Summer 1997), pp. 70–1 (emphasis added).
5. Leopold von Ranke, *The Theory and Practice of History* (Indianapolis, IN: Bobbs-Merrill, 1973).
6. See Tim Hicks, 'St. Helena: Controversy to the End', in Philip J. Haythornthwaite and others, *Napoleon: The Final Verdict* (London: Arms and Armour Press, 1998), pp. 191–220. Hicks concludes with the apposite thought that '[t]he only sure way of resolving the poisoning controversy would be to exhume the body and perform another autopsy' (p. 209). Candidate RMAs cannot be handed over to science for definitive resolution.
7. Steven Metz and James Kievit, *Strategy and the Revolution in Military Affairs: From Theory to Policy* (Carlisle Barracks, PA: Strategic Studies Institute, US Army War College, 27 June 1995), p. 10.
8. Richard K. Betts, 'Should Strategic Studies Survive?' *World Politics*, 50, 1 (October 1997), esp. p. 27.
9. Jeremy Shapiro, 'Information and War: Is It a Revolution?', in Zalmay M. Khalilzad and John P. White (eds), *Strategic Appraisal: The Changing Role of Information in Warfare* (Santa Monica, CA: RAND, 1999), pp. 136–8.
10. Arnold J. Toynbee, *A Study of History*, 12 vols (Oxford: Oxford University Press, 1934–61). Richard J. Evans, *In Defence of History* (London: Granta Books, 1997), pp. 54–6, is appropriately damning.
11. Arguments pertaining to my historical cases of postulated RMAs are employed at this juncture strictly to illustrate the salience of the questions about RMA provenance. As a consequence, and with only a few exceptions, I make no particular effort here to justify the summary judgements offered. Sources in support of my historical judgements are provided with the case studies in Chapters 6–8.
12. With thanks for inspiration to John Davidson, *Haig: Master of the Field* (London: Nevill, 1953), and Nigel Hamilton, *Master of the Battlefield: Monty's War Years, 1942–1944* (New York: McGraw-Hill Book Company, 1983).
13. Paul W. Schroeder, 'Napoleon's Foreign Policy: A Criminal Enterprise', *Journal of Military History*, 54, 2 (April 1990), pp. 147–61, must dent the armour even of the most forgiving among Napoleon's admirers.
14. The 'strategist's view' (following Shapiro, 'Information and War', p. 137) of the candidate information-led RMA is so indistinct that there was sense in Jeffrey R. Cooper's possibly rhetorical question, 'Should we pursue the RMA for its own sake? Because it could be done?': *Another View of the Revolution in Military Affairs* (Carlisle Barracks, PA: Strategic Studies Institute, US Army War College, 15 July 1994), p. 5. He does proceed to inherently less pejorative questions: 'Because it promises substantial advantages in addressing our evolving security challenges? Or, finally, because we may have no choice since potential competitors may decide to pursue the RMA regardless of its course' (pp. 5–6). Cooper usefully adds the thought that a state should think carefully about the consequences of leading an RMA if it already holds a dominant position in the marketplace of war-making prowess. Correctly enough, he cites the own-goal aspect to Britain's Royal Navy introducing a new class of all-big-gun battleships with the launching of HMS *Dreadnought* on 10 February 1906. Jon Tetsuro Sumida, *In Defence*

of Naval Supremacy: Finance, Technology and British Naval Policy, 1889–1914 (London: Routledge, 1989), is fundamental.

15. Trends and fashions in threat-set identification and evaluation can be monitored reliably in the annual (since 1995) 'strategic assessment' publication of the United States' National Defense University.

16. See R. V. Jones, *Most Secret War* (London: Coronet Books, 1979), pp. 269–70, 392–6; and Gerhard L. Weinberg, *A World at Arms: A Global History of World War II* (Cambridge: Cambridge University Press, 1994), pp. 568–74.

17. Stephen Peter Rosen, *Winning the Next War: Innovation and the Modern Military* (Ithaca, NY: Cornell University Press, 1991); Deborah D. Avant, *Political Institutions and Military Change: Lessons from Peripheral Wars* (Ithaca, NY: Cornell University Press, 1994); and Peter Trubowitz, Emily O. Goldman, and Edward Rhodes (eds), *The Politics of Strategic Adjustment: Ideas, Institutions, and Interests* (New York: Columbia University Press, 1999), all shed important light on the problems that military institutional culture can place in the way of possible adoption of new ideas and practices.

18. The green beret may be unconventional headwear, but the mind that it covers could be inappropriately conventional. For more detail, see Colin S. Gray, *Explorations in Strategy* (Westport, CT: Praeger Publishers, 1998), ch. 7; and idem, 'Handfuls of Heroes on Desperate Ventures: When Do Special Operations Succeed?' *Parameters*, 29, 1 (Spring 1999), pp. 12–13.

19. See Lawrence Freedman, *The Revolution in Strategic Affairs*, Adelphi Paper 318 (London: IISS, April 1998), ch. 3.

20. The literature is vast and, when of British origin, is inclined to err towards patriotic hagiography. That sin is avoided in Paddy Griffith's clear-eyed appraisal, 'Wellington – Commander', but is not wholly absent from the otherwise excellent essay by Correlli Barnett, 'Playing Into Wellington's Hands – Bonaparte's Mistakes', both in Griffith (ed.), *Wellington – Commander: The Iron Duke's Generalship* (Chichester: Antony Bird Publications, 1986), pp. 13–53, 127–38 respectively.

21. See Timothy T. Lupfer, *The Dynamics of Doctrine: The Changes in German Tactical Doctrine During the First World War*, Leavenworth Papers 4 (Ft. Leavenworth, KS: Combat Studies Institute, US Army Command and General Staff College, July 1981); Tim Travers, *How the War Was Won: Command and Technology in the British Army on the Western Front, 1917–1918* (London: Routledge, 1992); Paddy Griffith, *Battle Tactics of the Western Front: The British Army's Art of Attack, 1916–18* (New Haven, CT: Yale University Press, 1994); and especially Holger H. Herwig, *The First World War: Germany and Austria-Hungary, 1914–1918* (London: Arnold, 1997), chs 5–10.

22. See David Holloway, *Stalin and the Bomb: The Soviet Union and Atomic Energy, 1939–1956* (New Haven, CT: Yale University Press, 1994).

23. Not least among the ranks of military thinkers in China, the country most likely to find itself actively opposing American hegemony in the twenty-first-century. Michael Pillsbury (ed.), *Chinese Views of Future Warfare* (Washington, DC: National Defense University Press, 1997), rewards careful reading. Lloyd J. Matthews (ed.), *Challenging the United States Symmetrically and Asymmetrically: Can America Be Defeated?* (Carlisle Barracks, PA: US Army War College, Strategic Studies Institute, July 1998); and Ralph Peters, *Fighting for the Future: Will America Triumph?* (Mechanicsburg, PA: Stackpole Books, 1999), also warrant respectful attention. After 11 September 2001, of course, 'asymmetrical threats' came to mean terroristic threats. To date the outstanding dissection of asymmetry is Steven Metz and Douglas V. Johnson II, *Asymmetry and US Military Strategy: Definition, Background, and Strategic Concepts* (Carlisle Barracks, PA: Strategic Studies Institute, US Army War College, January 2001).

24. Spenser Wilkinson, *The French Army before Napoleon* (Aldershot: Gregg Revivals, 1991 [1915]), p. 22.

25. Williamson Murray, 'Military Culture Does Matter', *Strategic Review*, 27, 2 (Spring 1999), pp. 32–40.
26. Writing about the Roman Republic in the era of the Punic Wars, Alvin Bernstein informs us that 'Between his seventeenth and forty-sixth birthdays the Roman citizen owed the state sixteen years of active military service': 'The Strategy of a Warrior-State: Rome and the Wars Against Carthage, 264–201 BC', in Williamson Murray, MacGregor Knox, and Bernstein (eds), *The Making of Strategy: Rulers, States, and War* (Cambridge: Cambridge University Press, 1994), p. 60. Also see F. E. Adcock, *The Roman Art of War Under the Republic* (Cambridge, MA: Harvard University Press, 1940), ch. 1. Inspiration for the *levée en masse* rather closer to home than Republican Rome could be found in the much praised work, *My Reveries upon the Art of War*, written by Marshal of France Maurice de Saxe in the late 1740s (published posthumously in 1757). 'Would it not be better to prescribe by law that every man, whatever his condition in life, should be obliged to serve his prince and his country for five years. This law could not be objected to because it is natural and just that all citizens should occupy themselves with the defense of the nation': Thomas R. Phillips (ed.), *Roots of Strategy: A Collection of Military Classics* (London: John Lane, 1943), pp. 102–3.
27. Wilkinson, *French Army before Napoleon*; idem, *The Rise of General Bonaparte* (Aldershot: Gregg Revivals, 1991 [1930]); David Chandler, *The Campaigns of Napoleon* (London: Weidenfeld & Nicolson, 1967), pt 3; Peter Paret, 'Napoleon and the Revolution in War', in Paret, *Makers of Modern Strategy*, pp. 123–42.
28. In 1994, Michael J. Mazarr was in no doubt that 'We are in the midst of a revolution in military affairs (RMA). It is a post-nuclear revolution, a return to an emphasis on non-nuclear warfare, both conventional and unconventional': *The Revolution in Military Affairs: A Framework for Defense Planning* (Carlisle Barracks, PA: Strategic Studies Institute, US Army War College, April 1994), p. 3.
29. Peter Paret, *Understanding War: Essays on Clausewitz and the History of Military Power* (Princeton, NJ: Princeton University Press, 1992), ch. 5, 'Napoleon as Enemy', is particularly clear on this matter. '[T]he revolution in war that occurred at the end of the eighteenth-century was not consciously structured' (p. 75). Even if there had been a blueprint for success, in Paret's opinion that design could not have been invented by Napoleon or even by his immediate antecedents in command of the armies of revolutionary France. Paret advises that '[t]he French Revolution coincided with a revolution in war that had been under way through the last decades of the monarchy'. 'Napoleon and the Revolution in War', p. 124.
30. 'From late 1948 to 1957, Lieutenant General (later General) Curtis E. LeMay was the driving force behind SAC's [the Strategic Air Command's] early development': Samuel R. Williamson, Jr and Steven L. Rearden, *The Origins of US Nuclear Strategy, 1945–1953* (New York: St Martin's Press, 1993), p. 167. Also see Harry R. Borowski, *A Hollow Threat: Strategic Air Power and Containment before Korea* (Westport, CT: Greenwood Press, 1982), and William S. Borgiasz, *The Strategic Air Command: Evolution and Consolidation of Nuclear Forces, 1945–1955* (Westport, CT: Praeger Publishers, 1996). On the contribution of President Dwight D. Eisenhower see Colin S. Gray, 'The Defence Policy of the Eisenhower Administrations, 1953–1961', DPhil. thesis (Oxford: Rhodes House Library, 1970), and Saki Dockrill, *Eisenhower's New-Look National Security Policy, 1953–61* (London: Macmillan, 1996).
31. For Bernard Brodie, see Ken Booth, 'Bernard Brodie', in Baylis and Garnett, *Makers of Nuclear Strategy*, pp. 19–56; and Barry H. Steiner, *Bernard Brodie and the Foundations of American Nuclear Strategy* (Lawrence: University Press of Kansas, 1991). For Albert Wohlstetter, see Richard Rosecrance, 'Albert Wohlstetter', in Baylis and Garnett, *Makers of Nuclear Strategy*, pp. 57–69, and James Digby and J. J. Martin, 'On Not Confusing Ourselves: Contributions of the Wohlstetters to US Strategy and Strategic Thought', in

Andrew W. Marshall, Martin and Henry S. Rowen (eds), *On Not Confusing Ourselves: Essays on National Security Strategy in Honor of Albert and Roberta Wohlstetter* (Boulder, CO: Westview Press, 1991), pp. 3–16.

32. I. S. Bloch, *Modern Weapons and Modern War* (London: Grant Richards, 1900). See Michael Howard, 'Men Against Fire: The Doctrine of the Offensive in 1914', in Paret, *Makers of Modern Strategy*, pp. 510–26.

33. A. J. Wohlstetter and others, *Selection and Use of Strategic Air Bases*, R-266 (Santa Monica, CA: RAND, April 1954), undoubtedly was influential, but in its advocacy of a maximum feasible degree of US homeland basing for SAC it was pushing on an open door for an official client who wanted to be given that particular message. The same RAND team of systems analysts proved much less influential when it advocated housing SAC's long-range bombers in expensive concrete shelters (among other measures of base hardening). SAC ignored advice that it did not want to hear. General Curtis LeMay did not intend his forces passively to try to ride out a Soviet surprise attack. Kaplan, *Wizards of Armageddon*, ch. 6, 'The Vulnerability Study', is informative.

34. At least, so I argue at length in my *Modern Strategy* (Oxford: Oxford University Press, 1999).

35. Brian R. Sullivan, 'The Future Nature of Conflict: A Critique of "The American Revolution in Military Affairs" in the Era of Jointery', *Defense Analysis*, 14, 2 (August 1998), p. 92.

36. Early in 1940, Dr Vannevar Bush was President of the Carnegie Institution of Washington; formerly he had been at MIT. On 12 June of that year, Bush secured Roosevelt's approval of his bureaucratically somewhat imperial proposal to create, and of course head up, a National Defense Research Council which would guide, mobilise, and help to manage diverse scientific research for national security. 'To most of those who had a part in the revolution [in the relations among American scientists, politicians, and soldiers] it became a truism that Vannevar Bush was its indispensable man': McGeorge Bundy, *Danger and Survival: Choices About the Bomb in the First Fifty Years* (New York: Random House, 1988), p. 39. That indispensability proved nowhere more momentous than in his intermediary role between the worlds of science and politics in the case of atomic possibilities (p. 45). Also see Richard Rhodes, *The Making of the Atomic Bomb* (New York: Simon & Schuster, 1986), pp. 336–8.

37. See James R. Blaker, *Understanding the Revolution in Military Affairs: A Guide to America's 21st Century Defense*, Defense Working Paper 3 (Washington, DC: Progressive Policy Institute, January 1997), pp. 4–8. William J. Perry is a distinguished military scientist and administrator of military technological innovation. Whatever his more contestable credentials as a strategic thinker, there is no doubt that he was the right man at the right place at the right time to advance the supremely technological cause of an information-led American RMA. See William J. Perry: 'Desert Storm and Deterrence', *Foreign Affairs*, 70, 4 (Fall 1991), pp. 66–87; (with Ashton Carter and John D. Steinbruner), *A New Concept of Cooperative Security* (Washington, DC: Brookings Institution Press, 1992); 'Military Action: When to Use It and How to Ensure Its Effectiveness', in Janne E. Nolan (ed.), *Global Engagement: Cooperation and Security in the 21st Century* (Washington, DC: Brookings Institution Press, 1994), pp. 235–41; 'Defense in an Age of Hope', *Foreign Affairs*, 75, 6 (November/December 1996), pp. 64–79.

38. Le Corbusier, *Towards a New Architecture*, trans. Fredrick Etchells (London: Architectural Press, 1946), p. 261.

39. The synergism of person with opportunity to create radical, but apparently nonlinear, outcomes does not allow for the drawing of sharp lines of demarcation. The Bolshevik and Nazi revolutions were both very much manufactured, which is to say wilfully created, events and processes, but the 'wills' in question could only triumph in permissive contexts. For example, Ian Kershaw is highly persuasive when he claims flatly that

'Without the changed conditions, the product of a lost war, revolution, and a pervasive sense of national humiliation, Hitler would have remained a nobody': *Hitler, 1889–1936: Hubris* (London: Penguin, 1998), p. 132. One has to be careful lest a healthy recognition of the significance of context, or opportunity, leads to an unhealthy discounting of the value purposefully added by a particular individual, movement, or institution.

40. For example, in 1916–18 General Sir Douglas Haig and General Erich Ludendorff both served as enthusiastic, 'enabling' patrons to a revolution in the conduct of war effected by their subordinates. For Haig, see Michael Crawshaw, 'The Impact of Technology on the BEF and its Commander', in Brian Bond and Nigel Cave (eds), *Haig: A Reappraisal 70 Years On* (London: Leo Cooper, 1999), pp. 155–75; for Ludendorff, see Michael Geyer, 'German Strategy in the Age of Machine Warfare, 1914–1945', in Paret, *Makers of Modern Strategy*, pp. 527–97.

41. Thomas J. Welch, 'Revolution in Military Affairs: One Perspective', in Frances Omori and Mary A. Sommerville (eds), *Strength Through Cooperation: Military Forces in the Asia–Pacific Region* (Washington, DC: National Defense University Press, 1999), p. 122.

42. It is not necessarily entirely to Napoleon's credit to observe, as does Chandler, that 'most significantly of all, the form of the battle [Castiglione, 5 August 1796] proves beyond any doubt that Napoleon's master battle plan [including the idea of the *manoeuvre sur les derrières*] was already clear in his mind as early as 1796. In subsequent years he might polish and improve its technique – especially the crucial matter of timing the successive stages – but all the elements of the successful attacks carried out at Austerlitz, Friedland or Bautzen were already in existence and in operation at the battle of Castiglione': *Campaigns of Napoleon*, pp. 700–1. The thesis that Napoleon failed adequately to adjust his style in the conduct of war to sharply altered conditions, especially after 1809, is argued forcefully in Robert M. Epstein, *Napoleon's Last Victory and the Emergence of Modern War* (Lawrence: University Press of Kansas, 1994).

43. Herwig, *First World War*, pp. 416–28, 'The Turning Point'.

44. Eugenia C. Kiesling, *Arming Against Hitler: France and the Limits of Military Planning* (Lawrence: University Press of Kansas, 1996), is particularly persuasive on the relative importance of training. In common with logistics and medical matters, training is of so fundamental a significance to combat effectiveness that military professionals tend to believe that it needs no unusual emphasis. In their world everyone knows that quality and quantity of training is a sine qua non for high performance. In contrast, many amateur strategists are apt to overlook the importance of training – and discipline, logistics, and medical matters – because their professional expertise typically resides in ideas or technologies.

45. Carl von Clausewitz, *On War*, trans. Michael Howard and Peter Paret (Princeton, NJ: Princeton University Press, 1976 [1832]), p. 204; Antoine Henri de Jomini, *The Art of War* (London: Greenhill Books, 1992 [1862]), pp. 70–1. John Ellis, *Brute Force: Allied Strategy and Tactics in the Second World War* (New York: Viking Penguin, 1990), emphasises the importance of material superiority for Allied victory.

46. Bernard Brodie and Fawn Brodie, *From Crossbow to H-bomb*, rev. edn (Bloomington: Indiana University Press, 1973).

47. N. H. Gibbs, *History of the Second World War, Grand Strategy, I: Rearmament Policy* (London: HMSO, 1976), ch. 15; R. J. Overy, *The Air War, 1939–1945* (New York: Stein & Day, 1985), pp. 54–63; John Terraine, *A Time for Courage: The Royal Air Force in the European War, 1939–1945* (New York: Macmillan, 1985), esp. pp. 173–80. Also see Francis K. Mason, *Battle over Britain: A History of the German Air Assaults on Great Britain, 1917–18 and July–December 1940, and of the Development of Britain's Air Defences between the Wars* (London: McWhirter Twins, 1969); and Alan Beyerchen, 'From Radio to Radar: Interwar Military Adaptation to Technological Change in Germany, the United Kingdom, and the United States', in Williamson Murray and Allan

R. Millett (eds), *Military Innovation in the Interwar Period* (Cambridge: Cambridge University Press, 1996), pp. 265–99.

48. To invade Russia from peninsular Europe is to proceed into an ever-widening funnel-shaped domain. Even the largest of peninsular European armies – for the examples I cite, the German Östheer and the French Grande Armée – could register only modest force to space ratios, once an imaginary line connecting the Baltic and Black Seas was passed. The geographical dimension of strategy which must provide vital, and specific, context for RMA execution, is explored in Colin S. Gray, 'Inescapable Geography', in Gray and Geoffrey Sloan (eds), *Geopolitics, Geography, and Strategy* (London: Frank Cass, 1999), pp. 161–77. For the German and French cases cited, see respectively Horst Boog and others, *Germany and the Second World War, Vol. IV: The Attack on the Soviet Union* (Oxford: Clarendon Press, 1998); and Carl von Clausewitz, *The Campaign of 1812 in Russia* (London: Greenhill Books, 1992 [1st Eng. edn 1843]). The classic graphical presentation (by Charles Minard in 1861) of the diminishing size of Napoleon's army in Russia, plotted against time, distance, and temperature, may be located most readily in Michael I. Handel, *Masters of War: Classical Strategic Thought*, 3rd edn, (London: Frank Cass, 2001), opposite p. 194.

49. Sun Tzu, *The Art of War*, trans. Ralph D. Sawyer (Boulder, CO: Westview Press, 1994 [*c.* 400 BC]), passim.

50. Edward N. Luttwak argues that the more successful a tactical innovation, the more likely it is to be countered rapidly and effectively: *Strategy: The Logic of War and Peace* (Cambridge, MA: Harvard University Press, 1987), esp. ch. 2. To be successful is to attract attention and motivate an urgent hunt for countermeasures of all kinds.

51. Helmuth Graf von Moltke, *Moltke on the Art of War: Selected Writings*, ed. Daniel Hughes, trans. Hughes and Harry Bell (Novato, CA: Presidio Press, 1993), p. 45. Moltke continues with the observation that 'Only the layman sees in the course of a campaign a consistent execution of a preconceived and highly detailed original concept pursued consistently to the end.'

52. Alternative RMA life-cycle designs include Cooper, *Another View of the Revolution in Military Affairs*, which offers five steps (the right conditions, 'recognition of a revolution in the making', 'acceptance or validation that a revolution is in progress', 'institution-alization' by 'careful specification of the new problem ... that will be addressed', and exploitation, pp. 23–4), and Metz and Kievit, *Strategy and the Revolution in Military Affairs*, which suggests six steps ('initial stasis, followed by initiation, critical mass, consolidation, response, and return to stasis'), p. 12.

53. Jomini, *Art of War*, p. 48.

4

On Strategy, I: Chaos Confounded?

Strategy is difficult to do, but it is not impossible: chance always threatens to rule in war, but it does not reign. Clausewitz can mislead when he writes: 'In the whole range of human activities, war most closely resembles a game of cards.'[1] In emphasising rightly the roles of guesswork and luck in war, exactly because 'No other human activity is so continuously or universally bound up with chance',[2] he risks turning a sound point into an unsound one. It is almost mischievous for Clausewitz to hazard the analogy between cards and war, because there is a truly vital difference between them. Cards are dealt literally at random. By contrast, the dimensions of war and strategy include chance and uncertainty (perhaps gathered in the broad church of 'friction'),[3] but they do not reduce to them. Card players are obliged to perform with assets randomly selected, strategic players are not. To develop the analogy further, strategic performance is not akin to skill in poker. The superior poker player plays the person not the cards. The poker wizard will always win conclusively against inferior players, regardless of the cards that are dealt (at random of course), provided only that a series of hands is allowed. The luck of the cards has next to nothing to do with it. Needless to add, for players of equivalent skill, better cards could be the difference between them. In war, as in life, while a cruel and capricious fate may thwart rational calculation and predictability, by and large it does not. Ceteris tolerably paribus, objectively better armed forces tend to win wars.[4] Strategic skill is important, but unlike the case of poker, alone it is not a reliable foundation for victory. Inputs for strategic behaviour can reasonably be assumed to bear some usefully proportional relation to strategic outcomes. This is to say that strategic behaviour is substantially linear in character. None of this challenges the importance of chance, risk, accident, uncertainty, friction of all kinds, or guesswork. But it does challenge the strangely counterfactual and counterintuitive proposition that 'chaos rules' in war. Chaos does not rule. To paraphrase and expand on the biblical aphorism: 'the race is not always to the swift, nor the battle to the strong',[5] but that is the way to bet.

The discussion here and in Chapter 5 builds upon the brief remarks offered on strategy in Chapter 1. The purpose is to provide a theory usable for understanding how RMAs might work, and sufficiently flexible so that it can grow with feedback from analysis of historical data. Data as candidate evidence is deployed in Chapters 6–8. Succeeding sections below explain the meaning of strategy, pursue its nature and character, explore the central issues of chaos versus predictability, and conclude by posing and answering the vital question of whether, or to what degree, strategy is 'chaotic'. The second chapter devoted to developing a usable theory of strategy – Chapter 5 – considers RMAs as strategic behaviour and explains the multidimensional structure and dynamics of strategy. These two chapters stand or fall on their ability to present a theory of strategy which can help unlock the otherwise highly complex mystery that is the historical process of RMA. Chapter 3 outlined a fairly rugged theory of RMA, but that theory would hang as if it were suspended in a vacuum were it not employed and exploited by a theory of strategy.

Lest there be any confusion, the theory of strategy and the theory of RMA are not comparable in importance or existentiality. There is always strategic effect, whether or not the bridge of strategy is solidly built and well maintained. Strategy as the purposeful threat or use of force for policy ends has to matter. There is a sense in which even if strategy as 'a plan of action' appears to be missing from action,[6] strategic effect will occur anyway, albeit significantly unplanned. By contrast, RMA theory is eminently contestable both conceptually and empirically. It is much more important to understand strategy, what it is and how it works, than it is to develop RMA theory. However, the RMA hypothesis, for all its fragilities, has an intriguing potential to provide, slingshot-like, 'gravity-assist' acceleration to the spacecraft of the theory of strategy. That is the guiding principle behind this analysis. RMA theory can help us understand how strategy works. The point is well made by Roger Beaumont when, discussing 'nonlinearity–complexity–chaos research', he writes: 'Even if such concepts proved to be transient faddism, weighing fresh ideas can lead to a reconsideration of basic principles and assumptions.'[7]

WHAT IS STRATEGIC?

As Clausewitz insists, 'Everything in strategy is very simple, but that does not mean that everything is very easy.'[8] Perhaps strange to record, the most essential aspect of strategy, the core of its meaning, is easy to grasp yet seems everywhere to be resisted. That core of meaning is the instrumentality of the threat and use of force. It is quite common, though not always helpful, to think of strategy as a plan of action, as a plan for using military means to achieve political ends. Why introduce the implied formality of plans and planning into a working definition? So many people have difficulty comprehending the core notion of strategy as the use made of force, or military means, for the ends of policy, that the strictly redundant introduction of the idea of a *plan* of action introduces gratuitously a further source of potential distraction. The principal wrecking beacon for the understanding of strategy is the attractive power of the military instrument itself. The use of force is confused with the use made of force. The difference is small on the page, but cosmic in understanding.

There are many interesting and more or less useful definitions of strategy. For the purpose of this enquiry, to repeat the verbal formula offered in Chapter 1, strategy is understood as *the use that is made of force and the threat of force for the ends of policy.* Any fuzziness on the core meaning of strategy must impede progress in this analysis. Our approach to, and redesign of, RMA theory requires conceptual clarity. A great deal of the historical judgement on what is, and what is not, evidence for this or that RMA idea, lies in the realm of speculation and argument. It follows that special significance attaches to such navigation aids as are at hand. Sharp-edged and consistent employment of strategy and strategic is the leading such aid.

The strict idea of strategy as the bridge connecting the worlds of politics and military power, and expressing the consequences of the uses of military power, is extraordinarily important for research into RMA. My (neo-Clausewitzian) definition does not allow inherent, out-of-context, unusual importance to any particular kind of military instrument or mission. All forces are strategic in their effect, ergo none are distinctively strategic as a matter of general principle. As with *Qi* and *Zheng* in the Chinese military classics,[9] which is to say approximately the distinction between unorthodox and orthodox, so more strategic and less strategic is a difference that always must be determined locally. There are and can be no strategic forces *designated as such,* because strategic does not – at least, should not – mean (for example) nuclear-armed, long-range, or independently decisive. In each conflict, particular kinds of military forces will be relatively more significant than are others, but all forces generate strategic effectiveness on a sliding scale which registers near irrelevance at one end and close to the power of independent decision at the other.[10] Although strategy should be about attempting to achieve policy ends purposefully and hopefully in a predictable manner, in practice it is always about influencing the course of history. Plans may fail, assuredly they will need amendment in the real-time of unfolding events, but armed forces as threat and in action will help shape that course. When we dignify strategy to mean plans, as well as the use made of threatened action, we elect to emphasise the notion of value added by design to military behaviour.

It is significant for RMA theory that the understanding of strategy preferred here insists upon a holistic approach to military power. If one denies a necessarily strategic ascription to any particular character of military force – land, sea, air, space, mechanised, or whatever – then one is obliged to consider RMA in its full context. Recognition that all troops are 'strategic troops' and can,[11] in permissive conditions, perform the leading-edge role, should alert one to the possible limitations of some lines of RMA advocacy. Could troop- and support-carrying helicopters, as well as helicopter gunships, effect an RMA, at least in air–land warfare in Vietnam in the 1960s? That question could not be answered with narrow reference to the allegedly new 'dominant weapon' of army aviation/air mobility itself,[12] nor even with regard to land warfare in southeast Asia. No matter how sound it was tactically and technically in general terms, the possible RMA, certainly MTR, of the new 'air cavalry' concept, had to play in a particular conflict. US Army aviation in the 1960s could not offer unusual military effectiveness ultimately for strategic effectiveness just because it was a truly revolutionary idea which worked. Armed forces, including armed forces shaped to express the latest RMA, work more or less well as an instrument of the complex whole of strategy in the context of real historical struggles. Deborah Avant makes this point convincingly.

> The primary aim of counterinsurgency operations should be to secure the population and ever-greater amounts of territory. Helicopter units allowed Army units to arrive in an area, kill some guerrillas, then leave without securing territory or population ... In sum, the Air Cavalry, while a successful innovation, was of questionable importance for the counterinsurgency mission. Indeed, it was a successful innovation precisely because it was not designed for the counterinsurgency mission.[13]

Army Chief of Staff General Harold K. Johnson was surely sensible to advocate helicopter mobility because 'in the conduct of operations we are trying to escape the limitations that terrain imposes'.[14] The problem, as Johnson came to appreciate all too well, lay neither with helicopters nor with the air assault idea per se. Rather, the difficulty was that the US Army in Vietnam, commanded by General William C. Westmoreland, was conducting too many of the wrong sort of operations.

It is important to nest the theory and practice of RMA in the Clausewitzian understanding of strategy. Only as a consequence of that proper mental ordering is one likely to be suitably alert both to enemy options and to friendly synergies. Clausewitzian insistence on the instrumentality of 'engagements' helps counter the kind of goal displacement which sees armies promote their own organisational advantage as the supreme good. Sound strategy does not confuse means with ends, but the process of even honest promotion of much beloved means all but inevitably helps blur the distinction between the two. The political fight for a favoured RMA or MTR can hardly help but lead RMA visionaries, and then perhaps executors, to talk down rival, especially allegedly old-fashioned, military capabilities in order to promote the new.

Strategic understanding less than crystal clear on what is, and what is not, *strategic*, must risk misleading RMA debaters over the potential value of the novel capabilities at issue. Those challenged in their strategic comprehension also are likely to miss the synergistic benefit to be derived from using some of 'yesterday's' military capabilities in ways adjunct, or even integral, to more RMA-shaped forces. Above all else, inappropriate definition of *strategic* is very likely indeed to encourage unwise disdain for non-(or less)RMA forces and ideas, friendly and otherwise. A properly instrumental view of strategy and strategic enables us to construct the kind of scaffolding of theory necessary to explore historical RMAs fruitfully. That explanation should tighten our intellectual grasp on how strategy can work. If there is much that is mysterious about RMA phenomena, so a great deal remains to be explained about how strategy does its job.

PERMANENT NATURE, CHANGING CHARACTER

Strategy has a permanent nature, but an ever-changing character.[15] Nonetheless, the hypothesis of permanency can be challenged with respect to strategy's fit with both premodern and postmodern contexts. In addition, one can argue that in practice strategy tends to be captured by the structural dynamics of war, which is to say by war's very nature. Let us consider these points briefly.

First, challenge to the integrity of strategy's logic for premodern times focuses on the alleged inappropriateness of the concept of 'policy' in the means–ends nexus. The circular point is made that prior to the formation of modern states, the more or less organised violence that we identify as war quite literally could not serve the ends or objectives of such states (which did not exist).[16] 'War' could be conducted expressly as the expected social behaviour of a warrior class who waged it in large part because that was its function; it could be pursued to advance ideas of 'the right' (customary legal and religious); and it could be pursued for dynastic patrimonial advantage. But none of those long traditional premodern explanations of war fit comfortably within the strategic universe defined and explained by Clausewitz.[17] Premodern warfare does not pertain to a world wherein there is an inherently unstable equilibrium among the magnetic pulls of people, army and commander, and government with high policy.[18] Warfare as sacred duty, as existential expression of warriordom, as fun-filled energetic recreation, or as family aggrandisement, is not warfare as it was explained by Clausewitz as director of Prussia's Allgemeine Kriegsschule in the 1810s and 1820s.

Second, the postmodern challenge to the sense in strategy takes at least two forms. On the one hand, the point parallel to that just recorded for premodern times is noted: the arguably contemporary decline of the state allegedly means a dead-end for strategy as the bridge between a state's policy and its military power. The decline and fall of (major) inter-state warfare has to imply a like obsolescence in the relevance of theory for such warfare, and specifically an eclipse of the authority of the leading theorist, Carl von Clausewitz. On the other hand, new forms in warfare, especially of nuclear and cyber kinds (though with biological and biotoxin possibilities in mind also), could threaten either to sever the logical links that make strategy work, if only in principle, or to alter war's very nature. The basic problem with strategy for nuclear weapons is not conceptual, rather is it almost extravagantly practical. Arguably, strategy cannot work for nuclear weapons because the military *instrument* might not be able to function as such. Nuclear weapons are so destructive that they are not obviously usable in action, which should mean that their use cannot credibly be threatened purposefully.[19] On this logic, nuclear weapons cannot function through strategy to serve policy. Even if one ultimately rejects this line of argument, as I do, still it requires careful answer.

It can be argued that cyberwar, including the use of electronic weapons of mass disruption, menaces the very core of the integrity of the concept of strategy and war. If cyberwar is war without the direct infliction of physical pain, what merit attaches to the more traditional definitions of strategy and war, including those strongly favoured in this book? Can cyber*war* in cyberspace fit the world of the strategist who requires and expects the threat and use of force to be wielded for policy ends?[20] Is electronic warfare congruent with the idea of the threat and use of *force*? In what sense can cyberwar be an expression of organised violence for the objects of policy? The answer to questions such as these, and to the challenges to the theory of strategy cited above as respectively pre- and post-modern, lies in a functional approach to strategy's meaning and purpose.

There is some truth in each of the criticisms just noted of strategy *à la* Clausewitz. However, those truths really amount to little more than restatement of obvious and incontestable facts. Unquestionably, the character of the political context, of warfare itself (which is to say, of war's 'grammar'),[21] and therefore necessarily of strategy, has shown much evolution, and possibly the detailed working of occasional revolution, over the course of history. That granted, this author discerns no pressing reason to confine the applicability of strategy, even of strategy as explained in Clausewitz's theory of war, to a modern era book-ended neatly by the Peace of Westphalia and the Yalta and Potsdam settlements. Politics and policy do not have to translate as the kind of politics and policy characteristic of modern times (a wide range indeed)[22] for them to function well enough as the ends in the means–ends nexus key to strategy.

There is no obvious reason to be strictly, indeed somewhat mindlessly, literal in scoping the domain of strategy and war. The military strategist employs military means in order to coerce for the control that policy seeks.[23] But there is more to strategy than the military element, just as there is more to war than the organised and purposeful exercise of violence. If we are comfortable enough with the ideas of, say, political, psychological, and economic war, why not with cyberwar also? Each of those forms of warfare shares the characteristic of an absence of applied physical force. The policy-maker as grand strategist must choose among all the instruments available, including the military. My preferred definition of strategy – the use made of force and the threat of force for the ends of policy – signals unambiguously a focus upon physical coercion. That focus can be thought of as a beacon, a clear navigation aid. It is, however, compatible with the inclusion of matters that bear only functionally upon the subject. For discipline in analysis, it is helpful to assert some military centrality in the chosen definitions of strategy and war. Readers should interpret broadly both Clausewitz's reference to 'the use of engagements', and my resort to 'the use made of force and the threat of force'. Engagements need not mean battles, while the threat of force may loom more in the background to, than in the foreground of, events.[24]

Similarly, although war and warfare should not be divorced in our minds from the possibilities of organised violence as military force, they should be approached inclusively. For an apposite example, Norman Friedman writes contentiously but persuasively:

> There was never a victory parade, nor had there even been a declaration of war. Yet the Cold War was a real war, as real as the two world wars. It was not, as some imagined, an accident of misunderstanding. Conflicts such as those in Korea, Malaysia, Vietnam, and Afghanistan were all campaigns in the larger war. Throughout, the Cold War was shadowed by the hot war that might have been fought, the expected shape of which determined governments' reactions to unfolding situations.[25]

Third, in principle, war should be conducted by means of strategy to serve policy. In practice, policy can be conducted by strategy to serve war. This paradox is a political, but alas not a practical, absurdity. It is the core nature of strategy to be instrumental. Unfortunately, that inherent instrumentality is not tied to fixed identities for master and servant as between policy and war. An acute commentator notes that 'the nature of war is to serve itself'.[26] The same cannot be said of strategy. Strategy cannot even conceivably serve itself, because it is in its nature only to bridge, to be instrumental. Strategy inherently is an empty vessel, albeit one that is important and complex. Because of both apparent absurdity and inherent ambiguity, the effect of role reversal from Clausewitz's ideal type ('war is simply a continuation of political intercourse, with the addition of other means')[27] can be difficult to recognise, at least the extent of the reversal may be protected from full notice.

Although many scholars notice instances where war appears to drive policy, only rarely is such notice allowed to make more than a guest appearance in analysis. A reason for that slimness of recognition is simply definitional, indeed it works all but viscerally on what we know as that treacherous phenomenon, commonsense. Specifically, scholars usually define war as a political event. Because war is distinguished inalienably for reasons of its political motivation from brigandage or crime, the notion that it is the more independent of the two variables (i.e. war and policy) tends not to be pursued.

The other leading reason why it can be difficult to appreciate a role reversal from the Clausewitzian ideal between war and policy lies in the complexity and ambiguity of the nexus. In theory, policy's broad purposes and more specific objectives are clearly distinguishable. In practice, however, the conduct of war at the elevated level of grand strategy is a process in which political desirability is in constant dialogue with political feasibility as enabled by dynamic military opportunities (gained or lost, real or only apparent). Clausewitz advises:

> Once again: war is an instrument of policy. It must necessarily bear the character of policy and measure by its standards. *The conduct of war, in its great outlines, is therefore policy itself,* which takes up the sword in place of the pen, but does not on that account cease to think according to its own laws.[28]

He is correct, but possibly inadvertently misleading. Braving reification, perhaps even the pathetic fallacy, I am suggesting that although, following the great man, 'the conduct of war ... is therefore policy itself', that conduct can be directed more according to the needs of war and the unfolding opportunities that its course appears to offer than in the service of some distinctive source of guidance known as policy. Because strategy is a collaborative process – actually, many interdependent processes – it has to mediate between and, effectively if not efficiently, fuse political with military advisory inputs. In practice, the dialogue (admittedly a severely reductionist term) between the realms of policy and military power often evades empirical disentanglement. Policy, in most senses, has to serve war, if not always the war that it thought it had chosen, once the iron dice are rolled. Furthermore, conceptual clarity persistently is in a state of tension with real historical fuzziness. Soldiers and politicians, war and policy, the demands of war's grammar and the goals of policy; none of these three neat binary nexuses are as sharp-edged in practice as they are in theory. The truth is that there is a continuum in the relative influence of policy, as contrasted with the dynamics of war itself, over the conduct of war. This is not a straightforward case of either/or. The nature of strategy is not at issue, and neither are the structural dynamics of its 'working'. But whether strategy is more the bridge which enables military power to direct policy, or vice versa as the Good Book insists, is always determined in practice by actual circumstances and behaviour.

Much of the argument as just developed, if recognised at all, usually is cited as strategic pathology, really as the negation of strategy. Although I share the urge to reject as astrategic, even anti-strategic, role reversal between war and policy, still a nuanced approach is desirable. Definitional truths about strategy and war must not hold historical interpretation in thrall in the face of contrary evidence. Furthermore, it is not self-evident that strategy fuelled more by war's emerging opportunities than by policy's wishes must be oxymoronic. Such a case would balance means and ends, though the means would be policy and the ends advantage in war, and necessarily would have political meaning.

Overall, this third challenge to the integrity of strategy at best is only interesting and partially true. The threat or use of all forms of military power must have strategic effect. Similarly, that effect has political consequences for the course of history regardless of which sources of influence are dominant in the processes of strategy-making.

CHAOS AND PREDICTION

If the essence of strategy is instrumentality, the essence of instrumentality is predictability.[29] Strategists predict the achievement of desired outcomes through the threat or use of particular qualities and quantities of force. A series of defence budgets comprises financial expression of a dynamic prediction of the inputs (purchasable by the monies provided) judged adequate to enable the output in potential strategic effectiveness that should yield tolerable security. Strategy entails prediction at several levels. Defence communities have to predict how particular investments across many of strategy's dimensions (e.g. technology, new organisations, new operational ideas, infrastructure for training, fuel and ammunition for training and as ready war stocks) will reward the investors in enhanced potential for military effectiveness. Two critical levels of ascending challenge in predictability still lurk beyond the prediction problems of Clausewitz's 'preparations for war'.[30] The strategist has to predict how well his military power will perform in action against a live, distinctive, and reacting foe; that is the challenge of predicting military effectiveness. More difficult still is the need for the strategist to predict how much, and what kinds of, military effectiveness will be required to yield the strategic effectiveness that matches political goals.[31]

For good or ill, the strategist cannot purchase military or strategic effectiveness directly. As with love and happiness, strategic effectiveness has to be approached instrumentally in an exercise critically more artistic than scientific. A principal difficulty for strategy is the fact of disaggregation. Readers should resist the temptation to think of a country's military power as a machine that bursts reliably and smoothly into life when the policy-maker turns the key. The reality of military power is that it is hugely articulated, disaggregated, somewhat fluid and ultimately is atomised. For a mob to be an army order has to be imposed by leadership in common purpose, exercising firm yet not overbearing command. Control is achieved by the management of command, and generally by coordination in the face of all the causes of friction which the enemy, nature, and 'friendly' incompetencies will trip into action.[32] The titles of this book and chapter flag the significance of chaos, though neither is intended to encourage the view that chaos rules. Indeed, the book's main title implies that strategic behaviour is appropriate even in chaotic situations. The title of this chapter suggests that chaos might be overcome by strategy. If chaos rules, then strategy departs.

The social scientist confronted by an attractive-seeming menu of explanatory concepts deriving from other domains of knowledge needs to decide what aids understanding and what does not. More challenging still is the requirement to decide just how relevant and useful are novel-sounding concepts that unquestionably have some pertinence. More difficult still, the social scientist needs a measure of self-awareness and an alertness to herd behaviour, in order to help distinguish real, from fool's, gold. In Beaumont's all too apt words:

> Not all scientists have agreed as to whether chaos–complexity–nonlinearity is only a slight change of analytical perspective, or a fad, as opposed to being what Thomas Kuhn in *The Structure of Scientific Revolutions* called a 'paradigm shift', that is, a major fresh conceptual configuration that moves perspective to a whole new order.[33]

If scientists do not agree on the significance of chaos–complexity–nonlinearity for the natural sciences, it behoves social scientists to be especially alert when their conceptual snatch squads bring home these difficult ideas and theories as booty for exploitation in an alien landscape. That granted, still I contend that chaos, complexity, and nonlinearity speak persuasively to the nature of strategy and war. Almost as much to the point for this enquiry, those concepts and theories can help explain how RMAs work or fail to work, and they help suggest reasons why innovation and invention need not yield decisive military, for strategic, advantage. However, before the conceptual package of 'chaotics', of chaos–complexity–nonlinearity, can be unleashed for the better interpretation of strategic history, first it has to be tamed for local application.

As was lightly referenced in Chapter 1, there is a large and growing literature on chaos and complexity theory, and on the phenomenon of nonlinearity.[34] Scholarly as well as more popular science writing has been exploited by strategic theory in an attempt to apply these concepts in the dismal social science of strategic studies that deals with man's inhumanity to man. The relevance of chaos theory to this discussion of strategy and RMA is best explained with close reference to the evolving intellectual-historical context.

In common only with Thucydides among the greater theorists on war, Clausewitz emphasises that 'War is the realm of uncertainty; three quarters of the factors on which action in war is based are wrapped in a fog of greater or lesser uncertainty.' He claims that 'War is the realm of chance. No other human activity gives it greater scope; no other has such incessant and varied dealings with this intruder. Chance makes everything more uncertain and interferes with the whole course of events.'[35] He claims unambiguously that the problem is not only 'chance: the very last thing that war lacks',[36] because 'It is now quite clear how greatly the objective nature of war makes it a matter of assessing probabilities.' To that 'objective nature of war', 'the element of chance' adds 'guesswork and luck' which 'come to play a great part in war'. When Clausewitz overlays these claims for war's probabilistic, foggy, and chance-prone nature with his collective concept of friction, he leaves the eighteenth century's ideal type of a clockwork strategic universe far behind.

In the 1960s and 1970s some physicists, mathematicians, meteorologists, and biologists recognised and sought ways to explain – including ways to explain why some behaviour might be inexplicable in detail – 'the highly complex behaviour of apparently chaotic or unpredictable systems which show an underlying order'.[37] Extant mathematics and mathematical tools could not model the turbulent behaviour of some very complex systems. Chaos, complexity, nonlinearity, and turbulence became important ideas attracting effort in scientific research. Probably the most significant insight was captured by Edward Lorenz in his famous phrase, 'the butterfly effect'. A mathematician–meteorologist, Lorenz argued persuasively that even minute events could have huge consequences. More to the point, hugely different consequences – hurricanes, calm weather – would follow from sets of initial conditions that were only marginally distinctive.[38] This did not have to mean that in theory explanation–prediction is impossible. But it did mean that because all relevant initial conditions (in a highly dynamic universe) are in practice unknowable, accurate prediction in effect has to be impracticable.

In the 1980s and 1990s popular science writers picked up on chaos–complexity–nonlinearity. James Gleick's *Chaos* (1988) was a bestseller. In the mid-1990s, the dominant school of thought on RMA theory in the United States adhered to a notably orderly, mechanistically Newtonian view of strategic affairs. The holy writ of 'The American RMA', as proclaimed by Moses – Admiral William A. Owens – regarded the fog of war as a problem to be dispelled by the latest marvels of C⁴ISR, and indeed treated war itself as a challenge reducible to surgical application of precise remote bombardment.[39]

By the mid- to late 1990s, the extended US defence community contained scholars and practitioners who were distinctly uncomfortable with the vision of war implied by Admiral Owens' approach to the RMA, and as outlined schematically and authoritatively in the key JCS document, 'Joint Vision 2010'.[40] Some of these sceptics were historically trained, but virtually to a person they were steeped in the Clausewitzian worldview; at the least they were deeply respectful of what they believed the great Prussian had written. These sceptics noticed that Clausewitz had emphasised such un-Owens RMA-like factors as human beings, chance, uncertainty, fog (of war), guesswork, and luck.[41] It so happens that many of these people had not been, as it were, persuaded by Clausewitz's theory of war. Rather, that theory was persuasive because it matched the empirical evidence of those scholars' own military experiences (largely in Vietnam), and because it fitted like a glove what they understood to be the texture of strategic history at all levels.[42]

By a happy accident, in the late 1980s an American student of German history turned his considerable talent to the study of 'the implications of nonlinear science for the liberal arts', and the rest, as the saying goes, is history. Specifically, in the Winter 1992/93 issue of the leading journal in the field, *International Security*, Alan Beyerchen published a brilliant analysis which powerfully conflated 'Clausewitz, Nonlinearity, and the Unpredictability of War'. Beyerchen presents Clausewitz as a chaos theorist:

> The overall pattern is clear: war seen as a nonlinear phenomenon – as Clausewitz sees it – is inherently unpredictable by analytical means. Chance and complexity dominate simplicity in the real world. Thus no two wars are ever the same. No war is guaranteed to remain structurally stable. No theory can provide the analytical short-cuts necessary to allow us to skip ahead of the 'running' of an actual war.[43]

All of which is persuasive, *up to a point*. Unfortunately, Beyerchen's sound argument is imperilled by the excessive domain that he claims for nonlinearity. His impressive attempts to fuse Clausewitz and Lorenz (among others) were familiar to the critics of the Owens variant of RMA theory. It would be difficult to exaggerate the potency of the theoretical brew I am describing. Beyerchen provided just the argument for which many RMA sceptics were searching by the mid-1990s. He mixed the authority of Clausewitz with the excitement of the contemporary frontier of science, on behalf of a thesis that was an apparently perfect fit with the sceptics' personal military experiences, reading of history, and current debating needs. Of course, this is hindsight–foresight.

The error in Beyerchen and others' theory that war is chaos lies in its overly imperial essentialism. It is true that war is essentially nonlinear and chaotic. But war also is essentially economic, political, and even substantially predictable, which is to say compatible with purposeful strategy. When social scientists and historians boldly borrow concepts and theories from the mathematical and natural sciences, they need to be as daring in their use of the intellectual loot as they were in the initial inspiration to reach across the boundaries among disciplines. In practice, some strategic commentators have tried to be too faithful to the original scientific meaning of the borrowed concept, and have applied the ideas of chaos–complexity–nonlinearity uncritically. Chaos theory has been allowed undisciplined application against RMA advocacy of a mechanistically linear kind, because it packs such a potent punch.

As so often is the case, Clausewitz's *On War* is by far the best place to begin a search for balanced understanding of the nature of war and strategy. Bearing in mind that, uniquely among the authors of classic theories of war, Clausewitz allows full recognition of chance, uncertainty, risk, luck, guesswork, and friction,[44] does the great man believe that war is literally nonlinear and chaotic? 'War is the realm of chance', Clausewitz claims persuasively, indeed incontestably. But, by analogy, because the Great Australian Bight is the realm of the shark, it does not follow that swimming there is impossible. Similarly, the north and south polar regions are realms of cold lethal to man, but through extraordinary effort man can and does survive in both of them. A more apt analogy, perhaps, is the claim that even though a casino is quite literally 'a realm of chance', the playing field is structurally tilted to the advantage of 'the house'. An individual punter can win very big indeed, but 'the house' will always win, overall and eventually (i.e. on the all-important bottom line), against thousands of punters playing over a period of time. A punter, even a syndicate of punters, might threaten to 'break the bank at Monte Carlo', but it would be a truly historic event (against the odds) for a casino to be bankrupted by the good luck of its clients.

History, logic, and intuition all combine to advise that although war is a gamble, it is not a realm of pure chance. As the saying goes concerning performance in the US National Football League, 'on any given Sunday any team can beat any other team'. Nonetheless, there are objectively superior football teams, and – injuries permitting – consistently they win many more games over the course of a season than do the less good football teams. To return from flights of analogy, good armies can have bad days, but – that granted – as a general rule good armies beat bad armies quite reliably. Of course, what makes for the military and strategic effectiveness of any army must be analysed in full context. By way of simple illustration, the armed forces of Iraq were hopelessly outclassed as an opponent of the US-led UN coalition in 1991, much as the armies of France and Britain were outclassed by the German Army in 1940.[45] War is a realm of chance in that conceivably Iraq could have plucked some simulacrum of a face-saving victory from the jaws of impending defeat. However, chance, even in a realm defined significantly by it, needs notable assistance. For chance to have saved Iraq in 1991, the UN coalition would have to have committed strategic errors on an epic scale.[46] All things are possible, but they are not equally likely. The friends of chaos theory for strategic studies have to be careful lest what begins as a powerfully insightful idea is rapidly transformed into a simplistic, and *demonstrably false*, essentialist nostrum to the effect that 'chaos rules'. Clausewitz did not say that; at least he did not quite say that, and the qualification is vital.

What Clausewitz attempts, brilliantly and by and large successfully, is to explain why strategy is difficult to do well. By analogy, he advises that it is in the nature of the terrain to be crossed for it to present an array of hostile natural and human obstacles to our safe passage. We can add the thought that in order to win the traveller simply has to complete his mission and arrive safely at an acceptable destination. War is not like competitive ice skating, where points are gained for technique and artistic presentation. In war the choreography may be brutally inelegant, but if it achieves its goal it will be good enough. Norman Friedman is correct when he advises that '[w]ars are messy, murky affairs. The winner is usually the side that makes fewer mistakes, not the side which perfectly executes a masterly strategy'.[47] Clausewitz does not mislead the reader, but some readers have misled themselves. For all his warnings about the uncertainty of war, and his ominous advice that 'friction is a force that theory can never quite define',[48] he does not abandon hope for strategy. Quite the contrary, in fact, as this mature passage reveals.

> The good general must know friction in order to overcome it wherever possible, and in order not to expect a standard of achievement in his operations which this very friction makes impossible.[49]

To win a war you do not need to score a 'perfect ten' in military excellence, you just have to perform better, perhaps less badly, than the enemy. More telling even than Clausewitz's treatment of friction is his magisterial brief explanation of the quintessentially strategic character of a war intelligently conceived and conducted.

> War plans cover every aspect of a war, and weave them all into a single operation that must have a single, ultimate objective in which all particular aims are reconciled. No one starts a war – or rather, no one in his senses ought to do so – without first being clear in his mind what he intends to achieve by that war and how he intends to conduct it. The former is its political purpose; the latter its operational objective. This is the governing principle which will set its course, prescribe the scale of means and effort which is required, and make its influence felt throughout down to the smallest operational detail.[50]

It is most significant that Clausewitz could envisage war in so strategically rational a way, despite his full recognition of the chaotic possibilities. Later in the same chapter (Chapter 2 of Book 8) he rubs home the gritty realism that underlies the strategic aspiration just quoted. Writing about the variety both of war forms and war performance, Clausewitz advises:

> We must, therefore, be prepared to develop our concept of war as it ought to be fought, not on the basis of its pure definition, but by leaving room for every sort of extraneous matter. We must allow for natural inertia, for all the friction of its parts, for all the inconsistency, imprecision, and timidity of man, and finally we must face the fact that war and its forms result from ideas, emotions, and conditions prevailing at the time – and to be quite honest we must admit that this was the case even when war assumed its absolute state under Bonaparte.[51]

To say that war is the realm of chance and friction is not to say that war is the realm of those elements only. Although in the passages quoted Clausewitz struggles with only mixed success to reconcile his erstwhile fixation upon war's allegedly absolute nature with the historical experience of limited war, his struggle is revealing for our purposes. The following passage makes points central to our enquiry. Clausewitz argues that real historical, which is to say more or less limited, wars, have forms that express their origins, but that the inherent dynamics of war must reveal themselves in the particular detail of particular wars.

> [I]f we must admit that the origin and the form taken by a war are not the result of any ultimate resolution of the vast array of circumstances involved, but only of those features that happen to be dominant, it follows that war is dependent on the interplay of possibilities and probabilities, of good and bad luck, conditions in which strictly logical reasoning often plays no part at all and is always apt to be a most unsuitable and awkward intellectual tool. It follows, too, that war can be a matter of degree.[52]

In the context of this passage, the opposite of 'logical reasoning' is not necessarily, let alone principally, the idea in the preceding phrase, 'of good and bad luck'.

Against the backdrop of his theory of war, for Clausewitz strategy is possible, albeit difficult, even though his theory advises that 'war is the realm of chance'. Force can be used ('engagements') purposefully as an instrument of policy, despite the fact that attempts at such use frequently prove unsuccessful. What does chaos–complexity–nonlinearity theory add to our understanding of war and strategy? The starting point has to be recapitulation of the core meaning of these linked ideas that social science has borrowed.

- A system or phenomenon (e.g. war, strategy) is *complex* if it comprises several – more likely many – dimensions or elements, 'suggesting intricacy of structure and process, but not randomness, sometimes with a high degree of regularity in their dynamics up to a point of transition'.[53] Complexity 'usually implies a reasonable degree of predictability and controllability, which may quickly pass through a state-change into what is or seems to be "chaos"'.[54]
- A (complex) system or phenomenon is *nonlinear* when its performance shows radical discontinuities because of an apparent disproportion between inputs and outcomes.
- A system or phenomenon is *chaotic* when it shows both nonlinearity in performance and such extreme sensitivity to the downstream consequences of unknown variation in initial conditions, that predictive system behaviour is impracticable.
- In summary: *chaos* theory applies to (*complex*), *nonlinear* 'dynamical' systems, which is to say systems with large numbers of shifting components that exhibit a tendency to express an endogenous, 'self-organising criticality'. That criticality produces a new nonrecurrent (i.e. non-periodic) pattern of order. In other words, a process of nonlinear dynamics irregularly produces orderly patterns which are not easily predictable, if they are predictable at all.[55]

These ideas fit war and strategy, but they do not fit perfectly. Indeed, the measure of imperfection is critically important and, if underrecognised, vitiates much of the merit in their relevance for strategic studies. Before considering the strengths and weaknesses of chaos–complexity–nonlinearity theory for strategic studies, there is no evading the problem of language. Social scientists have never been backward in willingness to layer obscurity upon opacity by enfolding the fog of war in a fog of specialised language. Even when chaos theory is clearly written, it presents the social scientist with what amounts to a barrier of difficult concepts expressed unusually (and that is to ignore the communication difficulty posed by the challenging algebra of nonlinear equations).

Lest we lose the plot, it is necessary to emphasise that the ideas in chaos theory are adapted for use in this enquiry strictly because they draw attention to several of the most vital features in the nature of strategy and war. In no important sense is this discussion a general celebration of the relevance of chaos theory for social science. Why are the ideas of chaos theory important for the better understanding of strategy?

First, strategy is complex in the sense conveyed by the notion of complexity employed by chaos theorists. Strategy has several or many dimensions (or elements) which function synergistically in intricate ways. The product of that synergy is a course of consequences in military effectiveness for strategic effectiveness which cannot be exactly modelled for predictability.[56] At least, effectiveness cannot be modelled usefully if it is understood to be the linear product of attritional combat. Vice Admiral Arthur K. Cebrowski, the leading figure pressing for a network-centric approach to military operations and war,[57] argues for a model of conflict which accommodates the feedback from inter-action with the enemy (inter alia) and the influence of nonlinear dimensions of strategy. He explains thus:

> There are practical reasons why attritional models are still used [so-called 'Lanchestrian models', after Frederick W. Lanchester]: their inputs are easily measured, their model 'runs' are easily reproduced, and their MOEs [measures of effectiveness] are readily understood. Simplicity wins out over complexity. The chaos of war appears to be so far beyond measuring in any reasonable manner that we consider it best to ignore (or explain away) such influences as leadership, morale, cohesion, information quality, and command and control. This is what expands the gap between models and reality.[58]

The admiral insists that '[w]e must make new models and find new MOEs with which to evaluate them. We must change our mental model.'[59] He claims that

> Network-centric warfare is such a change. Network-centric warfare looks at war as a complex, adaptive system wherein nonlinear variables

continuously interact. Physical forces play a part, but so do cognitive and behavioral factors. Within the constant dimensions of war (force, space, and time), the domains of belief, knowledge, and the physical world must be portrayed.

Notwithstanding the negative reaction which the bumper-sticker term 'network-centric warfare' invites, Cebrowski's understanding of war and how to think about it is close in detail, and even closer in spirit, to the one that I advance.

Second, strategy is nonlinear in that strategic consequences, or effectiveness, can show radical discontinuities. Such discontinuities, RMAs for one class of example, are not random events or accidents. However, they may occur as the result of action on, and synergistically among, so many of strategy's different dimensions as to be effectively beyond prediction, confident or otherwise. The same argument applies to the history of the international political system.[60] The course of international history from 1919 to 1939, for example, is a perfect case of a nonlinear, but substantially deterministic, dynamical system. Nazi Germany and its consequences for world order was not a random outcome of the first 31 years of the twentieth century. The emergence of the Third Reich was, however, an outcome determined by so many factors, including so many genuinely unpredictable contingencies (e.g. in particular the fact, certainly the timing, of the Great Depression), that it was a surprising discontinuity, indeed a revolutionary surprise. Causation for many of history's great discontinuities has been suspiciously easy to identify long after the surprising event.

Third, strategy is chaotic because it can register both the radical disconti-nuities in outcomes characteristic of nonlinearity, as well as consequences that differ on a range apparently wholly disproportionate to the scale of the initial impetus. Familiar examples of such chaotic performance in the realm of strategy include two famous cases in the American Civil War: the death of 'Stonewall' Jackson at Chancellorsville (30 April–6 May 1863), and Robert E. Lee's 'lost order' before the battle of Antietam (17 September 1862). The former accidental event probably literally was to deprive Lee of victory at Gettysburg in July 1863, while non-occurrence of the latter contingency might well have saved Lee from having to campaign at all in 1863.

The death of Jackson on 10 May 1863 eliminated 'the army's most gifted corps commander and Lee's principal adviser and confidant'.[61] Given that battlefield command is a collaborative matter of teamwork, that Lee did not have a hands-on command style vis-à-vis his corps commanders, and also that the army of the Confederate States of America was not amply blessed with superior generals,[62] one can appreciate how severe the effects of the loss of Jackson were likely to be.

Going back eight months from Jackson's death, on 13 September 1862 General George B. McClellan, the commander of the Federal Army of the

Potomac, was handed a copy of Lee's 'Special Orders (SO) No. 191'.[63] SO191 was Lee's complete plan for the autumn campaign of 1862. This campaign, designed on a flood tide of battlefield victories, was intended to culminate in a major battle waged at a time and place in Maryland or, more likely, in Pennsylvania, of Lee's choosing, for the purposes of achieving foreign recognition and terminally discouraging the enemy. Such a success at that time would have the clear potential to end the war. The capture of the 'lost order' both destroyed Lee's plan to fight a battle in highly advantageous circumstances, and afforded McClellan one of history's more golden opportunities to destroy a dispersed enemy in detail. As it was, McClellan's timidity and procrastination enabled Lee to enforce at least a tactical draw at Antietam, even though the Army of Northern Virginia was obliged to fight at a two-to-one disadvantage.

A significant caveat has to be recorded concerning the counterfactuality assumption that tends to lurk under-recognised in chaos theory for history-based social science. Because (strategic) history is played only once, literally unrepeatably in real-time, strictly speaking an argument for chaotic behaviour can only be speculative. Theorists and historians may argue persuasively that history shows the chaotic features of nonlinearity and the sensitivity of outcomes to often indeterminate initial conditions. But they cannot know for certain that they are interpreting truly chaotic behaviour; history is played only once.

Human affairs are not meteorology, no matter how suggestive ideas expressed and developed mathematically for the latter are for the former. Edward Lorenz's set of nonlinear equations could explain why his 'butterfly effect' should be true. A small change in a particular value in the contributors to the weather at a particular point in time in a particular region, might have distinctive, and possibly traceably predictable, but hugely disproportionate, consequences at a later time in other regions. Notwithstanding the structural similarities for theory between global weather and global politics, consider the robustness or otherwise of chaos theory with reference to an especially dramatic counter-factual occurrence. Suppose Adolf Hitler had been shot in the mêlée which concluded the 'beer-hall putsch' (announced in the Bürgerbraukellar) in Munich on 7–8 November 1923.[64] Many people, including many scholars, are so convinced of the eponymous truth in the thesis that the Second World War was 'Hitler's war', that the death of just that one man in 1923 seemingly self-evidently would have had consequences for the course of history radically different from what actually occurred.

I select the fictitious death of Hitler in 1923 because it appears to yield the strongest imaginable case for strategic history as chaos unveiled. However, one can argue plausibly that the outbreak of the Second World War was, if anything, overdetermined. History is the realm of contingency, but it seems to this theorist, at least, that no Germany in the 1930s – Weimar, Nazi, restored Hohenzollern, or whatever – could accommodate itself peacefully to the

European order of the Versailles settlement.[65] Of course it mattered who ruled Germany, and how, but it is difficult to believe that a second round of *grande guerre* was avoidable. To suggest, as here, that a Second World War most probably was unavoidable, is not necessarily to suggest, its popular title notwithstanding, that it was simply 'round two' of a two-event series in a 'thirty years' war'.[66] The military–political outcomes in 1918–19 left vital questions of European and Asian order so unresolved that a rematch was probable. However, the character of the war at issue possibly depended hugely upon the many contingencies of 1919–39 (perhaps only of 1919–31). The Second World War might have been another balance-of-power struggle *d'après* 1914–18, rather than a war about preclusive German imperium in Eurasia (and perhaps beyond). In fact, 'Versailles Europe' had been thoroughly overturned *peacefully* in Germany's favour by 1939. This does not mean, however, that any German government other than one led by Hitler would have avoided another great war. Of course, a cynic could argue that the ostensible differences between German ambitions in 1914 and 1939 did not much matter. The reality of great-war dynamics flagged not entirely convincingly by Clausewitz with his writing about absolute war,[67] meant that both 1914–18 and 1939–45 were conducted by the leading belligerents with a view to achieving complete victory. Clausewitz observes:

> If war is part of policy, policy will determine its character. As policy becomes more ambitious and vigorous, so will war, and this may reach the point where war attains its absolute form. If we look at war in this light, we do not need to lose sight of this absolute: on the contrary, we must constantly bear it in mind.

The problem with this explanation is that it fails to recognise that policy is likely to become more 'ambitious and vigorous' because of the evolving costs and opportunities revealed by the course of war itself.

Because chaos theory has become quite fashionable, and because it is intelligent as well as 'methodologically correct' for scholars to acknowledge the role of contingency, or chance, there is some danger that super-stable conditions may pass unnoticed as such. The outbreaks of both world wars, though naturally highly contingent in the detail of their actual historicity, probably were systemically deeply *non*-chaotic outcomes. It is plausible to argue that the outcome, 'war', was super-stable in the 1910s and 1930s/40s vis-à-vis preceding streams of events, even many hypothetical, alternative such streams. This is not to deny that Hitler's ideology and demonic personality probably were vital for the character of war that the Second World War became.

For another example, a non-shooting outcome to the Soviet–American Cold War of 1947–89 lends itself to at least two rival explanations, neither of which is plausibly provable. On the one hand, Albert Wohlstetter, among other influential strategists, asserted that there was a 'delicate balance of terror'.[68] One deficiency, even one modest scale of deficiency, in nuclear-related defence preparation and deterrence could fail some truly historic road-test. On the other hand, some strategic theorists claimed that nuclear deterrence either did not much matter,[69] or was massively insensitive in its existentiality to competitive defence policy performance.[70] 'Normal accident' and organisation theory, as adapted by Scott D. Sagan, warns us that global nuclear peril might have occurred by reason of normally expected glitches in the performance of complex organisations over long periods of time.[71] The historical fact is, however, that although Soviet and US nuclear forces had many accidents, none led to a third world war. Thus we have a case allegedly systemically liable to exhibit chaos, but actually revealing what may be super-stable behaviour. It is only prudent to take the potential for chaos seriously. Nonetheless, a reasonable person could argue that Soviet–American strategic relations appear to have been accident-insensitive; at least they were obviously, *and indisputably,* critically insensitive to the accidents and many miscalculations which actually happened.[72] Given that the Cold War was a single, unique stream of historical events, we have to be cautious in explaining the facts of both the non-occurrence of a great hot war and the reality of cold war.

IS STRATEGY CHAOTIC?

Chaos theory is thus a useful tool for social scientists, provided it is not permitted unduly to shape strategic historical data as evidence so as to suit its arguments. Up to a point, and in some senses, strategy (and war) is chaotic, complex, and nonlinear. Moreover, focus upon chaos, complexity, and non-linearity should prove helpful in revealing how strategy and strategic history work, especially in the guise of hypothesised RMAs. There is nothing really new about this. The language of chaos theory may be novel, but the core ideas of complexity, nonlinearity, and many synergies, have long been understood. For example, General Sir Ian Hamilton, who was a profound thinker about war, even if he was less than stellar as a high commander, caught some of the essence of what today we call 'chaos theory' when he wrote about complexity and nonlinearity in 1921:

> From many points of view there has never been a moment when all the elements of the art of war have been so much in the melting-pot as at present. A little change in one direction and quality gets the complete whiphand of quantity; a little change in another direction and the hordes of Asia may swamp our Western civilisation; a tiny discovery in a third and the whole face of war will be altered and all its historical machinery be thrown upon the scrap-heap.[73]

Sir Ian appears to anticipate Lorenz's 'butterfly effect'.

Though certainly complex, strategy is not beyond meaningful planning and execution. Similarly, although strategy can be nonlinear, much of strategic behaviour actually is linear. The better armies, like the better football teams, though in principle ever liable to a defeat, will win the bulk of their operational tests. Strategic performance can be chaotic in that causes and consequences (inputs and outputs) appear disjointed. Nonetheless, the downstream impact of modest changes in input (change in generals, a new generation of fighter aircraft, and so forth) are not beyond all sensible prediction, even when one does not neglect to consider the independent will of the enemy. Overall, while alert to the domain of chaos and suitably respectful of the power of contingency, the scholar of strategic history is likely to be impressed by the limited scope of that domain.

I have suggested that the outbreaks of the world wars were overdetermined and as events probably were anything but chaotic. I would suggest similarly, and with high confidence, that in 1943–45 the defeat of Nazi Germany was entirely a linear process. I would suggest also, though much more cautiously, that in 1917–18 the defeat of Imperial Germany was linear and non-chaotic. Strategy was feasible in both cases. Indeed, notwithstanding the facts of chaos–complexity–nonlinearity, history generally allows purposeful strategy, as well as intended strategic effect, far more than a token walk-on role. Chaos can be confounded.

NOTES

1. Carl von Clausewitz, *On War*, trans. Michael Howard and Peter Paret (Princeton, NJ: Princeton University Press, 1976 [1832]), p. 86.
2. Ibid., p. 85.
3. Clausewitz does not fuse chance and uncertainty with friction (ibid., pp. 119–21), but it can be useful to do so. See Colin S. Gray, *Modern Strategy* (Oxford: Oxford University Press, 1999), p. 41. Chance occurrences plainly have the potential to produce friction, 'the force that makes the apparently easy so difficult': Clausewitz, *On War*, p. 121. For extensive commentary on Clausewitz' idea of friction, see Barry D. Watts, *Clausewitzian Friction and Future War*, McNair Paper 52 (Washington, DC: Institute for National Strategic Studies, National Defense University, October 1996); and Stephen J. Cimbala, *Clausewitz and Chaos: Friction in War and Military Policy* (Westport, CT: Praeger Publishers, 2001).
4. By 'objectively better' I do not mean to imply any foolish autarchy about foe assessment. Of course, the performance of armed forces ultimately can be measured only *strategically*, as means employed against a foe to achieve ends. However, it is sensible to compare, say, methods of recruitment, realism in training, and tactical effectiveness of equipment between armies, and, if appropriate, judge one party superior to the other. At least it is possible to make such comparison with specific reference to these important inputs to the generation of fighting power and military effectiveness.
5. *Ecclesiastes*, 9:11.

6. On strategy as a plan of action, see J. C. Wylie, *Military Strategy: A General Theory of Power Control*, ed. John B. Hattendorf (Annapolis, MD: Naval Institute Press, 1989 [1967]), p. 14. Readers in search of a whole menu of strategy definitions can consult Edward N. Luttwak, *Strategy: The Logic of War and Peace* (Cambridge, MA: Harvard University Press, 1987), pp. 239–41, and Colin S. Gray, *Modern Strategy* (Oxford: Oxford University Press, 1999), pp. 17–23.

7. Roger Beaumont, *War, Chaos, and History* (Westport, CT: Praeger Publishers, 1994), p. 12. One should not read Beaumont's and my praise of RMA theory for its potential value as stimulant to fundamental enquiry as a blanket endorsement of any and every seemingly glittering concept *du jour*. Scholars skilled in, indeed professionally rewarded for, theoretical invention often apparently for its own sake, can generate an awesome scale of pointless intellectual industry. RMA is an interesting concept, unlikely to prove transient even though it was certainly 'faddish' in the 1990s.

8. Clausewitz, *On War*, p. 178.

9. Sun Tzu, *The Art of War*, trans. Ralph D. Sawyer (Boulder, CO: Westview Press, 1994), pp. 147–50; and Chen-Ya Tien, *Chinese Military Theory: Ancient and Modern* (Oakville, Ontario: Mosaic Press, 1992), pp. 43–6.

10. Even if a particular kind of military instrument, air power for example, is judged to enjoy systemic most-case advantage in relative effectiveness over say, land power and sea power, that does not make it a uniquely strategic agent. Just such a claim for dominant status is made for (US) air power in Benjamin S. Lambeth, 'The Technology Revolution in Air Warfare', *Survival*, 39, 1 (Spring 1997), pp. 65–83.

11. 'We're strategic troops, so what we do behind enemy lines can have serious implications': Andy McNab, *Bravo Two Zero* (London: Bantam, 1993), p. 8.

12. I borrow the idea of the dominant weapon from J. F. C. Fuller. He argued that the dominant characteristic of a weapon is its range of action, which is 'the characteristic which dominates the fight. Therefore the parts played by all other weapons should be related to the dominant one. Otherwise put, the weapon of superior reach or range should be the fulcrum of combined tactics': *Armament and History* (London: Eyre & Spottiswoode, 1946), p. 21. For example, whether or not the belligerents recognised the fact, artillery was the dominant weapon in land warfare in 1914–18, a status much more arguably enjoyed by rotary-wing aviation in Vietnam.

13. Deborah D. Avant, *Political Institutions and Military Change: Lessons from Peripheral Wars* (Ithaca, NY: Cornell University Press, 1994), p. 69. Avant draws heavily upon the judgement of Sir Robert Thompson in his *No Exit from Vietnam* (New York: David McKay, 1969).

14. Harold K. Johnson quoted in Lewis Sorley, *Honorable Warrior: General Harold K. Johnson and the Ethics of Command* (Lawrence: University Press of Kansas, 1998), p. 170. The best treatment of most of the relevant issues remains Andrew F. Krepinevich, *The Army and Vietnam* (Baltimore, MD: Johns Hopkins University Press, 1986), esp. pp. 118–27, 168–72. Robert Mason, *Chickenhawk* (New York: Penguin, 1984), is a superior memoir of the helicopter war, written by a 'Huey' (Bell HU-1 Iroquois) pilot.

15. My thesis in *Modern Strategy*.

16. See Martin van Creveld: *The Transformation of War* (New York: Free Press, 1991); 'What is Wrong with Clausewitz?', in Gert de Nooy (ed.), *The Clausewitzian Dictum and the Future of Western Military Strategy* (The Hague: Kluwer Law Institutional, 1997), pp. 7–23; and *The Rise and Decline of the State* (Cambridge: Cambridge University Press, 1999).

17. The most unsympathetic of Clausewitz's current critics, John Keegan, offers a notably astrategic view when he suggests that 'war is collective killing for some collective purpose': *War and Our World* (London: Hutchinson, 1998), p. 72. Keegan proclaimed the obsolescence of Clausewitz's worldview, at least of that worldview as he understood it,

in his extraordinary work, *A History of Warfare* (London: Hutchinson, 1993). Clausewitz also figures as yesterday's theorist in Mary Kaldor's insightful study, *New and Old Wars: Organized Violence in a Global Era* (Cambridge: Polity Press, 1999). Impressive, if not wholly persuasive, speculation anticipating a notably non-Clausewitzian condition of widespread chaos pervades Ralph Peters, *Fighting for the Future: Will America Triumph?* (Mechanicsburg, PA: Stackpole Books, 1999).

18. Clausewitz, *On War*, p. 89.
19. Nuclear-armed polities may not be able to threaten to take action likely to have suicidal consequences. They can, however, behave dangerously and promise contingently to pose 'the threat that leaves something to chance'. Thomas C. Schelling, *The Strategy of Conflict* (Cambridge, MA: Harvard University Press, 1960), title of ch. 8.
20. Intellectually pioneering studies include: John Arquilla and David Ronfeldt, 'Cyberwar is Coming!' *Comparative Strategy*, 12, 2 (April–June 1993), pp. 141–65; Martin Libicki, *What Is Information Warfare?* (Washington, DC: Institute for National Strategic Studies, National Defense University, August 1995); idem, *The Mesh and the Net: Speculations on Armed Conflict in a Time of Free Silicon* (Washington, DC: Institute for National Strategic Studies, National Defense University, August 1995); and Roger C. Molander, Andrew S. Riddile, and Peter A. Wilson, *Strategic Information Warfare: A New Face of War* MR-661-OSD (Santa Monica, CA: RAND, 1996). See also James Adams, *The Next World War* (London: Hutchinson, 1998).
21. Clausewitz, *On War*, p. 605.
22. Periodisation is both eminently contestable and can imperil, as well as assist, understanding. The title of my book, *Modern Strategy*, contains a redundant adjective. Strategy is strategy, 'modern' or other. As to when modern war began, selection of the key diagnostic principle is all important. For example, the following doctor–historians diagnose the condition of modernity according to rather different principles: Robert M. Epstein, *Napoleon's Last Victory and the Emergence of Modern War* (Lawrence: University Press of Kansas, 1994), identifies modernity with war planning which integrates different theatres of operations, mobilises fully the resources of the state, and conducts war at the operational level; Edward Hagerman, *The American Civil War and the Origins of Modern Warfare: Ideas, Organization, and Field Command* (Bloomington: Indiana University Press, 1988), equates modernity with the military adoption and employment in mass warfare of the new technologies of the Industrial Revolution; while Jonathan Bailey, *The First World War and the Birth of the Modern Style of Warfare*, Occasional Paper 22 (Camberley: Strategic and Combat Studies Institute, Staff College, 1996), records the arrival of modernity with the technical achievement of three-dimensional warfare which allowed success for combined arms keyed to the near-perfection of predicted indirect (i.e. not directly observed) artillery fire. 'Modern war' began for these three authors in *c.* 1809 (Epstein), *c.* 1863 (Hagerman), and 1917–18 (Bailey) respectively. It is well to remember that one historian's periodisation is another's artificial barrier. Medievalist Jonathan Riley-Smith, for example, in a book review of a collected work, *Medieval Warfare: A History* (Maurice Keen (ed.), Oxford: Oxford University Press, 1999), complains that 'The collection ... gives the impression, heightened by the omission of any treatment of Byzantine warfare, that somehow Western medieval history was self-contained. It is assumed that what divided medieval from early modern warfare was primarily technological, but the use of gunpowder was relatively advanced by the middle of the fifteenth-century, and it is arguable that warfare remained fundamentally unchanged – except perhaps in scale – until the late eighteenth': 'The Uses of Violence', *Times Literary Supplement*, 28 January 2000, p. 27.
23. This formulation conflates the theorising of Wylie, *Military Strategy*, with that of the contributors to Lawrence Freedman (ed.), *Strategic Coercion: Concepts and Cases* (Oxford: Oxford University Press, 1998).

24. With reference to the kind of strategic effect intended, military force can function either as a 'general deterrent' or as an 'immediate deterrent', or as both. See Patrick M. Morgan, *Deterrence: A Conceptual Analysis* (Beverly Hills, CA: Sage Publications, 1977), ch. 2.

25. Norman Friedman, *The Fifty-Year War: Conflict and Strategy in the Cold War* (Annapolis, MD: Naval Institute Press, 2000), p. xi.

26. Richard Henrick, *The Crimson Tide* (New York: Avon Books, 1995), p. 75. I am grateful to Richard K. Betts for bringing this neat paraphrase of Clausewitz to my attention. See his inspired analysis, 'Is Strategy an Illusion?', *International Security*, 25, 2, (Fall 2000), p. 37 n74. On p. 87 of *On War*, Clausewitz writes thus: 'War, therefore, is an act of policy. Were it a complete untrammelled, absolute manifestation of violence (as the pure concept [of 'absolute war'] would require), war would of its own independent will usurp the place of policy the moment policy had brought it into being; it would then drive policy out of office and rule by the laws of its own nature.' He proceeds to explain why 'this view is thoroughly mistaken'.

27. Clausewitz, *On War*, p. 605.

28. Ibid., p. 610 (emphasis added).

29. Richard K. Betts hits the spot when he writes: 'Without believing in some measure of predictability, one cannot believe in strategic calculation', and 'Unless strategists can show that a particular choice in particular circumstances is likely to procure a particular outcome, they are out of business': 'Is Strategy an Illusion?', p. 16.

30. Clausewitz, *On War*, pp. 131–2.

31. A British Chief of the General Staff, Field Marshal Sir Nigel Bagnall, has written plaintively that 'over the centuries identifying a nation's future strategic priorities has proved to be a very imprecise art, and as a result peacetime force structures have seldom proved relevant when put to the test of war'. Foreword to Michael D. Hobkirk, *Land, Sea or Air? Military Priorities, Historical Choices* (London: Macmillan, 1992), p. x.

32. The literature on leadership, command, and control is vast. G. D. Sheffield (ed.), *Leadership and Command: The Anglo-American Military Experience Since 1861* (London: Brassey's (UK), 1997), is particularly educational. The editor's 'Introduction: Command, Leadership and the Anglo-American Experience' is most useful.

33. Beaumont, *War, Chaos, and History*, p. 11.

34. See ch. 1 above, n10.

35. Clausewitz, *On War*, p. 101.

36. Ibid., p. 85.

37. *Philip's Science and Technology Encyclopedia* (London: George Philip, 1998), p. 69.

38. See James Gleick, *Chaos: Making a New Science* (London: Penguin, 1988), pp. 11–31, 'The Butterfly Effect'; and Peter Coveney and Roger Highfield, *Frontiers of Complexity: The Search for Order in a Chaotic World* (London: Faber & Faber, 1995), esp. pp. 169–70.

39. William A. Owens: 'The Emerging System of Systems', US Naval Institute *Proceedings*, 121, 5 (May 1995), pp. 35–9; 'System-of-Systems', *Armed Forces Journal International*, January 1996, p. 47; and *Lifting the Fog of War* (New York: Farrar, Straus & Giroux, 2000).

40. Joint Chiefs of Staff, 'Joint Vision 2010: America's Military – Preparing for Tomorrow', *Joint Force Quarterly*, 12 (Summer 1996), pp. 34–49.

41. The respect for Clausewitz is worn as a badge of honour. Consider these titles: Watts, *Clausewitzian Friction and Future War*; Williamson Murray, 'Clausewitz Out, Computer In: Military Culture and Technological Hubris', *The National Interest*, 48 (Summer 1997), pp. 57–64; and Cimbala, *Clausewitz and Chaos*.

42. Many among the RMA sceptics have in common both a professional education in history and a personal 'strategic moment' in or (literally) over Vietnam. This may be a case of spurious correlation, but such prominent sceptics as Williamson Murray

(USAF), Barry D. Watts (USAF, F-4 pilot), Brian R. Sullivan (USMC), Allan R. Millett (USMC), Mackubin Thomas Owens (USMC), Paul K. Van Riper (USMC), F. G. Hoffman (USMC), and Robert H. Scales, Jr (USA) all feature Vietnam more or less prominently in their resumés. My first-hand knowledge of this group reinforces what common sense would suggest anyway: personal experience of the complexity and chaotic contingency of combat is apt to incline scholars to be sceptical of the promise of war as a near-faultless exercise in surgical bombardment. Murray goes so far as to suggest that the physical environment in which land forces (Army and Marine Corps) operate – as contrasted with those for the sea and air forces – shapes a distinctive institutional military culture 'friendly to a more Clausewitzian view of war'. He suggests that the Air Force and the Navy are predisposed by their geographical foci towards a 'mechanistic approach' to war, indeed 'towards a technological, engineering approach': 'Does Military Culture Matter?', *Orbis*, 43, 1 (Winter 1999), p. 36. While it is true that navies and air forces engage in capital-, as opposed to people-, intensive warfare in relatively simple environments (the terrain is much more uniform), the scope for Clausewitzian chance, uncertainty, and friction is common to operation in all geographies.

43. Alan Beyerchen, 'Clausewitz, Nonlinearity, and the Unpredictability of War', *International Security*, 17, 3 (Winter 1992/93), p. 90.

44. It is, however, a common error to exaggerate the differences between Clausewitz, Sun Tzu, and Jomini. This tendency is readily corrected by a reading of Michael I. Handel, *Masters of War: Classical Strategic Thought*, 3rd edn (London: Frank Cass, 2001), *passim*. I claim only that Clausewitz is uniquely insistent upon the importance of chance and friction, not that he is unique in recognising their salience.

45. The point is not that coalition forces in 1991, or German land–air forces in 1940, performed flawlessly. Rather is my argument that they were so much more militarily effective than their enemies, that virtually no sets of alternative real-time choices by those enemies plausibly would have saved them from defeat. In both cases the key to success lay not in technology, but in the ways in which technology was used. It is probably true to claim that Iraq suffered from a true, and truly lethal level of, technology shortfall. But it is no less plausible to argue that the US-led coalition would have won in 1991 even had it been fighting with the same equipment as the Iraqis. In 1940, German equipment of all kinds was good enough, but barely so. It is interesting that some potent analyses have made similar points about these two cases. James S. Corum claims flatly that '[t]he training factor alone would have proven decisive in 1940': *The Roots of Blitzkrieg: Hans von Seeckt and German Military Reform* (Lawrence: University Press of Kansas, 1992), p. 205. Looking at the French side of the equation, Eugenia C. Kiesling makes close to the same point: 'The connection between inadequate training and battlefield failure would be revealed in the 1940 campaign': *Arming against Hitler: France and the Limits of Military Planning* (Lawrence: University Press of Kansas, 1996), p. 82. The whole story is exceptionally well told in Alistair Horne, *To Lose a Battle: France 1940* (London: Macmillan, 1969). With respect to the Gulf War of 1991, Stephen Biddle has challenged the popular belief that Iraq was caught dramatically short by a foe on the leading edge of an information-led RMA. He argued instead that the extraordinarily lopsided military contest can best be explained as the result of synergy between very high military skills and advanced technology. Coalition military effectiveness was far greater than simply the *sum* of troops' skills and technology: 'Victory Misunderstood: What the Gulf War Tells Us about the Future of Conflict', *International Security*, 21, 2 (Fall 1996), pp. 139–79. Biddle's thesis is debated extensively by Dayl G. Press ('Lessons from Ground Combat in the Gulf: The Impact of Training and Technology'), Thomas A. Keaney ('The Linkage of Air and Ground Power in the Future of Conflict'), Thomas G. Mahnken and Barry D. Watts ('What the Gulf War Can (and cannot) Tell Us about the Future of Warfare'), and by Biddle again ('The Gulf War Debate *Redux*: Why Skill

and Technology are the Right Answer'), in *International Security*, 22, 2 (Fall 1997), respectively pp. 137–46, 147–50, 151–67, 163–74.

46. Israeli military intervention was the possible event with the greatest promise to fracture the coalition. Had that occurred it would have been the product not of chance, but of successful incitement by Iraq.

47. Friedman, *Fifty-Year War*, p. 486.

48. Clausewitz, *On War*, p. 120.

49. Ibid.

50. Ibid., p. 579.

51. Ibid., p. 580.

52. Ibid.

53. Beaumont, *War, Chaos, and History*, p. xiv.

54. Ibid.

55. 'Dynamical' and 'self-organising criticality' are terms of art for the priests of chaos theory. For example, see Stephen H. Kellert, *In the Wake of Chaos: Unpredictable Order in Dynamical Systems* (Chicago: University of Chicago Press, 1993), pp. 2–3, and Coveney and Highfield, *Frontiers of Complexity*, esp. ch. 6. Stephen R. Mann, 'Chaos Theory and Strategic Thought', *Parameters*, 22, 3 (Autumn 1992), pp. 54–68, is a brave venture in cross-disciplinary fertilisation.

56. On the limits of the theory of rational choice, and its associated models, see Stephen M. Walt, 'Rigor or Rigor Mortis? Rational Choice and Security Studies', *International Security*, 23, 4 (Spring 1999), pp. 5–48; and his reply to his critics, 'A Model Disagreement', *International Security*, 24, 2 (Fall 1999), pp. 115–30 (Walt's critics romp enthusiastically on pp. 56–114 of that same issue).

57. Arthur K. Cebrowski and John J. Garstka, 'Network-Centric Warfare: Its Origins and Future', US Naval Institute *Proceedings*, 124, 1 (January 1998), pp. 28–35; and Cebrowski and Wayne P. Hughes, 'Rebalancing the Fleet', US Naval Institute *Proceedings*, 125, 11 (November 1999), pp. 31–4.

58. Arthur K. Cebrowski, 'President's Notes', *Naval War College Review*, 52, 4 (Autumn 1999), pp. 5–6. For F. W. Lanchester's attritional models of combat, see his *Aircraft in Warfare: The Dawn of the Fourth Arm* (London: Constable, 1916), chs 5–6.

59. Cebrowski, 'President's Notes', p. 6.

60. A great deal of scholarly work needs to be done on the vexed question of world order(s) and the even more vexed question of the relationship between world order(s) and war. Torbjorn L. Knutsen, *The Rise and Fall of World Orders* (Manchester: Manchester University Press, 1999); T. V. Paul and John A. Hall (eds), *International Order and the Future of World Politics* (Cambridge: Cambridge University Press, 1999); and Andrew Williams, *Failed Imagination? New World Orders of the Twentieth Century* (Manchester: Manchester University Press, 1998), map the field for enquiry quite usefully.

61. Michael A. Palmer, *Lee Moves North: Robert E. Lee on the Offensive* (New York: John Wiley and Sons, 1998), p. 49. For the most extreme of recent claims for Jackson's indispensability, see Bevin Alexander, *Lost Victories: The Military Genius of Stonewall Jackson* (Edison, NJ: Blue and Gray Press, 1996). On the Stonewall Jackson hagiography industry, see William C. Davis, *The Cause Lost: Myths and Realities of the Confederacy* (Lawrence: University Press of Kansas, 1996), ch. 10, 'Stonewall Jackson in Myth and Memory'. The new standard biography is James I. Robertson, Jr, *Stonewall Jackson: The Man, The Soldier, The Legend* (New York: Macmillan Publishing, 1997). In my opinion, the death of Thomas J. 'Stonewall' Jackson did have fatal consequences for the military fortunes of the Army of Northern Virginia, and hence very directly for the cause of Southern independence. The issue is not so much the genius, or otherwise, of Jackson, but rather the vital role he played in helping Lee to be a better general. Generalship really mattered in the Civil War.

62. A crucial point developed well in Gary W. Gallagher, *The Confederate War* (Cambridge, MA: Harvard University Press, 1997), esp. pp. 152–3. Elsewhere Gallagher rather misses the point when he claims that 'Jackson never led a real army and proved sadly deficient in administrative and political acumen': "'Upon their Success Hang Momentous Interests": Generals', in Gabor S. Boritt (ed.), *Why the Confederacy Lost* (New York: Oxford University Press, 1992), p. 89. To win its independence in the 1862–63 period the Confederacy did not require another Lee, though that would have been welcome. What it needed was a lieutenant to Lee who would lift Lee's campaign, and particularly his battlefield, performance.

63. See Stephen W. Sears, *Controversies and Commanders: Dispatches from the Army of the Potomac* (Boston, MA: Houghton Mifflin, 1999), ch. 5, for a full account of the 'lost order' episode of Special Orders 191 of 9 September 1862.

64. For details of this shambolic event, see Ian Kershaw, *Hitler, 1889–1939: Hubris* (London: Penguin, 1998), pp. 204–12. Kershaw comments: 'Had the bullet which killed Scheubner-Richter been a foot to the right, history would have taken a different course' (p. 211). But would it? If so, in what ways?

65. The military continuities from Weimar to Nazi Germany were formidable. See Hans W. Gatzke, *Stresemann and the Rearmament of Germany* (Baltimore, MD: Johns Hopkins University Press, 1954); Wilhelm Diest, *The Wehrmacht and German Rearmament* (Toronto: University of Toronto Press, 1981); and Corum, *Roots of Blitzkrieg*.

66. Gerhard L. Weinberg, *A World at Arms: A Global History of World War II* (Cambridge: Cambridge University Press, 1994), ch. 1, 'From one war to another', convincingly demolishes at least a good fraction of the proposition that the two world wars can be viewed as two rounds of what really conflates to a single event. He is, however, insufficiently alert to the habit of war's grammar to produce similarities in scales of effort, even when the political stakes initially are somewhat different. Also, Weinberg risks missing the political action when he argues the case for the terms of the Treaty of Versailles being rather moderate. Excellent reappraisal of major aspects of Versailles is offered in Manfred F. Boemke, Gerald D. Feldman, and Elizabeth Glaser (eds), *The Treaty of Versailles: A Reassessment after 75 Years* (Cambridge: Cambridge University Press, 1998).

67. Clausewitz, *On War*, p. 606.

68. Albert Wohlstetter, 'The Delicate Balance of Terror', *Foreign Affairs*, 37, 2 (January 1959), pp. 211–34.

69. See John J. Mueller, 'The Essential Irrelevance of Nuclear Weapons: Stability in the Postwar World', *International Security*, 13, 2 (Fall 1988), pp. 55–70; and Kenneth N. Waltz, 'Nuclear Myths and Political Realities', *American Political Science Review*, 84, 3 (September 1990), pp. 731–45.

70. Robert Jervis, *The Meaning of the Nuclear Revolution: Statecraft and the Prospect of Armageddon* (Ithaca, NY: Cornell University Press, 1989).

71. Scott D. Sagan, *The Limits of Safety: Organizations, Accidents, and Nuclear Weapons* (Princeton, NJ: Princeton University Press, 1993).

72. Non-expert concerned citizens reading, say, Bruce G. Blair's superior study, *The Logic of Accidental Nuclear War* (Washington, DC: Brookings Institution, 1993), should not forget that somehow, notwithstanding Blair's exciting title, accidental nuclear war has not happened, at least not yet.

73. Ian Hamilton, *The Soul and Body of an Army* (London: Edward Arnold, 1921), p. 70. Sir Ian may not have shone while in command at the Dardanelles, but he was certainly no fool as a military philosopher. John Lee, 'Sir Ian Hamilton and the Dardanelles, 1915', in Brian Bond (ed.), *Fallen Stars: Eleven Studies of Twentieth-century Military Disasters* (London: Brassey's (UK), 1991), pp. 32–51, is a persuasively empathetic assessment.

5

On Strategy, II: The RMA Connection

How does strategy 'work'? This chapter marries RMA theory to the theory of strategy. Our intention is to shape a methodology appropriate for the focused comparisons undertaken as the case studies in Chapters 6–8. The discussion here proceeds from explanation of RMA phenomena as strategic behaviour, to present the essential elements of a theory of strategy. That theory should make sense of events claimed as RMAs, whether or not one is enamoured either of the RMA concept in general or of its application to a particular historical case. For example, there is no question but that the belligerents in the Great War behaved strategically in 1917–18. Whether or not they conceived of and implemented an RMA is another matter. Although the RMA concept is very much on stage in this chapter and those which follow, my principal focus and toolkit of enquiry is the structure and dynamics of strategic behaviour, not RMA theory.

If chaos frequently, though far from invariably, is confounded by strategy – the argument in Chapter 4 – how is that accomplished? The RMA practitioner develops and possibly employs the military instrument that in the hands of the strategist delivers strategic performance. US nuclear-armed forces in the Cold War, for example, expressed both an RMA (perhaps more than one RMA) and the strategic behaviour of a superpower. Just as there is much more to strategy and war than RMAs, even in periods when RMAs allegedly flourished, so also the RMA hypothesis cannot be understood sensibly outside the broad framework of the theory of strategy and war.[1] To understand RMA, certainly to develop RMA theory, first one must comprehend strategy. Such comprehension is an absolute requirement, not an optional extra. If an RMA does not work strategically, it simply does not work.

Previous discussion has explained that although strategy is always complex, it is not always nonlinear or chaotic. Strategic matters great and small can confound the expectations of chaos theory. With regard to great strategic matters, the course and outcome of a struggle is rarely even remotely traceable either to pure chance or to some initially only marginal advantage or disadvantage.[2]

Belligerent polities make much of their own luck. Otto von Bismarck isolated France diplomatically in 1870, a feat not repeated by his successors in 1914. French military performance initially was scarcely more impressive in 1914 than it had been in 1870,[3] but there were systematic reasons why Alfred von Schlieffen's probably largely mythical 'Plan' was unlikely to secure a repeat of Helmuth von Moltke's battlefield triumphs.[4] For apparently smaller strategic matters also, chaos does not regularly rule in strategy and war. Activity on some of strategy's dimensions, and the relations between them, lend themselves to calculation. For example, fuel, distance, and time; troops and food and water; indeed the whole vital realm of logistics warrants its usual definition as the *science* of supply and movement.[5] Because strategic performance is the product of a complex process involving many incalculables (such as discipline, morale, skill at all levels of military behaviour, lucky choices), it does not follow that calculation in strategy is either impossible or unimportant. From the Second World War to the present day, operations research has demonstrated that to many clearly defined military, not strategic, problems there are superior quantifiable answers. The prudent strategist accepts gratefully all the quantified answers that can be developed to problems which lend themselves to such analysis.[6]

Many RMA theorists have grasped at least a significant part of the nature of strategy. Indeed, virtually all definitions of RMA, whatever their other limitations, express recognition of synergy. It is the nature of strategy to reflect practical operation of the motto that Alexander Dumas *père* declared authoritative for his king's musketeers: 'All for one, and one for all!' Theorists associated with Andrew W. Marshall's ONA consistently have explained the RMA concept as a gestalt (synergy, or synergistic whole).[7] Andrew F. Krepinevich insisted that '[m]ilitary revolutions comprise four elements: technological change, systems development, operational innovation, and organizational adaptation.'[8] From the same intellectual stable, ONA's Associate Director Thomas J. Welch, informs us that '[f]or the Office of Net Assessments [*sic*], a revolution in military affairs occurs when technological change makes possible material, which *when combined with organisational and operational change*, result in a transformation in the conduct of warfare.'[9]

In common with strategy, RMA as *gestalt* must be viewed as a complex open system whose several, even many, parts always function holistically. Technology, or military organisation, or operational ideas, cannot perform in isolation. Each acts upon and through the others, and they all act together in the currency of more (or less) military effectiveness. In its turn, that military effectiveness translates into more (or less) strategic effectiveness. Hence the relevance of Dumas *père*'s 'all for one, and one for all'. Clausewitz writes that '[i]n war more than in any other subject we must begin by looking at the nature of the whole, for here more than elsewhere the part and the whole must always be thought of together.'[10]

So much of this analysis is inherently contestable that it is important not to miss such a bedrock of reliable knowledge as is available to provide a solid foundation for theory. The structure and basic functioning of strategy yields just such bedrock. Vital questions need to be posed and answered concerning the relations possible among strategy's different aspects, but the identity of those aspects and the nature of their interconnections fortunately are not contentious. Alas, the truly difficult task remains. The securing of a conceptual grip upon the nature, structure, and functioning of strategy is only akin to establishing base camp for an expedition up a high mountain. This conceptual base camp literally is essential, in that if it is wrongly placed and poorly equipped and provisioned, the expedition must fail. However, this base camp of explanation of the nature and working of strategy is strictly an enabler for the serious assault on some of strategic history's elusive peaks in the chapters that follow.

RMA AS STRATEGIC BEHAVIOUR

Strategy has many facets, each of which, though distinguishable, is penetrated by the practical implications of the others. Moreover, the many-faceted vehicle of strategy moves as a single entity, regardless of the complexity, even the chaotically performing complexity, of its structure and functioning. It is a minor challenge to understand the nature and working of strategy. It is a major challenge to exploit that understanding in order to explain how, why, and with what plausible consequences actual historical episodes occurred as they did. Clausewitz warns that although war has a permanent, if complex, nature, it 'is more than a true chameleon that slightly adapts its characteristics to the given case'.[11] Every conflict is different. War's enduring nature shows unique characteristics from historical case to case.

Of what does strategy consist? What are its facets, aspects, elements, or dimensions (these terms are synonymous)? How do the dimensions of strategy, individually and synergistically, relate to the theory and practice of RMA? Answers to these questions comprise the core of the methodology applied in Chapters 6–8. The paragraphs immediately below expose the reasoning that is the basis for that methodology.

Every historical passage of strategy is unique. But every strategic episode is also the same in its structure and functioning. The medical classic, *Gray's Anatomy*, explains our common human corporeality, an explanation entirely consistent with the fact of apparently infinite human individuality. Modern research in physical anthropology reveals that even the long-popular proposition that humankind comprises several distinctive races is scientifically untenable. There is a greater range of genetic variation within so-called races than there is between them. By analogy, we should beware lest scholarly attention to the apparent distinctiveness of some kinds of wars or other forms of strategic behaviour obscure the underlying unity of all strategic phenomena.

119

Strategy's anatomy can be variously dissected, depending upon the purpose of the exercise. On the principle of 'horses for courses', this analysis prefers an unusually granulated approach. The case studies in the next three chapters are developed by a methodological toolkit which favours no fewer than 17 dimensions of strategy, as contrasted with Carl von Clausewitz's five, and Michael Howard's four (see below).[12]

The dimensions of strategy are also the dimensions of an RMA. The conduct of an RMA, pre-planned or not, is an exercise in strategy; it is strategic behaviour. It is correct to argue in company with Krepinevich and many others, that an RMA entails 'the four elements: technological change, systems development, operational innovation, and organizational adaptation'. However, it is no less true to argue that the practice of RMA involves action concerning all of strategy's dimensions. RMA has political meaning; it may use or challenge cultural preferences; it must cope with intelligent and unique adversaries; and it must occur over time – to cite only four of the dimensions.

When securely nested in a holistic and persuasive theory of strategy writ large, RMA theory is protected against the inadvertent ascription of out-of-context magical qualities. The point is that for an RMA to work, it has to, indeed can only, work as strategy. If it is unsound to tie strategic excellence to an allegedly new and master technology or wonder weapon, to a genius in high command, or to some deeply cunning tactical or operational idea – in all but isolation – so must it be unsound to harbour great expectations of RMAs propelled thus narrowly.[13]

Clausewitz wisely warns us against attempting 'to develop our understanding of strategy by analysing these factors [his five elements of strategy, see below] in isolation, since they are usually interconnected in each military action in manifold and intricate ways'.[14] That admonition is repeated most usefully by Michael I. Handel when he notes, in commentary upon Clausewitz's holism, that in war 'unlike in the natural sciences, different variables or factors cannot be isolated and studied independently'.[15] The truth in that argument translates as the point that all forms and characters of military behaviour register on the scale of military effectiveness, which, in its turn, scores on the scale of strategic effectiveness (even if in a nonlinear way). Nonetheless, Clausewitz and Handel need to be read critically. Despite the fact that there is a necessary unity to strategy and war, and even though 'the parts [of war] can only be studied in the context of the whole, as a "*gestalt*" (or synergy)',[16] the 'parts' – elements or dimensions – can and must be studied. Without affronting the holistic nature of strategy (and war), and without denying the highly dynamic synergies that operate in its complex structure, the leading edge of my analysis is precisely the approach concerning which Clausewitz was so emphatic in his warning.

Every historical RMA comprises identical categories of ingredients; these are the standard dimensions of strategy. But each RMA is keyed to novelty on one or several in particular among those dimensions. For example, the

Napoleonic RMA was triggered by changes in French society, by the political meaning of those changes, and then by the military implications of such changes, when exploited by a commander with extraordinary gifts.[17] That RMA obliged France's enemies to respond as best they were able with a focus on those dimensions on which they could improve, and which offered a fair prospect of strategic success. The patterns of response comprised a mixture of symmetrical and asymmetrical behaviour, both generically on the adversary dimension of strategy, and in detail on the political, geographical, economic, temporal, and so forth dimensions. Although each of strategy's dimensions influences every other one, arguably implying a chaotic complexity overall, still it is sensible to seek relative excellence where best one can so as to structure conflict with favourable terms and conditions.

A MATTER OF DIMENSION

Clausewitz recommends five broad 'elements of strategy': 'moral, physical, mathematical, geographical, and statistical'.

> The first type ['moral'] covers everything that is created by intellectual and psychological qualities and influences; the second ['physical'] consists of the size of the armed forces, their composition, armament and so forth; the third ['mathematical'] includes the angle of lines of operation, the convergent and divergent movements wherever geometry enters into their calculation; the fourth ['geographical'] comprises the influence of terrain, such as commanding positions, mountains, rivers, woods, and roads; and finally, the fifth [statistical] covers support and maintenance.[18]

It would be a gross understatement to say that Clausewitz's approach, with its five broad elements of strategy, is both insightful and useful. That granted, and for all the elegance in its apparent simplicity, in my view it is too parsimonious to be useful enough for this enquiry. That judgement holds even if one superimposes upon the five elements his 'remarkable trinity' of passion, chance, and reason, which he associated respectively primarily with 'the people', 'the commander and his army', and the 'government'.[19] That trinity approximates identification of social, military, and political dimensions of war.

As an editor and translator of *On War*, Michael Howard applied a variant of Clausewitz's structural analysis in his seminal 1979 article, 'The Forgotten Dimensions of Strategy'. Howard argued persuasively that strategy's logistical, operational, and social dimensions had been seriously neglected by recent strategists in favour of the technological. It is no criticism of Howard's essay to say that his argument, though generally inspirational and exceptionally relevant to this enquiry in its indictment of an undue technicity in modern and contemporary strategic thinking, does not provide an analytical framework capable of bearing the traffic of the historical case studies in Chapters 6–8. As with Clausewitz, so for Howard, an explicitly more inclusive theoretical framework is necessary.

The 'third cut' at analysing strategy through a structural–functional lens, my tri-clustered 17 dimensions as listed in Figure 5.1, is of course the framework applied in my case studies. Admittedly, structural–functional intention can appear to be obscured by such naked itemisation. I believe that a full formal 'wiring diagram' for my approach to the analysis of strategy, though in principle feasible, would not be helpful (which is why Figure 5.1 is strictly illustrative). I am determined to avoid a characteristic error committed by many scholars of decision-making. Specifically, their 'wiring diagrams' of the (somewhat ide-alised) decision-making process tend simultaneously to be trivial because they reveal the obvious, and overcomplicated because of the mind-boggling com-plexity they demonstrate. Paradoxically, those diagrams are not complicated enough because the real world of decision-making contains nexuses and feed-back loops on a scale and of such a character as to warrant description as chaotic by any definition. As earlier discussion demonstrated, the periodicity and even the life-cycle of RMA can be shown by simple graphics. Such is not the case for the structure and working of strategy.

Strategy is both static and dynamic. It is an eternal phenomenon with permanent dimensions, yet also it is a process that unfolds over time. Time must be recognised explicitly as a strategic dimension.[20] Six points are vital for understanding strategy's structure and dynamics.

First, strategy's dimensions are analytically distinctive, but in practice each affects, or certainly could affect, the performance of the others synergistically for net positive or negative results. For example, a tactically peerless but short-range Wehrmacht, supreme in combat effectiveness, could no longer deliver campaign success when policy required it to perform in Russia in geography whose terrain was too extensive as well as a climate too extreme for its logistical infrastructure to be effective.[21] Several crucial disconnects proved fatal. The Germans simultaneously prosecuted their war in the east with too few troops to cope with the enemy in his geography and too many to be effectively supportable logistically. The military effectiveness of the Wehrmacht, measured as its combat power, had meaning only with reference to an historically specific time, place and adversary (inter alia).[22] In addition, distinctive though the dimensions are in principle, in reality there are many fuzzy boundaries between them. I choose to distinguish between people, society, and culture, for example, but the fences around these categories are low and contain many openings. Similarly, economics and logistics can be understood to merge with military administration, while the asserted dimensions of politics, organisation, and command assuredly overlap. This fuzziness is not a problem; it is just the way things are and acceptance of it is a price worth paying for the flexibility granted by recognition of many, rather than fewer, items.

122

Figure 5.1: The Elements/Dimensions of Strategy: Three Cuts

First cut: *Carl von Clausewitz (1832)*

1. Moral
2. Physical
3. Mathematical

4. Geographical
5. Statistical

(Also: passion, chance, reason; *or* social, military, political)

Second cut: *Michael Howard (1979)*

1. Logistical
2. Operational

3. Social
4. Technological

Third cut: *Colin S. Gray (2002)*

(a) **People and politics**

1. People
2. Society
3. Culture

4. Politics
5. Ethics

(b) **Preparation for war**

6. Economics and logistics
7. Organisation (defence planning)
8. Military administration
   (recruitment, training, procurement)

9. Information and intelligence
10. Theory and doctrine
11. Technology

(c) **War proper**

12. Military operations
    (fighting performance)
13. Command
    (political and military)

14. Geography
15. Friction and chance
16. Adversary
17. Time

Second, there is no hierarchy among the dimensions of strategy. Normatively one may argue for ethics, or people, or politics, but in practice there can be no rank order, at least not with reference to strategic effectiveness. Whether or not strategy should be ruled by moral or political values, the necessary strategic performance can be enabled or undone by advantage or disadvantage on any of the 17 dimensions. Several of the dimensions appear to stand out as extraordinary sources in the shaping of strategic behaviour. For example, people, the human element, in a key sense have to be the fundamental engine driving the strategic theme in history. That human element, though widely variable in performance, offers an unchanging range of characteristic patterns in behaviour. For another example, time is the one dimension that literally cannot be corrected: if it has gone, it has gone. Commanders can be changed, additional forces can be raised, equipped, and trained, but lost time is exactly that. Many categories among my preferred dimensions (such as politics, society, ethics, geography, military operations, technology, and the adversary) all but invite special pleading on their behalf.

Viewing strategy, and war, with Clausewitz as a gestalt, graphical representation of its structure must demonstrate an absence of hierarchy and an all but impossibly complex network of connections. Quite literally, in the world of strategy everything relates to everything else. Figure 5.2 offers a simplified description of the structure and working of strategy.

Commandant Jean Colin had the matter right when he wrote in 1912:

> There is no hierarchy among the elements of war; one cannot pretend that one is more important than another. One day Napoleon said, 'Victory is to the big battalions'; the next day he declared that 'in an army the men don't count', that 'one man is everything'. Genius triumphed over numbers at Dresden and succumbed at Leipzig.[23]

The claim that there is no hierarchy among strategy's dimensions is not a pedantic scholarly point. Instead it penetrates to the heart of the analysis required in the chapters below. A sustainable argument for such a hierarchy could amount to the thesis that there is one, perhaps several, dimensions in which relative weakness may be beyond compensation from elsewhere. The obverse argument, for effective functional equality among dimensions for overall performance, means that in principle compensation could be found for particular weaknesses. In other words, poor performance on any dimension has the potential to wreck the entire strategic enterprise.

Third, the second point, which argues against hierarchy, is true because strategy is a whole, a gestalt, comprising many inalienable elements. No dimension can be discarded for reason of its inconvenience. For example, strategy cannot be conducted 'beyond geography',[24] or in the absence of a technological story, or by people bereft of strategic culture. Every dimension is present with, is integral to, strategy, whether one likes it or not and no matter how one elects to slice the strategy pie into constituent parts.

Fourth, because every episode in strategic history is unique, the historical reference for each dimension must always be locally specific and to some degree variable (e.g. even the geography of a conflict may vary as campaigns ebb and flow). Although there can be no all-case ordering of rank among strategy's dimensions, there should be patterns in relative importance specific to particular episodes of conflict. Albeit subject to change over time, belligerents will show more or less persisting patterns of relative strength and relative weakness across the dimensions. For example, in the Napoleonic Wars, Britain's strategic performance benefited from economic strength, a typically sound enough foreign policy, a permissive geography, unmatchable (at least, difficult to match) naval strength, and eventually exceptional battlefield leadership at the tactical level.[25]

Fifth, strategy is a synergistic, sometimes even a chaotically nonlinear, enterprise wherein strength or weakness on any dimension can influence the strength or weakness of other dimensions. To illustrate: an insular national geography is a source of strength if one enjoys control of the sea. But if the national geopolitical situation is one combining insularity with maritime weakness, then the sea is likely to play geostrategically as a broad highway for invasion.[26] More contentiously, modern history provides possible examples of excellent, at least competent, fighting armies betrayed by incompetent policy-makers and higher military commanders on behalf of ethically enervating causes.

The German Army in the Second World War may fit this category. To identify German political, strategic, and operational incompetence is not a hard claim to sustain. Enervation caused by ethical weakness is more debatable. Although Nazi ideology had a dire effect upon the critical structure of Germany's war(s), and hence upon its prospects for victory, on the other side of the equation that ideology almost certainly enhanced the average potency of German fighting power. Soldiers have to be led as well as commanded, and leadership is all about inspiration and motivation. The cult of the *Führer* and its attendant racial and national ideology certainly helped many young Germans to be better warriors. Although historians try to study this topic in a scholarly way, we are still too close to the Second World War for scholarship on the influence of Nazism to be untainted by unhelpful attitudes.[27]

The case of American performance in Vietnam is especially complex, because it embraces generally incompetent, or worse, political and higher military leadership and command,[28] good enough tactical skills, too little sharp-end fighting power on the ground, what many considered to be a noble political cause, and a local ally seriously reluctant, if not unable, to conduct systemic reform. This discussion is not interested in the US war in Vietnam per se, only in establishing the principle that each dimension of strategy in a conflict influences every other one. The policy that governed the conduct of the war denied US soldiers a fair prospect of success, while the operational art practised in the field by the US Army rendered an already exceedingly difficult mission as close to impossible as makes no difference.[29]

Sixth, contrary to the message from some of the more distant shores of chaos theory, strategy's dimensions can be manipulated purposefully in the quest for advantage and the struggle against disadvantage. Such purposeful strategic manipulation is entirely normal; indeed it is business as usual for strategically competitive polities. For example, a belligerent that knows itself to be tactically disadvantaged could in principle seek compensation through excellence at the operational level of war: that is very much how the Red Army defeated Hitler's Östheer in 1942–45.[30] Such compensation will not always be possible. For example, arguably the US mission in South Vietnam in the 1960s and 1970s was so disadvantaged on that conflict's political dimension, that no measure of excellence in economic strength, in technology, or even in tactical combat effectiveness, could compensate. It is worth noting that weakness–strength vis-à-vis each dimension of strategy is a scale likely to register historical data on a bell-shaped curve. By that I mean that, for example, while a few military commanders are heroically incompetent, and a few warrant the label of genius, most occupy the bulge of the curve as being average and good enough, ceteris paribus. By and large one needs only to perform well enough on each dimension. Given the pervasiveness of friction and chance in strategic affairs, an enemy is more likely to be overcome by the consequences of his own errors than by purposeful brilliance on our part. Strategic performance inherently is a relational variable. One does not have to win elegantly: one just has to perform better on the day than does the enemy.

Figure 5.2: The 17 Dimensions of Strategy

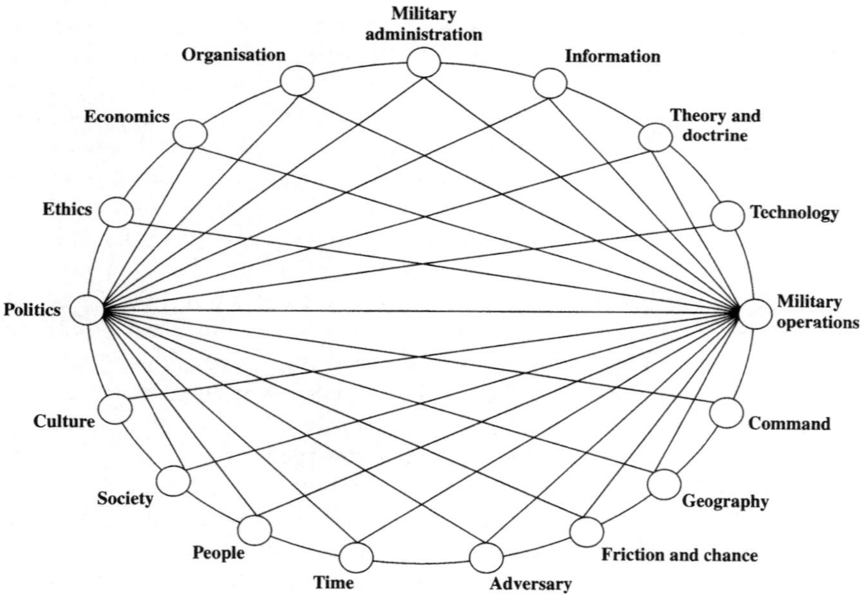

The 17 dimensions are displayed non-hierarchically.
Each dimension is always 'in play' and can influence every other dimension.
In this figure I have chosen simply to show the connections to and from two dimensions only, politics and military operations. Display of the nexuses for every dimension would result in a visually impracticable graphic.

This section concludes with the briefest useful description of the focus of each of my preferred dimensions. As a general rule the categories are close to

126

self-explanatory. However, it is well to be certain that every item in the toolkit of theory is properly identified formally.

1. *People* refers to the human face of strategy. There is a human face to all of strategy's dimensions. Strategy is decided upon and executed at every level of performance by real people who have all the strengths and weaknesses – physical, emotional, psychological – that people are wont to exhibit. Individuals matter in their individuality, and they can matter profoundly. At the sharp end, in military operations, strategy is done tactically by actual people performing as warriors, reluctantly or otherwise (not by generic, abstract 'armed forces').

2. *Society* means the social collective and the many ties of community which bind individuals as well as the processes that give them a sense of cultural identity. To date, sociology and social anthropology have not been well enough represented among the disciplines contributing to modern strategic studies.[31]

3. *Culture* refers to the ideals, the documents and other artefacts, and to the habits of behaviour (styles) characteristic of particular communities.[32]

4. *Politics* means the purpose(s) for which strategy is designed and executed. Also it refers to the consequences of military behaviour.[33] Politics can refer both to policy and the process of contention that produces policy (i.e. the policy process, writ large). This bifocality permeates Clausewitz's use of *Politik*.

5. *Ethics* encompasses the whole range of moral issues relevant, or believed by some to be relevant, to strategic behaviour.

6. *Economics and logistics* brackets the economic resources mobilisable for strategic purposes and the assets of supply and movement which comprise the vital enabling infrastructure for all military activities.

7. *Organisation* for the making of strategy and the direction and higher conduct of war refers to the structure and process of policymaking and of defence and force planning (including war planning). Plainly, this dimension shades into politics above, and military administration, command, logistics, and military operations below. The history of the twentieth century showed unmistakably the distinguishable importance of the quality of organisation for strategy.[34] The bridge that is strategy is very much made by the kind of structure and process represented by this dimension.

8. *Military administration* is by and large what Clausewitz means by 'merely preparations for war'.[35] This category refers to the recruitment, organisation, training, and equipment of the armed forces.[36]

9. *Information and intelligence* encompasses all aspects of information relevant to strategic performance. This dimension includes the dynamic states of knowledge – certainly the variable data and information – enjoyed by actual and potential belligerents. In addition, this category embraces all of the activities implied by the term 'intelligence'.

10. *Theory and doctrine* are the ideas current, including those officially authoritative, which purport both to explain strategic phenomena (theory) and to provide explicit guidance for behaviour (doctrine).

11. *Technology* refers to the quality of science and engineering expressed both in the machines that serve as weapons systems and in those that support such systems. To avoid apparent pedantry, from time to time technology will be employed analytically as shorthand for weapon systems, but only in contexts where that meaning is unambiguous.

12. *Military operations* covers all aspects of military performance in the field (or battlespace)[37] against the enemy. By analogy, a play may have an outstanding cast, a superlative script, an inspiring director, and an elegant theatrical venue. But the question remains, how well will the play be performed on the night? This dimension focuses upon the actual tactical doing of strategy by forces in action or threatening action. There is an obvious sense in which military operational performance is entirely a variable dependent upon the other dimensions of strategy. However, while the military effectiveness generated by strategy's elements can only be instrumental for strategic effectiveness on behalf of policy, that effectiveness is tied in to complex feedback loops. The pertinent values – of relative advantage and disadvantage – for strategy's dimensions are not simply the linear and perhaps nonlinear producers of military operational outcomes. By positive or negative feedback from the course of battle, those dimensional values change with events. For example, the geographical terms of conflict can change as battlefield success alters each side's geographical position. By conquering France and the Low Countries in May–June 1940, Germany advanced its air power and sea power – as well as its land power – to the Channel and Atlantic coasts. Clausewitz risks overstating the most essential of relevant truths when he insists that 'Combat is the only effective force in war; its aim is to destroy the enemy's forces as a means to a further end.'[38] It would be difficult to overemphasise the significance of his subsequent elaboration that 'If a decision by fighting is the basis of all plans and operations, it follows that the enemy *can frustrate everything through a successful battle*.'[39]

13. *Command* refers to the variable quality of performance by political and military leaders both as leaders and as commanders.[40] Obviously, this performance is tied closely to politics/policy and to organisation for strategy-making and execution, but still it is usefully distinguishable.

14. *Geography* is the playing field on which all strategic behaviour is conducted. It both shapes armed forces which must operate in particular physical regimes (land, sea, air, space, electromagnetic spectrum), it defines the belligerents,[41] and more often than not it is the stake in a conflict. Contrary to the argument of some unduly postmodern theorists of cyberwar, nothing occurs beyond geography.[42] Geography truly is inescapable.

15. *Friction and chance* conflate two themes from Clausewitz. Friction, both general and generic to the conduct of war (and defence preparation, one should add), as well as specific to unique situations, occurs in a context of uncertainty.[43] Chance embraces the accidents of bad luck and the opportunities for creative behaviour opened by good luck, neither of which could be anticipated in

detail. Although accidents do happen, many such events are preventable, and are prevented, by prudent strategic practice. For example, it is bad luck if a staff officer with campaign plans is captured by the enemy. However, although such a risk cannot be reduced to zero, elementary precautionary behaviour can greatly reduce this hazard.[44]

16. *Adversary* points to the quintessentially relational nature of strategy. Strategy is the intelligent bridge between means and ends which invariably is constructed in the context of a foe with an independent, albeit interacting, will who is out to thwart you. All references to strategy 'working' mean working against an adversary motivated, and in principle able, to deny you strategic success. Just as military action makes strategic sense only with reference to its political consequences, so strategic performance has to mean influence secured, or not, upon a foe. Even when strategy-making lacks for a dominant enemy, and instead is addressed only 'to whom it may concern', still it has to be conceived and planned with reference to a foe, albeit a generic one. Recall Clausewitz's telling metaphors. 'War is nothing but a duel on a larger scale. Countless duels go to make up war, but a picture of it as a whole can be formed by imagining a pair of wrestlers. Each tries through physical force to compel the other to do his will.'[45]

17. *Time* states an obvious constraint upon all strategic behaviour. In common with geography, and indeed with our (in)human nature, time is inescapable. However, unlike geography and human nature, time is rigidly unforgiving. In the apt words of Napoleon: 'Strategy is the art of making use of time and space. I am less chary of the latter than of the former; space we can recover, time never'; and '[t]ime is the great element between weight and force.'[46]

THEORY AND PRACTICE

Although theory and historical practice, explanation and historical evidence, must conduct a constant dialogue, theirs cannot be a partnership of equals. The facts of history may well be in dispute, while their meaning certainly will be, but nonetheless as potential evidence they are sovereign over ideas and methods. Chapters 1–5 of this book approximate what Clausewitz meant by 'preparations for war': Chapters 6–8 correspond to his meaning of 'war proper'. Strategy inherently has relational meaning as signified by its adversarial dimension. Similarly, theory in social science dangles senselessly in a vacuum if its authority is held to derive only from itself. While theory can be judged for its quality as theory, much as prose can be assayed for literary merit, both are mere verbiage if they do not say intelligent things. Methodologically elegant theory underconnected to evidence is akin to clever decoration in relation to art. Ken Booth made a cognate point when he wrote: 'Strategic studies divorced from area studies is largely thinking in a void.'[47] The test of the speculative theory in this text is its utility for plausible interpretation of the historical events presented in the next three chapters.

The tools of theory developed here are necessary because the alleged historical facts of RMA are anything but self-revealing, let alone self-revealing into orderly categories neatly interconnected for our enlightenment. This is not to say, however, that we are likely to be short of historical information. The case studies of RMA developed below present only modest problems of elusive information. The challenge rather is to interpret the information for some pattern in meaning, in this context as evidence of RMA, of how RMAs work, and of what that working suggests for the better comprehension of the dynamics of strategic performance.

I have joined the small bandwagon of social scientists who have borrowed the ideas of chaos theory from the mathematical and natural sciences. However, my borrowing has not been uncritical. To claim that strategy is complex, sometimes nonlinear, and prone to be chaotic, is hardly a bold assertion. The key issue is a matter of judgement. Is strategy *so* complex, *so* nonlinear, and *so* chaotic, that purposeful strategic behaviour is impracticable? That is the question that really counts. My answer is that strategic behaviour generally is possible, even though the true whole structure and dynamics of strategy are literally beyond anyone's comprehension. Should readers doubt this claim, they might care to reflect upon the network exposed only in highly simplified form in Figure 5.2. When policy-makers flash a green light and military leaders turn the key for military (ultimately for strategic) performance, the course and outcome of subsequent events are not entirely random. To be sure, strategic prediction frequently is shown to be vain. Nonetheless, strategy's often nonlinear working does not necessarily equate to unpredictability and we should not confuse either apparent or real disproportion between input and output with a consequentially chaotic opacity. For example, the age-old principle of 'economy of force', and its expression in the modern theory and practice of special operations, points to hugely useful and predictable intended chaotic effect. The core rationale for special operations forces is the promise of a massively favourable unequal military and strategic return from a relatively small investment of resources.[48] When in 1941 Lieutenant David Stirling of the Scots Guards suggested to General Sir Claude Auchinleck that with 66 men he could destroy most of the Luftwaffe in North Africa on the ground, he provided a glorious illustration of a vision of purposefully chaotic behaviour. That is to say, the raids promised a great disproportion between investment and return (i.e. they exemplify nonlinearity) and, as early failures proved, they were crucially sensitive to the details of initial conditions (i.e. they were chaotic).

Chaos in its everyday non-specialist sense can be confounded by purposeful strategic behaviour. That argument does, however, have only limited domain. Strategic history displays chaotic features in all senses. Because of what is both not known and is literally unknowable in strategy, a flight to the facts is not feasible as a comprehensive aid for the practical strategist. General strategic education in a superior theory of war, for the leading example as provided by Clausewitz, has to compensate for limitations in information and knowledge. Historical detail must be unique, but the practising strategist can cope with, indeed can employ, 'chaos', by understanding, for example, that 'warfare is the way of deception',[49] and that 'the best strategy is always *to be very strong*; first in general, and then at the decisive spot'.[50]

Lest the argument here appears unduly positive towards the prospect for success for the strategist, the following sobering judgement by MacGregor Knox serves well as a timely warning.

> In this bewildering world, the search for predictive theories to guide strategy has been no more successful than the search for such theories in other areas of human existence. Patterns do emerge from the past, and their study permits educated guesses about the range of potential outcomes. But the future is not an object of knowledge; no increase in processing power will make the owl of history a daytime bird. Similar causes do not always produce similar effects, and causes interact in ways unforeseeable even by the historically sophisticated. Worse still, individuals – with their ambitions, vanities and quirks – make strategy.[51]

Knox is correct, but only up to a point. As a historian he points rightly to the vanity of predictive theory. However, the strategist has no choice other than to act on the basis of such theory. The caveats of the scholarly historian have to be set against the practical necessity for strategy-making in the face of uncertainty. Fortunately, history does not reveal that purposeful strategy is impossible, just unreliable.

How best should the theory of strategy and the theory and practice of RMA speak to each other? That is the defining question for the next stage in this enquiry.

NOTES

1. The purposes pursued in this book and the methodology employed do not require me to trek into the wild terrain of war causation. That is fortunate, because even the daunting theoretical challenges tackled here in the endeavour to effect fruitful collaboration between strategic theory, chaos theory, and RMA theory pale by comparison with those which obtain in the realm of war causation. Readers are advised that I am fully aware of the necessity for political context(s), foreign and domestic, if actual historical strategic behaviour is to be understood. Where appropriate, the political dimension (inter alia) of strategy and war is accorded the importance it merits. Readers will find insightful the commentary on the connection between political and military analysis in the third volume of Henry Kissinger's memoirs. Describing his argument over strategic arms control policy with the intellectually and even personally abrasive

Secretary of Defense, James R. Schlesinger, Kissinger records, probably truthfully, that 'I was convinced that, at the end of the day, Schlesinger and I would come to an understanding because, in truth, our disagreements were essentially esoteric and technical or else bureaucratic.' Referring to their earlier, pre-governmental, personal relations as 'defense-intellectuals' in the 1960s, Kissinger writes of himself and Schlesinger: 'At that time, our views coincided on all essentials, the principal difference being that I was more concerned with geopolitical and he with technological challenges': *Years of Renewal* (London: Weidenfeld & Nicolson, 1999), p. 177.

2. I do not discount the role of contingency. In Chapter 4 I cited 'Stonewall' Jackson's death after Chancellorsville and Robert E. Lee's 'lost order' before Antietam as prime examples of truly accidental occurrences which probably had major strategic significance. Especially with respect to the strictly personal element in the human dimension of strategy, contingency can loom very large. Napoleon was not simply one among others in an interchangeable file of men on horseback ready and able to express and employ the energy of the France that emerged from the successive crises of revolution. Similarly, a British government headed by Lord Halifax instead of Winston Churchill in June–July 1940 might well have reached a (temporary) political settlement with Hitler. Such a settlement in the west, and by extension in the south, could have tipped the balance in Germany's favour with respect to the real war that Hitler intended, with the USSR. For yet another example, a peaceful outcome to the Cuban missile crisis of October 1962 may have rested vitally upon the characters of and relationship between the US president and his principal and most trusted adviser, his brother Robert. The truth of the matter is that the historian can rarely be certain just how sensitive is an outcome – in the case of the Kennedy brothers, of nuclear war or peace – to the details of the circumstances that produced it. This points to the potential relevance of chaos theory.

3. The most essential background on the French Army up to the disastrous Battle(s) of the Frontiers, 14–25 August 1914 (14–22 August, Battle of Lorraine; 20–25 August, Battle of the Ardennes; 22–23 August, Battle of the Sambre) is provided in Gerd Krumeich, *Armaments and Politics in France on the Eve of the First World War: The Introduction of Three-Year Conscription, 1913–1914* (Leamington Spa: Berg Publishers, 1984); and Douglas Porch, *The March to the Marne: The French Army, 1871–1914* (Cambridge: Cambridge University Press, 1981). The international context is laid out in David G. Herrman, *The Arming of Europe and the Making of the First World War* (Princeton, NJ: Princeton University Press, 1996). For the performance of the French Army in 1870, see Michael Howard, *The Franco-Prussian War: The German Invasion of France, 1870–1871* (London: Methuen, 1981).

4. Martin van Creveld claims that 'the sheer size and weight of the German Army in 1914 proved wholly out of proportion to the means of tactical transportation at its disposal. This was true even though the really great increase in consumption came only after the campaign of the Marne was over': *Supplying War: Logistics from Wallenstein to Patton* (Cambridge: Cambridge University Press, 1977), pp. 140–1. New research posing an existential challenge to the Plan is presented in Terence Zuber, 'The Schlieffen Plan Reconsidered', *War in History*, 6, 3 (July 1999), pp. 262–305. Zuber is not a man to mince words: he concludes: 'There never was a "Schlieffen plan"' (p. 305). In a war of 'the two Terences', Terence M. Holmes challenges with 'The Reluctant March on Paris: A Reply to Terence Zuber's "The Schlieffen Plan Reconsidered"', *War in History*, 8, 2 (April 2001), pp. 208–32. But Terence Zuber has the better of the duel – thus far, at least – in his 'Terence Holmes Reinvents the Schlieffen Plan', *War in History*, 8, 4 (November 2001), pp. 468–76.

5. George C. Thorpe, *Pure Logistics: The Science of War Preparation* (Washington, DC: National Defense University Press, 1986 [1917]), remains a classic. For further enlightenment see Archibald Wavell, *Generals and Generalship* (New York: Macmillan, 1943),

esp. pp. 10–11. Wavell laments: 'Unfortunately, in most military books strategy and tactics are emphasised at the expense of the administrative factors' (p. 11). See also van Creveld, *Supplying War*; Julian Thompson, *The Lifeblood of War: Logistics in Armed Conflict* (London: Brassey's, 1991); Joseph Sinclair, *Arteries of War: Military Transportation from Alexander the Great to the Falklands – and Beyond* (Shrewsbury: Airlife Publishing, 1992); John A. Lynn (ed.), *Feeding Mars: Logistics in Western Warfare from the Middle Ages to the Present* (Boulder, CO: Westview Press, 1993); and Thomas M. Kane, *Military Logistics and Strategic Performance* (London: Frank Cass, 2001).

6. The issue is never numerical calculation per se; always it is the feasibility and relevance of such calculation. Determined calculators are never bereft of 'data' to manipulate. Readers interested in the scope for numerical analysis in strategy could do worse than peruse Bernard Brodie, 'Strategy as a Science', *World Politics*, 1, 4 (July 1949), pp. 476–88; Kenneth A. Boulding, *Conflict and Defense* (New York: Harper & Brothers, 1962); E. S. Quade (ed.), *Analysis for Military Decisions* (Chicago: Rand McNally, 1964); and Roland N. McKean (ed.), *Issues in Defense Economics* (New York: National Bureau of Economic Research, 1967).

7. I am grateful to Michael I. Handel for his emphasis upon Clausewitz's insistence that war must be studied 'in the context of the whole, as a "gestalt" ': *Who is Afraid of Carl von Clausewitz? A Guide to the Perplexed*, 8th edn (Newport, RI: Department of Strategy and Policy, US Naval War College, Summer 1999), p. 4.

8. Andrew F. Krepinevich, 'Cavalry to Computer: The Pattern of Military Revolutions', *The National Interest*, 37 (Fall 1994), p. 30.

9. Thomas J. Welch, 'Technology and Warfare', in Keith Thomas (ed.), *The Revolution in Military Affairs: Warfare in the Information Age* (Canberra: Australian Defence Studies Centre, 1997), p. 28 (emphasis in original).

10. Carl von Clausewitz, *On War*, trans. Michael Howard and Peter Paret (Princeton, NJ: Princeton University Press, 1976 [1832]), p. 75.

11. Ibid., p. 89.

12. Ibid., p. 183; Michael Howard, 'The Forgotten Dimensions of Strategy', *Foreign Affairs*, 57, 5 (Summer 1979), pp. 975–86.

13. Once revealed in action, wonder weapons invite technical–tactical, operational, strategic, or even political offsets. Genius in high command is vulnerable to a stray bullet or deadly virus, not to mention the implementing performance by the staff and army. Cunning tactical or operational ideas lose their cunning once they are run on the field of play and thereby are revealed. This is because of the paradoxical logic of conflict. There is an interdependently, but critically independently, behaving adversary. On this central logical point, Edward N. Luttwak, *Strategy: The Logic of War and Peace* (Cambridge, MA: Harvard University Press, 1987), is unsurpassed, and probably unsurpassable.

14. Clausewitz, *On War*, p. 183.

15. Handel, *Who is Afraid of Carl von Clausewitz?*, p. 4.

16. Ibid.

17. See especially Peter Paret: 'Napoleon and the Revolution in War', in Paret (ed.), *Makers of Modern Strategy: From Machiavelli to the Nuclear Age* (Princeton, NJ: Princeton University Press, 1986), pp. 123–42; *Understanding War: Essays on Clausewitz and the History of Military Power* (Princeton, NJ: Princeton University Press, 1992), pp. 75–84; 'Napoleon as Enemy'; and 'Revolutions in Warfare: An Earlier Generation of Interpreters', in Bernard Brodie, Michael D. Intriligator, and Roman Kolkowicz (eds), *National Security and International Stability* (Cambridge, MA: Oelgeschlager, Gunn & Hain, 1983), pp. 157–69.

18. Clausewitz, *On War*, p. 183.

19. Ibid., p. 89.

20. See Ajay Singh, 'Time: The New Dimension in War', *Joint Force Quarterly*, 10 (Winter 1995–96), pp. 56–61. One need hardly comment that there are no new dimensions in war.

21. Van Creveld, *Supplying War*, ch. 5, and Harold A. Winters, *Battling the Elements: Weather and Terrain in the Conduct of War* (Baltimore, MD: Johns Hopkins University Press, 1998), chs 4 and 8 are useful. It is no longer fashionable to argue that 'The part played by the Red Army in 1941 in halting the enemy advance has been exaggerated by Soviet historians. Success was due mainly to geography and climate and thereafter to Stalin's determination ... The resistance of the Soviet armed forces was probably of only subsidiary importance': Albert Seaton, *The Russo-German War 1941–45* (New York: Praeger, 1970), p. 221. Nonetheless, Russian geography and climate were unforgiving of German material weaknesses and infirmity of operational purpose. Excellent recent studies are David M. Glantz and Jonathan M. House, *When Titans Clashed: How the Red Army Stopped Hitler* (Lawrence: University Press of Kansas, 1995); and Horst Boog and others, *Germany and the Second World War, Vol. IV: The Attack on the Soviet Union* (Oxford: Clarendon Press, 1998).

22. For example, with regard to the German Army in the Great War, General Sir Ian Hamilton has observed thus: 'In that force, created by Von Roon, a force which expired, so we hope, on the 11th November, 1918, we have the latest word on army manufacture – the typical army – and, for its own especial purpose of a short range, short time weapon, it stood supreme, enabling the German Empire to throw every iota of its strength into the contest from the moment the word mobilisation went forth. When the range and the time drew out longer and longer, the machine, and with it the nation, was, for the time being, absolutely used up – finished!': *The Soul and Body of an Army* (London: Edward Arnold, 1921), p. 34.

23. Jean Colin, *The Transformations of War*, trans. L. H. R. Pope-Hennessy (London: Hugh Rees, 1912), p. 348.

24. See Colin S. Gray, 'Inescapable Geography', in Gray and Geoffrey Sloan (eds), *Geopolitics, Geography, and Strategy* (London: Frank Cass, 1999), pp. 161–77.

25. Intelligent recent studies of British strategic performance include: Christopher D. Hall, *British Strategy in the Napoleonic War, 1803–15* (Manchester: Manchester University Press, 1992); A. D. Harvey, *Collision of Empires: Britain in Three World Wars, 1793–1945* (London: Hambledon Press, 1992), pt 1; and esp. Rory Muir, *Britain and the Defeat of Napoleon, 1807–1815* (New Haven, CT: Yale University Press, 1996).

26. Britain's premier maritime theorist, Sir Julian Corbett, has written that 'If we have gained complete command [of the sea], no invasion can take place, nor will it be attempted. If we have lost it completely no invasion will be necessary, since, quite apart from the threat of invasion, we must make peace on the best terms we can get': *Some Principles of Maritime Strategy*, ed. Eric J. Grove (Annapolis, MD: Naval Institute Press, 1988 [1911]), p. 239.

27. For example, in a generally excellent book, Martin van Creveld offered the politically very acceptable conclusion that '[the average German soldier in the Second World War] did not as a rule fight out of a belief in Nazi ideology': *Fighting Power: German and US Army Performance, 1939–1945* (Westport, CT: Greenwood Press, 1982), p. 163. A different tale emerges in Omer Bartov, *Hitler's Army: Soldiers, Nazis, and War in the Third Reich* (New York: Oxford University Press, 1991); while Stephen G. Fritz, *Frontsoldaten: The German Soldier in World War II* (Lexington: University Press of Kentucky, 1995), offers some correction to Bartov.

28. H. R. McMaster, *Dereliction of Duty: Lyndon Johnson, Robert McNamara, the Joint Chiefs of Staff, and the Lies that Led to Vietnam* (New York: HarperCollins, 1997), is truly damning. It can be supplemented by Robert Buzzanco, *Masters of War: Military Dissent and Politics in the Vietnam Era* (Cambridge: Cambridge University Press, 1996).

29. See Andrew F. Krepinevich, Jr, *The Army and Vietnam* (Baltimore: Johns Hopkins University Press, 1986); Michael A. Hennessy, *Strategy in Vietnam: The Marines and Revolutionary Warfare in I Corps, 1965–1972* (Westport, CT: Praeger Publishers, 1997); and Jeffrey Record, *The Wrong War: Why We Lost in Vietnam* (Annapolis, MD: Naval Institute Press, 1998). Should anyone be interested, I believe that the United States could have won in Vietnam. There is merit in Michael Lind, *Vietnam, The Necessary War: A Reinterpretation of America's Most Disastrous Military Conflict* (New York: Free Press, 1999); Lewis Sorley, *A Better War: The Unexamined Victories and Final Tragedy of America's Last Years in Vietnam* (New York: Harcourt Brace, 1999); and especially in C. Dale Walton, *The Myth of Inevitable US Defeat in Vietnam* (London: Frank Cass, 2002).

30. Glantz and House, *When Titans Clashed*. See also Jürgen E. Förster, 'The Dynamics of *Volkegemeinschaft*: The Effectiveness of the German Military Establishment in the Second World War', and John E. Jessup, 'The Soviet Armed Forces in the Great Patriotic War, 1941–5', in Allan R. Millett and Williamson Murray (eds), *Military Effectiveness, Vol. III: The Second World War* (Boston, MA: Allen & Unwin, 1988), respectively pp. 180–220, 256–76. For a helpful guide to sources on the Russo-German War of 1941–45, see Rolf-Dieter Müller and Gerd R. Ueberschär, *Hitler's War in the East: A Critical Assessment* (Providence, RI: Berghahn Books, 1997).

31. Bernard Brodie once wrote famously that 'good strategy presumes good anthropology and sociology. Some of the greatest military blunders of all time have resulted from juvenile evaluations in this department': *War and Politics* (New York: Macmillan, 1973), p. 332. Useful studies include Ken Booth, *Strategy and Ethnocentrism* (London: Croom Helm, 1979); and Robert B. Bathurst, *Intelligence and the Mirror: On Creating an Enemy* (London: Sage Publications, 1993). Much of the sociological scholarship that does have a military connection is thoroughly astrategic.

32. This dimension of strategy has been debated heatedly of recent years: Shu Guang Zhang, *Deterrence and Strategic Culture: Chinese–American Confrontations, 1949–1958* (Ithaca, NY: Cornell University Press, 1992); Alastair Iain Johnston, *Cultural Realism: Strategic Culture and Grand Strategy in Chinese History* (Princeton, NJ: Princeton University Press, 1995); idem, 'Strategic Cultures Revisited: Reply to Colin Gray', *Review of International Studies*, 25, 3 (July 1999), pp. 519–23; Peter J. Katzenstein (ed.), *The Culture of National Security: Norms and Identity in World Politics* (New York: Columbia University Press, 1996); Michael C. Desch, 'Culture Clash: Assessing the Importance of Ideas in Security Studies', *International Security*, 23, 1 (Summer 1998), pp. 141–70; Colin S. Gray, 'Strategic Culture as Context: The First Generation of Theory Strikes Back', *Review of International Studies*, 25, 1 (January 1999), pp. 49–69; Keith R. Krause (ed.), *Culture and Security: Multilateralism, Arms Control and Security Building* (London: Frank Cass, 1999).

33. Military behaviour – threats and deeds in the field – has to have strategic effect, which in its turn must have political consequences. These are not simply trivial definitional truths. Even if you regard some conduct of warfare as more cultural, including recreational, than purposively strategic, strategy and politics still are relevant. Strategic effect is strategic effect, regardless of whether or not the soldiers in question enjoyed the activity. Martin van Creveld, *The Transformation of War* (New York: Free Press, 1991), and John Keegan, *A History of Warfare* (London: Hutchinson, 1993), are seriously confused on these basic matters.

34. Organisation for strategy-making is emphasised most effectively in Williamson Murray and Mark Grimsley, 'Introduction: On Strategy', and MacGregor Knox, 'Conclusion: Continuity and Revolution in the Making of Strategy', in Murray, Knox, and Alvin Bernstein (eds), *The Making of Strategy: Rulers, States, and War* (Cambridge: Cambridge University Press, 1994), respectively pp. 1–23, 614–45 (esp. 615–21).

35. Clausewitz, *On War*, p. 131.

36. Michael Glover, *Peninsular Preparation: The Reform of the British Army, 1795–1809* (Cambridge: Cambridge University Press, 1963), is a superior example of an excellent study of military administration.

37. Readers behind the curve of current military jargon are advised that war now is waged in 'battlespace'. For example: Stuart E. Johnson and Martin C. Libicki (eds), *Dominant Battlespace Knowledge* (Washington, DC: Institute for National Strategic Studies, National Defense University, April 1996). The concept of, or at least the word, battlespace, pervades the leading US military vision statements of the 1990s: Joint Chiefs of Staff, 'Joint Vision 2010: America's Military – Preparing for Tomorrow', *Joint Force Quarterly*, 12 (Summer 1996), pp. 34–49; and Joint Chiefs of Staff, *Joint Vision 2020* (Washington, DC: US Government Printing Office, June 2000).

38. Clausewitz, *On War*, p. 97.

39. Ibid. (emphasis in original).

40. In an outstanding essay, Michael Howard explains the vital distinctions between command, control, and leadership. He advises that 'The first two demand a capacity for comprehending often highly complex factors and thus require minds of above average intelligence. The last consists almost entirely of what Clausewitz termed "moral qualities", of a kind that can often coexist with a complete absence of any significant intellectual capacity at all': 'Leadership in the British Army in the Second World War: Some Personal Observations', in G. D. Sheffield (ed.), *Leadership and Command: The Anglo-American Military Experience since 1861* (London: Brassey's (UK), 1997), p. 117.

41. For classic, indeed classical, graphical representation of the geopolitical geometry of enmity and alliance, see Kautilya, *The Arthashastra*, trans. L. N. Rangarajan (New Delhi: Penguin, 1992), pp. 557–8.

42. Martin C. Libicki, 'The Emerging Primacy of Information', *Orbis*, 40, 2 (Spring 1996), pp. 261–74. I take issue with the thesis that technology is demoting the significance of geography, in 'The Continued Primacy of Geography', *Orbis*, 40, 2 (Spring 1996), pp. 247–59, and in 'Inescapable Geography'. The editors of *Orbis*, not I, picked 'primacy' for my title. Geography is important, but cannot claim 'primacy'.

43. Barry D. Watts, *Clausewitzian Friction and Future War*, McNair Paper 52 (Washington, DC: Institute for National Strategic Studies, National Defense University, October 1996), is outstanding, if difficult. For the master's argument, see Clausewitz, *On War*, pp. 85–6, 101, 119–21.

44. For example, was it good luck or sound practice that enabled British armoured cars of the Tank Corps' 17th Battalion to capture documents containing vital details about the central section of the Hindenburg Line, when they exploited the success of the 5th Australian Division on 8 August 1918, the first day of the Battle of Amiens? See J. P. Harris, *Amiens to the Armistice: The BEF in the Hundred Days' Campaign, 8 August–11 November 1918* (London: Brassey's, 1998), pp. 91–2.

45. Clausewitz, *On War*, p. 75.

46. Napoleon, quoted in Peter J. Tsouras, 'Napoleon and his Words', in Philip J. Haythornthwaite and others, *Napoleon: The Final Verdict* (London: Arms and Armour Press, 1998), p. 294.

47. Booth, *Strategy and Ethnocentrism*, p. 147.

48. See Colin S. Gray, *Explorations in Strategy* (Westport, CT: Praeger Publishers, 1998), pp. 164–5, 168–74; idem, 'Handfuls of Heroes on Desperate Ventures: When do Special Operations Succeed?' *Parameters*, 29, 1 (Spring 1999), pp. 2–24. See also William H. McRaven, *SPEC OPS, Case Studies in Special Operations Warfare: Theory and Practice* (Novato, CA: Presidio Press, 1995); John Arquilla (ed.), *From Troy to Entebbe: Special Operations in Ancient and Modern Times* (Lanham, MD: University Press of America, 1996); and Susan L. Marquis, *Unconventional Warfare: Rebuilding US Special Operations Forces* (Washington, DC: Brookings Institution Press, 1997).

49. Sun Tzu, *The Art of War*, trans. Ralph D. Sawyer (Boulder, CO: Westview Press, 1994), p. 168.
50. Clausewitz, *On War*, p. 204 (emphasis in original).
51. Knox, 'Conclusion: Continuity and Revolution in the Making of Strategy', p. 645.

6

Case Study I: The Napoleonic RMA

Historians are right to be uneasy about the way in which social scientists approach historical evidence. On the one hand, when historical truth is not an end in itself, historical data may be processed and selected as evidence to meet the needs of a perilously commanding theory.[1] On the other hand, unscholarly bias (otherwise simply called judgement) in an evidentiary quest for support of a favoured explanation is as prevalent among historians as among social scientists. Such caveats matter because this chapter and the next two present in outline analytical histories of three RMAs, and also explain how each RMA worked strategically. These discourses must be rather more constructed than is usual for historical presentation, because the episodes whose stories are narrated are each defined by the contested concept of RMA. To illustrate: historians are by no means agreed on the relationship between the causes, effects, and feedback loops that explain the course of the First World War. How much more difficult is it to secure a convincing grip on the historical narrative of the RMA of the First World War? The same point applies to each case study.

The cases chosen for analysis have been selected because, regarded all together, they meet at least the minimum essential standards for potentially valuable evidence. First, everyone agrees either that these are RMAs, or that these are worth debating as such. Second, two and a quarter centuries, embracing a wide range of different political, social, economic, and especially technological, contexts, comprise a reasonable period for temporally keyed diversity to make its mark.[2] Third, the RMAs selected were each so dominant in their period that they can stretch and fully test the theory of strategy. If RMAs are radical changes in the character and conduct of war, then the (French Revolutionary and) Napoleonic Wars, the First World War, and nuclear war all plainly qualify.

It is important for a study such as this to be aware of historians' controversies. It is no less important to avoid being misled by professional arguments among historians on matters which are either literally beyond answer, and hence are unproductive, or are unimportant for our purposes. With reference to the former caveat, it is easy to sympathise with Michael Crawshaw when he writes as follows:

> It has been suggested that the advances in artillery during the First World War amount to a 'revolution in military affairs', that presently overworked term. Certainly there was a technical revolution with major operational implications; it is perhaps better to leave the discussion there rather than indulge in semantics.[3]

Sic transit the lengthy debate in the 1990s about MRs, RMAs, and MTRs. However, it is easier airily to dismiss apparently trivial historians' disputes (e.g. did Captain André Laffargue inspire German stormtroop tactics?[4] – or, who invented the 'rolling,' or 'creeping', barrage?[5]), than it is to consider the deeper questions that those disputes may help us to probe. Some essentially unanswerable questions, though in a sense trivial for that reason, nonetheless are hugely important. For example, was the 'Napoleonic' RMA really effected in the early 1790s (before Napoleon commanded the Army of Italy),[6] or by the Grande Armée in 1805–07, or at some time in between? The timing ascribed to an RMA is likely to shape the explanation of its parentage and even its character and identity. Specialists' arguments can range from expression of the truly semantically trivial, all the way to the zone of fundamental existential disagreement. Many of the defence analysts who today agree that an RMA (or two, or three) is under way do not agree on the identity of that alleged revolution.[7]

The structure of enquiry is identical for all three case studies. The history of the RMA in question is first presented in the framework provided by the nine-step life-cycle specified in Chapter 3. The discussion then proceeds to apply the theory of strategy outlined in Chapter 5 in order to examine how the RMA in question 'worked'. The findings on the working of the three RMAs are marshalled and processed in Chapter 9, primarily, though not entirely, with reference to RMA activity as *competitive* strategic behaviour. A study such as this must be meaningless if the concept and reality of the enemy – i.e. of competition – does not haunt its pages. In postmodern terms, if there is no 'other', however notional, RMA behaviour is absurd.[8]

Given the focus on competition and conflict that strategy mandates, the question of point of view cannot be evaded. Whose RMA narrative(s) should the case studies analyse? Because our selected cases are all on the imperial wing of the range of possible domain, all major belligerents (or major potential belligerents), and many minor ones, were affected by the RMAs at issue. In practice, innovative responses to a fairly common challenge – for example, the tactical crisis of 1914–16 – could take somewhat different forms and courses in different countries and could be out of time-phase with each other. Strategic and military contexts and cultures differ. The solution preferred here to these kinds of difficulties for orderly analysis is the following: (1) to allow the RMA leader(s) to drive the narrative (i.e. 1792–1815, France; 1917–18, Germany and Britain; 1945–60, United States and USSR); (2) to accommodate responses to the feedback of battlefield experience (and its peacetime equivalents in competition and crisis) in the life-cycle story (as step 9); and (3) explicitly to analyse RMA behaviour in the face of the foe strategically.

NAPOLEON AND MODERN WAR

Between 1792 and 1815, more precisely in 1805, Revolutionary, then Napoleonic, France led the way in a transformation of the character and conduct of *grande guerre* on land. The new way of war, though unmistakable in roughly symmetrical contests between armies, did not extend impressively to small wars and neither did it have noteworthy implications for war at sea,[9] save arguably politically and with reference to grand strategy. French victories on land meant that after 1795 the coastline of continental Europe by and large was in hands hostile to British seapower. It is a fact potentially of some significance for the strategic assessment of RMA, however, that French landpower failed to secure a lasting victory over British seapower.[10] At its apogee, the Napoleonic way of war threw armies of unprecedented size on country-smashing campaigns of conquest through decisive manoeuvre and, usually, battle.[11] The forces employed to accomplish such heroic tasks were an assemblage of professional soldiers, fairly patriotic French conscripts, and sundry (but increasingly reluctant foreign) mercenaries.[12] The soldiery was articulated into autonomous *corps d'armée* and led with variable operational artistry by the Zeus of modern war, the Corsican 'mastermind' himself,[13] variously aided and frequently abetted by his Imperial Headquarters (*very* approximate general staff) and – after 1804 – his Marshalate.[14] In its prime, which is to say in 1805–07, the Napoleonic style at least appeared to restore the power of swift decision to war as an instrument of foreign policy.

RMA LIFE-CYCLE

Preparation
Being careful of the toils of teleology, it is not difficult to identify a period of preparation for the Napoleonic RMA extending back as far as the 1740s. In an insightful threefold explanation, historian Jeremy Black finds the origins of this RMA in

> first, widespread demographic and economic expansion in Europe from the 1740s; second, the emphasis on the values of reform and the rational approach to problems that characterized the Enlightenment thought; and, third, the impact of the protracted warfare of 1740–67. The first pro-

duced the resources for military expansion, the second encouraged an emphasis on novelty, and the third, a period of testing, led to a determination to replace what had been found deficient and to ensure that armies (and societies) were in a better state for future conflicts.[15]

Napoleon's genius for war was charismatically personal, occasionally tactical, generally operational, and only rarely strategic or political. It is with no intent to diminish his fame that one must appreciate that Napoleon, as general and emperor, largely was not responsible for the creation of the military machine that he employed. Even to phrase it thus is to risk misunderstanding. Napoleon's charismatic leadership, his energy, and his operational brilliance were, of course, the ingredients that transformed French military power from the status of sometimes first among equals, into a *Grande Armée sans pareil*. Nonetheless, Napoleon found more than he made in the French Army of his glory years.[16]

As noted above, one must beware of the teleological mode of explanation. As a general rule, Napoleon's antecedents were simply seeking to improve the potency of French arms; they were not self-consciously preparing the way for an RMA. The Comte Hippolyte de Guibert was an exception. He understood very well that for an army to be a fast-moving and reasonably agile instrument of decision, it had to be composed of citizen soldiers who, for reason of political loyalty, could be trusted outside the bounds set by a rigid and tactically limiting discipline.[17] Guibert's 1772 text, *Essai général de tactique*, was only the most impressive among a notable array of writings and experiments in the field of military reform. The eponymity of the 'Napoleonic' RMA is entirely appropriate, but the phase of preparation was long and cumulatively fruitful.

If the Napoleonic RMA enjoyed its 'strategic moment' arguably at one or other among the bridge at Lodi in 1796, Marengo in 1800, and Ulm–Austerlitz in 1805, that moment assuredly was enabled by a half-century of preparation. The Napoleonic spark was vital – though even that is not beyond all challenge[18] – but the materials were too hard for him to ignite into a consuming instrument for his political and personal ambition. Napoleon's RMA in action can be regarded as the final product of five essential elements which, holistically, yielded the preparatory work cited here as step one in the life-cycle of an RMA.

Two additions are needed to the three 'sources of ... change' cited persuasively by Black: the growth in human and economic resources, the spirit of rational enquiry, and extensive military experience. While Black's 'elements' take us to the late 1780s, the brew for an RMA threatens criticality when we add both the social, economic, and political mobilisation effected and enabled by the dynamics of the Revolution, and a strategic context permitting extraordinary talent to show its worth. In addition to the 'division square' invented by Napoleon to resist Mameluke cavalry in Egypt,[19] he made at least two major contributions to the art of war: the massing of a more agile artillery park into grand batteries, and the assembling of divisions into the *corps d'armée* that were, in effect, armies in miniature. The system of *corps d'armée* was a vital enabler for the conduct of operational manoeuvre with a very large force. Nonetheless, his genius lay more in military execution than in military conception. That overall judgement carries no pejorative implication. It is true that Napoleon did, or attempted, military action faster, on a grander scale, and more frequently, than any of his recent predecessors had attempted or even envisaged. But it is also true that every aspect of his military instrument, and of the art with which he governed its behaviour, was invented by others. However, Napoleon took others' ideas and made them work; at least, he made them work as well as they could under the constraints of the time (especially the logistical limitations).[20]

Who and what prepared the way for what eventually was to be the magnificent Grande Armée of 1805? Set against the backcloth of no little French military success in the 1740s, but then of humiliating failure in the Seven Years War (1756–63), a series of reforming theorists, most with extensive combat experience, prepared the way for what was to become, full-blown, the Napoleonic RMA. Marshal Maurice de Saxe, Jean-Charles Folard, and Jean de Mesnil-Durand developed ideas to enhance battlefield performance – including placing emphasis upon the shock value of attack columns and stressing the importance of logistics.[21] Those, and ancillary, notions were propelled forward in the 1760s, 1770s, and 1780s by the military experiments and writings of the Duc de Broglie, Bourcet, and Guibert. Broglie tried the divisional system of military organisation as early as 1761, the system was adopted at least administratively in 1787–88, and it became standard practice by 1793. Divisional organisation allowed an army to move far more swiftly than would be the case were it obliged to move and manoeuvre as a single unarticulated body. Rapid marches and agile descents upon the enemy's lines of communications, operations envisaged by Bourcet and Guibert, would be impracticable were the French Army not organised into autonomous divisions of all arms.

General Bonaparte, an artilleryman, inherited the finest artillery service in the world. The modernity of the French artillery park of the 1790s was not simply fortuitous, rather was it the result of more than thirty years of inspired and systematic reform and improvement. Lineage can be instructive. The creator of the modern French artillery park, the Comte de Gribeauval, trained a brilliant pupil in the Baron du Teil, who – in his turn – trained a yet more apt student in the person of Lieutenant Napoleon Bonaparte at the artillery school at Auxonne in 1788–89.[22]

When General Napoleon Bonaparte secured his first independent command in 1796, courtesy of the patronage of Paul Barras of the Directory, the French Army was nearly ready for prime time (which is not to deny that Napoleon's Army of Italy was in a rough condition indeed). As well as owning the finest artillery in Europe, the French Army of the mid-1790s also possessed the most advanced drill-book (of 1791), which is to say tactical doctrine, and had both suffered and benefited from the domestic political and social turbulence of the Revolution. While politics had wrecked the French Navy, on balance it *eventually* fostered a far more potent army.[23] Revolutionary enthusiasm, supplemented carefully by an approximation (in practice admittedly only a poor approximation) of universal conscription, and augmented by a new and sustained patriotism, combined to provide military manpower on a scale that an inspired leader with a sound enough doctrine could turn to ambitious account. Napoleon's sometimes masterly orchestration of the grand batteries (100-plus guns) of artillery, *l'ordre mixte* of attack column and line, and of clouds of skirmishers (to protect the battalion attack columns before they deployed into line, inter alia), was manipulation of an already superior military instrument and art of war.

Recognition of challenge

The Napoleonic RMA was a response both to pressing necessity and to apparently glittering opportunity. In truth, the RMA led by the French Army in the late 1790s and early 1800s was the product of a cumulative series of perceived challenges.

First, as noted above, from the 1740s to the 1780s thoughtful soldiers in France recognised a strategic need (the quest for favourable decision by battle) to reform the army. What could be done was done, given the highly restrictive political, legal, and social context of Bourbon France. Though heavily populated and in some senses extremely wealthy, the France of the *ancien régime* was walking wounded in terms of its mobilisable military power. The wounds included the aristocratic near-monopoly of commissioned ranks, the fact that the rank-and-file were by no means citizens, and the inability of the crown to raise the revenue from taxation to pay for the army and navy. These weaknesses were not, of course, unique to Bourbon France.[24] On the eve of the Revolution – a revolution ironically triggered by the calling of the States-General to resolve the fiscal problems caused, or at least accelerated dramatically, by the unsustainable costs of assisting the American colonies – French military reformers had met the challenge of potentially bloody indecision posed by inflexible army organisation and tactics. By 1789, French tactics were of the best and their military equipment was either superior (artillery) or ordinary but good enough (the standard infantry flintlock musket, the model '1777').[25]

Having met the challenge to reform whatever was politically reformable by 1791, next the French had to meet the challenge of bare political–military survival. From 1792 to 1794 the cry most genuinely was *la patrie en danger*. Military misfortune, merited or not, and political nonconformity, real or suspected, resulted in Revolutionary France cashiering (and sometimes guillotining) no fewer than 593 general officers in 1792 and the first half of 1793.[26] To succeed, even just to survive, as a French general in 1793, one needed to be politically correct in the eyes of the Committee of Public Safety and its flying representatives *en mission*, as well as fortunate in battle.[27] Defeat was often interpreted as evidence of treason.

Both helped and hindered by the insistence upon total political reliability on the part of its generals, as well as by the somewhat indiscriminate cull of those aristocratic officers who did not flee abroad on their own initiative, Revolutionary France improvised its way through the great crisis of 1793. Much assisted by the typical incompetence of its coalition of foreign (and domestic) foes, the Revolution fought in the only way that it could. The much famed Battle of Valmy (20 September 1792) was won with superior artillery and such elements from the 1791 drill-book that an unstable mix of regular and volunteer soldiers jointly could implement. Against more determined, better led, and more united foes, the French armies of 1792–94 surely would have gone down in well-deserved defeat. Strategic history can be kind, however, in that it does not require an absolute superiority as a condition for victory, but rather only that the total performance be better than that of distinctly flawed enemies. The French armies that combated the multinational forces of the First Coalition (of seven) were but a shadow of what was to appear collectively as the Grande Armée a decade later: nonetheless they were good enough to see off the enemies of the Republic. The French Army of 1796, by then shorn of most of the political baggage that had hampered performance in 1793, and hardened and honed by four years of sometimes desperate warfare, *arguably* was the finest fighting instrument in Europe. One must write 'arguably', because French military performance against the First Coalition (26 June 1792–17 October 1797) was decidedly uneven. T. C. W. Blanning provides a valuable corrective to still orthodox opinion among historians, when he argues that 'the five years of fighting between 1792 and 1797 seemed to suggest that a military solution to the problem of revolutionary France was still feasible'. He continues by pointing out that

> If they [the Austrians] had lost Belgium after their defeat at Jemappes on 6 November 1792, they had won it back again after their victory at Neerwindern on 16 March 1793. If they had lost it again after their defeat at Fleurus on 26 June 1794, who was to say that they would not win it back again at some future date? If the French had been able to conquer the left bank of the Rhine, they had been repelled every time they tried to cross the river. Even the campaigns of 1796 could be interpreted in more than one way: certainly General Bonaparte had been triumphant in Italy, but in the main German theatre the Archduke Charles had defeated the Rhin-et-Moselle and Sambre-et-Meuse armies and had chased them back over the Rhine again. In short, the revolutionary armies had *not* proved to be the all-conquering irresistible force of Brissotin ante-bellum oratory. Whenever the Austrians had been able to take the field with roughly equal numbers, their superior discipline and training had proven more than a match for revolutionary *élan*.[28]

The third challenge, following those to reform and then simply to survive, was posed by the opportunity to conquer. If the Napoleonic RMA that eventually was expressed instrumentally in the Grande Armée was forged in the fire of long antecedent military reform, and out of a period of desperate improvisation for political survival, its mission was conquest, pure and simple. As a military instrument of then unequalled striking power, the Grande Armée of the 1800s met the challenge of the open door which beckoned. That army could do, at least could credibly attempt, what Napoleon craved to achieve. In addition, the more that the Grande Armée could do, the more that would be asked of it. The challenge of conquest was unbounded, because the owner of this RMA-in-action was committed for entirely personal reasons to an open-ended quest for glory.[29]

Parentage

Who made the Napoleonic RMA, or is this question akin to asking who is buried in Grant's Tomb? If by eponymous titular definition Napoleon effected 'his' RMA, who, or what, were the parents? It is possible, and at least generally satisfactory, to argue that the Napoleonic RMA, and indeed the meteoric military–political career of the man himself, was sired by the Revolution. As described above, much preparatory work was undertaken from the 1740s to the 1780s for what would appear under Napoleon's guidance as a radical change in the conduct of war. However, such practitioner-theorists as Saxe, Broglie, Bourcet, Guibert, and Teil, among others, did not make an RMA. Their military ideas and experiments helped forge a more potent French Army, but that army, in the service of the Bourbons, could not have implemented what became the Napoleonic RMA. That RMA was not simply a great non-linearity just waiting to happen.[30]

Impressive were the possibilities for much improved military performance presaged in the words and deeds of the pre-revolutionary reformers. But for possibilities to be transformed into probability, two vital enablers were required. First, there had to be the parentage provided by a Revolution (or some close simulacrum thereto) which could augment technical military excellence with political velocity and human and material mobilisation. Second, leadership was required to use the new military instrument to the limits of its potential. The second of these transformational variables, the 'enabling spark', is discussed immediately below.

To risk reductionism, the dynamics of the Revolution enabled French military power to be all that it could be, while the leadership provided for good and ill by Napoleon Bonaparte enabled that military power to achieve all that it could achieve. Napoleon eventually could lead the Grande Armée to death and glory because the Revolution: (1) opened promotion to talent and republican political patronage (even to Corsican opportunists); (2) performed well enough, on balance, in marrying military professional competence to political enthusiasm; (3) unintentionally began to systematise the raising of exceptionally large armies; (4) descended periodically into the kind of political chaos which is an invitation to ambitious generals to restore order and confidence and to advance themselves.

In an immediate and political sense uniquely appropriate to this RMA, we should probably assign responsibility for parentage by choosing among: (1) the Revolution itself; (2) Paul Barras, the political commissar at Toulon, later a member of the Directory, who was Napoleon's patron at vital moments; and (3) General Lazare Carnot, who, as the member of the National Assembly, and later the Committee for Public Safety, most responsible for military affairs, devised the *levée en masse* of August 1793 and the (political commissar) system of *députés-en-mission*. Carnot was the individual most responsible for the administration and logistics of the military machine which Napoleon came to command.

Enabling spark
It is not the contention of this study that an RMA – even an RMA bordering on MR – requires antecedent political revolution; such a political context is judged neither necessary nor sufficient. Rather is it the case simply that with respect to the Napoleonic RMA the great crisis of 1793, a crisis triggered by revolutionary French statecraft (to dignify an amateur hour), set in train a response to that challenge which assumed the character of an RMA. Virtually by definition, an RMA worthy of the ascription has to be a response to a perceived crisis. Armed forces do not rapidly effect radical change in their approach to the conduct of war unless their owner-operators are seriously alarmed. As we shall see, the RMAs of the First World War and of the nuclear era were both licensed and propelled by that same spirit of extreme worry about *la patrie en danger* which gave birth to a new French military reality in 1793–94. The absence of any such suitable crisis today (i.e. one not involving an opaquely asymmetric global terrorism) is one among several reasons why the contemporary alleged I-led RMA may fizzle rather than explode.[31]

Napoleon Bonaparte, personally, was the enabling spark for his eponymous RMA. As Owen Connelly asserts with admirable directness, 'If there was a Napoleonic military revolution, he was it.'[32] Whether or not Napoleon invented a new way of war is arguable, while we can assert with confidence that he did not create a new model army. He did, however, perfect the military instrument that he found (up to a point, at least, with major reservations necessary about logistics and staffwork generally), and make far more of it as an instrument for conquest than the sum of its parts would have suggested probable.[33] Even allowing for the limitations of evidence which hobble the authority of virtual history,[34] it is still plausible to insist that Napoleon was necessary, rather than merely sufficient, as the enabling spark for an RMA. Of course, there were other competent French generals who could, indeed did, menace Napoleon's reputation: Moreau, Jourdan, and Desaix, for example (nor should we forget

General Charles Dumouriez, the co-victor at Valmy, who self-destructed through excessive ambition). We cannot be certain that those ambitious, militarily gifted, opportunists would not have created a Grand Armée and proceeded upon an imperial rampage comparable with that actually effected by Napoleon. It does, however, seem unlikely that the French Army would have been much more than a first among rough equals in hands other than Napoleon's. Napoleon was not just a part of the RMA, interchangeable with several other candidate leaders. He unified the French Army as *his* army, much as Adolf Hitler was to do with the German armed forces nearly a century and a half later.[35]

Strategic moment

Usually there is a moment, dignified here as 'strategic', when an emerging RMA first reveals itself unmistakably. In principle, the only difficulty for this enquiry is at the secondary level, of deciding which moment most warrants the 'strategic' label. In practice, the strategic moment is seriously debatable only for the RMA case of the First World War (Cambrai – November 1917, or Hamel – July 1918, or Amiens – August 1918?). For the Napoleonic RMA the strategic moment has to be the campaign by the Army of Italy in 1796–97. If that is unduly sweeping, then one might select the pre-battle manoeuvres and the combat itself at Castiglione (5 August 1796).[36] Castiglione showed Napoleon using his favoured strategy of the central position (the interior lines so highly praised by Jomini),[37] concentrating his dispersed forces for battle, seeking local superiority at the decisive place and time in order to exploit the effect of a *manoeuvre sur les derrières*. In short, the Napoleonic warfare of the 1800s was presaged in miniature in the Po valley in summer 1796. In David Chandler's apposite words, 'Castiglione is important as showing the development of Bonaparte's concept of the "strategic battle", and its grand tactical sequences would be repeated with variations (and greater success) on many future occasions.'[38]

There is a sense in which Paddy Griffith is correct when he asserts that the RMA was completed by 1794, with the significant French victory at Fleurus (26 June).[39] By mid-1794, most of the French Army (but not the cavalry) had largely recovered from the damage wrought by the Revolution and, on a good day, was competitive with or better than any in Europe. The Napoleonic RMA, however, was all about an operational elegance (albeit a brutal elegance) in the conduct of war that even General Jourdan doing well, as at Fleurus, could not anticipate convincingly.

Institutional agency

The military instrument expressing the Napoleonic RMA was the creation of the French Republic, then the Empire and the extended imperium. That bald statement is not quite the truism it may appear. It is not misleading to say that the institutional agency for Napoleon's RMA was the French state, French society, and as much of the rest of Europe as could be suborned and exploited. Of course, the proximate institutional agent for this RMA was what became the Grande Armée,[40] but that often magnificent military machine did not exist to serve the interests of France. Instead, it was formed and used to serve Napoleon's ambition, and the ultimate purpose assigned to France and its satellites by the Emperor was to satisfy it in all its needs. This claim is not the mundane point that armies necessarily are the products of the states and societies that man, equip, feed, and pay for them. The point, rather, is that the object of Napoleonic warfare, of the Napoleonic RMA in battlespace action, was to set the stage for yet more warfare in the future. Paul W. Schroeder in particular among contemporary historians has captured the truly criminal insatiability that lurked behind the Napoleonic dazzle.[41]

As the politics and grand strategy of Napoleonic warfare were deeply personal, so also were the institutional agencies for Napoleon's will. This proved to be a potent source of both strength and weakness. The First Consul, then Emperor, unified French land power into the Grande Armée, of which he was sole lord and master. In theory, the Grande Armée, articulated after 1800 into *corps d'armée*, each approximately 30,000 strong, and commanded by the Marshalate, marched to the emperor's tune. In practice, Napoleon's overcentralised command system broke down under the stress of distance, friction of all kinds, and the incompetence of key subordinates undertrained for their responsibilities. Defence analysts today have to beware of the pitfall of inappropriate standards. The wonder is not that Napoleon's military system often functioned poorly: rather is it little short of amazing that it worked as well as it did. After the winter of 1808–09, for example, the emperor was running both many aspects of the Empire and from time to time (1809, 1812–14) active military campaigns simultaneously on the Danube and in south Germany (1809, 1813) and in the Iberian peninsula (1809–14). Even with some good metalled roads[42] and a few key lines of semaphore-telegraph,[43] the factors of time and distance posed insuperable difficulties for a command system which could operate decisively only with authority from the hub that was Imperial Headquarters (wherever the emperor happened to be).

Napoleon was a practical man in all regards save, fatally, those of high-level statecraft and grand strategy. Under his fairly enlightened and rational governance, the impressive administrative architecture of rules and institutions that was the French state actually worked; at least, it worked well enough. Again to risk apparent circularity of argument, it is true to claim that war itself was a vital institutional agency that enabled the general, and then the emperor, to wage yet more war. Following the ancient principle of making war pay for war, in 1796 Napoleon inspired the ragged heroes of the Army of Italy with the promise of pillage and loot. For Napoleon war was an end in itself, while for France war, certainly the occupation of foreign lands, was an economic necessity.

Instrument

It is essential to distinguish the military instrument which must expressly 'do' the RMA in combat – or in peacetime and crisis for general and immediate deterrence – from its institutional agents of several kinds. This aspect of the RMA life-cycle refers simply and inescapably to the quantity and quality of fighting forces acquired, maintained, and sustained to implement the revolution in question.

There was a potent synergy between the sheer size of the French Army in the 1790s and 1800s, and the sophistication of its way of war. To be militarily effective, a French Army that expanded in size nearly fivefold between 1791 and 1794 simply had to be articulated into divisions, and then corps, and needed trained staffs at divisional, corps, and army levels of command.[44] The relationship between an RMA and its political, social, and military contexts requires nuanced treatment. The military instrument of this RMA, the French Army, differed greatly in scale and quality over the period of interest, and those differences were critical to how the RMA worked for the army strategically, including how well it fought.

The RMA produced when the political dynamics of the French Revolution overlay a notably technically (but not socially) reformed military machine, was implemented by a succession of different French armies. The Grande Armée of the high glory years of 1805–12 was preceded by armies in the 1790s which combined the regulars of the ancien régime with improvising and variably enthusiastic amateurs, and then by the battle-hardened professionals whom General Bonaparte led in Italy and somewhat misled (and abandoned) in Egypt and Syria. That Grande Armée, destroyed in Russia, was succeeded first by a huge mob of a hastily gathered 'army' in 1813 (which was largely demolished at Leipzig), next by a small and largely amateur force in 1814, and then finally by a collection of all the talents for the last hurrah at Ligny–Waterloo in 1815. It should be unnecessary to add that 'the French Revolutionary and Napoleonic RMA' had to adapt to, as well as guide, the highly variable scale and quality of military assets available to it.[45]

We can identify at least three military–instrumental contexts for this RMA. First, there was the French Army which literally saved the Revolution between 1792 and 1794, from Valmy to Fleurus. That army was an unreliable combination of regular professionals, volunteer amateurs (sometimes rabble-in-arms), and conscriptees; it was also very large by general European standards. Second, there was the French Army of, say, 1795 to 1800, and then of 1814 and 1815, which – in its direct Napoleonic connection, at least – was modest in size and hence, in principle, was readily well commanded by a single person superior in generalship. Third, there was the Grande Armée of 1805–12, which, flaws acknowledged, stands comparison with the finest armies in all of history.

The Revolution yielded the political system which enabled French society to provide, and keep providing, the largest and most modern army in Europe.

There is much to be said in praise of genius in command, creative operational artistry, superior tactics, and up-to-date equipment, but as Horatio Nelson said, 'numbers only can annihilate'.[46] The ability to mobilise, and keep mobilising, large armies, enabled French generals to be profligate in their expenditure of manpower. Quite suddenly in the 1790s, soldiers became cheap. Many operational and tactical problems could be solved or alleviated by paying a high price in casualties. The France of the Revolution and Empire could seek bold solutions through trial-by-battle, because it had an all but limitless supply of human cannon fodder. Thus could Napoleon pursue high ambitions in statecraft, and seek direct answers by decisive combat. The Napoleonic RMA pointed to a way of war that mandated armies of a scale unprecedented in European history. In part, though only in part, this RMA was an adaptation of the best military thinking of the eighteenth century to new political, social, and economic circumstances. Those circumstances enabled war to be conducted on a much larger scale than hitherto. The campaigns and battles of the Grande Armée from 1805 until 1813, which is to say from Ulm–Austerlitz to Leipzig, showed two step-level increases in scale. Whereas battles in the 1790s in the principal theatres of operations (the Rhine and Flanders) typically saw the total number of soldiers on both sides approximating 100,000 (94,000 at Valmy, 1792; 58,000 at Jemappes, 1793; 127,000 at Fleurus, 1794), the early and the high years of Empire registered new magnitudes of effort. In 1805 at Austerlitz, a total of 155,000 men took the field; Jena-Auerstadt in 1806 was conducted by 241,000 men; and Eylau in 1807 by 149,000. The period 1809–13 witnessed the maturity of a new scale of modern warfare. The armies took the field with 290,000 men at Wagram in 1809; 246,000 at Borodino in 1812; and an all but mind-boggling 560,000 in 1813 at Leipzig, the largest battle of the nineteenth century.

It is perhaps ironic, though really it is just a reflection of strategy's inherently competitive and paradoxical nature,[47] that the military instrument for this French-led RMA, the Grande Armée, should prove self-defeating in several respects. The political vision and programme which were its enabling spark were bound to motivate the generation of countervailing strength abroad. Furthermore, the very scale of the Grande Armée which gave it army- and country-smashing potential was also a scale which, in adversity, could rebound to smash its political owner. Moreover, the size of the Grande Armée and its admittedly imperfect foreign imitators came hugely to reduce the operational tempo and dexterity that was key to the Napoleonic way of war. The new nationalism and administrative system which enabled French resources to be mobilised to create and sustain – with assistance from loot and indemnities abroad – enormous armies, could be used wisely only by a leadership respectful of practical limitations as well as open to the exploitation of opportunities. Napoleon's attempts at RMA-in-action could be a brilliant, even if often a brilliantly 'scrambling',[48] holistic conception, which fused cunning operational manoeuvre with decisive battle. After 1807, however, the reality increasingly was a Grande Armée unimpressively led by much of the Marshalate, poorly commanded and controlled via unreliable communications, and logistically fragile or much worse. By 1809 and certainly beyond, Napoleon's battlefield foes could have a bad day, but still remain in or close to the field and sufficiently undefeated as to be certain to return for another bout.

The Napoleonic RMA translated as a military gigantism that led to a fatal imbalance between the art of war and that '*science* of the art of war' to which reference has been made. Napoleon's appalling political and grand strategic leadership, commanding the resources mobilisable because of the events of the 1790s, produced what became typically an attritional style in war. Even when enemies could be beaten in battle, or decisively outmanoeuvred, as Napoleon achieved for a while on a small scale in spring 1814 and on a large scale, albeit lethally incompletely, in the Hundred Days campaign of 1815, *decision* worthy of the name could not be secured. Even a French victory at Waterloo probably would only have postponed Napoleon's demise. The political odds against him were just too high by 1815, both abroad and in war-weary France itself. As Geoffrey Wawro observes, probably with some exaggeration:

> From the moment the seventh and final coalition was assembled at Vienna in March 1815 until the last shot was fired at Waterloo in June, the allied armies had operated smoothly and efficiently. Even had Bonaparte won at Waterloo, he would have met a second wave of Austrian and Russian troops, which invaded France to reinforce the British and Prussians in June.[49]

The valid point is not that Napoleon necessarily would have lost to other Allied armies in 1815, even had he won at Waterloo; rather is it that a Napoleonic France would *always* have new wars to wage and that one day there would be a conclusive defeat.

Execution and evolving maturity
Isolated elements of what the world was to think of as the Napoleonic way in warfare can be located from the 1740s onwards. Indeed, there is not much about that 'way' which was not as old as warfare itself. Achievement of potential flexibility and high tempo through subdivision of the army into autonomous units (divisions, then corps); concentration of those units on the battlefield and the value of superior numbers at the 'decisive point'; manoeuvre upon the enemy's rear, possibly to set him up for a breakthrough of his front; logistics 'on the hoof', as it were, living off the enemy's land; the massing of firepower in great batteries; fluidity of tactics as between column, line, and skirmishing; the use of spies and the intent to deceive – such supposedly signature features of Napoleonic warfare as these were all ancient history in the discourse of conflict. Napoleon's greatness lay not in the innovative and

creative uncovering of the deepest truths about the conduct of war – Jomini the competent scribbler could imagine himself uniquely able to do that[50] – but rather in his skill in execution.[51] Many good soldiers knew most of what Napoleon knew about war. The key difference lay in the facts that Napoleon usually could execute effectively with his knowledge and they could not, while he had, and helped temper, an army that could do the RMA of the period where it mattered most, on the field of honour. In the practical realm of strategic history, excellence is one-third knowledge, but fully two-thirds execution. To pass high in a written examination in generalship at a war college is no guarantee of practical success as a general. Generals need to be resilient in mind and body, as well as skilled at their trade. In the apt words of General Sir Archibald Wavell, 'the first essential of a general [is], the quality of robustness, the ability to stand the shocks of war'.[52]

Where the Duke of Wellington's excellence primarily lay in tactics, administration, and – above all – logistics, Napoleon's peculiar genius for war was all but invariably charismatic, characteristically operational, and only occasionally tactical.[53] The RMA-in-action that was the Napoleonic way in warfare was first made manifest, at least in adolescent form, in his Italian campaigns of 1796–97, was evident in his handling of the Egyptian–Syrian adventure in 1798–99, was plainly apparent to all observers in his second Italian campaign in 1800, and reached full maturity in his use of his new Grande Armée to defeat the armies of the Third and Fourth Coalitions in 1805 and 1806–07.[54]

With the Grande Armée of 1805–06, Napoleon enjoyed untrammelled centralised, political, and military command authority over a unified national army; 'his' substantially derivative system of war had been battle-tested for much of a decade, though not yet on a truly grand scale; and his foes were either great powers enfeebled by the politics of coalition, or an isolated great power as yet not really ready for the modern style of war as conducted by its French exemplar. Where at Ulm the Austrians were defeated by operational manoeuvre that brilliantly obviated the need for combat, at Austerlitz the bickering Austro-Russian forces were smashed both by inspired operational art and by the tactical *coup d'œil* of Napoleon at his peak. The double battle of Jena–Auerstadt of 14 October 1806 would rate close to the top of the short list of Napoleon's most impressive demonstrations of operational artistry, were it not demoted by the poor quality of the Prussian foe, at least in its competence at the operational level of war. The conduct of battle at Jena–Auerstadt, though successful for the French, was by no means an unalloyed tactical triumph.[55]

Great victories for France still lay ahead, but the desperate drawn (at best) battle of Eylau (7–8 February 1807), and even the expensive victory at Friedland (14 June 1807), could indicate to those perceptive enough to see that some fissures were appearing in the Napoleonic way of war. The leading such fissure provides the leitmotiv for the ninth and final step in this discussion of the

Napoleonic RMA; it is the working and implication of what Edward N. Luthwak so aptly terms the paradoxical logic of strategy.[56]

Feedback and adjustment

The paradoxical logic of strategy holds that that which works today is unlikely to work tomorrow, precisely because it works today. There is an adversarial dimension integral to the structure, functioning, and very purpose of strategic behaviour. Therefore it follows that RMAs-in-action are always conducted not only in the face of an enemy, but also in the face of an enemy motivated, and possibly capable, of finding good enough solutions to the problems posed by the RMA(s) *du jour*. So it was for the Napoleonic RMA. Furthermore, one cannot overemphasise the point that RMA, indeed RMA as enhancer of military effectiveness, does not work in a political and strategic vacuum. Fighting power, that engine essential for military effectiveness,[57] makes sense only with reference to the fighting power of the enemy and to the brutally quantitative demands placed upon it by statecraft.

There is little room to doubt Robert M. Epstein's claim that Napoleon's Grande Armée of 1805 was 'the first truly nineteenth-century army'.[58] The most intriguing strategic questions, however, are (1) 'for how long would "first" mean "only"?'; and (2) 'would there be enough of this uniquely modern army to do the job that its owner would demand of it?' By 1809 at the latest it was evident that the answer to the first question was 'not long at all'. By 1812 (especially after Borodino, 7 September), few could doubt that even the Grande Armée was not grand enough.

An RMA leader in time of war needs to move rapidly to exploit a notable initial military advantage to the point where a favourable political order can be won and secured. If an RMA-forged lead cannot be thus exploited, the consequence has to be that undefeated, or inadequately defeated, foes will learn the modern trade of war and find ways to become strategically competitive. For example, the fact that Nazi Germany lost the Second World War on a Trojan scale does not mean that the mechanised warfare RMA the Wehrmacht practised in 1939–42 was fatally flawed,[59] far from it. What it does mean is that a style in war successful against incompetent enemies who lack the geographical depth or the reserves to ride the attack, may not work against opponents able both to trade space for time for military education on the job, and to mobilise societal assets in depth.

Notwithstanding the standard measure of war's frictions, including human error and sheer bad luck, Napoleon's RMAed Grande Armée was briefly every bit as potent as misty-eyed admirers affirm. In 1805–06, reliably, and in 1807–12, by and large, the Grande Armée and its leader with his modern style of war were indeed the epitome of contemporary strategic lethality. So much is not at all the issue. The question, rather, is how well or poorly did Napoleon and his army adjust to changing circumstances, both exogenous and endogenous?

Two points in particular stand out from an examination of the entire executive record of the Napoleonic RMA. First, whether or not military systems and commanders in general are capable of learning by experience in linear or non-linear ways,[60] the years 1796–1815 do not demonstrate strongly a process of military, let alone strategic, learning by Napoleon. He was frequently operationally brilliant with small and ill-trained forces in 1814, while he proceeded in the Hundred Days initially to win the Ligny–Waterloo campaign operationally, only to lose it, narrowly, through monumental operational and tactical incompetence.[61] Unfortunately for a commonsense theory of learning cumulatively by experience, Napoleon was no more brilliant in 1814, say, than he had been in his Italian campaigns of 1800 or even 1796. His 'battlecraft' as tactical commander often was unsure, but time and again his erratically reliable *coup d'oeil,* and a healthy measure of luck, enabled him to scramble to victory, or blunder to glory, as one historian has expressed the matter.[62] Overall, he was not obviously a better commander in 1814–15 than in 1796–1800.

Second, whatever that was new and of benefit that Napoleon may have learned over the years about the art of waging war was ironically more than offset in its positive effects by the evolution of his military instrument and its strategic context. As, following Clausewitz, there is a culminating point of victory,[63] so there was a point in 1807–09, beyond which lay an increasing entropy. Aside from particular improvements by Napoleon's enemies, who were learning how to raise their military and strategic game,[64] the Emperor's enterprises were too many and too vast, and his Grande Armée became too large even for his prodigious talents to command competently through his marshals, let alone use wisely.

There were several reasons why the Napoleonic RMA ultimately failed to deliver success to France. First, enemies learned how to perform well enough so as to frustrate the Napoleonic way of war. Second, the Grande Armée, though large in size through 1813, sustained losses (especially in 1812 and 1813, at a level of approximately 500,000 in both years) that blunted its effectiveness. Paradoxically, it was too large to be an agile and compliant tool of Napoleon's erratic genius, but it was not large enough to dominate the space that he coveted (from the Tagus to the Moskva rivers). Third, this RMA, at least in its leading French guise, was fatally flawed from the head downwards, because its owner-operator was incapable of using military success to achieve a lasting peace.[65] Napoleon the statesman–strategist was akin to a gambler so addicted to the game that he cannot walk away from the table and count his winnings. No success ever is sufficient, and every reverse might be overturned by the next fall of the cards.

Like courage, excellence in command appears not to be a steady value for an individual. Higher military education, either by experience or by history books,[66] cannot eradicate or even much alleviate the ill consequences of flaws in character. Moreover, even some strengths have the potential to become net sources of weakness. Napoleon's supreme self-confidence and focused and utterly selfish force of will were key to his success. However, they were also key to his downfall, because they rendered him unable to appraise objectively the political and military competence both of his foes and even of vital subordinates. In addition, the insatiable egotistic nature of his career meant that he was incapable of empathising sufficiently with France's enemies and potential enemies so as to be able to devise a militarily attainable European order which would serve French *and others*' interests well enough to be sustainable. For the RMAed forces of France under the Emperor the goal in war always was yet more war.

Napoleon's battlefield tactics were influenced by his judgement about the changing quality of the army that he led. After 1809, though some claim even before the Wagram campaign, the decline in the quality of the ordinary French infantry of the line (*les fantassins*) mandated heavier reliance upon simpler tactics and the seeking of combat compensation in a yet larger artillery contribution.[67] Following the catastrophe in Russia in 1812, the French Army was so deficient in cavalry that even prudent reconnaissance and screening, let alone swift pursuit to rout and destroy, became unachievable luxuries (approximately 200,000 horses were lost). These points granted, still there is scant evidence to suggest that Napoleon examined his way of war in order to adjust in a discretionary manner to changing times. Above all else, it is quite apparent that he did not take a grip upon his evolving military and strategic problems. France's principal continental enemies fielded ever larger armies which were highly variably reformed into uneven facsimiles of the French exemplar. Reform in Prussia, Austria, and Russia admittedly was limited. It was, however, genuine, and was founded upon the educational experience of defeat by a superior French model.

Military adversity, inter alia, led Napoleon down the same road that imperial and Nazi Germany would take. Specifically, his army was notably divided into an ever-growing, and hence ever more diluted, élite Imperial Guard, *and the rest*, which more and more often was a quite ragged, under-trained militia.[68] In strong contrast to Erich Ludendorff and Adolf Hitler, though, who respectively expended their stormtroopers (and the 'attack divisions' as a whole) and the Waffen-SS with almost reckless abandon,[69] Napoleon repeatedly chose to hoard his Guard way beyond the bounds of military (if not political) prudence. From Jena to Waterloo, the Guard (particularly the 'Old' Guard) was not permitted to earn its pay at the right time at the decisive point.

The final judgement on the life-cycle of the Napoleonic RMA has to be that after 1806–07 the Emperor too often failed to register feedback from military experience, and was either unwilling or unable to adjust his way of war to the increasing scale of combat or to the improved competence of his foes. Genius, almost no matter how genuine, is always flawed, usually declines, if nonlinearly, with age and strategic mileage, and inspires its foes.

STRATEGIC BEHAVIOUR

This focused comparison among cases of RMA is both enriched and perilously complicated by the fact that of the RMAs selected for analysis here, two are tested in, indeed in good part emerge as, responses to the immediate needs of war (Napoleonic, First World War), while one is tested in real political, but only virtual military, combat (nuclear). This diversity of candidate evidence is welcome because such is the true complexity of strategic history. An elegant simplicity in analysis would be as convenient as it would risk doing undue violence to the apparent evidence. The only uniformity imposed here and in the succeeding chapters is that of analytical method. Genuine ambivalence and fuzziness is registered as such.

Table 6.1, like similar efforts for the historical RMAs in Chapters 7 and 8, summarises how the Napoleonic RMA functioned strategically. The table expresses a test of the Napoleonic way of war according to the theory of strategy provided in Chapter 5.

Table 6.1: The Napoleonic RMA: Strategic Dynamics

Dimensions	France
People	DS/W
Society	DS
Culture	
Politics	S/W
Ethics	W
Economics and logistics	W
Organisation	W
Military administration	S
Information and intelligence	
Theory and doctrine	S/W
Technology	
Military operations	S
Command	DS/W
Geography	W
Friction	S/W
Adversary	
Time	W

Key: DS   Defining strength of this RMA
DS/W Both relative strength and weakness
S   Strength in this dimension
W   Weakness in this dimension

As we argued there, although strategy has many dimensions, all of which interpenetrate and work together holistically, still it is feasible and useful to distinguish among these factors because their relative influence varies widely.

Because the same analytical approach is employed for all the case studies, a few general explanatory points need to be provided just once. These points therefore should be kept in mind with reference to the strategic behaviour that is each historical RMA.

1. Every one of the 17 identified dimensions is always in play, integral to strategy's *holistic* working.

2. Although a political/policy dimension is distinguished as endogenous to strategic behaviour, one must remember that there is an exogenous political context for every strategy episode for an RMA. To risk caricaturing the point, one should note the familiar aphorism, 'right method, wrong war'.[70] Rephrased, a particularly RMAed military machine may perform superbly in a limited military–technical and tactical–operational sense, yet the consequences might be catastrophically awful if the policy–historical context for such application is not suitable.[71]

3. The adversary is listed as just one distinctive dimension among the 17, but in truth it is what the RMA as strategic behaviour is all about. If the RMA does not battle-test well enough against the adversary of the day, the RMAed forces in question fail.

4. Competent net assessment, which is to say studying the enemy carefully and taking it seriously, is usually difficult. Because of the wide range of alternative approaches to strategy, many countries have allowed fallacious strategic theory and doctrine to mislead them. The skilful strategist, by analogy, may play the person rather than the person's apparent assets. For example, a net assessment of the relative strengths of contemporary US I-led armed forces could be fatally off-cue if an opponent is able to wage a style of war which places many US strengths at a discount.

5. When feasible, our analysis is of an RMA in action strategically against real historical foes, not simply of an RMA as a theory of, or presumed capability for, war. To illustrate, the German version of the First World War RMA contained a signally impressive combined arms, infantry-led, assault doctrine. The fact is, however, that a large fraction of the German infantry which conducted Ludendorff's 'Peace Offensive' in March, April, and May 1918, did not follow that doctrine in practice.[72]

6. Some strengths, even some RMA-'defining strengths', also can be a source of weakness. When all, or nearly all, depends upon the genius in command, what happens when that genius is absent, sick, has a bad day, or simply suffers some decline in his powers?

7. Strengths and weaknesses can change places as a conflict proceeds. Geography was a relative strength in the German context in 1939–41, but as the territorial domain of the war expanded, and as it lost command of the air, Germany found itself perilously overexposed and overextended.

8. A country can register both strongly and weakly on a particular dimension of strategy at the same time, when the conflict in question is conducted in

different ways in different geographies. Napoleon's 'Spanish ulcer', which cost him 40,000 troops a year for nearly six years, provided a semi-self-contained examination of the Napoleonic RMA, which the French failed miserably.[73]

9. RMAs are never strictly unilateral, and differing sequential, endeavours. Instead, when there is a clear RMA leader, as usually is so, other polities, some of like general strength, soon will produce their own RMA (or counter-RMA) variants. This enquiry accommodates the point by identifying both German and British versions of the First World War RMA, and US and Soviet variants of the nuclear RMA.

The story lurking starkly in Table 6.1 can be explained in terms of eight broad points.

First, the Napoleonic RMA is defined by a fusion of unusual advantages on the human (people), social, and command dimensions of strategy, married to enabling political, military administrative, military theoretical, and military operational strengths. And, need one add, the synergisms that created this highly personalised RMA could work their partially nonlinear magic because revolutionary France in the 1790s truly was the land of political opportunity for competent and lucky military adventurers. Crisis was ever a time of opportunity. The military methods, ideas, and weapons with which Napoleon 'did' his RMA in the field were, as noted, by no means personal to him or known only to the French.[74] What made Napoleon's way of war, therefore, was not superior insight into the mysteries of the military art. Instead, 'his' RMA mainly was propelled by the human and material mass mobilised by the new nationalism, the talent liberated to rise by the destruction of the former class system, and the personal charisma and command attributes which allowed him to seize and keep the authority to execute the leading military ideas of the day on a heroic scale.

Second, the military potency of this RMA was yielded to France synergistically by many factors. They include Napoleon's truly extraordinary gifts as operational artist, his adequate – if unsteady – competence in tactics, his inheritance and acceptance of cutting-edge military theory and doctrine, the legacy of Europe's finest artillery park, and the availability of many combat veterans. The fact that France was the most populous (apart from Russia) and in theory (i.e. when properly administered) wealthy country in Europe lent the potential impulsion of mass to the military quality just noted.[75]

Of course, the military story is not all positive. The cavalry, the arm vital for reconnaissance, security, and pursuit, took years to recover from its collapse when most of the (more or less aristocratic) officers defected or fled from the Revolution. That brief period of recovery in the mid- to late 1800s was reversed abruptly and definitively by the catastrophic loss of 200,000 horses in Russia in 1812, as noted already.[76] Battle-hardened veterans are an asset, but protracted exposure to battle and, especially, to the risks of disease endemic to the wars of the period, eventually must translate into dead or crippled veterans.[77] Like his spiritual, though certainly not political or strategic, military successor, Robert E. Lee, Napoleon waged war in a style extravagant with the lives of his men. Even Napoleon's successes typically were hard-fought and extremely bloody affairs for the victor. After 1806–07 he had either to adjust his tactics to suit a generally less skilled soldiery, or he had to find compensation in areas of strength to exploit so as to offset the enervating effects of that ever blunter military instrument.

Third, it was the power of politics which lifted Napoleon to the threshold of greatness and also which provided him with the ability to mobilise the human and material resources necessary for his pursuit of glory. However, while there was strength in a political dimension to strategy which placed France at the head of the march of progress and modernity, the ugly side of French political dynamism, its chauvinistic nationalism, inevitably sparked emulative and countervailing nationalism elsewhere. The consequence abroad of the aggrandising impact of French political nationalism-in-arms, French statecraft in the unlovely guise of the Napoleonic RMA, was, of course, a counter-vailing mobilising nationalism which enabled other versions of RMA to be attempted, if not always to flourish.

Fourth, the weakness in the strength of the political dimension of French strategic behaviour prompted what is worth calling an ethical vulnerability. To be fair to the French nation, the 'criminality' of Napoleonic statecraft was more personal to its generally domestically popular leader than it was endemic in the national enterprise of the period. As Paul W. Schroeder argues convincingly, an important reason why Napoleon and his (leading) French version of the contemporary accessible RMA ultimately failed was because he was all but universally reviled in moral terms outside France.[78] The goodwill for France gained in some quarters abroad by the ideals of the Revolution, and later the respect for General Bonaparte as the bringer of order out of political chaos, were both, *seriatim*, dissipated by repeated campaigns for naked conquest and loot. Even by the standards of a cynical age which accepted war unquestioningly as a legitimate instrument of policy, Napoleon's strategic ventures were judged illegitimate and intolerable. Eventually, even had Napoleon at last genuinely been willing to settle for some particular definition of a European Order, none of his opponents would trust him to abide by its requisite terms of conduct.

Fifth, Table 6.1 logs geography as a weakness, because Napoleon sought to exercise his RMA in action over distances, and hence with the problems of time, that were apt systematically to promote severe loss of strength at the sharp end of campaign activity.[79] Because of personality and politics, Napoleon sought to command all behaviour by the Grande Armée, no matter where its articulated corps were deployed.[80] A super-centralised command system, with the commander's military household and staff acting only as narrow experts, clerks, or messengers, is fraught with peril even when the relevant battlespace is constricted and the forces are relatively small and unitary in organisation.

However, when the commander-in-chief seeks to command by remote control quite regularly over hundreds, and occasionally over thousands, of miles, across mountains, and through the hazards of enemy action, disaster is foreordained. A near-constant refrain about the Napoleonic conduct of war on the scale and over the distances characteristic after mid-1805, is the perennial damage wrought by breakdowns in command. Aside from the unhelpfully unhistorical and humanly impractical point that Napoleon should not have attempted to conduct wars simultaneously at opposite ends of the continent, and should have either selected or trained more competent corps commanders for the Marshalate, the fact remains that the communication technologies of the day were endemically a weak link in his RMA.

The sixth point follows inexorably from the fifth: the Napoleonic RMA proved logistically impracticable. Disaster was eventually certain if Napoleon's version of the contemporary RMA-in-action required consistent swift success through operational art over great distances. The days of reckoning occurred most damagingly in Russia in 1812, but they had put in brief, albeit survivable, appearances long before (particularly in Egypt, Spain, Portugal, and Poland). The failures in Napoleon's command system referred to above resulted four times in his inability to trap the principal Russian armies close to the frontier.[81] The logistical catastrophe of the extended Russian campaign, as indeed, on a much smaller scale, of the campaigns in Spain and Portugal, was borne of military operational failure. One can improvise for a short successful campaign or war. However, if it is one's strategic style to conduct campaigns without end, for unbounded political goals, over all relevant distances, eventually the sense in which 'war is the realm of chance' will prove fatal,[82] and so indeed it proved.

Seventh, we cite the compound strategic dimension of 'friction' as both a strength and a weakness of the Napoleonic RMA.[83] Such ambivalence refers to more than simply the truism that friction hinders all belligerents. Rather is the meaning here that the creation of friction of a particularly debilitating kind was central to the Napoleonic way in warfare. Napoleon, the quintessentially operational-level military artist, sought by deceptive and cunning campaign manoeuvre, as well as by grand tactics designed to unhinge the enemy on the battlefield, to unravel the opponent's plans and shatter his nerve. In short, Napoleon tried to wrong-foot the foe operationally and tactically. The Ulm manoeuvre, Austerlitz, the *bataillon carré* of corps advance before Jena-Auerstadt, and the surprise *Aufmarsch* and uncertainty (to foes) of *Schwerpunckt* before Ligny-Waterloo in 1815, all exemplify the positive effect of the creation of operational- (and grand-tactical) level friction. But friction has to be labelled a weakness as well as a strength, even in the restricted operational application accorded it here. When intended operational dexterity is executed clumsily or not at all, the friction suffered is likely largely to be suffered by its perpetrator. When superiority in command of military activity at the level of operational art is the cutting edge of an RMA-in-action, as with Napoleon's, then failure or accident bearing on this centre of gravity is fraught with a lethal level of peril.

Eighth, and finally, organisation for strategy-making and for the monitoring of strategy execution is categorised as a weakness for Napoleon because, unpoliced by a respected staff and subordinate commanders tasked or licensed to offer strategic advice, there was literally no person or process to check the Emperor's self-destructive impulse to gamble unreasonably. In common with Wilhelmine and Nazi Germany, Napoleonic France had no strategy-making organisation worthy of the name.[84] Napoleon was not obliged to listen to, let alone heed, unwelcome advice on the strategic subject of means and ends. He was, of course, sensitive to public opinion, and that opinion periodically made known its liking for the blessings of peace. Directly put, the Napoleonic RMA self-destructed because, for all its advantages, it was directed by a leader who neither knew when to stop nor had the innate good sense to protect himself by inventing an organisation that could and would tell him. One must add that Napoleon would have been as unlikely as would Adolf Hitler to have tolerated genuinely strategic advisers.

In this chapter, as in Chapters 7 and 8 to follow, the author's ambition is limited to explanation of what occurred in an RMA, historically and functionally. The vital step that remains is the one which proceeds from the explanation of 'what' to the understanding of 'why'. These case study chapters yield the data for evidence of how strategy works, inherently competitively, in the presence of an enemy with an independent, at least interdependent, will. Now we move on from the first appearance of modern war to its full-blown maturity a century later.

NOTES

1. Alarm bells should ring with an unusual insistency when one comes across a grand theorist who, disingenuously but engagingly, admits that 'This is a hunt for truly general "laws" of history': Spencer A. Weart, *Never at War: Why Democracies Will Not Fight One Another* (New Haven, CT: Yale University Press, 1998), p. 8. The most satisfactory, which is to say sceptical, treatment of 'democratic peace' theory to date, is Miriam Fendius Elman (ed.), *Paths to Peace: Is Democracy the Answer?* (Cambridge, MA: MIT Press, 1997).

2. My historical range here may not impress those who would like RMA case studies to reach back to the two military revolutions in Ancient Greece (see Victor Davis Hanson, *The Wars of the Ancient Greeks and Their Invention of Western Military Culture* (London: Cassell, 1999), chs 2, 4), but still they should serve well enough as fuel for modest theory building. We will not demonstrate the probable truth in 'truly general "laws" of history' (see n. 1 above), but an empirical base for RMA theory that includes Valmy – 1792 – and the Cuban Missile Crisis – 1962 – does offer some grounds for confidence.

3. Michael Crawshaw, 'The Impact of Technology on the BEF and its Commander', in Brian Bond and Nigel Cave (eds), *Haig: A Reappraisal 70 Years On* (Barnsley: Leo Cooper, 1999), p. 164. Benjamin S. Lambeth has made much the same point. 'Rather than wasting further energy in quarrelling over whether or not a "revolution in military affairs" is upon us, there may be merit in simply acknowledging the appearance of what used to be called, in a different context, strategic superiority': 'The Technology Revolution in Air Warfare', *Survival*, 39, 1 (Spring 1997), p. 76.

4. In 1915, Captain André Laffargue wrote a pamphlet, *The Attack in Trench Warfare*, a copy of which was captured by the Germans in a trench raid in summer 1916 and subsequently was translated and distributed to units in the field. Laffargue's ideas bore some, but only some, relation to German stormtroop tactics as they were to evolve from 1916 to 1918. See Bruce I. Gudmundsson, *Stormtroop Tactics: Innovation in the German Army, 1914–1918* (New York: Praeger, 1989), pp. 193–6. See also Timothy T. Lupfer, *The Dynamics of Doctrine: The Changes in German Tactical Doctrine During the First World War*, Leavenworth Papers 4 (Fort Leavenworth, KS: Combat Studies Institute, US Army Command and General Staff College, July 1981), pp. 38–9.

5. The sophisticated rolling or creeping forward of an artillery barrage which the infantry would hug closely was standard practice in 1918. In 1915–16, however, this idea was novel and its attempted practice perilous (to the cooperating infantry). The 'creeper' of 1918 apparently had its origins in a 'lifting' barrage at Loos in 1915 – when the barrage would lift a wall of shells from one parallel trench line to another, and then another, and so on. See J. B. A. Bailey, *Field Artillery and Firepower* (Oxford: Military Press, 1987), pp. 132–4; Paddy Griffith, *Battle Tactics of the Western Front: The British Army's Art of Attack, 1916–18* (New Haven, CT: Yale University Press, 1994), pp. 142–53; and Robin Prior and Trevor Wilson, *Command on the Western Front: The Military Career of Sir Henry Rawlinson, 1914–18* (Oxford: Blackwell, 1992), pp. 164–5. The truly creeping barrage was an innovation on the Somme in 1916.

6. As claimed in Paddy Griffith, *The Art of War of Revolutionary France, 1789–1802* (London: Greenhill Books, 1998), p. 277.

7. For example, the very title of Lawrence Freedman's well-argued and influential monograph is a challenge to much of the assertion and counterassertion in the extant RMA debate: *The Revolution in Strategic Affairs*, Adelphi Paper 318 (London: International Institute for Strategic Studies, April 1998).

8. The 'other' need not be a formally identified foe, a dominant threat, but all defence behaviour, including RMA behaviour, requires some idea of threat (external or internal). Strategic performance is only possible if there is a foe, even if it lurks only as a possibility over the horizon.

9. To employ and extend Clausewitz's distinction, the grammar, if not the policy logic, of war at sea differed from that of war on land: *On War*, trans. Michael Howard and Peter Paret (Princeton, NJ: Princeton University Press, 1976 [1832]), p. 605.

10. Historians can always find plausible reasons of personality, chance, and other contingencies why a country lost a war that it appeared to have a more than fair prospect of winning. Individuals and luck certainly can matter greatly. Nonetheless, geopolitical and geostrategic factors often point to a playing field that was far from level. In other words, while history could proceed chaotically, it was more likely than not that a Napoleonic France, or a Nazi Germany, would fail to stay the course against maritime-led foes. I seek to explain why this should be so in *The Leverage of Sea Power: The Strategic Advantage of Navies in War* (New York: Free Press, 1992), esp. ch. 5. On the British struggle with France in our period of most interest, see Piers Mackesy, *War without Victory: The Downfall of Pitt, 1799–1802* (Oxford: Clarendon Press, 1984); A. D. Harvey, *Collision of Empires: Britain in Three World Wars, 1793–1945* (London: Hambledon Press, 1992), pt 1; Christopher D. Hall, *British Strategy in the Napoleonic War, 1803–15*

(Manchester: Manchester University Press, 1992); and Rory Muir, *Britain and the Defeat of Napoleon, 1807–1815* (New Haven, CT: Yale University Press, 1996).

11. The evidentiary base for my treatment of the Napoleonic RMA and of the RMA of the First World War is somewhat, though only somewhat, different in kind from my treatment of the nuclear-led RMA. The historically earlier cases rest upon a lifetime's reading; the later case adds to reading a participatory quality. It is almost invidious to cite particular historiographical sources for the Napoleonic RMA, and thereby risk implying the exclusion of others, but the following have been especially useful on the Napoleonic way of war: J. Colin, *The Transformations of War* (London: Hugh Rees, 1912); Peter Paret, *Yorck and the Era of Prussian Reform, 1807–1815* (Princeton, NJ: Princeton University Press, 1966); David Chandler, *The Campaigns of Napoleon* (London: Weidenfeld & Nicolson, 1967); Gunther E. Rothenberg, *The Art of Warfare in the Age of Napoleon* (Bloomington: Indiana University Press, 1980); Peter Paret, 'Napoleon and the Revolution in War', in Paret (ed.), *Makers of Modern Strategy: From Machiavelli to the Nuclear Age* (Princeton, NJ: Princeton University Press, 1986), pp. 123–42; Archer Jones, *The Art of War in the Western World* (Urbana: University of Illinois Press, 1987), ch. 6; Russell F. Weigley, *The Age of Battles: The Quest for Decisive Warfare from Breitenfeld to Waterloo* (Bloomington: Indiana University Press, 1991), pt 3; Robert M. Epstein, *Napoleon's Last Victory and the Emergence of Modern War* (Lawrence: University Press of Kansas, 1994); Rory Muir, *Tactics and the Experience of Battle in the Age of Napoleon* (New Haven, CT: Yale University Press, 1998); Griffith, *Art of War of Revolutionary France*; Owen Connelly, *Blundering to Glory: Napoleon's Military Campaigns*, rev. edn (Wilmington, DE: Scholarly Resources, 1999); Vincent J. Esposito and John R. Elting, *A Military History and Atlas of the Napoleonic Wars*, 2nd edn (London: Greenhill Books, 1999); and Jay Luvaas (ed.), *Napoleon on the Art of War* (New York: Free Press, 1999).

12. Charles J. Esdaile places great emphasis upon the professionalism of Napoleon's armies. He argues persuasively that Napoleon 'did not in any sense preside over a "Nation-in-Arms", it being clear that, had he attempted to rely on this principle, his whole political system would have collapsed, which is precisely what occurred in 1814. On the contrary, raised by mass conscription though it largely was, his military machine was wholly professional, this greatly accentuating its undoubted technical merits': *The Wars of Napoleon* (Harlow: Longman, 1995), p. 54.

13. With thanks to Homer and Robert Fagles, 'That mastermind like Zeus, Odysseus led those fighters on': Homer, *The Iliad*, trans. Fagles (New York: Penguin, 1990), p. 120.

14. For Napoleon's Grand Quartier-Générale Impérial (Imperial Army Headquarters) see John R. Elting, *Swords Around a Throne: Napoleon's Grande Armée* (New York: Free Press, 1988), ch. 5. The Marshalate is scrutinised carefully in David G. Chandler (ed.), *Napoleon's Marshals*, 2nd edn (London: Weidenfeld & Nicolson, 1988).

15. Jeremy Black, *Warfare in the Eighteenth Century* (London: Cassell, 1999), p. 192.

16. Exceptionally useful treatments include Steven T. Ross, *Quest for Victory: French Military Strategy, 1792–1799* (Cranbury, NJ: A. S. Barnes, 1973), chs 1–3; John A. Lynn, *The Bayonets of the Republic: Motivation and Tactics in the Army of Revolutionary France, 1791–94* (Urbana: University of Illinois Press, 1984); Spenser Wilkinson, *The French Army before Napoleon* (Aldershot: Gregg Revivals, 1991 [1915]); and Griffith, *Art of War of Revolutionary France*.

17. 'But suppose there should arise in Europe a people endowed with energy, with genius, with resources, with government; a people which combined the virtues of austerity with a national militia and which added to them a fixed plan of aggrandisement; which never lost sight of this system; which, as it would know how to make war at small cost and subsist on its victories, would not be compelled by calculation of finance to lay down its arms. We should see that people subdue its neighbours and upset our feeble

contributions as the north wind bends the slender reeds': Jacques Antoine Hippolyte, Comte de Guibert, quoted in Wilkinson, *French Army before Napoleon*, pp. 80–1. For a freer translation, see Gérard Chaliand (ed.), *The Art of War in World History: From Antiquity to the Nuclear Age* (Berkeley: University of California Press, 1994), p. 624.

18. Although General and then First Consul Bonaparte plainly emerged in a linear way from the opportunities opened by the circumstances of the 1790s, I believe that one moves into the realm of chaotic nonlinearity after the Republic becomes the Empire in 1804. In other words, one can suggest fairly plausibly that the France which survived the protracted crisis of 1792–94 was both going to be governed by an authoritarian leader and that it was going to pose grave problems for the European balance of power. However, to cede the point is not necessarily to argue that the great French rampage which lasted for the better part of 20 years simply happened to be led (after December 1799) by Napoleon Bonaparte. Of course, Napoleon was not the only ambitious and competent military commander in Revolutionary France; he was, however, certainly in a league of his own when compared with such potential rivals as Marshal Jean-Baptiste Jourdan (1762–1833), the victor at Fleurus in July 1794, or General Jean Victor Moreau (1763–1813), the victor at Hohenlinden in December 1800, or General Charles François Dumouriez (1739–1823), who won at Jemappes in November 1792. A different judgement might apply to General Louis Charles Desaix (1768–1800), of whom Chandler comments that 'his talents were not obviously inferior to those of Bonaparte' (*Campaigns of Napoleon*, p. 229), but his early death at Marengo in 1800 cut short a glittering career.

19. Ibid., pp. 176–7.

20. This must be a matter for judgement, but in the opinion of this author a revealing contrast can be drawn between the ways of war of Napoleonic France and Nazi Germany. In the case of the latter, self-inflicted political, strategic, and operational wounds created a lethal logistical weakness. Awesome though the logistical problems were of campaigning in Russia, they were certainly surmountable by Germany in the 1940s, as had been demonstrated a generation earlier in 1917–18. By way of quite sharp contrast in circumstances, though not in outcome, Napoleon's preferred style of war inherently was logistically unsound when applied in the geography of eastern, and indeed east-central, Europe in the 1800s and 1810s. To extend the contrast, it may be recalled that both Republican France and Nazi Germany lost armies in Africa because of logistical embarrassment created and enforced by the British Navy. The points claimed here are, first, that Nazi Germany lost in the east in the 1940s because it fought incompetently, notwithstanding the theoretical feasibility of victory. Second, Napoleon lost in Russia in 1812 because he could not win. The relatively poor quality of his communications and the ponderousness of his logistics were militarily fatal. Both French and German examples cited here were cases of armies apt to be commanded in such a way that typically they campaigned on the edge of a logistically mandated oblivion. Napoleonic France was overwhelmed by the *science* of the art of war; Nazi Germany proved, no less fatally, to be largely indifferent to it. I am indebted to Elting for the telling phrase, 'the science of the art of war', *Swords Around a Throne*, p. 81.

21. The outstanding work of the period was Maurice de Saxe, 'My Reveries upon the Art of War', in Thomas R. Phillips (ed.), *Roots of Strategy: A Collection of Military Classics* (London: John Lane, 1943), pp. 95–162. See also Jeremy Black, 'Eighteenth-century Warfare Reconsidered', *War in History*, 1, 2 (July 1994), pp. 215–32, and *Warfare in the Eighteenth Century*, pp. 194–5.

22. See Chandler, *Campaigns of Napoleon*, ch. 1, and Spenser Wilkinson, *The Rise of General Bonaparte* (Aldershot: Gregg Revivals, 1991 [1930]), ch. 1.

23. Wilkinson, *French Army before Napoleon*, and Griffith, *Art of War of Revolutionary France*, are particularly useful.

24. And, if Jeremy Black is to be believed, neither were these weaknesses believed widely at the time to inhibit fatally the power of military decision. See his persuasive argument in 'Eighteenth-century Warfare Reconsidered', to the effect that, prior to the French Revolution contemporaries perceived no widespread 'crisis of strategy' caused by military ineffectiveness. Black challenges the long-held orthodox belief that eighteenth-century warfare typically was indecisive. He is especially plausible when he warns against the passing of historical judgement based upon the uncritical application of modern strategic ideas to a different strategic era.

25. Wilkinson, *French Army before Napoleon*, p. 141.

26. The .69-inch (in theory) calibre Charleville musket was in service from 1777 until 1840. Rothenburg, *Art of Warfare in the Age of Napoleon*, p. 63.

27. The Committee of Public Safety was established by the National Convention on 6 April 1793. For the system of representatives *en mission*, see Griffith, *Art of War of Revolutionary France*, ch. 3.

28. T. C. W. Blanning, *The Origins of the French Revolutionary Wars* (London: Longman, 1986), p. 174 (emphasis in original). 'Brissotin' oratory refers to the demagogic rhetoric of Jacques Pierre Brissot de Warville, who, in a speech to the Legislative Assembly on 20 October 1791, began a political campaign to have Revolutionary France seek through war a lasting solution to its security problems.

29. The Napoleonic RMA broke in the hands of its owner-operator most essentially for the same reason that the Nazi German way of war failed to deliver strategic success; both were required by the ambition of a political leader to attempt the militarily impossible. Long overdue straight talk about Napoleon's statecraft is provided by Paul W. Schroeder: 'Napoleon's Foreign Policy: A Criminal Enterprise', *Journal of Military History*, 54, 2 (April 1990), pp. 147–61; and *The Transformation of European Politics, 1763–1848* (Oxford: Clarendon Press, 1994), esp. pp. 388–95.

30. Peter Paret advises that 'the new forms of fighting [in the military revolution of the period] did not evolve in the isolation of staff college and drill-field, *nor did they follow as a matter of course from technological and political developments*. They were the expression of numerous, often conflicting, elements in their societies ...': *Yorck and the Era of Prussian Reform*, p. 3 (emphasis added). Paret is warning against the sweeping explanation which discounts contingency and what today scholars label a chaotic complexity.

31. This is not to deny that some, perhaps many, RMA proponents assert a contemporary state of crisis in US defence preparation. For example, in his latest book Admiral William A. Owens argues forcefully that 'the US military is in serious trouble today', and that 'We have a topflight force that is running on empty, performing admirably with a growing number of weapons systems ... that are twenty to twenty-five years old and are becoming obsolete.' The admiral predicts that '[t]his situation ['burnout' of service people from too high an operational tempo with aged equipment] probably cannot go on for much longer without dire results': *Lifting the Fog of War* (New York: Farrar, Straus & Giroux, 2000), p. 4. Other commentators believe that a goodly part of such a state of crisis as may afflict the US armed forces at present is the product of ill-considered RMA thinking of the kind expressed by Admiral Owens. Michael O'Hanlon, *Technological Change and the Future of Warfare* (Washington, DC: Brookings Institution Press, 2000), both rejects the RMA hypothesis and denies that there is a crisis in need of RMA treatment.

32. Connelly, *Blundering to Glory*, p. 2.

33. Given the fact that most of the literature on Napoleon as general, rather than as statesman, is strongly admiring, Frank McLynn performs a useful service when he argues that 'A close analysis reveals that he [Napoleon] has also [in addition to the legend of Napoleon the "political saviour"] been severely overrated as a military commander.'

McLynn is willing to concede that 'There can be no denying that Napoleon occupies a high rank in the military history of the ages, but he cannot be counted among the handful of peerless commanders': *Napoleon: A Biography* (London: Jonathan Cape, 1997), p. 665. McLynn has a point, as does Connelly when he argues in *Blundering to Glory* that Napoleon was a great 'scrambler', a peerless military opportunist. Neither point of view is entirely convincing, but both can contribute usefully to a properly nuanced approach to the subject.

34. For virtual historical speculation about Napoleon, see Alistair Horne, 'Ruler of the World: Napoleon's Missed Opportunities', in Robert Cowley (ed.), *What If? Military Historians Imagine What Might Have Been* (London: Macmillan, 2000), pp. 201–19.

35. The Grande Armée was a largely professional instrument of Napoleon's personal will, rather than the army of France. For the comparison, see Omer Bartov, *Hitler's Army: Soldiers, Nazis, and War in the Third Reich* (New York: Oxford University Press, 1991). Napoleon and Hitler had in common the corrupting practice of buying, perhaps renting, the loyalty of favoured military subordinates by titles, baubles of decoration, land, and plenty of hard cash.

36. See Chandler, *Campaigns of Napoleon,* pp. 191–201.

37. Antoine Henri de Jomini, *The Art of War* (London: Greenhill Books, 1992 [1862]), p. 114.

38. David Chandler, *Dictionary of the Napoleonic Wars* (Ware: Wordsworth Editions, 1999), p. 83.

39. Griffith, *Art of War of Revolutionary France,* p. 277.

40. Elting is persuasive enough when he asserts that 'The birth of the Grande Armée may be set at May 18, 1803, when England repudiated the Treaty of Amiens (signed March 27, 1802) and declared war on France'. *Swords Around a Throne,* p. 59. Also see Chandler, *Campaigns of Napoleon,* ch. 32.

41. Schroeder argues that 'one cannot understand Napoleon's foreign policy without reckoning with its essential criminality, recognizing the dark void at its center. It is not true that Napoleon merely continued or somewhat extended the normal amoral lawlessness of eighteenth-century international politics … All the eighteenth-century international crimes, including the partitions of Poland, had some system of rules, some notion of European order, however brutal and defective, in mind. Napoleon did not; that is why he could lie about it so freely on St Helena': 'Napoleon's Foreign Policy', p. 158.

42. Wilkinson reminds us that 'Between the Seven Years War and the Revolution [1763–89] metalled roads were made all over central Europe, and their creation is one of the explanations of Napoleon's rapid marches': *French Army before Napoleon,* p. 52.

43. Elting, *Swords Around a Throne,* pp. 103–6.

44. The figures are not to be entirely trusted, but the French Army has been estimated to have had a pre-war – summer 1791 – strength of approximately 155,000. By 1794 the total numbers have been estimated at 633,000 for January, 732,000 for April, and 749,000 for September: Wilkinson, *French Army before Napoleon,* pp. 139–40. According to Chandler, Napoleon's Grande Armée totalled close to 700,000 – in the field, in garrisons, and in depots – while by 1812 close to a million men were under arms for France (*Campaigns of Napoleon,* p. 333).

45. This is deliberately to ignore, for the present, Griffith's contention that there were two RMAs, French Revolutionary *and* Napoleonic. 'He presided over what was in effect only a "second" military revolution, which was neither as dramatic nor as fundamentally important as the first. It consisted of the gradual improvement of the French war machine from its very low ebb in 1792 to its eventual "finest hour" at the Boulogne camp of 1804–05, and subsequent operations on the Danube and the Saale': *Art of War of Revolutionary France,* p. 277.

46. Horatio Nelson, dispatch to Rt Hon. Sir George Rose, 6 October 1805, quoted incorrectly in A. T. Mahan, *The Influence of Sea Power upon the French Revolution and Empire, 1793–1812*, II (Boston, MA: Little, Brown, 1892), p. 186. In his *The Campaign of Trafalgar* (London: Longmans, Green, 1919), Julian S. Corbett quotes the dispatch accurately as 'Numbers can only annihilate [*sic*]' (pp. 327–8). Napoleon on land and Nelson at sea both appreciated the principle that quantity has a quality all its own. Great military enterprises require application of a great scale of *concentrated* military/naval force.

47. See Edward N. Luttwak, *Strategy: The Logic of War and Peace* (Cambridge, MA: Harvard University Press, 1987).

48. Connelly, *Blundering to Glory*.

49. Geoffrey Wawro, *Warfare and Society in Europe, 1792–1914* (London: Routledge, 2000), p. 22.

50. 'I lay no claim to the creation of these principles [of war], for they have always existed, and were applied by Caesar, Scipio, and the Consul Nero, as well as by Marlborough and Eugene; but I claim to have been the first to point them out, and to lay down the principal chances in their applications'. Jomini, *Art of War*, pp. 127–8. Rarely was false modesty so false.

51. A claim well expressed by Colin. 'If we take any of the most brilliant of Napoleon's projects, and compare them with the corresponding plans of his adversaries, we shall hardly perceive any difference. What decided victory was the manner of execution, promptitude in resolutions and in movements': *Transformations of War*, p. 253.

52. Archibald Wavell, *Generals and Generalship* (New York: Macmillan, 1943), p. 3.

53. In addition to the works cited in this chapter thus far, see Paddy Griffith (ed.), *Wellington Commander: The Iron Duke's Generalship* (Chichester: Antony Bird Publications, 1984); David G. Chandler, *On the Napoleonic Wars: Collected Essays* (London: Greenhill Books, 1994); Philip J. Haythornthwaite and others, *Napoleon: The Final Verdict* (London: Arms and Armour Press, 1996); Jac Weller, *On Wellington: The Duke and his Art of War* (London: Greenhill Books, 1998); and Gordon Corrigan, *Wellington: A Military Life* (London: Hambledon & London, 2001). Because of the meteoric pace of his rise to power, Napoleon, an artilleryman, never commanded infantry at the regimental level. For most of his career he dealt in grand strategy, strategy, and grand tactics (operational art), not in tactics for troops. His lack of feel for the handling of infantry in battle was to punish him with real severity at Waterloo. See Andrew Roberts, *Napoleon and Wellington* (London: Weidenfeld & Nicolson, 2001), pp. 12–13.

54. For the course of military events there are no adequate substitutes for Chandler, *Campaigns of Napoleon*, and Esposito and Elting, *Military History and Atlas of the Napoleonic Wars*.

55. Owing to poor intelligence and command and control, Napoleon overwhelmed 64,000 foes with nearly 100,000 men at Jena, while Marshal Davout brilliantly defeated the bulk of the enemy army at Auerstadt, when only 27,000 soldiers of the Grande Armée defeated no fewer than 50,000 Prussians and their allies.

56. Luttwak, *Strategy*, p. 4.

57. 'Within the limits set by its size, an army's worth as a military instrument equals the quality and quantity of its equipment multiplied by what, in the present study, will be termed its "Fighting Power". The latter rests on mental, intellectual, and organizational foundations; its manifestations, in one combination or another, are discipline and cohesion, morale and initiative, courage and toughness, the willingness to fight and the readiness, if necessary, to die. "Fighting Power", in brief, is defined as the sum total of mental qualities that make armies fight': Martin van Creveld, *Fighting Power: German and US Army Performance, 1939–1945* (Westport, CT: Greenwood Press, 1982), p. 3. For military effectiveness, see Allan R. Millett and Williamson Murray (eds), *Military Effectiveness*, 3 vols (Boston, MA: Allen & Unwin, 1988).

58. Epstein, *Napoleon's Last Victory*, p. 24.
59. It is interesting to see two first-rate historians appearing to drive on both sides of the street at the same time with respect to the German style in war in 1939–42. On the one hand, Williamson Murray and Allan R. Millett advise us that 'In no sense did German success represent a revolution in military affairs; rather, an evolutionary process of developing a combined arms doctrine for mobile warfare and committing their forces to hard training provided the German advantage.' But, on the other hand, they discuss the evolution of German methods for land warfare in a chapter suggestively entitled 'The Revolution in Military Operations': *A War to be Won: Fighting the Second World War, 1937–1945* (Cambridge, MA: Harvard University Press, 2000), p. 82 and ch. 2 respectively.
60. The idea of inconsistent learning, even of apparently chaotic learning and forgetting, has not received much attention by scholars. Three models of learning dominate studies of generalship: (1) degree of competence is assumed to be steady over time; (2) learning is assumed to be cumulative and linear; (3) learning and competence are judged or assumed to ascend steadily, then to peak (a 'prime' time of skill), and then to decline. An important study of First World War generalship refutes all three models. 'It appears, then, that the exercise of command on the Western Front was not a consistent process of learning. To the misfortune of those required to carry out these operations, lessons already mastered might then go disregarded and have to be learned all over again': Prior and Wilson, *Command on the Western Front*, p. 88.
61. In this campaign, Napoleon achieved a surprise forward concentration, and then he deceived Wellington and wrong-footed him as to his operational intentions. Having set the stage brilliantly, Napoleon proceeded to lose the plot. He demonstrated a fatal lack of grip for tactical control over his key subordinates (who were poor selections, anyway, albeit from an admittedly shrunken list of candidates in 1815), he showed a lethal lack of energy, he failed to complete the hard-fought victory he achieved over Marshal Blücher at Ligny, allowing the Prussians to retire in tolerably good order *towards* the Allied Anglo-Dutch army of Wellington, and he waged – actually permitted Marshal Ney to wage – a tactically awesomely incompetent (not merely unimaginative) battle at Waterloo. And yet still Waterloo was nearly a French victory.
62. Connelly, *Blundering to Glory*.
63. Clausewitz, *On War*, pp. 566–73.
64. See Paret, *Yorck and the Era of Prussian Reform*; Rothenberg, *Art of Warfare in the Age of Napoleon*, esp. ch. 6; idem, *Napoleon's Great Adversary: Archduke Charles and the Austrian Army, 1792–1814* (New York: Sarpedon, 1995); Epstein, *Napoleon's Last Victory*; and Esdaile, *Wars of Napoleon*.
65. Brian Bond, *The Pursuit of Victory: From Napoleon to Saddam Hussein* (Oxford: Oxford University Press, 1996), ch. 2, is outstanding in perception and clarity.
66. According to Napoleon these are the only sources of 'knowledge of the higher parts of war': Luvaas (ed.), *Napoleon on the Art of War*, p. 24.
67. On this issue, compare the contrasting opinions in Chandler, *Campaigns of Napoleon*, p. 340, and Epstein, *Napoleon's Last Victory*, pp. 168–9. It is Epstein's view that the Austrians, in particular, improved, rather than that the Grande Armée deteriorated, as veterans left the colours and as more and more foreigners entered the ranks.
68. At its creation in May 1804 the Imperial Guard totalled 8,000 men. In 1814, it peaked at the size of an army: 117,482. Chandler, *Campaigns of Napoleon*, p. 338.
69. Ludendorff divided the German Army on the Western Front into 'attack' and 'trench' divisions. The former comprised fully a quarter of the total and suffered catastrophic losses in the four great offensives of 1918. The German Army suffered close to 2,760,000 casualties (dead, seriously wounded, prisoners of war, and deserters) in 1918. As Tim Travers reminds us, 'The highest losses occurred in the Mobilisation or Attack

divisions, containing the elite of the German Army': *How the War Was Won: Command and Technology in the British Army on the Western Front, 1917–1918* (London: Routledge, 1992), p. 154. In the Second World War, from a modest beginning with the organisation of three divisions in November 1939, the Waffen-SS by 1945 had grown to be a semi-autonomous army of 38 divisions (21 of which were foreign-manned) and close to 800,000 soldiers. S. P. Mackenzie, *Revolutionary Armies in the Modern Era: A Revisionist Approach* (London: Routledge, 1997), ch. 9, is interesting.

70. Of course, this aphorism is oxymoronic. If military method and political context are severely out of phase, that method cannot be 'right'.

71. It is ironic that 'German' strategic history in the nineteenth century shows both sides of this problem. On the one hand, Napoleon failed to solve his German challenges by military means. His treatment of Prussia, inter alia, in 1806–07 created an ultimately fatal political, then military, set of difficulties for France which matured in 1813–15. On the other hand, not understanding its own recent history, the new Imperial Germany after 1871 followed the Napoleonic path by seeking a military solution to its political, and geopolitical, difficulties of security.

72. Travers, *How the War Was Won*, pp. 99, 175.

73. David Gates, *The Spanish Ulcer: A History of the Peninsular War* (New York: W. W. Norton, 1986), remains exceptional among modern studies. For a strictly military history of French problems in the Peninsula, viewed from the perspective of its British foe, Jac Weller, *Wellington in the Peninsula, 1808–1814* (London: Greenhill Books, 1992), merits classic status.

74. Jeremy Black risks exaggeration, but is generally persuasive, when he writes as follows: 'The French Revolution did open up new possibilities, and it was these logistical and manpower factors rather than any significant tactical changes that explain early French victories. Later French defeats resulted not from France's opponents adopting her tactics, but rather from their copying French methods of raising larger armies, particularly in the case of Austria and Prussia. Tactics, while modified, remained essentially the same. Corps and divisions were evolutionary developments with roots in the eighteenth century, not products of Revolutionary France': 'Eighteenth-Century Warfare Reconsidered', pp. 231–2.

75. In 1800 France had a population of 33 million, whereas its most persistent foes, Austria and Britain, had populations of only 10 and 15 million respectively.

76. Chandler, *Campaigns of Napoleon*, p. 853.

77. Paradoxically, as noted earlier in the text, Napoleon was unduly solicitous of the lives and general wellbeing of his Imperial Guard, which truly was an army within the army. Membership of the 'Old Guard' required experience in two campaigns and five years' service (ibid., p. 339).

78. Schroeder, 'Napoleon's Foreign Policy'.

79. On what is known as the loss-of-strength gradient, see Kenneth E. Boulding, *Conflict and Defense: A General Theory* (New York: Harper & Brothers, 1962), pp. 245–9.

80. For an insightful analysis notably empathetic to the Napoleonic purpose and method in command, see Martin van Creveld, *Command in War* (Cambridge, MA: Harvard University Press, 1985), ch. 3.

81. Chandler, *Campaigns of Napoleon*, p. 856.

82. Clausewitz, *On War*, p. 101.

83. Ibid., pp. 119–21.

84. See MacGregor Knox, 'Conclusion: Continuity and Revolution in the Making of Strategy', in Williamson Murray, Knox, and Alvin Bernstein (eds), *The Making of Strategy: Rulers, States, and War* (Cambridge: Cambridge University Press, 1994), esp. pp. 615–21.

7

Case Study II: The RMA of the First World War

The First World War has no close rivals as a theatre of controversy for combative historians. Despite the passage of more than eighty years since the guns fell silent at 1100 hours on 11 November 1918, intellectual firepower ranging over many aspects of the war is livelier that ever. To the longstanding debates on the war's origins and precipitating causes,[1] and the merits or otherwise in its characteristic higher generalship,[2] have been added disagreements about the skill with which the war was conducted tactically and operationally. To a social scientist whose professional focus typically is on the near future (e.g. the contemporary RMA debate), it can be quite startling to realise that virtually every major question one can ask about the First World War is as yet not settled beyond reasonable doubt by scholarship. Citing a stream of innovative studies which began to appear in the 1980s, Williamson Murray claims persuasively that it was only with the appearance of those recent works

> that we have finally began to understand the World War I battlefield. We still do not have an equivalent work [to those by Lupfer and Travers] for the French, Italian or Russian armies. If historians who possess the documents and unlimited time have taken seventy years to unravel the changing face of the battlefield, one should not be surprised that the generals had some difficulty during the war.[3]

Fortunately for our study, much of the historians' combat about the First World War, though fascinating, falls short of posing a potential threat to the integrity of these proceedings. Indeed, some of the more traditionally active zones of historians' contentions seem notably unlikely to shed much useful light on strategic history. For example, it is not obvious that further argument about Sir Douglas Haig's style of command, and performance in generalship, can yield more nuggets of clarification – unless such argument is tied closely to study of the effectiveness of his army.[4] Similarly, finely grained comparison of German and Allied (especially British) military–technical competencies as contributions to combat proficiency also stand in dire peril of missing the all-important strategic point. Specifically, the armed forces of the Allies did their strategic job well enough, while those of the Central Powers did not. It is all too easy for careful historians of the tactical and the operational conduct of the First World War so to lose the plot of a necessary strategic perspective that ironically they mirror in their errors those of their German subjects. Some of the new scholarship on the First World War, heralded by the appearance in 1981 of Timothy Lupfer's paean of praise for the changes in German tactical doctrine, has been vastly impressed by German military excellence. In defence and on offence, we are told, the German Army had the combat edge. The literary arguments are powerful, while the unilateral detail of German achievement is telling indeed. There is, however, a need somehow to account for the embarrassingly inconvenient fact of German defeat. To staple together in an analytically convincing way the odd couple of alleged tactical excellence and strategic incompetence is a task beyond most historians. For example, there is something deeply unsatisfactory about these summative thoughts by Bruce Gudmundsson:

> That the excellence that was achieved in the realm of tactics did not win the war for Germany does not make the revolution that occurred between 1914 and 1918 any less significant.[5]

Gudmundsson sacrifices a major strategic truth – that German arms did not fight well enough to win – in order to record a minor one – that a revolution in tactics was effected. Semi-plausibly he proceeds to argue that

> The failure of the German Army in 1918 was not a failure then of German tactics at the squad, platoon, company, battalion, regimental, division, or even army level, but a failure of German operational art, German strategy, and German national policy.[6]

By analogy, a sports journalist might extol at great length the multi-dimensional skills of a football team in all aspects of the playing of the game, while blaming the strange fact of persistent defeat on the coach, team management, and the schedule. If tactical superiority should have led the way to operational and then strategic, for ultimate political, success in any great conflict, it was in the First World War.[7] Armies that reliably win tactically, which is to say fight more effectively than do their enemies, win wars. It is really as simple as that. They may not win elegantly or cheaply, but still they win. A relevant moral of this analysis is to the effect that when we read expert studies which purport to show the amateurishness and general clumsiness of the British Expeditionary Force (BEF), contrasted with Teutonic military skill and dexterity, what seems not to add up truly does not compute. We need to remember not only what Clausewitz wrote about war being a duel but also that History, unlike some historians, does not award marks for style.

The test of an army is how well it fights. The test of strategy is how well it uses force to meet the demands of policy. Our focus here is upon how, and how well, the major belligerents in the First World War learned the trade of modern warfare. More specifically, across the many dimensions to strategy what choices were made which were intended to exploit areas of relative strength and offset those of relative weakness? The RMA theme itself usefully directs enquiry to military performance overall. The theme of strategic behaviour emphasised here provides a constant reminder that military performance cannot be assessed intelligently save with reference both to the enemy and to the possibly fluctuating political purpose of it all.

Although one needs to be alert to the temptations and sins of patriotic historiography, it is scarcely surprising that the reputation of the BEF of 1914–18 should have grown by leaps and bounds as the result of the close scrutiny it has received by historians of recent years.[8] One would like to say it was inevitable that a new breed of military historians eventually would notice that there was something askew about the orthodox picture. How did upper-class Edwardian bumblers,[9] rigidly and unimaginatively leading a docile mass of wartime amateurs (volunteers and then conscripts),[10] manage to beat the supposedly tactically excellent principal military force of the continental superpower of the period? Obviously, the favourable (im)balance of resources of most kinds was important. But could it be that among the British 'butchers and bunglers' of 1914–18 were men who were indeed up to their jobs of leading an army which knew its business by 1917–18?[11] Today, the 'butchers and bunglers' image of 1914–18 generalship has been belatedly demolished as the nonsense that it largely is. Nonetheless, some military historians are prone to veer towards judgements which implicitly appear to rest upon a beau-ideal notion of proper generalship for the period,[12] while conceptual rigidities can bedevil historical assessment. Just as the grand idea of a First World War RMA is a long retrospective scholar's invention, so the idea that by 1918 two substantially rival concepts of warfare – traditional infantry and artillery-led, versus mechanical – contended for dominance, also is the product of speculative theory. Tim Travers, the leading advocate of the thesis that two styles of war beckoned the BEF in 1918,[13] commits a classic scholarly error by criticising the British High Command for failing to pursue more consistently a character of combat packaged conceptually by himself in the 1980s and 1990s.

This chapter proceeds schematically as did Chapter 6. The candidate RMA of the First World War is advanced for understanding within the framework of the standard nine-step RMA 'life-cycle' presented earlier. That functional, but also substantially historical and largely descriptive, discussion[14] is succeeded by brief commentary on how this alleged RMA worked as strategic behaviour.

THE GREAT ARTILLERY WAR[15]

The leading edge of military-historical scholarship on the First World War today engages in sharp fire-fights on everything save for the relative significance of its subject. J. P. Harris is not especially controversial when he states as fact that 1914–18 'witnessed the most rapid evolution in the art of war yet known'.[16] Though now near-orthodox among scholars, this claim would have seemed no less than startling as recently as 1980. Needless to add, perhaps, the new tactical and operational scholarship on the First World War has yet to penetrate far into the coffee-table and documentary television markets, or indeed into a general public consciousness educated by the supreme awfulness of the worst day in British military history (after King Harold's defeat in 1066), 1 July 1916, the first day on the Somme.[17] Harris's judicious claim repeats the opinion expressed by Jonathan Bailey in an extraordinarily influential study. Bailey, significantly a very serious artilleryman as well as a bold historian, has asserted that

> Between 1917 and 1918, a Revolution in Military Affairs (RMA) took place which, it is contended, was more than merely that; rather it amounted to a Military Revolution which was that most significant development in the history of war to date, and remains so. It amounted to the birth of what will be called the Modern Style of Warfare with the advent of *'three dimensional'*, artillery indirect fire as the foundation of planning at the tactical, operational and strategic levels of war. This was indeed so revolutionary that the burgeoning of armour, airpower and the arrival of the Information Age since then amount to no more than complements to it – incremental technical improvements to the efficiency of the conceptual model of the Modern Style of Warfare – and they are themselves rather its products than its peers.[18]

Far from Bailey's argument being challenged, the years that have elapsed since he wrote the words quoted have seen his view extensively endorsed. His conceptualisation of what was effected in 1917–18 was, so it seems, just what the world of historical scholarship was waiting for.[19] It required an artilleryman–historian to have the confidence to place the 'revolutionary' label on what widely had come to be appreciated as a period of exceptionally rapid change. So what did occur in the art of war in those terrible four years, and why?

The RMA of the First World War was invented and carried through by great military machines which found themselves baffled and frustrated by the failure of the extant legacies of previous RMAs to deliver tactical and operational, let alone strategic, success. The character of warfare which failed in 1914–16 may be described as Napoleonic with an industrial base. Following the Napoleonic model, 'the German method of strategy' of the second half of the nineteenth century produced swift army-, even regime-, smashing victories.[20] The method

embodied excellence in staffwork, in short-range logistics, much hard march-
ing, mobile firepower, and some bold operational artistry (not to mention the
good fortune of truly incompetent foes). German military studies believed
they had found in classical sources, but above all else in Napoleon's signature
manoeuvre sur les derrières, the magical elixir which guaranteed success.
Envelopment, even double envelopment (*après* Hannibal's bloody triumph at
Cannae), was vital for annihilation. As was to happen again, in 1940–41,
German military planners before the First World War exaggerated the degree
to which their (not so recent) victories were achieved by the genius in Prussian
method, rather than by luck and enemy folly. However, even if Germany's high
military reputation at home and abroad was entirely well merited, a familiar
pattern of competitive emulation had asserted itself by 1914.

> After 1870 every European army adopted the Prussian formula. They
> introduced conscription, expanded their railways and telegraphs, procured
> magazine rifles, machine guns and quick-firing artillery, set their general
> staffs the task of planning *offensive* wars in painstaking detail, and assigned
> a recklessly bowdlerised version of Clausewitz to their war colleges ...
> Forgetting that the Napoleonic 'revolution in military affairs' had lost
> its punch once every other army in Europe adopted it, these generals
> went to war in 1914 labouring under the 'short war illusion'; they were
> somehow convinced that their planning, armaments and tactics would
> defeat the enemy, even though the enemy possessed virtually the same
> technologies and doctrines that they did.[21]

Geoffrey Wawro, whose words those are, captures most of the relevant
context for the military crisis of 1914–18. The problem was not simply that
the mainstays of the German method of war had been copied abroad, but
also that that method could no longer succeed in the confines of the strategic
geography of western Europe, unless, that is, the enemy made *and persisted
with* operational level errors of truly Homeric proportions.[22] In August 1914,
with its operational and tactical recklessness, France did its best to flatter the
potential of a style of warfare which ordinary military competence should thwart
without great distress.[23] By imperfect analogy, the mass armies of industrial
Europe that marched to war in 1914 (having detrained at their frontiers) were
not unlike the armies of 1809–12, or perhaps the great nuclear war machines
of the superpowers from the late 1950s to the close of the Cold War. In each
of those historical cases, there were reasons structural to the context why rapid
and decisive military victory either could not be achieved at all, or in the
nuclear regard could not be secured at tolerable cost. With hindsight–foresight
it is child's play for historians to identify solutions to problems which, to the
historical actors, were revealed as such only cumulatively, piece by piece. In
practice, the RMAs of the early 1800s, 1914–18, and 1945–89, all carried the
seeds of their own self-limitation. The Napoleonic RMA could not overcome

its technical and human problems of operational-level command in its gigantic, but disaggregated, armies; the RMA of the First World War was limited by technical problems of real-time battlespace command and especially by the absence of robust means for rapid exploitation of initial tactical success; while the nuclear RMA, as we shall see, was substantially confined in its strategic utility by the sheer, excessive, destructiveness of its weapons.

This chapter tells how yet another modern style of warfare was invented, perhaps discovered – since almost all of its constituent elements already were present in 1914–16 – when the contemporary model failed dismally in the field in war. As noted already, the dominant paradigm of modern war in 1914 was thoroughly Napoleonic. Field guns laid directly over open sights would soften up the enemy's infantry; friendly infantry in waves or columns would then advance alone to the assault; and finally cavalry would try to exploit the infantry's success and turn the enemy's retreat into a rout (that is, if he was not double-enveloped, i.e., surrounded, and compelled to surrender). By 1918 that paradigm was long lost and buried together with its victims. From spring 1917 to the end of the war, an increasingly mature new paradigm of land warfare had indirect artillery fire enable decentralised combined-arms combat teams of infantry to seize and hold bite-size chunks of the enemy's defended zone. Tanks may or may not be used to crush barbed wire, depending upon the army in question, the task, and the terrain, while aircraft are variably useful, depending upon the weather and time of year (in daylight). This 'modern style of warfare' of 1917–18 vintage has been the model for regular land–air (or air–land) combat until the present day. Such modern war takes as a given the likelihood that the enemy has no flanks to be menaced (which is not always the case, of course). Instead, the mission is to achieve penetration of what amounts to a continually fortified zone.

Unlike some other military historians who are quick to award more points to one, rather than another, variant of this new paradigm of land warfare, Bailey wisely argues that:

> The interaction between the strategic setting and available technology still governs the fundamental choice – discerned in 1918 – at the operational and tactical levels of war; between manoeuvre supported by firepower and firepower supported by manoeuvre.[24]

In other words, there was no set formula, no all-cases correct way, to employ the tactical elements in 1918 for superior military effectiveness.[25] Nonetheless, strategic history does record unambiguously that the Allied practice of RMA, inter alia, in 1917–18 as strategic behaviour proved conclusively superior to the rival German effort. One must never forget that history crowns as victor neither the belligerent who achieves understanding of the most elegant style of contemporary war that is feasible, nor even necessarily the belligerent who can best practice that style. War is not only about superior military art. After all, military art has to serve a political master via strategic direction. The need to emphasise this point is one reason why RMA theory (and practice) is apt to mislead if it is developed in isolation from the theory (and practice) of strategy.

Preparation
By way of sharp contrast with the Napoleonic RMA, the RMA of the First World War did not amount to the inspired command of a well-nigh ready-fashioned military instrument. Rather did the parents of RMA between 1914 and 1918 have to make the revolution (in fairly distinctive national variants) in response to the manifest military crisis created by the abject failure of existing ways in war. A wide gulf divided British (maritime) from German (continentalist) strategic history in the century separating Waterloo from First Ypres. In part as a consequence, large differences separated British and German strategic and military cultures. The RMA effected in the First World War nonetheless was to reflect a generally common military enlightenment. A multi-year (we will not say long) war is a great equaliser of military skills. An RMA carried through in wartime enjoys a pace and conclusive realism in field testing that precludes scope for much of the debate that peacetime innovation can attract.

This RMA was not the product of one man, or even of several men (note its lack of eponymity), and it did not have as its centrepiece some arguably 'dominant' new weapon or technology. It did, however, have a dominant category of weapon, albeit not a new one, in the artillery. It would be technically true, but trivialising, to claim that just about every machine and military method or skill that played a significant team role in the RMA of 1917–18 either existed physically in earlier form, or at least had been conceived by fertile imaginations (e.g. the tank), prior to the war.[26] With respect to this RMA, although we can label developments over the course of the preceding century as RMA-preparatory, it would be more correct to see those years as preparation for what occurred in action as a general military crisis in 1914–16. The raw material from which the RMA would be fashioned in the midst of war was of course more or less present as potentialities in earlier years.

The political, social, technological, and industrial forces that found expression in the battle-shaped competitive military instruments of RMA of 1917–18 were the same forces which, *guided by a different paradigm of large-scale modern war*, produced the 'trenchlock' of 1914–16. If firepower especially in the forms of indirect artillery bombardment and automatic weapons was key to the unravelling of fortified fronts, it was the developments in firepower that had enabled flankless fortified fronts to be held against the assault craft of the day.

It follows that the war waged in late 1917 and 1918 can be traced in its fundamental preparation to the great changes which gave birth to the modern state, to the modern idea of the national security community, and the industrial revolutions of coal and iron, and then steel, oil, and electricity. The Military Revolutions, or RMAs, of *c.* 1600 to *c.* 1900 ultimately found military expression in mass conscript armies, which were mobilised and then supported by rail, were equipped with the best weapons that modern science and technology could devise, and were commanded and administered by general staffs of variable excellence. Alas, the factors just cited comprised the fuel of military, leading to strategic, and political, crisis. The new weapons and other useful devices (e.g. barbed wire) invented and developed from Waterloo to Ypres, when employed in warfare on a large scale against a fairly symmetrical foe, had the cumulative effect of denying the power of decision to the fight.

Preparation for what, in retrospect, well warrants ascription as the RMA of 1917–18, took the form of three years of trial and error on offence and defence as the belligerents struggled to design, test, and rearm for a practicable paradigm of flankless land warfare. That brief period of wartime preparation provided both new tactics for combined-arms warfare and, no less essential, the quality and quantity of machines and munitions necessary for new tactics to be applied. Focus on the RMA of the First World War must not obscure the significance of mass. By 1918, the two very tired sides in the war in the west were by and large more than competent in the tactical conduct of land warfare,[27] with each national army inventing and practising the form of RMA that best fitted its circumstances. Probably it is no exaggeration to claim that although neither had a notable edge in military prowess after four years of war, that condition of rough equality enabled the superior resources of the Allies to function as an uneven playing field. It would be difficult to exaggerate the importance of the conclusions reached by Ian Malcolm Brown in his path-breaking study of British logistics.

> Geddes's reforms of the winter of 1916 and spring of 1917 [brought in as Director-General of Transportation to reorganise BEF communications] released the constraints on both operations and strategy. From 1917 onwards, and particularly in 1918, the very excellence of the BEF's administration largely freed Haig and his subordinates to innovate and make offensive plans much more rapidly … the impact of administration in 1918 may be called subtly profound – it is not obvious, but it allowed the BEF to launch a series of material–heavy offensives in 1918 that, along with the rest of the allied effort, made clear to the German high command that the allies had become capable of winning the war on the battlefield.[28]

The BEF's logistical and general administrative excellence became deadly as the British Army overall became truly competitive with the Germans in fighting skills.

One should not need to add that the campaigns of 1914–16 were not intended as preparation for an RMA in 1917–18 which would resolve the tactical problems of taking and holding ground in the face of modern firepower. Such teleology is a conceit of the retrospective historian or theorist. In the successive years from 1914 to 1917, either both sides (1914, 1916) or the Allies only (in 1915, France; in 1917, France then Britain) believed that it had cracked the code for strategically decisive military success. Grim though it is to characterise the war in this way, the four years of the conflict can be seen as a race for each belligerent between, on the one hand, the acquisition of education in modern war and the raising of the military instrument to apply that education and, on the other hand, the progressive depletion of the moral and material resources to prosecute the combat. War weariness at home and at the front could impose a lethal enervation upon armies which had, at last, found fairly reliable tactical ways to fight well.

Recognition of challenge
It would be a grave teleological error to work backwards from the new style(s) of land warfare of 1918 to the point of departure in 1914, and interpret the intervening four years of bloody military education as a race to be first to a finishing line called competence in modern war. At first, the armies of 1914 did not know that they were not competent. Moreover, when all parties' ways in warfare failed to deliver even a remote semblance of victory, it was less than self-evident to nearly everyone that the necessary course of instruction and softening up of the foe must extend over three to four years.[29] To clarify that point yet further by analogy: the task of frustrated military men in 1914–17 can be likened to the mission of mountaineers committed to ascend Mount Everest, except that they do not, *and cannot*, know the height of the mountain. By way of an unsettling postmodern thought, *our* Mount Everest for the Great War analogy has no stable altitude. With the inestimable value of hindsight, we can appreciate much of the whole scale and difficulty of the climbs that the military machines were ordered by policy to attempt from 1914 to 1918. Such knowledge is strictly a privilege granted by historical perspective.

Objectively speaking, certainly the German, British, and French Armies recognised and rose as far as conditions allowed to meet the challenge of modern war. But that claim represents an Olympian overview. As late as September 1918, for example, it was less than crystal clear to Allied soldiers just how much of a challenge the German Army still posed (e.g. must we fight on through the winter and into 1919?).[30] Contrary to the argument of some historians, Tim Travers in particular, it is not persuasive to suggest that in the Hundred Days campaign of August–November 1918 the BEF demonstrated a lack of reliable grip on the challenge of modern war.[31] That only modest use of tanks was made by the BEF in the closing three months of the war reflected battlefield conditions and the availability of machines, not an absence of enthusiasm for a properly 'mechanical' style of modern war.

RMA theory has yet to offer much worth reading on the subject of 'revolutionary' behaviour as a response to challenge that is explicitly acknowledged. Writing historically, one size does not fit all cases. It can be difficult to 'get the RMA right', perhaps even to effect the right RMA, if one is not sure of the question. For example, if the atomic bomb was the answer, was there a question worth addressing with respect to German and Japanese atomic weapon research?[32] Recall that although early in the Second World War there had been excellent grounds to be anxious about German (and Japanese) research in atomic physics, the grounds were notably less solid for actually detonating the nuclear RMA in action in August 1945 – by which time the Allied policy rationales included military expediency and diplomatic effect, not plausibly possible Japanese atomic bombs. Fast forwarding with the same question, 'if an information-led RMA is the answer today, what is the strategic question?' How well defined, persuasive, and important is the challenge that the makers of a particular RMA acknowledge and strive to overcome?

Of the candidate great RMAs (or MRs) examined in some detail in this book, that of 1914–18 was directed literally at the most concrete of existential challenges. The tactical, and hence the operational and strategic, stalemate on the Western Front presented a clear and all too present danger to political goals. The Napoleonic RMA was pulled full-throttle into life by the ambitions of one man who inherited a military system which did not need to raise its game very far in order to be in a league of military effectiveness all its own, for a while at least. The nuclear RMA was pushed into reality by political fears which, though rational and reasonable, rested upon evidence and argument about enemy activity of a decidedly speculative kind. In the 1990s, the information-led RMA occurred, if it did, apparently bereft of significant political or strategic propulsion. The RMA of 1914–18 could hardly be more different.

The fundamental challenge in 1914–18 was supremely tactical in nature and scarcely required active probing thought for its recognition. The belligerent armies in the west could not outflank each other laterally, or vertically over-head. It followed that they needed to discover reliable means to penetrate the enemy's front and then exploit the break-in to secure a breakthrough for the achievement of operational-level success. Definition of challenge to tactical success emerged rapidly from the time when Helmut von Moltke issued the order to 'entrench and hold' above the River Aisne on 10 September 1914.[33] Though conceptually constant, the tactical challenge that the RMA of 1914–18 had to overcome was supremely dynamic. As the belligerents learned fitfully how to attack, so also they learned how to defend. Moreover, given that the defence is structurally advantaged in land warfare, and never in modern times more so than when railways could provide operational reinforcement more rapidly than footpower could penetrate deep battlezones,[34] the side typically playing defence (the German on the Western Front) characteristically was playing on a field with a favourable tilt. As the Allies' art in attack improved, impressively if unsteadily, from 1914 to 1918, so – alas – did the Germans' art in defence.

The challenge recognised in late 1914 was to devise ways, and acquire the military means, to break into and through a thinly scraped broken line of trenches. But by spring 1917 the task was to penetrate a three-zone elastic defence averaging seven miles in depth wherein a thinly held forward outpost realm served as a breakwater for a 'battle zone' or main line of resistance (MLR), comprising probably three lines of trenches and other (all around) fortified positions, which covered the artillery and the counterattack divisions which were held in and behind a 'rearward zone'.[35] Where feasible the 'battle zone' would be sited in terrain masked (dead ground) from the Allied attacker, and artillery would be well integrated with the defensive scheme. The Germans' emphasis was on flexibility. By way of a sharp contrast with their expensive tactical practice in 1916 at Verdun, and especially on the Somme, the new German defensive doctrine after winter 1916–17 sought to defeat Allied assaults on the MLR, not to hold on to, or promptly recapture, every last foot of lost territory. Defending infantry could disperse into shell holes to avoid much of the enemy's barrage, if it was of the 'lifting' kind (from one linear target to another). They would hold their positions in the battle zone pending the arrival of counterattack formations, which should be able to defeat an enemy that had achieved an offensive break-in. That enemy would be heavily attrited in numbers, exhausted, and unable to mount a cohesive defence. Such was the core of the theory of defence. Every zone in the defence system would be protected by ever more expansive aprons of barbed wire. As just noted, where geographically practicable the more serious elements of the defence would be sited on reverse slopes, hidden in the remains of woods, or built into the ruins of the urban architecture of the region.

The fact that all war is a duel, and that there is a constant dialectic between offence and defence, meant that the RMA of the First World War was a race to innovate so as to make strategic progress towards a receding finishing line. The hastily improvised defences of 1914 were a poor joke when compared, say, with what Friedrich von Lossberg designed for the so-called Hindenberg Line in winter 1916–17. But so also was the art of attack of 1914–15 when compared with the complex orchestration of all-arms (sometimes) in 1917 and 1918. While the ignorant armies learned how to prevail, they learned also how to deny victory to the foe.

Parentage

The RMA of 1914–18 was authored by a cast of thousands. The tactical re-education of armies millions strong effected over the course of four years was very much driven 'from below' at what, following a literally Homeric suggestion, might well be called the working level of the war machines.[36] The rival high commands merit respect for not notably impeding innovation, indeed for providing such positive encouragement as their respective military cultures permitted. It should be unnecessary to add that military failure or disappointment on the grand scale yielded a context which proved a great enabler for bold experiment. With more or less assistance from on high, the RMA cumulatively was constructed and implemented by relatively junior officers, rather than by the names familiar to domestic publics from the newspapers (synonymous with 'the media' for 1914–18).

We are not short of names for the honour roll of parents of the RMA of 1914–18, but to provide such a listing risks misleading the reader. In both the German and the British Armies (the twin foci for the purposes of this case study) the process of tactical reform entailed constant dialogue between 'line' and 'staff'. Moreover, that dialogue was hugely decentralised, as regiments/ battalions, divisions, specialised corps, and armies each applied their experience in gargantuan training networks. Behind the static lines, 'trench (-zone) locked' from the North Sea to Switzerland, a complex architecture of battle and other training schools of all varieties proliferated.[37]

The RMA was never pursued according to a clearly articulated unified vision or doctrine. The contribution of no single person, document, or even concept of operations, neatly captures the revolution holistically. The theory and practice of direct *and predicted* artillery fire, preferably delivered unpre-registered (on the real targets), for Jonathan Bailey's three-dimensional way of war, is the closest approximation provided to date to what lies at the heart of the RMA of 1917–18.[38] His artillery-oriented interpretation of the course of the war is by far the most convincing explanation of what changed militarily, and why, in those years. Eighty-plus years of memoirs and scholarship have delivered no better theory than Bailey's.

Following Bailey, we should recognise the leading artillery colonels and generals as most truly the parents of this RMA. Haig and Ludendorff, even such army commanders as Hubert Plumer, John Monash, and Henry Rawlinson, are not the heroes of this revolution. Instead, if names we need, the roll of honour must include, for the Germans, Colonel Georg 'Durchbruch' ('Break-through') Bruchmüller (*Der Durch Bruchmüller*) and Captain Erich Pulkowski,[39] while for the British the names of most note include Generals Birch, Holland, Uniacke, and Tudor. The latter certainly were senior men, GHQ, Army, and corps-level Royal Artillery advisers, but they were not, and have not become, household names.[40] Given that there was an important mechanised dimension to the British and French version of this RMA, it is appropriate to add to the list of parents of the RMA the names of Ernest Swinton of the Royal Engineers, most plausibly described as the inventor of the 'tank', and J. F. C. Fuller, the leading theorist on the use of the tank.[41] With respect to the increasingly decentralised and combined-arms focus for infantry attack, the best-known name for theory remains Captain André Laffargue of the French Army, whose modest study, *The Attack in Trench Warfare*, probably has been accorded undue significance.[42] The practice of infantry attack, emphasising flexibility in the co-ordination of combined arms from the battalion down to the platoon and even squad levels, is associated most closely by repute with Captain Willi Rohr, the leading spirit in the German development of stormtroop tactics.[43] For the defence, although the initial inspiration (in 1915) allegedly was French, the principal nominee for the hall of fame has to be Colonel Fritz von Lossberg, who as Chief of Staff of the German Third Army in 1915–16, and subsequently wherever his expertise was most needed, served as the quint-essential 'fireman', designing and effecting systems of elastic defence in depth.[44] The Hindenburg Line of universal eponymous note should really be known as the 'Lossberg Line'.

The true parents of the RMA of the First World War were thus not commanding generals, or civilian politicians, who demanded the invention of a new, more effective, style of land warfare. Instead, they were the captains, majors, colonels, and one- and two-star generals who developed, or at least encouraged, the best contemporary military practice, as unfolding experience revealed to be the case, and who led intra-war reform by a process of example, laissez-faire and persuasion. However, no matter how widely we cast the net to recognise the vast and diverse scope of this wartime RMA enterprise, it is important not to dilute appreciation of the central, literally essential role of indirect (i.e. unobserved) and increasingly unpreregistered predicted artillery fire, and hence of the men who innovated with that arm of service.

Enabling spark
Artillery was the adjustable tool which, more than any other complementary element, unlocked the linear fortresses of 1917–18. The artillery key required both quantity and quality, and it needed skilful, certainly averagely competent, infantry to exploit its success. However, it would not be correct to argue that artillery was *the* decisive weapon in 1914–18. Artillery did not decide who won the war. But Allied competence, and better, in artillery did decide that their overall advantages in resources could be translated into military effectiveness for a strategically favourable outcome. Such was German and Allied artillery prowess by late 1917 that, ceteris paribus, limited military success became fairly reliably feasible.[45] When gross tactical errors were made, as for example when the French crowded their forward line of defence along the Chemin des Dames with troops (27 May 1918), then the artillery 'enabler' truly could open a dazzling prospect of operational victory. To enable victory to be won is not, of course, to ensure its achievement. British and German artillery in 1917–18 could create an opening for the manoeuvre force to exploit for decisive operational-level advantage, if only that force had been truly able to manoeuvre to win the deep battle.

The artillery of 1917–18 could enable success *if* the best technical practices making for accuracy were followed; *if* it was employed in sufficient mass; *if* it was controlled flexibly as the shape of battle altered; *if* geographical–tactical circumstances were permissive; *and if* the co-operating arms played their combined combat roles with sufficient skill and adequate weight.[46] In other words, the near-perfection of artillery techniques and material by 1917–18 did not constitute a silver bullet certain to deliver victory. The leading reason was that here, as historically so often, belligerents engaged in a protracted conflict could not unilaterally invent, and then with the element of surprise practise, a devastatingly novel way in war. In wartime the enemy is alert to tactical change and already is mobilised to cope with it. Isolated changes in tactical practice – for example, the German introduction of chlorine gas at Second Ypres in 1915 – typically yield only isolated and temporary advantage. The Great War did not follow any discernibly nonlinear course as a result of some individual technical tactical catalyst.[47]

Full demonstration of the belated triumph of comprehensively scientific gunnery was achieved almost serendipitously. The BEF planned a great raid at Cambrai in November 1917 to breach the Hindenburg Line, a raid designed primarily to test the massed use of tanks for the first time. The terrain in front of Cambrai was judged to be good tank country, but only if the ground was not pitted with thousands of shell holes prior to the effort of the tanks to advance. A further reason to eschew any version of the ever more monumental artillery bombardment characteristic of the material 'massification' of the war in 1916–17 was the need to preserve surprise for the tank-led assault. The BEF secretly gathered a total of 478 tanks for the raid. By the close of the first day of the battle, 179 were out of action, though only 65 because of enemy action.[48] The story of the initial success at Cambrai (nearly four miles gained) appeared principally to be the tale of the tank. However, useful though the tank had proved to be when employed in large numbers, particularly for crushing belts of barbed wire, the real story of Cambrai was about combined arms. If any one element threatened to unlock the German front at Cambrai, and show the way 'to the green fields beyond', it was the artillery. The key tactical 'enabler' was the artillery rather than the tank. While Cambrai had been intended to showcase the potential of the tank, in fact it demonstrated – to risk exaggeration – a near perfection of predicted artillery fire. As much by accident as by wise intent, the grand design for Cambrai, shaped to privilege the tank, happened to require the artillery to make a statement about how far it had progressed since the Somme in 1916 in scientific gunnery.[49]

Military effectiveness for strategic effectiveness is made from all of the dimensions of strategy. The argument at this juncture amounts to the claim that certainly British, and generally also German and French, artillery could 'unlock' field-fortified armies by late 1917 and 1918, *other factors permitting*. The qualification is vital, not merely dutiful or decorative. The best gunnery minds, methods, and equipment enabled military success: they sparked what now is known as the RMA of the First World War. But this artillery-led RMA could not succeed in the field by means of artillery knowledge, method, and material acquisition alone. In the same way that some corps in the BEF offered cultural resistance which impeded adoption of German- (and French-) style tactics of defence in depth,[50] so notably large elements in the German Army in the west declined in practice to obey orders and adopt the 'Pulkowski method' to achieve accurate predicted (unpreregistered) artillery fire.[51] It is one thing to know how to wage modern war, it can be quite another actually to be able to do it across the whole army. For another example, the excellence of German infantry assault technique in 1918 is well established: indeed, it was demonstrated on a modest scale in 1917 at Caporetto (20 October) and in the counterattack at Cambrai (30 November). The problem was, first, that most of the German follow-on infantry attacks in the great offensives of 1918 did not employ so-called stormtroop tactics, and, second, that elite stormtroopers suffered unsustainable losses.

If the artillery revolution of 1917–18 that sparked the RMA was to be allowed to enable victory to be won, then the whole army, and the society and government behind it, had to play their parts also. At least until the age of the nuclear-tipped ICBM (and probably not even then), wars could not be won by artillery conducting deep battle in isolation. With reference to the artillery, it is quite apparent that this 'enabling spark' for RMA taught itself through more than three years of war, 1914–17, how to do the job that the persisting stalemate unexpectedly revealed to be necessary. The artillery required scientific method, the right equipment and ammunition, sufficient quantity for quality to tell, and competence by co-operating arms for success in the whole team endeavour of modern land warfare.

Most of the scientific techniques needed by the artillery in the conditions of 1914–18 were not invented in those years. Nonetheless, it required the necessities of what amounted to siege warfare for theory and what once had been only exceptional practice to be adopted as standard operating procedure. Recall that in 1914

> Artillery training was based on the assumption that the normal method of shooting would be over 'open sights' – that is, much as a man would fire a rifle. The gun layer would look along his sights at a target that he could see from where he was standing. Obviously it was expected that the enemy would do the same.[52]

Such practices proved suicidal, even in August–September 1914. 'Direct fire was given up and virtually never used again.' But if the enemy – infantry, guns, or whatever – could not be seen, how could guns be laid upon him? The answer was summarised thus by a superior study-memoir:

> In conditions such as those of the last war artillery could only be used *effectively* if they had (1) good maps, (2) their own position accurately

located, (3) the position of enemy guns accurately located, and (4) means of laying their guns accurately on these targets without previous registration.[53]

How were these facilities to be provided? The answer, for the BEF, was the 'Field Survey Battalions, R.E. – (1) by the Map Sections, (2) by the Topo. Sections, (3) by the Observation Groups [for gun 'flash spotting'] and Sound Ranging Sections'. As contrasted with the 'open sights' firing at Le Cateau in August 1914, the state of the art in artillery use in 1918 would achieve 'an accuracy of 80 metres at a range of 4,000 metres through prediction, a similar performance (in terms of accuracy if not range) to modern guns [1987]'.[54] For the perfection of the military instrument, calibration to check for barrel wear on each gun became standard. Ammunition batches were tested for variations in manufacture. Meteorological reports were consulted for changes in air temperature (and hence density) and for wind speed and direction. Gun sites were surveyed scientifically and accurate bearings were taken from known locations in enemy positions.[55] Accurate maps of enemy-held terrain were drawn and updated as aerial reconnaissance allowed photography from above. Enemy guns – typically not a target in pre-1914 artillery doctrine, and not a priority as late as the Somme in 1916 – were located by sound and muzzle flash, as well as by direct observation from the air. The quantity, quality, variety, and sophistication of ammunition (including shell fusing) was a revolution itself in 1914–18, while the number of heavier guns, especially of the howitzer type (for higher-trajectory plunging fire), was increased exponentially.[56] Similarly, the ratio of artillerymen to infantry in armies shifted dramatically, as the artillery's role changed from a useful adjunct to infantry battle to a literally vital enabler if the infantry was to move forward at all or hold its ground.

Whatever the exact character of RMA favoured by different belligerents from battle to battle in 1917–18 (i.e. allegedly mechanised, or infantry–artillery), or stamped with approval by later armchair generals, one feature they all share is dependence upon the artillery fire-plan. In 1917–18, as in any period, there was an abundance of reasons why grand military designs might fail on the day. Distinctively unique to this RMA of the First World War is the fact that if the artillery performance was poor, the prospects for success would hover between improbable and impossible.

Strategic moment
The idea of a strategic moment can sit oddly with a long view that might rather regard such particular instances more as false dawns than as the reliable herald of revolutionary effectiveness through new ways in warfare. The reason for the apparent paradox that a strategic moment can be, indeed usually is, succeeded by military disappointment, resides in the very nature of conflict as a bilateral

(or more) struggle. Some of the theoretical writing about RMA misses the Clausewitzian point that 'war does not consist of a single short blow'.[57] Definitions of RMA that require 'a dramatic increase – often an order of magnitude or greater – in the combat potential and military effectiveness of armed forces', in Andrew Krepinevich's words, do not fit well with historical evidence which expresses the paradoxical logic of strategy.[58] Airy generalisations about RMA are prone to mislead theorists into the error of forgetting that technological and tactical transference,[59] as well as more or less parallel discovery,[60] will reduce the longevity of Krepinevich's optimistic 'dramatic increase' in military effectiveness.

Even quite plausible strategic moments can herald military performance which fizzles after a flashy start, rather than continues to dazzle as its executive military instrument matures in prowess. Indeed, because military effort is not autarkic, but is applied in a contest, it is always possible, and sometimes is probable, that a strategic moment genuinely worthy of the title will raise the curtain only on a more modern version of attrition.[61] The merit in this argument is illustrated with unusual clarity in the case of the First World War RMA. Several candidates vie for coronation as the strategic moment in this RMA. There are three German and also three Allied candidates for the strategic moment. The possible German strategic moments were: Oskar von Hutier's attack on Riga (1 September 1917); the attack by Otto von Below's Fourteenth Army (with six German and eight Austro-Hungarian divisions) at Caporetto (24 October 1917); and Ludendorff's great 'Michael' Peace Offensive (opened on 22 March 1918). The Allied candidates were: the attack by General Julian Byng's Third Army at Cambrai (20 November 1917); the relatively modest assault by General John Monash's Australian Corps (under the command of General Henry Rawlinson's Fourth Army) at Hamel (4 July 1918); and Rawlinson's spectacular offensive at Amiens (8 August 1918). Other candidates could include French (and American) performance at the opening of the Second Battle of the Marne (18 July 1918), or the breaking of the Hindenburg Line by Rawlinson's Fourth Army (with the set-piece action commencing on 29 September 1918).

The relative abundance of supportable candidates for election as the strategic moment of the First World War RMA is of no particular significance. Indeed it would be a trivial endeavour to devote space and energy to a detailed comparison of the merits in each candidate. What really does matter for our analysis is that fact that each side had a strategic epiphany. Unfortunately, the approximately parallel strategic epiphanies meant that neither side was likely to be able to exercise and then exploit its particular versions of the RMA *du jour* into the zone of decisive military effect. For the Allies (in this case, the British), the balance of argument supports the consensus among RMA theorists that Cambrai was the moment, notwithstanding the painful disappointment suffered with the successful prompt German counterattack and then the temporary, albeit frightening, defeats of spring 1918. For the Germans, the most plausible strategic moment was the enormous, though ultimately empty, victory at Caporetto.[62] These choices are not only historically persuasive in the light of long hindsight, but they endorse dominant contemporary opinion also, which is much more gratifying. The BEF's tank-led, but artillery enabled, brief triumph at Cambrai, following the undisguisable failure of Third Ypres, prompted the British prematurely to ring their church bells for the first time since 4 August 1914. As for Caporetto for the Germans, in Bruce Gudmundsson's telling judgement: 'The successful exploitation of the breakthrough at Caporetto proved to Ludendorff that the German Army had developed a tactical system capable of breaking the deadlock of trench warfare and thus permitting the resumption of manoeuvre at the operational level.'[63]

Operationally reviewed, Caporetto and Cambrai in October and November 1917 led nowhere directly. But both events showed the way forward to responsible soldiers at the time. They showcased new styles in land warfare which, with the errors of novelty reduced, might (perhaps should) deliver the overly long-anticipated strategic victory. Whereas von Hutier's success at Riga overwhelmingly was an operational-level triumph[64] – albeit with the vital assistance of sound artillery technique centrally directed by Bruchmüller – both Caporetto and Cambrai were, for the time, quite extraordinary tactical victories. They can be seen as dress rehearsals for the main event that was to be Ludendorff's four-step grand offensive in 1918. However, such teleology would be unwise. These two German successes were both shaped vitally by unique circumstances. Caporetto, for all its impressiveness, was a success in mountainous terrain against an Italian Army, which, though adequately equipped, suffered from appalling leadership. To defeat a demoralised Italian Army, led by one of the war's least competent commanding generals (General Luigi Cadorna), offered no guarantee of later success against the Anglo-French legions in France. At Cambrai, on 30 November, General von der Marwitz's Second Army applied the best in current artillery and infantry practice to pinch out the salient (five and a half miles) seized by Byng's Third Army between 20 and 29 November. Whereas the German artillery on the Isonzo at Caporetto had been concentrated in counter-battery duties against the extensive Italian artillery,[65] at Cambrai the principal task was to provide a creeping barrage in direct support of the infantry. Between them, Caporetto and the Cambrai counterattack told the German High Command that at last they had a winning ticket. Specifically, they had found and practised a method of offensive war with centralised, but tactically flexible, artillery prowess and decentralised infantry assault skills. It seemed probable to the Germans that, working well together, their new infantry and artillery tactics, when effected in the necessary mass, should reliably produce so significant a level of tactical success as to deliver operational victory. Strategic and political triumph logically and inexorably should follow.

187

The great British Cambrai tank raid on 20 November 1917 was the Allies' strategic moment, even though it showcased a more mechanised vision of future land warfare than would be the general experience in 1918.[66] If the German use of artillery at Riga, Caporetto, and then in the Cambrai counter-attack, was typically excellent, then the BEF's artillery performance at Cambrai was awesome. With no preliminary bombardment, or even registration firing, which could alert the enemy, British artillery secured a firepower dominance that allowed the tanks and infantry to advance further, and more cheaply, than had been possible in the war to date on the Western Front. This limited attack, and the German counterattack, encouraged both sides to dream and plan for success tomorrow. However, the operational, strategic, and political context of 1917–18, as well as the very nature of strategy, would limit the scope of practicable achievement.

Institutional agency
The military instrument that conducts an RMA at the sharp end in the face of battle is the product and expression of organisations with cultures which both help and hinder the effective conduct of warfare. The temporal and human dimensions of strategy and war impact upon strategic performance in ways that historians frequently neglect to notice. The RMA of the First World War showed institutional and intellectual-doctrinal adaptation in the face of temporal and human constraints unprecedented before or since.

In order to rate the strategic performance of German and British Armies in 1914–18, it is important to recognise how steep was the learning curve they had to ascend, how short a time they had in which to adapt, and how severe were the impediments of all kinds which generated friction for them. On the temporal front, it is sobering to appreciate that the executors of this RMA had only two to three years in which to complete their task. The agents for RMA in the French Revolutionary/Napoleonic and nuclear cases enjoyed respectively 23 and 42 years in which to adapt to modern war. The information-led RMA of current controversy is today a story with an active life of more than a decade, and is still running. The contemporary RMA debate may be suffering from terminal enervation, but its real-world referents are very much alive.[67] What is so impressive about the organisational and tactical-doctrinal adaptations of 1914–18 is that they were implemented under duress in wartime conditions.

It is true, of course, that large-scale intensive battle was not continuous, and that the two sides showed different (though naturally interlocking) patterns in primary operational and tactical focus upon offence or defence. Nonetheless, innovation had to be effected either in the actual, or in the anticipated, shadow of battle. The states, societies, and military organisations with their preferred doctrines were allowed the better part of two decades to learn how to wage modern war in the 1790s and 1800s. They had a similar span of years to identify the requirements of what was hoped to be 'safe (enough) nuclear strategy'.[68] Moving on, states have now had a decade and still counting to comprehend the information-led RMA. By way of contrast, the leaders in 1914–18 had to perform literally while under the gun (that was firing). Even when we turn to the mechanised RMA(s) of the Second World War, we find that the German Army enjoyed two potentially useful 'time-outs' for doctrinal second thoughts, in 1939–40 and 1940–41.[69] The British Army in that war was not tested on the grandest of scales between June 1940 and June 1944, notwithstanding the educational traumas experienced in north Africa and Italy.[70] The US Army, and especially the US Army Air Forces, were granted ringside seats to observe the dos and don'ts of modern war as perpetrated by others. In the Second World War, only the Soviet Red Army was obliged by an unforgiving temporal necessity to adapt, borrow, and innovate, much as had the armies of 1914–18.[71]

An important consequence of the temporal dimension of the First World War shows itself also in a human dimension which registers as a cumulatively enervating, even operationally disabling, level of casualties. The armies of 1914–18 had to adapt organisationally and doctrinally while under extreme time pressure and with an instrument that was suffering transformative casualties.

Readers must judge for themselves where they pitch their opinions between admiration and criticism for the strategic performance of the military profession in 1914–18. The experience of the Second World War and then the nuclear-shadowed Cold War can promote an unhistorical loss of perspective. In less than four years, in the Great War, the principal belligerents effected a scope and scale of societal and economic mobilisation for as total a war effort as it was judged social stability could stand. Looking to the sharp end of the effort, the military institutions of state had to adapt to a character and style of war for which they were utterly unprepared. Then, having discovered the awful facts of mass warfare, they had to innovate a style of combat to break out of the stalemated box of that mass warfare. It is amazing that both sides succeeded in large measure.

The fact that the Allies won attests more to a nature of strategy and war that commands respect for quantity, than it does to any inherent superiority in the Allied, as contrasted with the German, way in war. Dennis Showalter is almost exactly correct when he argues that '[n]one of the combatants succeeded in establishing a clearly decisive, clearly superior style of war by November 1918.'[72] We must say 'almost', because wars cannot be won by style, superior or offensive. Indeed, many historians believe that the German Army waged tactically the better war, if one may so express it, even though it lost in the end. It is a vital theme of this book that strategic behaviour is a holistic undertaking and can be assessed properly only in that way. The Allied, especially the BEF's (of 1918), way in land warfare was not always elegant, but it did express a style that their total resources could support satisfactorily, while the German way did not.

The institutions and ideas needed to wage the Great War, as the character of that conflict revealed itself sequentially in 1914–16, were invented in improvised fashion from organisations and cultures that set out in August 1914 to wage a quite different kind of war.[73] Although much of the administering and tactical behaviour was the product of initiatives at local working and fighting levels, states and armies had to adapt to the prolonged conduct of war on the grandest of scales judged feasible. Jerky newsreel film of quaint uniforms, suicidal-looking linear infantry assault, and well-fed senior generals – in the context of the terrible casualty statistics – is frequently deployed to illustrate a commentary alleging monumental incompetence by nearly all those in charge. With an omniscient hindsight, latter-day would-be Haigs and Ludendorffs rush to negative judgement. Notwithstanding the passage of more than 80 years since 1918, it is noticeable that no-one as yet has been able to identify practicable short-cuts to victory in 1914–18. Some scholars argue that victory, and defeat, should have been served at lower cost. It is claimed that the Allies ought to have made more regular and extensive use of a 'mechanical' style in combat, and should have limited their offensive ambitions to try to 'bite and hold', rather than effect a breakthrough for deep exploitation.[74] The former was doable in 1917–18, while the latter was not.

It is no part of this analysis to engage directly with today's critics of German and Allied performance in the war. However, it is our purpose to show that both sides effected an RMA, perhaps a military revolution, and that their strategic behaviour was impressive by any plausible historical standard. Dennis Showalter is persuasive when he argues that

> European systems ... adjusted rapidly, comprehensively, and successfully to the demands of mass warfare. States and armed forces manifested throughout 1915 a palpable sense of wonder that conscripts were reporting, factories were producing, and fighting was continuing, at least for the moment. They projected as well the image – and to a great degree the reality – of *a culture of competence.*[75]

A BEF scheduled to contribute six divisions to co-operate with the French, if the Cabinet agreed, grew to comprise 60 (British and Empire) divisions. French and German armies, anticipating an operational level replay of the swift campaign of 1870, had to recover their balance after the definitive failure of their (pre-) war plans in 1914 and adjust to the certainty of action for another campaigning year. We must be alert to the historians' trap of, in this case, judging leaders in 1914–15 in the light of our knowledge that the war lasted until 11 November 1918. First 1914 was to be the year of decision (for both sides), then 1915 (for France and Britain, and Germany in the east), then 1916 (for both sides), then 1917 (for the British, at least), then 1918 (for the Germans, and ultimately the British), and even 1919 (for the French and Americans).

Both sides adjusted to the extended conduct of mass warfare, and then they adjusted impressively to the limitations of mass, of sheer quantity, and had to learn how to manage, integrate, and use the new technologies and tactics by the mass armies that had been created. It is true that the German Army was always infantry-led in its style of war, notwithstanding wide recognition of the artillery expertise of Bruchmüller (and his methods).[76] Also, it is true that the Allies adjusted to the stalemate of mass versus mass with a more machine-led style of combat.[77] November 1918 tells us who adjusted most effectively to the realities of modern war: in other words, whose strategic (*means*–ends) behaviour was superior. That point aside, each principal belligerent performed prodigies of military, inter alia, innovation while under fire.

Although there were notable differences between the German and British variants of the RMA of the First World War, they both coped plausibly and generally effectively with the novel common tactical problems of the era. Both learned: how to use machineguns in large numbers (even to the point where a machinegun barrage would fire indirectly for unobserved effect, creating a 'bullet storm' to protect an advance);[78] how to use (and oppose) tanks; how to conduct trench and counter-bunker warfare entailing the development of mortars, 'bombs', hand and rifle grenades, flamethrowers, and light machine-guns; how to use gas cylinders and then gas shells; how to lay artillery indirect fire, preferably without prior local registration; how to conduct air warfare of all kinds, and much more. Both sides taught themselves decentralised combined arms tactics (with many new weapons) at platoon and section levels, and how to combine infantry, artillery, and aircraft in offence and defence. In addition, to mention dimensions frequently taken for granted by historians of tactical, operational, and strategic art, the entire enterprise of *grande guerre* had to be financed and efficiently supplied with the necessary human and material resources. Needless to say, perhaps, the requisite administrative and logistical skills for the war which unfolded in real time for the belligerents, had to be invented, borrowed, or discovered near-instantly.[79] We also should note that political leadership of a high order of competence was necessary to keep the combatant societies up to the mark for a trial which, even as late as early autumn 1918, appeared to have no end.

Instrumentality
The previous, current, and next steps in our RMA life-cycle (institutional agency, instrumentality, and execution) may be likened successively to sword-making, large-scale sword production, and swordplay. It was suggested immediately above that the institutional agents on both sides for the First World War RMA performed miracles of organisation, administrative innovation, and doctrinal adaptation. However, miracles take time. No matter how generally praiseworthy were the organisational agents of RMA, and regardless of the military merit in the new ideas discovered and honed in 1915–16, not until quite late in 1917

did either side on the Western Front begin to command a plausibly potentially winning scale of military power *of requisite combat competence.*[80]

It would be foolishly reductionist and therefore misleading to claim that the technological dimension of war was decisive in the conflict. It would not be misleading, though, to refer to the First World War as the great artillery war, at least in the sense that artillery proved to be the only key that reliably opened the tactical door to tactical success (and any operational success, should that prove feasible). Technology for superior artillery performance was by no means synonymous with that performance. The guns of 1914–18 certainly needed technological support from metallurgy, chemistry, electronics (for communication), meteorology, survey, and aviation. They also needed rigorous industrial quality control for consistency in high-quality manufacture, technical competence in gunlaying, and tactical excellence for the devising of fire plans which would work synergistically with the other elements in the combined-arms team (infantry, tanks, cavalry, aircraft). Knowledge and technology, though vital, could not produce tactical success. To win, the armies also needed numbers (of everything).

The German and Allied military instruments which carried through the First World War RMA demonstrated time and again in 1914–17 that they were not (yet) instruments for victory. Although one can point plausibly enough to poor, even some plainly awful, tactical and operational performances year after year in 1915, 1916, and 1917, it is extremely unlikely that either side all but threw away by incompetence a genuinely glittering opportunity to win. On the geography of the Western Front, neither side enjoyed a net military effectiveness between 1914 and 1917 such that victory was reasonably probable. Battles, even campaigns, could be lost, certainly drawn, but tactical gain and loss had no immediately major operational, let alone strategic, consequences. Attritional warfare is like that.[81] The Germans were beaten on the Marne in September 1914, but they retired in good order and dug in for four years. They failed to turn, or break through, the left of the Allied line around Ypres in October–November, but the outcome was a stalemate born of exhaustion, not any significant German retreat. Franco-British offensives were entirely repulsed in 1915; they tested most expensively the solidity of the territorial status quo in the war. In 1916 on the Western Front, everybody failed in their sundry objectives; the Germans and French at Verdun; the British, French, and Germans on the Somme. In 1917, the French failed miserably on the Aisne, while the British did well at Arras and Messines, but fought themselves to a standstill in the mud at Third Ypres in the autumn. Cambrai in late November saw tactical success, first for the BEF's surprise tank raid, and then for the Germans' counterattack; but again brief tactical success for each side led precisely nowhere, operationally and strategically – or at least so it seemed. Since decisive operational manoeuvre was not possible on the flankless Western Front, it is hardly surprising that dramatic evidence of military progress was not easy to find in the phase that Douglas Haig called 'the wearing out fight'.[82]

It took both sides three years to learn sufficient of what they needed to know about the changing character of modern war so as to have ready to hand a method, actually methods, to win. That comprehension was bought with the casualties and material resources expended from 1914 to 1917. The RMA of this great war, as applied in the conditions of the period by its authors (i.e. not as it can be assessed today for the quality of its lasting contribution to the art of war),[83] could deliver in the west strictly tactical-level success which could only cumulate by attritional results to show operational, and then a clear strategic and political, outcome (an armistice reflecting the fact of German military defeat). The essential quality in military method necessary to win was of course dynamic, as both sides learned comprehensively the trade of modern war. The rival armies improved in their absolute military prowess from 1914 to 1917, but unfortunately for the prospects for swift decision, military effectiveness in war is always a relational variable. As military solutions evolved, so alas did the military problems.

Properly holistic appreciation of how and why the war was won (lost) in 1918 underlines how essential it is to approach an RMA as strategic behaviour. It is necessary, but not sufficient, to argue that the Allied armies, led by the BEF,[84] won because they had mastered the art of war for 1918; neither is it sufficient to claim that the BEF was the leading military instrument of victory because of the relative material abundance behind it. Nonetheless, J. P. Harris is right to remind us that 'British artillery in 1918 also had the luxuries of seemingly limitless quantities of ammunition and an abundance of guns.'[85] The superiority of mobilised resources was strategically significant because by late 1917 Allied armies were 'proficient enough', or better, in the skill with which those resources were used in battle. On the 'adversary' dimension of strategy, in 1918 the Allies fought not only with a German Army effecting an infantry–artillery (i.e. unmechanised) version of the common RMA of the time, but also, critically, with an enemy increasingly short of manpower and eventually increasingly low in fighting spirit. Morale will not defeat steel, as the campaigns of 1914 and 1915 demonstrated, but if it is in short supply it lowers the quantity and quality of performance required of an enemy for victory. Manpower and morale were in perilously short supply in all armies on the Western Front in 1918, save only for the Americans (who had other problems – lack of skill and equipment in particular). The outcome in November speaks eloquently to many of the critics of the Anglo-French 'way of war' who forget that war is about the entirety of strategic effect and its consequences. Victory in 1918 was achieved by the overall superior raising and combat direction of military means.

The 'German RMA' of the First World War, for all its much lauded elegance in stormtrooper infantry tactics and the 'Pulkowski method' in silent artillery registration, unarguably failed the strategic test when exercised in 1918.

Between March and November of that year the German Army literally bled to death. That massive haemorrhage was not the result of ill-fortune, rather was it the inevitable consequence of the adoption of a style of infantry-led assault in a tactical context that predictably did not allow for operational exploitation for victory by manoeuvre. On top of the butcher's bills from the hideous attritional struggles of the first three years of the war, 'the German RMA' squandered the surviving strength of the army. It is worth quoting Tim Travers at some length on the fate of the German military instrument of RMA in the last nine months of the war.

> It is not always recognised how depleted the German Army on the Western Front had become by late 1918. The German Official History estimated that from 18 July to the Armistice, the German Army had lost 420,000 dead and wounded, and a further 340,000 as prisoners of war, for a total of 760,000 casualties, plus an unknown number of desertions or refusals to serve, which may have been as high as 750,000 to 1 million. This was on top of the 1 million or so lost between March and July 1918, during the German offensives, so that the German Army suffered a possible total loss of some 2,760,000 casualties and deserters during 1918. Moreover, the highest losses occurred in the Mobilisation or Attack divisions, containing the elite of the German Army.[86]

Ludendorff committed his army to a desperate offensive with what amounted to reckless abandon in 1918, transferring a million men in 62 divisions from the East (though leaving half a million second-line troops), to give himself a temporary numerical advantage on the Western Front before the Americans could arrive in war-winning numbers.[87] He demonstrated conclusively, if inadvertently, that when military means and ends are out of balance, defeat must ensue if the enemy is good enough at modern war to stay on its feet and weather the initial storm. Germany's lack of depth in mobilisable manpower in 1918 rendered its preferred style of infantry-heavy RMA a desperate adventure, given the tactical conditions of the time (including the particular strengths of the enemy).[88]

Execution and evolving maturity
The British and German Armies were both, in their distinctive ways, highly competent and adaptable organisations. On the British side, prewar, the embarrassing early errors in South Africa in 1899–1900 were rapidly corrected and the Boer republics were decisively defeated militarily in 1901–02.[89] As a generalisation, the quaint notion that the British Army in the early years of the century was officered by professionally slothful amateurs, more interested in gentlemanly sporting pursuits than the theory and practice of war, is an absurd canard. This allegedly ill-officered army, comprising large numbers of hard-case regulars who were all-but civilian unemployable, successfully waged

continuous small-unit warfare around the globe against a bewildering array of military cultures. Zulu warriors in Natal, Waziri tribesmen along India's north-west frontier,[90] Boer irregulars on the high veldt, fanatical Dervishes in the Sudan – the British Army took on these, and scores of others, and almost invariably won. It mastered mountain, desert, high-plains, littoral (amphibious), and jungle warfare.[91] If these were military incompetents, they must have been extraordinarily lucky to emerge victorious as often as they did.

Of course, the British Army, the principal military instrument of one version of the First World War RMA, had some signature weaknesses. In point of fact it had the kind of weaknesses one would expect from an 'army' that year in and year out did not operate as such. It functioned by regimental garrison around the Empire, only occasionally needing to concentrate force at a divisional (let alone multi-divisional) level. The army was parochial, in-bred, and so ridden by 'cap badge' loyalties as seriously to inhibit inter-arm co-operation. Nonetheless, it was a flexible and effectively economical instrument of imperial rule. It is worth repeating some facts central to our story. First, this British Army between 1906 and 1914 prepared an expeditionary force for possible European continental employment comprising six all-arms (primarily infantry) and one cavalry division, approximately 120,000 men.[92] On mobilisation in August 1914, the BEF initially was composed of just 110,000 men. For some comparison, in November 1918, notwithstanding suffering two and a half million total casualties (world-wide) – dead (723,000), wounded (1,662,625), and POW's (170,389) – Sir Douglas Haig commanded a BEF ration strength of 1,794,000.

The bare statistics are startling enough, but it is worth noting that this BEF of 1914–18 which '[i]n technical, tactical, operational and administrative terms ... developed into an army of great sophistication, more advanced in some respects than any of its contemporaries',[93] had to be rebuilt comprehensively after the opening rounds of fighting. The Official History tells us that '[i]n every respect the Expeditionary Force of 1914 was incomparably the best trained, best organised, and best equipped British Army which ever went to war.' Unfortunately, as it notes also, '[w]here it fell short of our enemies was first and foremost in numbers.'[94] Both British and Germans (and, of course, French, Russians, and Austro-Hungarians) suffered grievous loss in 1914, but the impact was disproportionately severe upon the much smaller army. That BEF which deployed to France with only 110,000 men in mid-August suffered casualties totalling 86,237 by 30 November (official close of the First Battle of Ypres).[95] German losses naturally were much higher,[96] fighting as they were all along what had become a Western Front, as well as in the east, but then the German Army mobilised nearly four million men in early August. The German Aufmarsch towards the west was effected by no fewer than 1,600,000 men.[97] In 1914, the Germans were defeated operationally, and noticeably bloodied, but most of their prewar regular army was intact: not so for the BEF.

Both the BEF and the German Army had to learn how to wage land warfare on the greatest of scales, and in so doing they carried through different variants of an RMA. The benefit of a wartime context is the prompt feedback on relative effectiveness of new tools and methods, and the self-evident urgency of military need for change. A downside of wartime is that real-time pressures to do well enough today, especially when – as in the BEF case – one is learning for the first time how to provide for and run a mass army, can leave little time or inclination to think systemically. In other words, while an RMA is likely to require the reconceptualisation of military problems, the pressures of real-time war encourage getting on with the familiar job (e.g. if 500 guns firing for two weeks were insufficient, let us try 1,000 guns for three weeks). Also the problem of conceptual innovation, and then detailed execution, is compounded if the limited stock of the most effective people continually suffers from combat attrition on a large scale.

In some opposition to the argument advanced immediately above, it can be argued that radical change into the RMA zone is greatly facilitated by the fact that armies can be transformed by heavy casualties in a prolonged conflict (not that the First World War was a long war by *grande guerre* standards). One can suggest that although the BEF temporarily lost much of its erstwhile (highly professional) tactical skill in 1915–16 because of 'massification' by the sudden huge civilian influx, the exponential expansion of 1914–17 did create opportunities for new men to learn new skills for a new context.[98] The Official History quoted above concedes that the British Army of 1914, for all its virtues, could not stand comparison with the Germans 'in the matter of co-operation between aeroplanes and artillery, and use of machineguns'.[99] By summer 1918 the BEF was probably the most skilful army on the Western Front at the combining of arms in the offensive mode in land warfare. It is well worth noting that the most justly celebrated element in the German RMA of this period, the raiding style of stormtrooper infantry tactics, was developed by the Pioneers (each corps had a Field Pioneer Battalion), who were not unduly burdened by prior notions of proper infantry tactics and weapons.[100]

The Allied and German RMAs of the First World War were invented and applied, piece by piece, including some steps backwards, throughout the war. Scholarly efforts to compare the quality of, say, the British and German ways in war of 1917–18, let alone to consider in isolation how well each did absolutely, are thoroughly misconceived. Just as no country (except possibly the United States today) is likely to be equally militarily proficient on land, by sea, and in the air, so the BEF and the German Army had distinctive areas of relative strength and weakness. Those areas could change somewhat over time with mobilisation, experience, casualties, and the performance of the foe. For maximum clarity, let us identify the most salient facts.

By 1918, both sides in the west had learned by the most painful of educational experiences all that they could realistically be expected to know about the 'grammar' of modern land warfare.[101] Each knew the contemporary trade of war. The BEF and the German Army of 1918 had mastered the contemporary art of the offensive, while the BEF was still improving in its grasp of how best to defend. With British defensive weakness admitted, and plainly demonstrated (March and May 1918), still German military effectiveness on the offensive was insufficient to turn tactical into operational success. Each national army implemented as generically common an RMA as its geopolitical, material, and military-cultural contexts allowed. Finally, viewed properly as strategic behaviour, the Allied, especially the BEF's, RMA, better matched available means to desired ends than did the German variant.

Year after year from 1914 to 1918 the two sides were learning roughly in parallel how to attack and how to defend. Because the Germans had seized so large and important a fraction of French territory (and virtually all of Belgium), they enjoyed the tactical and operational advantages of being, as it were, in possession. The Allies had to attack if the Germans were to be expelled, and they had to attack frontally because there were no operationally exploitable flanks to the Western Front. It is unsurprising that by necessity the Germans became true masters of the defence; they launched great offensives in the west only in 1914 and 1918.[102] The attack at Verdun in 1916 was designed to seize easily defensible terrain that would oblige the French Army to bleed itself to death trying to recapture. Unfortunately for their performance according to the grand means–ends equation of strategic accounting, for two years (1914–16) the German Army adhered to a tactical doctrine of prompt counterattack to recover all lost ground, a doctrine which had the inexorably nasty consequence of roughly equalising the levels of casualties suffered. From 1915 until early 1918 the German experience on the Western Front tended to the defensive, while the Allies were primarily on the offensive. This contrast mattered, and never more than in what transpired to be the year of decision, 1918. The way in which it mattered most was with respect to artillery. German artillery was good and better than good, especially when directed centrally by Bruchmüller, but it was not as good on the offensive as was the artillery of the BEF, and neither was it as numerous (though of course it was assembled to provide local superiority to support attacks). Everything matters in combined-arms warfare, but in the First World War artillery for the side on the offensive mattered more than anything else.

As indicated much earlier, strategic performance is the product of the values on all of strategy's dimensions. As with the belligerents coping with the Napoelonic RMA discussed in the previous chapter, and the leading partici-pants in the nuclear RMA in the next one, the contestants in 1914–18 were working fungibly with substitutions. Neither side wanted or needed strictly the best infantry, or artillery, or air corps, rather did it require sufficient military effectiveness to secure strategically significant advantage. In greater or lesser measure, with few exceptions both sides engaged in, or at least attempted, the same activities. This is not surprising. After all, in all significant respects, the belligerent great powers were members of the same 'civilisation'. The 'German way' in military matters had been extensively, even slavishly, copied abroad between 1871 and 1914. What were the most significant features of the RMA of the First World War which were executed by trial and error over such a short span of years? In summary form they were as follows.

1. Infantry tactics devolved from centralised synchronised movement by battalions, down to company, platoon, and even section (squad, in US terminology) levels.[103]

2. The decentralised 'combat team' platoons of late 1916 to 1918 were microcosms of combined-arms warfare.[104] Rifle platoons were yesterday's story. The platoons of 1917 and 1918 had cross-trained specialists in the (light) machinegun (Lewis gun), rifle-grenade and hand grenade, and rifle. Infantry tactics in theory differed little among the armies on the Western Front. Both sides employed linear 'waves' and columnular 'worms' as tactical conditions mandated, while an insistence on low density in attack and also in the outpost zone of a multi-zone elastic defence system was common to all armies.

3. The artillery that prior to 1914 was regarded as, and shaped to be, a useful precursor to infantry action on an infantry-dominated battlefield was by 1917–18 transformed into 'queen of the battlefield'. It was the artillery, vastly augmented in numbers and improved almost beyond recognition in its effectiveness against all kinds of targets (especially other artillery), that functioned as the key to the tactical breaking opens of the Western Front for both sides. However, no matter how improved it became by 1918, artillery could not open the front to decisive operational-level manoeuvre. Much of the artillery's effectiveness in 1917–18 depended upon care in set-piece preparation which could not be achieved in the real-time flow of battle, beyond the initial assault. Even if the ground was not too boggy for the artillery to advance in support of the infantry, time was required for preparation and co-ordination of each new fire plan for the guns in combined-arms combat. The time needed to bring up the field artillery and to prepare fresh fire plans was time that the enemy generally could employ to even better effect improvising new defences and bringing up reinforcements (including the advance of locally held counter-attack formations). The logic of this tactical situation was that, given the absence of any practicable means of speedy mobility in exploitation by assaulting infantry, offensives could only proceed step by halting step, or by 'bite and hold', as the method of the limited offensive came to be known.

4. Finally, the RMA of the First World War depended vitally upon the large-scale acquisition of new, or greatly improved, weapons and weapon support systems.[105] Although this RMA was about the skilful combination of arms and the competent administration of huge armies and their infrastructure, it was all enabled by achievements on the technological dimension of war. The artillery needed the right kinds of ammunition to deny mobility to enemy

troops, to neutralise hard targets, and (with the '106' instantaneous surface 'graze' fuze available in 1917) to be effective against resilient surface objects (e.g. barbed wire). Even if the ammunition were appropriate, the artillery had to be able to hit targets that it could not observe directly; moreover, it needed to be able to do so at the first attempt, without the registration firing which revealed operational intentions. The accurate maps, the ability to locate enemy batteries (from the ground and the air) and take accurate bearings on them, and the means and methods for centralised (at division, corps, and army levels) command and control of the guns simply did not exist early in the war. Suitably sensitive microphones for the crucial task of sound-ranging on the noise of enemy firing, for example, were available only late in 1917. For the all-important infantry platoon, *the* building block of manoeuvre by 1918, this RMA provided new LMGs, new hand grenades and rifle-grenades, and flamethrowers. Battalions acquired the new three-inch 'Stokes' mortar, a vital aid to the infantry against an enemy which often could be reached only by a plunging trajectory of fire, and which could not be supported in follow-on assaults by howitzer-type guns, because the soft or cratered ground precluded their rapid forward movement. In addition, we must note the development of air power for all purposes,[106] generically the invention and application of modern chemical warfare, the invention and exploitation of the tank, the (very incomplete) process of motorisation of army transport, and the extraordinary – but still modest – development of radio.

German failure to develop the tank is not difficult to explain, but it was to prove costly. It is scarcely surprising that a Germany typically on the defensive in the west from November 1914 until March 1918, acutely disadvantaged in the contest of mobilisable resources and strongly confident in the skills of its infantry, should have decided not to try to emulate Allied efforts to construct large numbers of tanks. However, given that Germany's gun park was none too abundant, the absence of tanks meant that imprudently heroic performance was required of the infantry and the artillery. Tanks crushed barbed wire; in their absence the wire barrier zones had to be overcome either by prolonged bombardment – which sacrificed surprise and impeded mobility in the infantry assault and forward advance of field artillery – or by the infantry themselves, which cost time and unsustainable casualties (as the offensives in 1918 were to demonstrate).

With the exception of the tank, the Allied and German variants of this RMA showed a persuasive parallelism. Intellectual and technological transfer, as well as independent near-simultaneous discovery, meant that both sides came to share a generally common understanding of how modern land warfare had to be waged for successful offence and defence. By preference and in part by necessity, the Germans were relatively more dependent on the tactical skills of their infantry than were the British or French. But both sides waged a style of war in which new weapons and new technical skills with older weapons were literally essential. By 1918, elite assault infantry in all the armies in the west, well down to the platoon level, carried their own diverse fire support forward into the attack. As noted earlier, the winning margin for the Allies in 1914–18 lay not in development of an inherently superior style in warfare, a 'better' variant of RMA. Rather did the Allies win because in their refinement of an RMA they enjoyed a decisive edge in mobilisable resources which enabled them to press on to the point of military victory.

Feedback and adjustment

Simple models of RMA have to be so reductionist as to be simply misleading. In one of the wisest brief commentaries on the process of innovation, Vice Admiral Arthur K. Cebrowski advises that 'transformation is a journey, not a destination – a process, not a goal – a continuum, not an achievement'.[107] That statement conceals its profundity under a cloak of apparent banality. When applied to the historical experience of RMA in the First World War, Cebrowski's rhetorical dictum rapidly shows its mettle. The RMA of the period truly was a journey without a predetermined, or pre-determinable, destination. Although the leading belligerents had mastered the art of war of their day by 1918, that day evolved as conditions moved on. Moreover, if there is merit in the long retrospective view of some historians that by mid- to late 1918 the BEF had created, indeed had become, 'an entire weapons system' of all arms (with the emphasis upon firepower),[108] RMA and strategic performance can be disjoined. Only experience could teach the armies of 1914, 1915, 1916, 1917, and early 1918 that they had yet to 'get it right enough'. Elegance in combat style does not guarantee success. A considerably flawed (by what standard?) way in warfare might have produced sufficient military effect in 1916 or 1917 to meet the strategic requirement for victory.

The perspective I am contesting is that which reflects a characteristically teleological historians' fallacy: specifically, that the belligerents invented and all but perfected the modern style of warfare in 1916–18. The Commander in Chief of the BEF, Sir Douglas Haig, certainly believed that his forces were good enough at fighting for expansive goals to be envisaged for 1916, 1917, and 1918. In common with social scientists attempting to peer into the future, historical figures cannot know where the winning tape is for achieving full maturity in a contemporary RMA. Indeed, since that RMA is apt to appear seriatim in real time, it may even be less than self-evident to its contemporaries that revolution is not evolution and that there is a winning tape in a military contest of finite duration. Conflicts are only exactly finite to historians, who can look and note how long they lasted. It is useful both to think of some historical experiences as cases of RMA, and (as here) to postulate a life-cycle to those cases. But also it is necessary to soften the categories of such analysis with recognition of the sense in Cebrowski's reminder that 'transformation is a journey'.

The RMA journey explored in this chapter was pursued under the active discipline provided by a competent enemy which itself was embarking on that RMA quest. In Chapter 6 we showed how the grand French rampage of 1792–1815 in part was thwarted militarily by the fact of eventually offsetting RMA behaviours. Such also is the story of 1914–18. Both sides learned how to conduct modern warfare, and neither enjoyed a sufficient lead in overall military effectiveness (for strategic effectiveness) as to be able to short-circuit a process of cumulative decision by attrition. Whether or not German infantry and combined-arms skills were superior is an issue of no real moment. The unarguable fact is that the Allies were always good enough in the totality of military effectiveness to ensure that their military quality and quantity remained tolerably competitive with the enemy. In due course, the Allies evolved a modern style of warfare that was good enough, or better, to make conclusively effective use of their superior mobilisable resources.

It is true, as Robin Prior and Trevor Wilson argue in their pathbreaking biographical study of contemporary operational art, that military learning could be erratic.[109] This is attributable to individual human flaws, certainly to weaknesses in how armies process new information, but it is also the result of the very structure of war. Manifest failure in the field, as by the BEF in 1915 and 1916, revealed readily enough what did not work in particular cases. However, that failure is less likely to reveal what should work well enough tomorrow. For the BEF, the principal military lesson of 1915, and even 1916, appeared to be that it needed more of everything: more men, more guns, more shells (at least more shells that exploded). Although the value of new technologies and improved methods was not at all discounted, the quantitative deficiencies, particularly the need for higher material quality (for example, in shell reliability), were so apparently obvious as to risk overshadowing the relative significance of the need for an RMA keyed to better methods in warfare.

Both sides had to adjust to changing military conditions not only as post-combat assessment suggested to be optimal, but as resources and changes by the enemy allowed. The conduct of an RMA in battle experience therefore required adjustments in two directions. German and Allied strategic behaviour each had to express a dynamic adjustment to the behaviour of the other. In addition, each side's strategic behaviour expressed a dynamic adjustment between its evolving 'warcraft' and its domestic context. The BEF in particular adjusted to its growing manpower crisis in 1917–18 by adopting a style of firepower-led, sometimes mechanised, warfare which played to Allied industrial strengths. Germany, under Ludendorff's strategic misdirection, adjusted to the conditions of 1917–18 by adopting a style of elite infantry-led warfare which lacked the quantity and even quality of firepower (given the lack of mechanisation) to hold casualties down to a bearable level.[110]

STRATEGIC BEHAVIOUR

Table 7.1 reveals the case for thinking about RMA on the one hand in the contexts of particular time and place (i.e. historical agent), and on the other hand in the context of strategy and war as a whole. The table asserts the strengths and weaknesses not so much, at least not primarily, of the generic RMA of the First World War, but rather of that RMA as developed and executed by Germany and Britain. Some of the strengths and weaknesses signalled in the table were not inherent in this RMA, but instead were endemic to the particular condition of Britain or Germany as historical agents of revolutionary military change. For example, Germany's debilitating weakness in the dimension of organisation for strategy-making and conduct did not derive in any sense from the character of the RMA. Germany simply did not possess policy-making, policy-advising, or policy-reviewing machinery worthy of the name. German policy, and grand and military strategy, such as they were, emerged from the shaky personal choices of the Kaiser as Supreme War Lord as shaped, and by mid-1916 as definitely bypassed, by whichever military faction was on top of the High Command. The appalling performance of imperial Germany in high policy and grand strategy must not be confused with the merit or otherwise in the German variant of the contemporary RMA. Our insistence upon examining RMA experience as strategic behaviour protects us against the twin fallacies of RMA analysis pursued either free of the contexts of actual historical agency, or innocent of strategy's nature. That nature to which, for example, organisation for strategy-making is vital, always has the potential to explode the nominal promise in RMA.

As in Chapter 6 the discussion here highlights the story coded in the table. Seven points serve to explain the judgements expressed in the table.

First, both German and British societies proved remarkably adaptable to the unprecedented demands of what became near-total war.[111] Both had large, industrially disciplined workforces, and as the character of the war altered in favour of technology under the pressure of RMA, so the peasants and other country lads who had been regarded as prime soldier material before 1914, were overtaken in desirability by those more familiar with machinery. The efficacy of social control was certainly strained by the experience of (fairly) protracted war, but it did not fail significantly until summer 1918 for Germany, and it never did fail for Britain. Notwithstanding anti-nationalist socialist ideology, increasingly severe civilian economic hardship, sharp military disappointments, and general war-weariness, the domestic truce (*Burgfriede*) of August 1914 just about held through the 'turnip winter' of 1916–17 and into the following year.[112] Germany did not lose the war because its army was stabbed in the back by traitors at home. It is true that the Allied blockade, and poor official handling of the prolonged food crisis, in the context of a seemingly endless and unwinnable war, caused domestic demoralisation. Also, it is true that many soldiers returned from the east after the winter 1917–18 more than a little infected with Bolshevik slogans and attitudes. Nonetheless, insofar as one can distinguish cause from consequence, both German society and its army (and navy) suffered a crippling blow to their morale not because of a general war-weariness, but rather because the hopes and even expectations for final victory in the unfortunately named *Kaiserschlacht* (Kaiser's battle) of the great Peace Offensive of 1918, were so cruelly and unexpectedly dashed.

Table 7.1: The RMA of the First World War: Strategic Dynamics

Dimensions	Britain	Germany
People	S	S
Culture		
Politics	S	W
Ethics		W
Economics and logistics	DS	W
Organisation	W	W
Military administration	S	S
Information and intelligence	S	S
Theory and doctrine		DS
Technology	DS	S
Military operations	S	DS
Command	W	DS/W
Geography	S	W
Friction		
Adversary		
Time	S	W

Key: DS   Defining strength of this RMA
DS/W Both relative strength and weakness
S   Strength in this dimension
W   Weakness in this dimension

Evidence of societal unrest is easy to locate, but less easy to interpret. For example, an undoubtedly war-weary Britain lost six million working days to strike action in 1918; the comparable figure for Germany was only 1.452 million. Niall Ferguson claims on good evidence that '[w]ith the exception of Russia, British labour relations were quite simply the worst in the war: neither Germany, not Italy, nor France suffered as many strikes.'[113] But what is unarguable is that both German and British societies proved willing enough to take the strain necessary to see through the conduct of their particular contemporary variants of RMA. As also had been the case with the Confederate States of America, the belligerent that lost suffered a truly combat-damaging loss of morale only as a result of military failure in the field. The rival armies were allowed ample scope by their respective societies to show what they could and could not do.

Second, although the political, ethical, and organisational weaknesses of Germany tell us nothing about this RMA per se, they do reveal a great deal both about why Germany was obliged to implement the RMA at all, and why it was unable to exploit the consequent military effectiveness to the point of victory. The principal belligerents of 1914–18 were obliged by military necessity to discover and give very large-scale expression to 'the modern style of warfare'. This RMA occurred, certainly occurred when it did, because of the bilateral campaign failures of 1914. We can trace the duration of the First World War to many causes, but poor quality of German policy- and strategy-making assuredly merits high ranking among them. German policy created a truly strategic conundrum. Its high ambitions overshot its military means, while its ability to improve those military means in the course of the fighting was never sufficient to bridge the strategic gap. Germany attempted to do too much with too little, and then proved unable or unwilling either to adapt policy to military reality or to shift military effectiveness to meet the political demand. This is what strategy is all about.

The operational expedient of the invasion of France through Belgium in the so-called Schlieffen Plan all but guaranteed that Germany would add the global sea power that was the British Empire to the list of its active enemies. Such an addition translated as a foe that Kaiser Wilhelm's Grande Armée could not defeat in continental warfare (recall Napoleon's like dilemma and, later, Hitler's).[114] As if that were not strategic peril enough, in 1917 the operational expedient of unrestricted U-boat warfare brought into the enemy's column the extra-European great power which could restore an Allied cause that was financially bankrupt, short of moral uplift, and becoming desperately pressed for manpower for soldiering and war industries.

Although Germans could be confident that their belt buckles were right to assert *Gott mit uns*, repeatedly they placed themselves ethically on the back foot by, to give the leading examples: invading neutral Belgium; behaving initially with exemplary brutality in that invasion; introducing poison gas to the battlefield; initiating the 'strategic' bombing of civilian centres; and sinking merchant (including passenger) ships without the warning required by international maritime law. German self-description as 'huns', on top of the kinds of misbehaviour just cited, greatly aided Allied efforts to demonise the foe. Nonetheless, it is worth noting that except in the Balkans and the Turkish Empire, the First World War never became the kind of ideologically sanctioned total war to which the Second World War in the East (and the Pacific) descended.[115] The doctrine of strategic (and military) necessity has some practical authority, but appeal to its grim sanction imposes moral costs, that then become material costs, on strategic performance.

Third, in a war that operational art cannot win in one or two smashing campaigns, logistical–economic and administrative excellence is likely to be promoted to the status of key enablers of victory. Prussian, then German, war planning was rightly widely admired in the nineteenth century. As the saying goes, the Prussian/German way in war preparation was the market leader, because the market follows success. Indeed, to be competitive in the front rank of belligerents in European land warfare, states and their armies often had no other practicable choice than to copy the Prussian/German example. Employing railways, the telegraph, and new small arms (rifles, generically – and field artillery), general staffs learned how to conscript, train, equip, feed, and move as much of the male population of the nation as political culture and social anxiety could tolerate.

Unfortunately, 'the battle is the payoff'. The whole object of the military expressions of the industrial and political nationalist revolutions that were the armies of 1914, was to serve as the instrument of swift operational decision. The general, if modest, superiority of German logistical skills for mobilisation and the organisation of the *Westaufmarsch* (and much smaller eastern),[116] was negated by much multi-level ineptitude (political, strategic, operational). It transpired that logistical planning for the great war-winning offensive in the west was a geographical and military absurdity. As Martin van Creveld argued, German logistics was 'the wheel that broke'.[117] To its cost, Germany learned that although modern Britain had no experience in continental warfare on the largest of scales, in its civilian society that great commercial and industrial empire had all the skills necessary for the mobilisation and administration of a quite extraordinary war effort.[118] As British military skills improved in 1916–18, so the strategic significance of superior economic strength asserted itself.

Fourth, to list information and intelligence as a relative strength of both sides is probably the most debatable of all the judgement calls in this comparative assessment. There were operational-level surprises in August 1914: the advance of the German armies on the right wing across the Meuse and Sambre (and the deployment of reserve with regular divisions),[119] and the German decision not to hazard the nominally greatly outnumbered battle line of the High Seas Fleet in the southern North Sea.[120] Subsequently, however, both sides prosecuted their RMA variants with typically increasingly accurate information about the enemy. This was to be expected, given that the principal battlespace comprised a near-static condition of siege warfare for four years. Variably aggressive trench raiding (particularly to take prisoners for interrogation), aerial reconnaissance by tethered balloons and aircraft, and signals interception (of telegraph, telephone, and radio),[121] as well as enemy activity of all kinds, eventually yielded a minutely detailed picture of the foe. Operational surprise was attainable (e.g. by the BEF at Cambrai on 20 November 1917), but more often than not the best that could be achieved was tactical.

Intelligence could be poor, as when Douglas Haig was misled by his senior intelligence adviser in 1916–17, Brigadier General John Charteris, into believing that the morale of the German Army was critically fragile. Vital tactical information could be erroneous, as when the BEF's infantry advanced on the

Somme on that fatal 1 July 1916, confident that the unprecedented quantity (but alas not quality) of the preceeding artillery bombardment had erased much of the German wire.[122] Considered overall, however, the structure of land warfare in this period was strongly resilient to the effect of advantage and disadvantage in the intelligence arena. Both sides performed well enough in this dimension of war. Even when they performed poorly, the ability of a defender to recover tactically and operationally from a setback, or to exploit an advantage, was so limited by the contemporary deficiencies in cross-battlespace mobility and communications that defeat was not likely.

Fifth, if intellectual superiority in 'warcraft' could assure victory, then Germany should have won the First World War (and then a Second World War, which of course it would not have needed to wage) in short order. If we bracket for unified consideration theory and doctrine, military operations, and command, we have in view the core of German military excellence. It was Germany's performance on these three among strategy's dimensions which enabled it to stand off close to the rest of the world *in both wars*, all the while allied to junior partners who were a net strategic liability. German military culture encouraged a happy marriage between centralised military theory and doctrine and decentralised discretion in command. That discretion, expressed as *Auftragstaktik*, or mission command, was prudent because the army was educated by and in authoritative doctrine and tactical battle drills.

The German Army had planned to win the Great War by excellence in operational art.[123] Operational envelopment was not merely the leading method, it was close to an article of faith. In practice, when the grand envelopment in the west attempted in August–September 1914 failed, the Germans had to discover how to wage and win the war tactically. This they did, with an imagination and determination that many recent historians have judged impressive indeed. The German Army excelled in combined-arms tactics, especially in infantry-led methods for effective attack and the defence in depth, while it was second to none in its grasp of artillery methods (though the BEF actually practised those methods better).

In some contrast to the Germans, the preferred British way in war was characterised by the fairly *ad hoc* and local development and adoption of such theory and doctrine as experience revealed to be useful, and by the rough equation of command with centralised control at the operational level. As David French, among others, has observed, the British were far less tolerant, and were far more fearful, of the prospective chaos of battle than were the Germans.[124] Whereas the German Army's answer to the systemic challenge of chaos was devolution in command discretion for well-trained soldiers,[125] the British answer was an attempt at firm control from above (division, corps, and army levels). Given the persisting strength of the German Army in doctrinal development, hard training, and tough selection for troop leadership positions, there can be no doubt that its style of decentralised military operations yielded a systematic advantage in the conduct of continental military operations. The German problem, of course, is that victory in war is not awarded by an impartial judge to the belligerent that fights most elegantly. War is waged both holistically, on all dimensions simultaneously, and most probably against an enemy which, though inferior in some respects of style in warcraft, still is competent enough almost to hold its own, ceteris paribus. So it was with the belligerents and their rival RMA variants in the First World War. The relative weakness of the BEF in its style of battlefield command found ample compensation in material and financial strengths. Neither side's personnel in truly high command (military *and political*) qualifies for elevation to the history's Hall of Fame of Great Captains. Nonetheless, German political–military leadership repeatedly proved itself singularly strategically incompetent, while Allied leaders were adequate. That difference was decisive.

Sixth, the armies that had gone to war in 1914 comprised essentially a rifle-armed infantry mass lightly assisted by field artillery and cavalry. The technology then applied to the task of securing military decision was only modest. No army was ignorant of the tactical implications of the technological changes of the previous half-century for modern war, though all were found severely wanting when the great test came. Each army believed that it had found a good enough solution to the age-old structural problem of combining fire with movement. This terrain has been well ploughed by historians. Suffice it to say that the advent of breechloading magazine-fed rifles using smokeless powder, machineguns, quick-firing (i.e., recoilless) field artillery, and barbed wire, appeared to point to a solution lying in the synergy between decisive operational (flanking) manoeuvre, and, once fire superiority was established, offensive spirit in tactical dash (when frontal assault could not be avoided).[126]

Both sides were obliged by 'trenchlock' evident in the west by the winter 1914–15 to invent or refine both light, infantry-portable weapons suitable for the assault and also the heavy plunging firepower necessary to destroy – later, to neutralise – bunkers and concrete blockhouses. Similarly, both sides had to acquire the heavy artillery capable of conducting 'deep battle' against the enemy's artillery and counterattack formations (held well to the rear). Bailey summarises thus:

> A '*rule of thumb*' developed, that reserves should be held 9 kilometres to the rear, capable of counter-attacking within two hours of the start of the attack. The shape of the battle-field thus came to be determined by the range of artillery.[127]

As noted already, the artillery had to learn not only how to fire accurately at targets it could not itself observe directly, but also – for surprise effect – how to fire accurately without prior registration shots against those targets. British military organisation, technology, and methods achieved a modest level of superiority in artillery effectiveness over the Germans by late 1916 (the close of the Battle of the Somme), an advantage that grew in weight and significance in 1917 and in 1918.

Although the Great War was an artillery war, perhaps the artillery war, still there were significant limits to what even excellent artillery could achieve. No matter how modern the artillery technology and technique in 1917–18, the guns could only strike reliably with precision when they knew exactly where they themselves were, and where the enemy was. Advancing infantry, no matter how well supported by artillery, must soon outdistance the range of that support. While the infantry consolidates its limited gains, waiting for the artillery to advance so it can support the next phase of attack, the enemy has time to move troops up by train to reinforce the crumbling sector of its front (tanks were not an adequate substitute for artillery). Both sides employed aircraft in the ground attack role. The Germans were especially systematic about it, using 'battle flights' (*Schlachtstaffeln*) literally in waves, wingtip-to-wingtip, as a form of flying assault artillery at Cambrai in 1917 and in spring 1918 to help punch holes in the British front.[128]

German and British performance on strategy's technological dimension is recorded here respectively as a strength and a defining strength. Although the Germans did well, the BEF did better. Given that the BEF had to expand from six to sixty divisions, enjoyed no recent tradition of excellence in the conduct of large-scale continental combined-arms warfare, and lost most of its 'regular' military expertise with the casualties suffered in the battles of 1914–15, it is unremarkable that it settled upon firepower in its several variants as the key to unlock the German front. The German Army did not despise firepower, but the combination of relative disadvantage in material resources and a great tradition of victory through operational (largely infantry) manoeuvre in combined-arms combat, led to a style of warfare rather less dependent upon firepower than that of the BEF. This generalisation ceased to hold as summer turned to autumn in 1918. Infantry losses in the offensives of March–July meant that the fighting power of the German Army depended more and more upon the artillery and machinegun assets of a defence starved of troops (certainly starved of troops willing to stand and die).

From rifle-grenades through light machineguns, to sensitive microphones for sound-ranging on enemy artillery, to gas shells, (fairly) mobile radio sets, and specialised combat aircraft – to cite but a handful of items from the short list – the First World War was a conflict of invention.[129] The most obvious technological differences between the belligerents in the west lay in the (near-) absence of tanks on the German side. This deficiency mattered tactically, but it does not even begin to explain why the Allies won the war. The outcome of the conflict was not determined technologically; both sides performed well enough, or better, in that regard. It was the case, however, that the modest Allied advantage in artillery skills, wedded to the greater depth of their resources pockets, enabled them to persist with a style of combat that must win by attrition – always provided their societies would be willing to continue paying the bill.

Seventh and finally, the strategic geography of the First World War translated as a playing field systematically tilted to the German disadvantage. Germany's geostrategic constraints had unfortunate temporal implications for its prospects of success. The location of Germany, that yielded the nominal advantage of the central position (or interior lines) – Napoleon's preferred situation, as interpreted by Jomini[130]– also meant actual or potential war simultaneously (and geometrically eccentrically) on two fronts. To compound the problems created by a statecraft which failed to prevent a Franco-Russian alliance (1891, 1894), Germany proceeded to pursue a hollow *Weltpolitik* in part via the grand-strategic instrument of a High Seas Fleet, which had the obvious potential to add Britain to its list of enemies.[131] Shackled to the 'corpse' that was its Austro-Hungarian ally,[132] Germany in 1914 required of its military machine a quite extraordinary performance if its comparative structural weakness in strategic geography was not to have lethal consequences when exploited over time by its enemies. The strategic geography of the war allowed Germany close to a single-front focus only in August–September 1914, and then in 1918 after the Russian collapse. Even in those contexts, Germany lacked the military weight to win in the west. Selectively superior military skills could not deliver victory in 1914–18, unless, that is, the enemy buckled from within or committed egregiously awful operational-level errors. The truth is that from 1914 to 1918 Germany either did not know how, or was unwilling, to extricate itself from a multi-front war that it could not win against a stronger coalition, which, courtesy of its dominance of the sea lanes, commanded access to most of the world's economic assets.

Jonathan Bailey is right: the RMA of the First World War was the birth of the modern style of warfare.[133] But novel as the truly combined-arms combat of 1918 was when compared with the largely sequential use of artillery, then infantry in 1914, the rules and lore of strategy applied to both. It is true that the national variants of the RMA as practised by the German Army and the BEF in 1917–18 were each absolutely militarily more effective than the older combat style. The significance of that claim is much diminished, though, by the recognition that each belligerent needed to be more effective in the field, given the near-parallel improvements scored by the enemy. The German way of war arguably was more elegant than the British, as these matters might be marked by a military purist, but such a claim would be a double absurdity. First, we know that the British (and Allied) RMA worked best *strategically*, because the Allies won. Second, the German and the British Armies did not really pick a preferred form of RMA; rather did each side's distinctive social–cultural and economic–material contexts settle upon the form of accessible RMA that it found fitted best its geostrategic and military–cultural conditions.

It was no accident, as Marxist writers used to observe, that the British style in land warfare – cautious, centrally controlled, firepower-led, and heavily mechanised – showed marked similarities between the two world wars. A similar claim for the Germans also is persuasive. As the belligerent weaker in resources of all kinds, yet enjoying the central position in Europe, Germany showed little more than commonsense in its dominant desire to win wars by dazzlingly swift and decisive operational manoeuvre.

We have seen how the RMA of the First World War, in common with its Napoleonic predecessor, did not confer decisive strategic advantage. Both of the historical studies presented thus far support the proposition that RMA, defined in Chapter 1 as a radical change in the character or conduct of war, is governed by strategy. Napoleonic France and Ludendorff's Germany failed to innovate in ways that would allow a new style in war to dominate the total means–ends nexus of strategy. We turn next to our third and final case, the nuclear RMA, to see if the strategic meaning of its life-cycle has been as revolutionary in practice as half a century of theory and commentary typically has asserted.[134]

NOTES

1. See Luigi Albertini, *The Origins of the War of 1914*, 3 vols (Oxford: Oxford University Press, 1952–57); H. W. Koch (ed.), *The Origins of the First World War: Great Power Rivalry and German War Aims*, 2nd edn (London: Macmillan, 1984); James Joll, *The Origins of the First World War* (London: Longman, 1984); and R. J. W. Evans and Hartmut Pogge von Strandmann (eds), *The Coming of the First World War* (Oxford: Clarendon Press, 1988).

2. For contrasting views of probably the most controversial of reputations of the 'Great Captains' of the war, see John Terraine's classic defence, *Douglas Haig: The Educated Soldier* (London: Hutchinson, 1963), and the effort at professional demolition in Denis Winter, *Haig's Command: A Reassessment* (London: Viking, 1991). There is considerable merit in Robin Neillands' sympathetic popular treatment, *The Great War Generals on the Western Front, 1914–18* (London: Robinson, 1999); while the essays in Brian Bond (ed.), *The First World War and British Military History* (Oxford: Clarendon Press, 1991), cover the British ground admirably, if not always persuasively.

3. Williamson Murray, 'Armoured Warfare: The British, French, and German Experiences', in Murray and Allan R. Millett (eds), *Military Innovation in the Interwar Period* (Cambridge: Cambridge University Press, 1996), p. 8 n. Murray cites Timothy Lupfer, *The Dynamics of Doctrine: The Changes in German Tactical Doctrine During the First World War*, Leavenworth Papers 4 (Fort Leavenworth, KS: Combat Studies Institute, US Army Command and General Staff College, July 1981); Timothy Travers, *The Killing Ground: The British Army, the Western Front and the Emergence of Modern Warfare, 1900–1918* (London: Allen & Unwin, 1987); and idem, *How the War Was Won: Command and Technology in the British Army on the Western Front, 1917–1918* (London: Routledge, 1992). To that short list of outstanding innovative studies, one should add the following: Shelford Bidwell and Dominick Graham, *Fire-Power: British Army Weapons and Theories of War, 1904–1945* (London: George Allen & Unwin, 1982); Bruce I. Gudmundsson,

Stormtroop Tactics: Innovation in the German Army, 1914–18 (New York: Praeger, 1989); Robin Prior and Trevor Wilson, *Command on the Western Front: The Military Career of Sir Henry Rawlinson, 1914–18* (Oxford: Blackwell, 1992); idem, *Passchendaele: The Untold Story* (New Haven, CT: Yale University Press, 1996); Bill Rawling, *Surviving Trench Warfare: Technology and the Canadian Corps, 1914–18* (Toronto: University of Toronto Press, 1992); David T. Zabecki, *Steel Wind: Colonel Georg Bruchmüller and the Birth of Modern Artillery* (Westport, CT: Praeger, 1994); Paddy Griffith, *Battle Tactics of the Western Front: The British Army's Art of Attack, 1916–18* (New Haven, CT: Yale University Press, 1994); Jonathan Bailey, *The First World War and the Birth of the Modern Style of Warfare*, Occasional Papers 22 (Camberley: Strategic and Combat Studies Institute, Staff College, 1996); J. P. Harris, *Amiens to the Armistice: The BEF in the Hundred Days' Campaign, 8 August–11 November 1918* (London: Brassey's, 1998); and Gary Sheffield, *Forgotten Victory: The First World War: Myths and Realities* (London: Headline Book Publishing, 2001).

4. J. M. Bourne is thoroughly persuasive when he argues that 'In future there seems little doubt that Haig's reputation will be finally determined not by studies of the man himself, but of the man in the context of the armies which he commanded, and especially by detailed operational analyses at the army, corps, divisional, brigade, and even battalion level. It is equally clear that the day has not yet arrived': 'Haig and the Historians', in Brian Bond and Nigel Cave (eds), *Haig: A Reappraisal 70 Years On* (London: Leo Cooper, 1999), p. 5.

5. Gudmundsson, *Stormtroop Tactics*, p. 177.

6. Ibid.

7. In a justly celebrated essay, Paul Kennedy wrote that 'it seems worth claiming that it was at the *tactical* level in this war (much more than in the 1939–45 conflict) that the critical problems occurred': 'Military Effectiveness in the First World War', in Allan R. Millett and Williamson Murray (eds), *Military Effectiveness: Vol. 1, The First World War* (Boston, MA: Allen & Unwin, 1988), p. 330 (emphasis in original).

8. For example: Prior and Wilson, *Command on the Western Front*; Griffith, *Battle Tactics of the Western Front*; Paddy Griffith (ed.), *British Fighting Methods in the Great War* (London: Frank Cass, 1996); Harris, *Amiens to the Armistice*; and John Lee, 'Some Lessons of the Somme: the British Infantry in 1917', in Brian Bond and others, *'Look to Your Front': Studies in the First World War by the British Commission for Military History* (Staplehurst: Spellmount, 1999), pp. 79–87.

9. The British Army as caricatured in Travers, *Killing Ground*.

10. See Leon Wolff, *In Flanders Fields: The 1917 Campaign* (New York: Time Book Division, 1958), and Alan Clark, *The Donkeys* (London: Hutchinson, 1961), for classics of the genre. Both works are powerful and well written; they just happen to purvey poor history.

11. Lest I be accused of unfair portrayal, see John Laffin, *British Butchers and Bunglers of World War One* (Gloucester: Alan Sutton Publishing, 1988).

12. With characteristic disrespect for conventional judgements, John Terraine vigorously defends the 1914–18 cohort of generals in *The Smoke and the Fire: Myths and Anti-Myths of War, 1861–1945* (London: Sidgwick & Jackson, 1980). It was fashionable for many years to rank Lt. General John Monash, Commander of the Australian Corps in 1918, as a military genius who deserved much higher command. Terraine's demolition of the case for Monash as an alternative to Haig (ch. 21) is amply supported in the (Australian authored) excellent biography, P. A. Petersen, *Monash as Military Commander* (Carlton: Melbourne University Press, 1985). Petersen shows clearly enough that Monash had superior military talent, but then so did Douglas Haig. Generalship in the First World War is discussed with insight in Correlli Barnett, *The Swordbearers: Studies in Supreme Command in the First World War* (London: Eyre & Spottiswoode, 1963), and Bond, *The First World War and British Military History*.

13. Travers, *How the War Was Won*, p. 8.
14. Such history as I offer is for the purpose of supporting analysis of the RMA hypothesis. Readers in search of a thoroughly reliable narrative history of the war will, alas, look in vain. The better histories are by no means the most recent, notwithstanding the revolution in tactical and operational study of the war achieved over the past twenty years. In descending order of merit, Cyril Falls, *The Great War, 1914–18* (New York: Perigee, 1959); John Terraine, *The First World War, 1914–1918* (London: Leo Cooper, 1983 [1965]); and C. R. M. F. Cruttwell, *A History of the Great War* (Oxford: Clarendon Press, 1934), constitute the premier league. Other histories worthy of note include Martin Gilbert, *First World War* (London: Weidenfeld & Nicolson, 1994), which is workmanlike if less than brilliant; Holger H. Herwig, *The First World War: Germany and Austria-Hungary, 1914–18* (London: Arnold, 1997), which provides a depth of solid treatment of the Germans and (even more rare) Austro-Hungarians unavailable elsewhere in the English language; John Keegan, *The First World War* (London: Hutchinson, 1998), which contrives to be simultaneously brilliant, idiosyncratic, and episodically thoroughly unreliable; and Spencer C. Tucker, *The Great War 1914–18* (London: UCL Press, 1998), which is a wonderfully competent, unpretentious textbook. Hew Strachan's monumental new study is as ambitious as it certainly delivers high quality thus far (only Vol. I to date): *The First World War, Vol. I: To Arms* (Oxford: Oxford University Press, 2001). The dust jacket blurb promises that 'This is the first truly definitive history of the First World War.' It may well prove to be the best history, but 'truly definitive' I doubt. Strachan's approach is almost extravagantly non-Anglocentric, treating the war as a global event.
15. I am pleased to adopt Jonathan Bailey's usage of this title: *First World War*, p. 16.
16. Harris, *Amiens to the Armistice*, p. 23.
17. For studies focusing on the human dimension, see Martin Middlebrook, *The First Day on the Somme, 1 July 1916* (New York: W. W. Norton, 1972); John Keegan, *The Face of Battle* (London: Jonathan Cape, 1976), ch. 4; and Lynn Macdonald, *Somme* (London: Michael Joseph, 1983), pt 2.
18. Bailey, *First World War*, p. 3 (emphasis in original).
19. It is noteworthy that the editors of the work likely to be regarded as the gold standard of historical scholarship on RMA selected Bailey to write the case study on the First World War. Bailey: 'The First World War and the Birth of Modern Warfare', in Williamson Murray and MacGregor Knox (eds), *The Dynamics of Military Revolution, 1300–2050* (Cambridge: Cambridge University Press, 2001), pp. 132–53. Endorsing Bailey's argument, the editors claim that 'The First World War had the most profound impact of all [five – modern nation state, French Revolution, Industrial Revolution, First World War, and nuclear weapons] Western military revolutions to date': Murray and Knox, 'Introduction: Thinking About Revolutions in Warfare', p. 10.
20. Geoffrey Wawro, *Warfare and Society in Europe, 1792–1914* (London: Routledge, 2000), p. 116.
21. Ibid., p. 225 (emphasis in original).
22. German method for future war is well portrayed in Joshua Wallach, *The Dogma of the Battle of Annihilation: The Theories of Clausewitz and Schlieffen and Their Impact on the German Conduct of Two World Wars* (Westport, CT: Greenwood Press, 1986); Arden Bucholz, *Moltke, Schlieffen, and Prussian War Planning* (New York: Berg Publishers, 1991); and Dennis Showalter, 'From Deterrence to Doomsday Machine: The German Way of War, 1890–1914', *Journal of Military History*, 64, 3 (July 2000), pp. 679–710. With reference to German operational intentions in 1914, see Terence Zuber's archivally based full-frontal challenge to orthodox views of the Schlieffen Plan: 'The Schlieffen Plan Reconsidered', *War in History*, 6, 3 (July 1999), pp. 262–305; and idem, 'Terence Holmes Reinvents the Schlieffen Plan', *War in History*, 8, 4 (November 2001), pp. 468–76.

23. Michael Howard, 'Men Against Fire: The Doctrine of the Offensive in 1914', in Peter Paret (ed.), *Makers of Modern Strategy: From Machiavelli to the Nuclear Age* (Princeton, NJ: Princeton University Press, 1986), pp. 510–26. See also S. R. Williamson, 'Joffre Reshapes French Strategy, 1911–1913', in Paul Kennedy (ed.), *The War Plans of the Great Powers, 1880–1914* (London: George Allen & Unwin, 1979), pp. 133–54; and Douglas Porch, *The March to the Marne: The French Army, 1871–1914* (Cambridge: Cambridge University Press, 1981), esp. ch. 11.

24. Bailey, 'First World War', pp. 152–3.

25. In *Amiens to the Armistice*, pp. 297–8, Harris is plausible in expressing some scepticism about Prior and Wilson's argument that the BEF had discovered 'a formula for success, June–July 1918': *Command on the Western Front*, esp. ch. 25.

26. Three superior surveys are John Terraine, *White Heat: The New Warfare, 1914–18* (London: Sidgwick & Jackson, 1982); Guy Hartcup, *The War of Invention: Scientific Developments, 1914–18* (London: Brassey's Defence Publishers, 1988); and Hubert C. Johnson, *Breakthrough! Tactics, Technology, and the Search for Victory on the Western Front in World War I* (Novato, CA: Presidio Press, 1994). Griffith, *Battle Tactics of the Western Front*, pt 3, and Michael Crawshaw, 'The Impact of Technology on the BEF and its Commander', in Bond and Cave, *Haig*, pp. 155–75, also are helpful.

27. Travers highlights the difficulties encountered by the BEF in winter 1917–18 both in understanding and in executing the concept of a three-zone defence in depth copied from the German example. Travers, *How the War Was Won*, ch. 3. The official history is revealing: see James E. Edmonds, *History of the Great War: Military Operations, France and Belgium, 1918, Vol. 1* (London: Macmillan, 1935), esp. pp. 254–9.

28. Ian Malcolm Brown, *British Logistics on the Western Front, 1914–19* (Westport, CT: Praeger Publishers, 1998), p. 238. Travers' caricature of the British Army does not fare very well in the face of Brown's meticulous study. Brown advises that '[t]his administrative success rested in large measure on the basic pragmatism and professionalism of the prewar British officer corps and its willingness to make changes to deal with problems as they arose. Ultimately, however, the reason was the willingness of these officers to turn to civilian professionals both as an adjunct to military men and, in the case of Sir Eric Geddes, as the means by which the entire transportation system was to be restructured. The successful administration of the BEF during the Great War hinged on the rise of the professional administrative officer' (p. 231).

29. Recent historiography has slain the myth that prior to 1914 the military experts on both sides expected a very short war. For the state of the art on this important matter see David French, *British Strategy and War Aims, 1914–1916* (London: Allen & Unwin, 1986). French reports that 'As early as 1909 he [Lord Kitchener] had decided that an Anglo-German war would last at least three years' (p. 24). To the best of my knowledge no-one has yet laid a critical glove on French's claim (writing about late 1914 and early 1915) that 'The New Armies were not just intended to win the war for the Entente but to win the peace for Britain. Kitchener wanted the British Army to reach its maximum strength in early 1917. In the meantime the Central Powers and Britain's continental allies would have fought each other to a standstill' (p. 25). For the German side, Herwig's book attests to the lack of expert confidence in the victorious short-war option that was Alfred von Schlieffen's 'obsession': *First World War*, pp. 49–50.

30. But Haig had got it right. 'By 11 August he had conceived the possibility of terminating hostilities in 1918, being apparently the first senior figure on the Allied side to do so': Harris, *Amiens to the Armistice*, p. 301.

31. The major indictment in Travers, *How the War Was Won*.

32. The answer was a resounding 'yes'. See Richard Rhodes, *The Making of the Atomic Bomb* (New York: Simon & Schuster, 1986), chs 10, 11.

33. Keegan, *First World War*, p. 195. The official history cited 14 September 1914 as 'the beginning for the British, of trench warfare': James E. Edmonds, *History of the Great War, Military Operations: France and Belgium, 1914, Vol. 1*, 3rd edn (London: Shearer Publications, 1984 [1935]), p. 396.

34. Gudmundsson hits the mark when he writes: 'If we focus on the operational level, we can see that the weapon that kept the Germans from winning a war of maneuver on the western front was not the machine gun but the railroad': *Stormtroop Tactics*, p. 178.

35. 'The OHL [*Oberste Heeresleitung*: Supreme Army Command] abandoned the linear trench system roughly 1 mile in depth ... in favour of a killing zone that ranged between 6 and 8 miles in depth': Herwig, *First World War*, p. 247. The course of the tactical dialectic between offence and defence can be studied in William Balck, *Development of Tactics – World War*, trans. Harry Bell (Fort Leavenworth, KS: General Services Schools Press, 1922); Pascal M. H. Lucas, *The Evolution of Tactical Ideas in France and Germany During the War of 1914–1918*, trans. P. V. Kieffer (Paris: Berger–Leorault, 1925 [1923]); G. C. Wynne, *If Germany Attacks: The Battle in Depth in the West* (Westport, CT: Greenwood Press, 1976 [1940]); and Lupfer, *Dynamics of Doctrine*. The German prewar debate is analysed superbly in Antulio J. Echevarria II, *After Clausewitz: German Military Thinkers Before the Great War* (Lawrence: University Press of Kansas, 2000).

36. Reflecting on the meaning of the story told in Prior and Wilson's book, *Command on the Western Front*, J. M. Bourne has observed persuasively that '[General Sir Henry] Rawlinson [C.-in-C. Fourth Army] was part of the BEF's learning process, not the cause of it. No one individual was the cause of it. The expeditionary force was too big and the endeavour in which it was engaged too complex for that ... Experience was the BEF's greatest teacher, not GHQ': 'British Generals in the First World War', in G. D. Sheffield (ed.), *Leadership and Command: The Anglo-American Military Experience Since 1861* (London: Brassey's, 1997), p. 111. Homer persistently describes war as work. For example: 'But once Zeus had driven Hector and Hector's Trojans hard against the ships, he left both armies there, milling among the hulls to bear the brunt and wrenching work of war': *Iliad*, trans. Robert Fagles (New York: Viking, 1990), p. 341.

37. Griffith conveys the scope and scale of the activity when he refers to 'an archipelago of training schools designed to bring all ranks up to the high standards demanded by modern warfare': *Battle Tactics of the Western Front*, p. 188.

38. Bailey, *First World War*; and 'First World War'. Also see his *Field Artillery and Firepower* (Oxford: Military Press, 1989), esp. ch. 14, and his contribution, 'British Artillery in the Great War', in Griffith, *British Fighting Methods in the Great War*, pp. 23–49.

39. See Zabecki, *Steel Wind*, esp. pp. 48–50, on the 'Pulkowsky Method' for achieving accurate predicted artillery fire, and Bruce I. Gudmundsson, *On Artillery* (Westport, CT: Praeger Publishers, 1993), ch. 6.

40. Recent scholarship argues convincingly that the most vital organisational link in the chain of innovations necessary to promote a dominance in artillery was the introduction of the corps-level Counter-Battery Staff Office (CBSO). The BEF invented the CBSO as a response to its experience on the Somme in 1916. In the winter of 1916–17, GHQ BEF required every corps to establish a CBSO. Noting that 'World War I was fundamentally a gunner's war', and that 'of the artillery's various responsibilities counter-battery became the most essential', Albert P. Palazzo claims that 'The German failure to emulate the CBSO system placed their artillery at a disadvantage, a liability from which they were unable to recover': 'The British Army's Counter-Battery Staff Office and Control of the Enemy in World War I', *Journal of Military History*, 63, 1 (January 1999), p. 57. See also Bailey, 'British Artillery in the Great War', pp. 44–5 n20.

41. See the classic study, Frank Mitchell, *Tank Warfare: The Story of the Tanks in the Great War* (Stevenage: Tom Donovan Publishing, 1987 [1933]); Robert H. Larson, *The British*

Army and the Theory of Armoured Warfare, 1918–1940 (London: Associated University Presses, 1984), ch. 2; and J. P. Harris, *Men, Ideas, and Tanks: British Military Thought and Armoured Forces, 1903–1939* (Manchester: Manchester University Press, 1995). On Fuller, see: J. F. C. Fuller, *Memoirs of an Unconventional Soldier* (London: Ivor Nicholson & Watson, 1936), chs 4–13; Anthony John Trythall, *'Boney' Fuller: The Intellectual General, 1878–1966* (London: Cassell, 1977), ch. 3; Brian Holden Reid, *J. F. C. Fuller: Military Thinker* (New York: St Martin's Press, 1987), ch. 2; and idem, *Studies in British Military Thought: Debates with Fuller and Liddell Hart* (Lincoln: University of Nebraska Press, 1998), ch. 2.

42. André Laffargue, *The Attack in Trench Warfare: Impressions and Recollections of a Company Commander*, trans. by an officer of infantry (Washington, DC: US Infantry Association, 1916). The claim that Laffargue's 1915 pamphlet was to be adopted as the basis for German stormtroop doctrine is roughly handled in Gudmundsson, *Stormtroop Tactics*, pp. 193–6. Although the Germans captured a copy of the pamphlet in 1916, this is not evidence that it had any notable doctrinal impact. All the major players in the First World War made approximately the same discoveries at approximately the same time about infantry tactics for the offensive. Small-scale experiments in 1915 were reinforced massively by the large-scale practical education provided in 1916 at Verdun and on the Somme. If the tactical enlightenment was fairly common, the lessons actually adopted by national armies expressed both the individual circumstances of those armies and, of course, their distinctive military cultures. Martin Samuels is not to be trusted in his denigration of the fighting power and combat skills of the British Army in 1914–18, but he is certainly right to emphasise the difference between dominant German and British approaches to command, control, and battle. See his interesting books: *Doctrine and Dogma: German and British Infantry Tactics in the First World War* (Westport, CT: Greenwood Press, 1992); and *Command or Control? Command, Training and Tactics in the British and German Armies, 1888–1918* (London: Frank Cass, 1995).

43. In August 1915, Captain Rohr assumed command of the experimental Assault Detachment (*Sturmabteilung*), manned by pioneers, of the Eighth Army Corps: Gudmundsson, *Stormtroop Tactics*, ch. 3.

44. From 1914 to 1918, Colonel Fritz von Lossberg served successively as a corps Chief of Staff (1914–15); as Deputy Chief of Staff at *OHL* (1915); and then as Chief of Staff to the Third, Second, First, Sixth, and Fourth Armies. Lupfer captures the matter exactly when he writes: 'For the rest of the war [1915–18] von Lossberg was legendary as the fireman of the western front, always being sent by *OHL* to the area of crisis': *Dynamics of Doctrine*, p. 10.

45. See especially the balanced judgements in Prior and Wilson, *Passchendaele*, ch. 19. This is not to deny that (British) offensives were pressed beyond the zone of initial success into the realm of follow-on failure (and Pyrrhic victory, such as that secured by the Canadians in the mud at Third Ypres).

46. Prior and Wilson offer a parallel argument when they write about operations in mid-September 1918 that '[i]n the absence of the full range of expertise which the British army was now in a position to employ in delivering their attacks, no operation was assured of success': *Command on the Western Front*, p. 357.

47. See Edward N. Luttwak, *Strategy: The Logic of War and Peace* (Cambridge, MA: Harvard University Press, 1987), chs 3, 5–6.

48. Falls, *Great War*, p. 318.

49. If the progress in artillery effectiveness was startling as between the bombardment which preceded the 1 July assault on the Somme in 1916 and that which opened the door for the tanks and infantry at Cambrai on 20 November 1917, the contrast with 1914 was near-magical. As J. M. Bourne has noted, prior to the war 'The British Army

had no tradition of "scientific" gunnery': *Britain and the Great War, 1914–1918* (London: Edward Arnold, 1989), p. 165. He proceeds to point out that 'In the Royal Field Artillery and the Royal Horse Artillery everything was subordinated to speed and to the need to maintain close support for the infantry. This left little time for calculation and often no call for it.' Looking to the progress secured by 1917–18, Bourne argues that 'The conversion of the Royal Regiment of Artillery as a whole to the principles of "slide-rule" gunnery [previously practised only by the 'despised Royal Garrison Artillery'] was one of the fundamental British achievements of the war.'

50. Travers, *How the War Was Won*, ch. 3.
51. Zabecki, *Steel Wind*, ch. 6.
52. John R. Innes, *Flash Spotters and Sound Rangers: How They Lived, Worked and Fought in the Great War* (London: George Allen & Unwin, 1935), p. 19.
53. Ibid., p. 30 (emphasis in original).
54. Bailey, *Field Artillery and Firepower*, p. 150.
55. The vital role of scientific survey for military effectiveness in the First World War is well explained in Peter Chasseaud, 'Field Survey in the Salient: Cartography and Artillery Survey in the Flanders Operations in 1917', in Peter H. Liddle (ed.), *Passchendaele in Perspective: The Third Battle of Ypres* (London: Leo Cooper, 1997), ch. 9.
56. By November 1918, some 30–40 per cent of the BEF were gunners: Griffith, *Battle Tactics of the Western Front*, p. 147. With respect to the size of the gun parks: 'In 1914, the British Army could find 72 field batteries but only six heavy batteries. By November 1918, there were 568 field batteries and 440 siege or heavy batteries': Bailey, 'British Artillery in the Great War', p. 24. The comparable figures for Germany were 642 field batteries and 138 fort (heavy) batteries in 1914, and, respectively, 873 and 550 in 1918: Zabecki, *Steel Wind*, pp. 161–3.
57. Carl von Clausewitz, *On War*, trans. Michael Howard and Peter Paret (Princeton, NJ: Princeton University Press, 1976 [1832]), p. 79.
58. Andrew F. Krepinevich, 'Cavalry to Computer: The Pattern of Military Revolutions', *The National Interest*, 37 (Fall 1994), p. 30; Luttwak, *Strategy*, pp. 4–17.
59. Dennis E. Showalter writes that 'What one state had or did, others could readily imitate. Dreadnoughts, quick-firing cannons, collapsible entrenching tools – all were manifestation of a copycat effect that by 1914 made Europe's armed forces mirror images of each other in terms of their technology': 'Mass Warfare and the Impact of Technology', in Roger Chickering and Stig Förster (eds), *Great War, Total War: Combat and Mobilization on the Western Front, 1914–1918* (Cambridge: Cambridge University Press, 2000), p. 75. Showalter's judgement about conditions before 1914 applies even more strenuously to the war years themselves.
60. For example, British nuclear physicist James Chadwick once said: 'I remember the spring of 1941 to this day [in 1969]. I realised then that a nuclear bomb was not only possible – it was inevitable. Sooner or later these ideas could not be peculiar to us. Everybody would think about them before long, and some country would put them into action.' Quoted in Rhodes, *Making of the Atomic Bomb*, p. 356.
61. David French's writings are particularly helpful in understanding the strategy of attrition in the First World War. See 'The Meaning of Attrition, 1914–1916', *English Historical Review*, 103, 407 (April 1988), pp. 385–405; *British Strategy and War Aims, 1914–1916*; and *The Strategy of the Lloyd George Coalition, 1916–1918* (Oxford: Clarendon Press, 1995).
62. Cyril Falls, *Caporetto, 1917* (London: Weidenfeld & Nicolson, 1966); Gudmundsson, *Stormtroop Tactics*, ch. 8; and Herwig, *First World War*, pp. 336–46, are particularly helpful.
63. Gudmundsson, *Stormtroop Tactics*, p. 139.
64. Ibid., p. 121.

65. Ibid., p. 141.
66. See Falls, *Great War*, Book 4, ch. 7; Wilfrid Miles, *History of the Great War, Military Operations: France and Belgium, 1917*, Vol. III (London: Imperial War Museum, 1991 [1948]); A. J. Smithers, *Cambrai: The First Great Tank Battle, 1917* (London: Leo Cooper, 1992); and the intelligent brief analysis in Johnson, *Breakthrough*, pp. 200–9.
67. See James J. Wirtz, 'QDR 2001: The Navy and the Revolution in Military Affairs', *National Security Studies Quarterly*, 5, 4 (Autumn 1999), pp. 43–60; Michael O'Hanlon, *Technological Change and the Future of Warfare* (Washington, DC: Brookings Institution Press, 2000); and Bill Owens, *Lifting the Fog of War* (New York: Farrar, Straus, & Giroux, 2000).
68. That is to say, 'safe' enough against most potential sources of miscalculation and accidents. The master concept was stability in its several forms (e.g. crisis stability, command stability, arms race stability).
69. The Germans made excellent use of their first 'time-out' (October 1939–April 1940) to correct the weaknesses in their military prowess revealed by the victory in Poland. Their second 'time-out' (June 1940–June 1941), by way of stark contrast, saw them bask in the artificial glow of the conviction that they had become unbeatable (in continental warfare, at least). This contrast is brought out effectively in Williamson Murray and Allan R. Millet, *A War to be Won: Fighting the Second World War* (Cambridge, MA: Harvard University Press, 2000), pp. 54–5, 115–20.
70. See David French, *Raising Churchill's Army: The British Army and the War against Germany, 1919–1945* (Oxford: Oxford University Press, 2000); and Tim Harrison Place, *Military Training in the British Army, 1940–1944: From Dunkirk to D-Day* (London: Frank Cass, 2000).
71. David M. Glantz and Jonathan House, *When Titans Clashed: How the Red Army Stopped Hitler* (Lawrence: University Press of Kansas, 1995), tells the story.
72. Showalter,'Mass Warfare', p. 90.
73. There is probably merit in the argument that 'the fact that the British were unprepared for war in 1914 meant that institutional adjustments took place as the nature of these "inconceivable problems" [of managing society in the conduct of near total war] became clearer': Roger Chickering, 'World War I and the Theory of Total War: Reflections on the British and German Cases, 1914–15', in Chickering and Förster, *Great War, Total War*, p. 53.
74. The 'mechanical' option is much favoured in Travers, *How the War Was Won*; while Haig's pursuit of impracticably grand objectives is criticised in Prior and Wilson, *Passchendaele*, and in David R. Woodward, *Field Marshal Sir William Robertson: Chief of the Imperial General Staff in the Great War* (Westport, CT: Praeger Publishers, 1998).
75. Showalter, 'Mass Warfare', p. 81 (emphasis added).
76. Bailey insists that in the Germans' infantry–artillery relationship, 'the supported arm [infantry] remained supreme': 'British Artillery in the Great War', p. 47 n41.
77. In a much debated analysis, Michael Geyer claims that the German Army responded to the challenge of modern warfare by developing '[a] more machine-assisted behavior', which is interesting but less than thoroughly convincing: 'German Strategy in the Age of Machine Warfare, 1914–1945', in Peter Paret (ed.), *Makers of Modern Strategy: From Machiavelli to the Nuclear Age* (Princeton, NJ: Princeton University Press, 1996), p. 543.
78. On the Allied side, the machinegun barrage (i.e. using massed machineguns on artillery principles) was a Canadian innovation in 1915. Griffith, *Battle Tactics of the Western Front*, pp. 124–5; Rawling, *Surviving Trench Warfare*, pp. 115–214.
79. Brown, *British Logistics on the Western Front, 1914–1919*.
80. Dominick Graham offers this elegantly economical and plausible summation of Haig's defence of his military stewardship: 'It took from 1915 until the Hundred Days in 1918 for the Army to acquire the means and learn how to use them effectively. This was the

main theme that Haig emphasised in his final despatch': 'Observations on the Dialectics of British Tactics, 1904–45', in Ronald Haycock and Keith Nielson (eds), *Men, Machines, and War* (Waterloo, Ontario: Wilfred Laurier University Press, 1988), p. 59. Haig's 'Final Despatch (21 March 1919)' is reprinted in J. H. Boraston (ed.), *Sir Douglas Haig's Despatches (December 1915–April 1919)* (London: J. M. Dent & Sons, 1979 [1919]), pp. 311–57. Haig's understanding of his war seems to me generally superior to the rival analyses yielded by more than 80 years of second-guessing by historians and others. This is not to register an uncritical approval by any means. Prior and Wilson are persuasive when they argue that the BEF could and should have performed better in 1917, had it been 'allowed to operate in appropriate weather and [were it] provided with suitably limited objectives' (*Passchendaele*, p. 197). It remains a probable fact that the British offensives of 1917 – preferably more prudently conducted than was the actual case, especially at Arras and Third Ypres – were necessary to attrite German combat power. In the words of Nigel Steel and Peter Hart: 'One thing was certain, the Germans certainly knew they had been in a fight at Ypres and Ludendorff's retrospective conclusions fully supported the strategic basis claimed for the battles of attrition and even for the idea that the Germans had been pushed some considerable way towards their collective breaking point': *Passchendaele: The Sacrificial Ground* (London: Cassell, 2000), p. 301.

81. Luttwak, *Strategy*, pp. 92–3, is outstanding in the clarity of its explanation of the nature of an attritional style in warfare.

82. Haig, 'Final Despatch'. Haig has been strongly criticised for unimaginatively applying a template of a 'structured' battle, with rigidly discrete successive phases, to his challenge of command in the First World War. The template was allegedly a product of his miseducation at the Staff College in 1896–97. See Travers, *Killing Ground*, ch. 4.

83. As in Bailey's seminal study, *First World War and the Birth of the Modern Style of Warfare.*

84. Although only the third-largest army on the Western Front by November 1918, after the French and the Americans, comparative statistics on POWs taken and guns captured show clearly that 'on 11 November 1918 the British Armies represented by far the largest share of the combat power of the forces ranged against the Germans': Harris, *Amiens to the Armistice*, p. 292.

85. Ibid., p. 45.

86. Travers, *How the War Was Won*, p. 154.

87. Historians continue to disagree about the scale and significance of the westward transfer of German divisions in late 1917 and early 1918. In a persuasive review of the debate, Giordan Fong makes the all-important point that '[i]n essence OHL was bent on throwing every unit it could into the titanic battles that convulsed the western front during the spring of 1918, in the hope that German arms might still prevail after four years of almost unendurable loss and suffering. Whether or not the divisions brought from the Ostheer fought directly in those battles is beside the point, for even if not directly engaged they enabled the release of dozens of other divisions. Without the divisions from the east or Italy the Germans would have found it exceedingly difficult to muster the size of force assembled for the initial attack on 21 March 1918, or to keep the battle going for as long as they did': 'The Movement of German Divisions to the Western Front, Winter 1917–18', *War in History*, 7, 2 (April 2000), pp. 232–3. Fong argues that '59 infantry and 3 cavalry [divisions were sent from the east] between 1 November 1917 and 30 April 1918' (p. 234).

88. For an interesting, but notably non-strategic, view of weapon-power and casualties, see Niall Ferguson, *The Pity of War* (London: Allen Lane, 1998), ch. 10, 'Strategy, Tactics, and the Net Body Count'. He is generally to be trusted only on the net body count, not on strategy and tactics.

89. See Brian Bond, *The Victorian Army and the Staff College, 1854–1914* (London: Eyre Methuen, 1972), ch. 6; Stephen M. Miller, *Lord Methuen and the British Army: Failure*

and *Redemption in South Africa* (London: Frank Cass, 1999); and John Gooch (ed.), *The Boer War: Direction, Experience and Image* (London: Frank Cass, 2000).

90. See Brian Bond (ed.), *Victorian Military Campaigns* (London: Hutchinson, 1967); Edward Spiers, 'The Late Victorian Army, 1868–1914', in David Chandler (ed.), *The Oxford Illustrated History of the British Army* (Oxford: Oxford University Press, 1994), ch. 9; and T. R. Moreman, *The Army in India and the Development of Frontier Warfare, 1849–1947* (London: Macmillan, 1998). Most readers should enjoy the ultimate in culturalist explanations for Western military success provided in Victor Davis Hanson, *Why the West Has Won: Carnage and Culture from Salamis to Vietnam* (London: Faber & Faber, 2001), esp. ch. 8, on Rorke's Drift.

91. C. E. Callwell, *Small Wars: A Tactical Textbook for Imperial Soldiers*, 3rd edn (London: Greenhill Books, 1990 [1906]) distils the wisdom gained by the British Army in its varied campaigns against irregular foes.

92. John Gooch, *The Plans of War: The General Staff and British Military Strategy c. 1900–1916* (London: Routledge & Kegan Paul, 1974). Samuel R. Williamson, Jr, *The Politics of Grand Strategy: Britain and France Prepare for War, 1904–1914* (Cambridge, MA: Harvard University Press, 1969); and David French, *British Economic and Strategic Planning, 1905–1915* (London: George Allen & Unwin, 1982), also are useful.

93. Harris, *Amiens to the Armistice*, p. 23.

94. James Edmonds, *History of the Great War, Military Operations: France and Belgium, 1914* (London: Macmillan, 1925), Vol. I, p. 10.

95. Edmonds, *History of the Great War, 1914*, Vol. II, p. 467.

96. The British official history estimates British and German casualties in the First Battle of Ypres (and adjunct areas in Flanders) as respectively 58,155 and 134,315: ibid., pp. 466, 468. There are problems of comparability between these statistics.

97. Herwig, *First World War*, p. 75.

98. On the outbreak of war the regular British Army comprised 247,432 men, with an additional 486,082 on the rolls as territorials and other kinds of reservists. Between August 1914 and December 1915, 2,446,719 men enlisted in the Army; a further 2,504,183 enlisted between January 1916 and November 1918 – for a grand wartime total of 4,970,902. In total, 5,704,416 served in the British Army in 1914–18: Ian Beckett, 'The British Army, 1914–18: The Illusion of Change', in John Turner (ed.), *Britain and the First World War* (London: Unwin Hyman, 1988), pp. 98–116.

99. Edmonds, *France and Belgium, 1914*, Vol. I, p. 10.

100. Gudmundsson, *Stormtroop Tactics*, pp. 35–8.

101. See Clausewitz, *On War*, p. 605, for war's grammar.

102. Nontheless, Bourne makes an important point when he emphasises the persistence of a German military opinion 'deeply imbued with the spirit of the offensive'. As he argues, the 'German instinct was for rapid and decisive success'. Bourne proceeds to suggest that '[t]he German conduct of the war in the west in 1916 and 1917 was an aberration. In 1918 the German High Command simply reverted to type': *Britain and the Great War*, p. 82. Notwithstanding a traditional instinct favouring an offensive way in war, in late 1917 Ludendorff was worried lest the years of defensive emphasis might have robbed the German soldier of initiative and offensive dash. For the obverse of that coin, there can be little doubt that by early 1918 three years of an offensive emphasis had left the BEF somewhat shaky in its grasp and practice of effective defence.

103. See William Balck: *Tactics: Vol. 1: Introduction and Formal Tactics of Infantry*, trans. Walter Krueger (Westport, CT: Greenwood Press, 1977 [1911]); and *Development of Tactics – World War*. Gudmundsson, *Stormtroop Tactics*, pp. 1–26, and Echevarria, *After Clausewitz*, also are helpful. For the British Army, C. E. Callwell, *Tactics of Today* (Edinburgh: William Blackwood & Sons, 1902), shows the impact of Boer War

experience and an intelligent readiness to reject some German tactical practices. Callwell notes wisely that 'it admits of no dispute that modern firearms render the attack of one body of troops across open ground upon another in position, and nearly matching it in strength, almost an impossibility. The magazine rifle, firing smokeless powder, is the main cause of this development' (p. 31). At Ypres in 1914 the BEF was to demonstrate just how correct Callwell had been in his 1902 book – even when the (British) defending force was not nearly matching the attacker in strength.

104. Harris, *Amiens to the Armistice*, p. 37.

105. Hartcup, *War of Invention*.

106. Much work remains to be done on the role of air power in the war. Informative studies include Richard P. Hallion, *The Rise of the Fighter Aircraft, 1914–1918* (Baltimore: Nautical & Aviation Publishing Company of America, 1988); idem, *Strike from the Sky: The History of Battlefield Air Attack, 1911–1945* (Washington, DC: Smithsonian Institution Press, 1989); Lee Kennett, *The First Air War, 1914–1918* (New York: Free Press, 1991); and John H. Morrow, Jr, *The Great War in the Air: Military Aviation from 1909–1921* (Washington, DC: Smithsonian Institution Press, 1993).

107. Arthur K. Cebrowski, 'President's Forum', *Naval War College Review*, 53, 4 (Autumn 2000), p. 8.

108. Prior and Wilson, *Command on the Western Front*, p. 309.

109. Ibid.

110. See Herwig, *First World War*. Geyer's 'German Strategy in the Age of Machine Warfare' could mislead. Germany could not compete in 'machine warfare' in 1914–18.

111. 'Total war' is a troublesome concept which is pursued generally to advantage in two fine sets of studies: Manfred F. Boemeke, Roger Chickering, and Stig Förster (eds), *Anticipating Total War: The German and American Experiences, 1871–1914* (Cambridge: Cambridge University Press, 1999); and Chickering and Förster (eds), *Great War, Total War*.

112. See Herwig, *First World War*, esp. ch. 7; and Marc Ferro, *The Great War, 1914–1918* (London: Routledge & Kegan Paul, 1973), ch. 14.

113. Ferguson, *Pity of War*, p. 275. An excellent study of the economic history of the war is Gerd Hardach, *The First World War, 1914–18* (Berkeley: University of California Press, 1977).

114. This argument is pursued in Colin S. Gray, *The Leverage of Seapower: The Strategic Advantage of Navies in War* (New York: Free Press, 1992). A brilliant period piece, truly a neglected classic, is C. R. M. F. Cruttwell, *The Role of British Strategy in the Great War* (Cambridge: Cambridge University Press, 1936).

115. Showalter, 'Mass Warfare', esp. pp. 92–3.

116. Bucholz, *Moltke, Schlieffen, and Prussian War Planning*. But see Zuber, 'Schlieffen Plan Reconsidered', for an important and unusually well documented revisionist view.

117. Martin van Creveld, *Supplying War: Logistics from Wallenstein to Patton* (Cambridge: Cambridge University Press, 1977), ch. 4.

118. Brown, *British Logistics on the Western Front, 1914–1919*.

119. Willamson, *Politics of Grand Strategy*, pp. 220–1; William James Philpott, *Anglo-French Relations and Strategy on the Western Front, 1914–1918* (London: Macmillan, 1996), p. 5.

120. Paul G. Halpern, *A Naval History of World War I* (London: UCL Press, 1994), p. 27. Strachan, *First World War*, ch. 5, is particularly useful.

121. For a classic tale see Patrick Beesly, *Room 40: British Naval Intelligence, 1914–1918* (Oxford: Oxford University Press, 1984).

122. Apart from the facts that up to one-third of the shells were duds, that (until spring 1917) it lacked fuses for its shells optimised to destroy barbed wire, that its rigid command and control rendered it inflexible as a support to the infantry, that it was

not accurate, and that it was not capable of neutralising the German artillery with counterbattery fire, the British artillery fire plan for the Big Push on the Somme suffered from a fatal weakness in its force (weight of projectile) to space ratio. Input was confused with output. The hugely impressive bombardment for the Somme was impressive only with reference to its – essentially meaningless – raw, militarily unilateral, statistics. In truth, the quantity and quality of the bombardment was fatally inadequate for the job assigned. See Bailey, *Field Artillery and Firepower*, pp. 134–9. Griffith records that '[a]s the war progressed, tacticians began to understand that a definite number of guns and shells would be needed to neutralise or destroy any given length of the enemy's trenches, and that this number could be discovered by a direct mathematical formula. Trial and error showed that there should be less than ten yards of friendly frontage for every gun, and 400 pounds of shell – or more – for every yard of enemy trench within the area to be attacked': *Battle Tactics of the Western Front*, p. 149. In the bombardment prior to the Somme, the relevant statistics were 15 yards of BEF frontage per gun, and 132 pounds of shell per yard – both plainly inadequate according to these dubious rules.

123. Gudmundsson puts the matter precisely: 'The German Army had entered World War I with the expectation that the conflict would be won at the operational level, that the fighting of battles was of secondary importance to the winning of campaigns. As a result, the German Army's brain power was concentrated in the General Staff in order to produce excellence in operational art; the "best and the brightest" focused on railroads rather than fire fights': *Stormtroop Tactics*, p. 177. The German understanding of operations and the implications for command is well explained in Bradley John Mayer, 'Operational Art and the German Command System in World War I', Ph.D. dissertation, Ohio State University, 1988.

124. This is a theme in French, *Raising Churchill's Army*.

125. James S. Corum believes that as well as entering the First World War with 'the best trained army in Europe', the Germans 'managed to keep its training advantage through the war': *The Roots of Blitzkrieg: Hans von Seeckt and German Military Reform* (Lawrence, KS: University Press of Kansas, 1992), pp. 10–11.

126. See Michael Howard, 'Men against Fire: The Doctrine of the Offensive in 1914', in Paret, *Makers of Modern Strategy*, pp. 510–26, offers fair judgement, as does Echevarria, *After Clausewitz*.

127. Bailey, *First World War*, p. 13 (emphasis in original).

128. Richard R. Muller, 'Close Air Support: The German, British, and American Experiences, 1918–1941', in Williamson Murray and Allan R. Millett (eds), *Military Innovation in the Interwar Period* (Cambridge: Cambridge University Press, 1996), pp. 146–52.

129. With thanks to the excellent Hartcup, *War of Invention*.

130. Antoine Henri de Jomini, *The Art of War* (London: Greenhill Books, 1992 [1862]), esp. pp. 102, 114.

131. See Paul Kennedy, *The Rise of the Anglo-German Antagonism, 1860–1914* (London: George Allen & Unwin, 1980).

132. Herwig, *First World War*, takes a notably unsympathetic view of Austria-Hungary as an ally. Also see Samuel R. Williamson, Jr, *Austria-Hungary and the Origins of the First World War* (London: Macmillan, 1991).

133. Bailey, *First World War*.

134. French, *Raising Churchill's Army*, is outstanding.

8

Case Study III: The Nuclear RMA

Lawrence Freedman concludes his celebrated history of nuclear strategy with a ringing declamation: '*c'est magnifique, mais ce n'est pas la stratégie*'.[1] The analysis here offers a full-frontal challenge to Freedman's judgement. In this book the nuclear revolution, actually revolutions, is treated as strategic behaviour, generically identical to the Napoleonic and First World War RMAs. Of course, Freedman has a good point to convey. Writing towards the end of the Cold War, he reasons as follows:

> At the end of over 40 years of attempts at constructing nuclear strategies one is forced to the conclusion that there has been a move to the analysis of second- and third-order issues. If strategic thought in the future is to consist of no more than permutations of old concepts in response to new military capabilities, or the exigencies of arms control negotiations in a desperate attempt to preserve the *status quo*, then it may have reached a dead end. For the position we have reached is one where stability depends on something that is more the antithesis of strategy than its apotheosis – on threats that things will get out of hand, that we might act irrationally, that possibly through inadvertence we could set in motion a process that in its development and conclusion would be beyond human control and comprehension.[2]

There is probably much wisdom in those words, but the case for nuclear weapons as anti-strategy most emphatically is not well made, appearances to the contrary notwithstanding. On the contrary, nuclear strategy, so called, passes the two most significant tests for strategic behaviour. First, it is plainly captured by the definition employed for this book: strategy is about the use made of (nuclear) force and the threat of (nuclear) force for the ends of policy. Second, empirically viewed, nuclear strategy has been purposeful behaviour intended to provide a bridge between nuclear means and political ends. In practice, strategic behaviour using nuclear weapons in action could lose that all-important instrumental nature, and instead cause a descent literally into military–technical chaos, wherein war serves only its own insatiable nature. However, no one knows that that would be the case, and most assuredly such is not the purpose of nuclear strategists. Freedman is unduly academic in his understandable, pejorative characterisation of a condition of stability which rests upon the possibility of loss of control, of irrationality, and of inadvertent catastrophe. Thomas C. Schelling's clever *reductio ad absurdum*, which Freedman paraphrases, is a half-truth at best.[3] Neither superpower planned to 'leave something to chance'. Even if the psychological reality of nuclear deterrence depends upon the fears just mentioned, both superpowers in the Cold War were obliged to assume a strategically purposeful foe, purposeful even beyond the threshold of nuclear use.

The story in this third case study is very much a strategic one, despite the not implausible claim that nuclear fusion weapons effected an historic decoupling of military means (in prospective use) from political ends. The critical claim extends to the point that surely weapons which one dare not use must lack credibility, and hence political utility. That line of logic leads one to the brilliant Schellingesque conceptualisation referred to immediately above, that nuclear deterrence works through 'threats that leave something to chance'. In other words, one may threaten to behave so dangerously that one could stumble into disaster, but one could not credibly threaten to commit collective societal suicide. This theoretical excursion is important because to the scholar the nuclear RMA suffers from a lack of finality. In common with the Napoleonic and First World War cases, the nuclear RMA was associated with a great conflict, but in this instance not with one that came to military closure. The meaning of the nuclear RMA in relation to the Cold War of 1945–89 forever must remain essentially contestable. This RMA certainly functioned strategically in and upon the behaviour of friends and foes, but after August 1945 it never saw actual military combat. One reason why many scholars have confused strategic ideas and official declarations with authoritative nuclear strategy is because that strategy has not been 'done' violently in tactical behaviour.

It is a working premise of this chapter that 'the Cold War was a real war, as real as the two world wars'.[4] But because the strategic history of the Cold War did not provide military milestones marking relative advantage in demonstrated combat prowess, the scope for speculation is much wider here than it was for the other case studies. Whereas Ligny–Waterloo and the 1918 Hundred Days' Campaign dropped unarguable final curtains on the contending RMA behaviours of 1792–1815 and 1914–18, the meaning of the nuclear RMA for the course and final outcome of the Cold War is notably debatable. The Soviet Union was not defeated in combat, nuclear or otherwise, by the United States directly. But was there an important sense in which it was beaten into political collapse by the nuclear-framed (if not necessarily nuclear-led) superpower military competition? If it is plausible to answer either 'yes', or even just 'perhaps in part', then the history of the Cold War might be teased into revealing how well each belligerent conducted its variant of the nuclear RMA.

TWO REVOLUTIONS

The nuclear RMA comprised two distinct, if linked, revolutions, not one.[5] It is tempting to confirm the popular conception of a single nuclear revolution, one first demonstrated as reality in July–August 1945. So great was the novelty of 'the bomb', and so close was its scientific–engineering story to that of the later 'super' (hydrogen) bomb, that many people even today would deem it scholarly pedantry to insist upon two nuclear revolutions. Pedantic or not, such insistence must mark these pages. Although the general public in the 1940s was awestruck by the atomic revolution, many military experts and some politicians decided that they were underwhelmed by the much heralded atomic RMA. John Lewis Gaddis may, or may not, exaggerate when he writes:

> The 'atomic revolution', therefore, was not particularly revolutionary. Once they got over the initial shock that such a thing was possible, early Cold War statesmen found ways to incorporate atomic bombs within existing frameworks of thought. With the possible exception of Truman, they did not significantly alter their conviction that war among great powers could still be a rational act. They may well have regarded a new world war as a remote prospect; certainly all of them saw it as an undesirable one. But they still thought it possible to fight and win such a conflict.[6]

What is more, they were probably correct, at least in the 1940s. If a Soviet–American third world war waged between 1945 and, perhaps, 1949, was expected by most of the strategic cognoscenti to resemble the Second World War, only with a unilateral US atomic add-on, a third world war waged from the late 1950s onwards was expected to be very different matter indeed. The thermonuclear revolution, step two of the catch-all 'nuclear RMA', was triggered by the development of weapons a thousand times more powerful than the 23 kiloton 'Gadget' implosion weapon tested at Alamogordo on 16 July 1945, a very close copy of which was dropped by a B-29 on Nagasaki on 9 August. As the US stockpile of atomic weapons climbed into the hundreds by 1949, so it became increasingly difficult for either side in the Cold War to discount their potential as *the* instrument of military decision. But once true thermonuclear (and not merely 'boosted-fission') capability was demonstrated – by the United States in 1952 and the Soviet Union in 1955[7] – there was no scope left for argument over whether or not a nuclear RMA was in train. If the introduction of deliverable weapons with energy yields in the megaton range did not signify a 'radical change in the character or conduct of war', one wonders what would.

A complication unique to this among our case studies is the weapon distinctiveness of the eponymous RMA elements among the whole panoply of national and coalition military power. Whereas both the Napoleonic and First

World War RMAs embraced in theory, and generally in practice also, the entirety of the military effort for land warfare, after a while the nuclear RMA was held by most Western theorists to mandate a strict divide between the nuclear and non-nuclear elements of military power.[8] In principle, at least, the effectiveness of a country's execution of the nuclear RMA might be measured in good part by what it could achieve strategically without having resort to nuclear use. More to the point, perhaps, would be what it could achieve strategically without triggering nuclear use by an enemy.

RMA LIFE-CYCLE

Preparation
The test of the 'Gadget' at the Trinity site in New Mexico on 19 July 1945 was the culmination of 50 years of progress in physics and chemistry by the international community of nuclear scientists. Whereas the atomic bomb itself was the product of a most deliberate and expensive (US$1.9 billion in 1945, $21.6 billion in 1996) wartime programme,[9] the science behind the bomb had advanced fitfully by serendipity, synergy, and plain luck.

The way for what became the nuclear RMA was prepared by three streams of behaviour: in transnational scientific research (the pursuit of truth); in methods of war; and in politics and ideology. Each was essential. First, as just noted, and for reasons that had nothing whatsoever to do with any official recognition of military need, nuclear physics was ripe for military exploitation by the end of the 1930s. H. G. Wells had conceived of, and written about, atomic bombs in 1911, an inspiration that impacted directly on the imagination of emigré Hungarian physicist Leo Szilard in 1933. Szilard understood theoretically (and intuitively) that the recently discovered (only in 1932) neutron might enable an explosive chain reaction to be triggered. If the pre-history of nuclear physics ended with the discovery of the all-important electrically neutral particle, the neutron,[10] its military history probably can be said to have begun when Otto Hahn and Fritz Strassmann achieved nuclear fission of uranium atoms in January 1939. Initially they did not know what they had accomplished. It took the skills of Lise Meitner and Otto Frisch to interpret their experimental results. Armed with Albert Einstein's theory of relativity which can explain the values achievable when mass is converted into energy ($E = MC^2$, of course), the world's physicists grasped the theoretical possibility, albeit only a distant possibility, that neutron bombardment of appropriate velocity (fast or slow?) of suitable material could produce a self-sustaining fission chain reaction for a very large explosion.[11] In the same way in which there was a constant dialogue between experimental and theoretical physics – with first the one, then the other, in the lead – so in the middle and later years of what became the Second World War the dialogue was expanded and transformed by the acquisition of a third player in the bid to secure practicable weaponisation – a major state-sponsored project.

The story of the Manhattan Engineering District, or Manhattan Project, is too well known to need repetition here. Suffice it to say that among the leading belligerents in the Second World War, only the British, and even in their case belatedly, showed early enthusiasm for a programme to develop an atomic bomb (partly because they needed a 'miracle' in 1940–41, partly because they were obliged to subscribe to a long-war theory of victory, and partly because science and government were tolerably well in harness in wartime Britain).[12] For reasons that only recently have become clear, Nazi Germany made poor scientific and technical choices and never in reality threatened to weaponise nuclear physics.[13] At least until August 1945 the Soviet Union, meaning Stalin, underrated the military and political significance of an atomic bomb, had other much more pressing needs for its scarce resources, and simply lacked the means (though not too much of the science) to proceed expeditiously.[14] It can be difficult to persuade countries struggling desperately to survive today to invest in deeply uncertain, and extraordinarily expensive, military–scientific projects which cannot possibly produce usable weapons in less than three or four years. For Germany and the Soviet Union in 1942–45, the years of the Anglo-American Manhattan Project, the future was now.

The second field of preparation for this RMA lay in methods of war. The way for the atomic bomb was prepared generally by the mass mechanisation of warfare, and in particular by the experience of strategic bombing. The artillery-led RMA of 1916–18 analysed in the previous chapter was the first wave in a process which was to see the wholesale mechanisation of warfare.[15] As the rival armies invented modern combined-arms land warfare in those years, so their air arms undertook the fairly systematic bombing of essentially civilian targets far behind the lines.[16] The course of 'strategic' bombing that culminated in the dropping of atomic bombs on Hiroshima and Nagasaki in August 1945 began with Zeppelin raids against England in 1916 and Gotha (heavy bombers) raids in 1917. There were raids before and after those times, but those were the years of most intensive bombing activity. Following the preordained failure of the pathetic World Disarmament Conference of 1932–34 to ban military aviation (or, indeed, anything else),[17] the military practice of the next ten years registered an erratic slide to 'terror' bombing on the greatest of scales, notwithstanding the paying of much formal homage at the altar of discriminate, precision targeting. Military necessity drove both RAF Bomber Command in Europe, and the USAAF's 20th Air Force in the Pacific, to adopt with wholehearted enthusiasm the operational concept of area (i.e. indiscriminate) bombing (especially with incendiaries from low altitude).[18] Shocking though Hiroshima and Nagasaki may be when reviewed in absolute terms, they appear somewhat less so when approached in historical context. The US air power that dropped the atomic bombs was beginning to be embarrassed by the fact that it was running out of substantially undamaged Japanese cities to burn down. As for the strategic bombing of Germany, by 1945 it is not inappropriate to comment that the aerial heavy bombardment instrument was employed more because it existed, and could not be left idle while the war was still on, than because it still had a vital role to play. If the atomic bombing of two Japanese cities marked a new stage in the barbarisation of warfare, then that barbarisation already was far advanced by August 1945.

Finally, we can find political – ideological – cultural preparation for the nuclear RMA and its implicit promise of an unparalleled level of destruction, in the phased shift from limited to absolute war aims in the era of the two world wars. The change from the destruction of great cities by a succession of near-thousand-bomber raids to their prospective demise caused by only handfuls, or less, of atomic bombs delivered by a few B-29 Superfortresses, was a change in means and methods, but arguably not in character of behaviour. The moral distinction between Dresden and Hiroshima is elusive. In both cases, Allied strategic air power was committed to inflict a pulse of maximum destructive effect upon an urban area. The sorting of innocent victims from guilty warriors was left to God, since the task manifestly could not be accomplished in real time from altitude. In both instances, the military, though not the strategic, rationale for the attacks was, to be polite, thin. However, the political underpinning of the nuclear RMA, which is to say the bedrock strategic explanation of its means–ends nexus, had been well prepared from 1916 to 1945.

In 1914, the great powers went to war for limited objectives, though certainly with the maximum means immediately available. Germany sought to protect its power position and the settlement of 1871, both of which it believed, incorrectly, to be in growing peril. Britain, our other RMA principal in Chapter 8, fought strictly to deny Germany continental hegemony.[19] Both countries had limited and defensive policy goals. While British war aims in practice remained modest – notwithstanding the public hatred fanned by the propagandistic demonisation of the wicked Hun – by 1918 Ludendorff's Germany had endorsed a policy of extraordinary continental expansion and imperium, especially in the east. Germany's eastern programme of 1918 was a pale precursor of the war objectives of the Third Reich a generation later.[20] The political management of the Great War in 1916–18, and then the effectively total political objectives pursued in the phase of the Second World War which commenced in June 1941, had set the stakes in modern war as high as they could be, well before the status of the atomic bomb changed from scientific possibility to realised weapon. The Soviet–German war of 1941–45 was conducted as a war of annihilation, certainly as a war without any rules beyond expediency, and it would allow of only two possible outcomes, total victory or total defeat. In short, the nuclear RMA burst upon a world already habituated to the pursuit of absolute ends by military means as absolute as contemporary prowess allowed.

Recognition of challenge

As usual, the Thucydidean formula of 'fear, honour, and interest' provides a satisfactory, if tantalisingly general, explanation of motive in statecraft. The double revolution of the nuclear RMA was driven pre-eminently by fear in both phases. The challenge recognised by scientists and officials working in the United States was to develop an atomic bomb before Nazi Germany. The long-subsequent US decision to proceed with the 'super', or hydrogen bomb project, was similarly fuelled by fear.[21] In the latter case, the fear was that the Soviet Union would proceed to weaponise the science of hydrogen fusion, regardless of US policy in that regard. Prudently, President Truman decided on 31 January 1950 that it would be strategically intolerable were the Soviet Union alone to acquire hydrogen bombs.

Fear, though both necessary and indeed sufficient to explain US (and Soviet) pursuit of the nuclear RMA, does not capture the whole of the story. To understand why atomic, then hydrogen, weapons were developed in the 1940s and early 1950s, the interdependent roles of 'honour and interest' and scientific invention have to be acknowledged as well as fear. In composite form, the challenge to which the nuclear RMA was the practical solution had the following principal elements: fear of German atomic research; determination that the United States should acquire the most powerful weapons as support for its predictable postwar international ordering role; and the sheer excitement of the innovation chase – scientific, engineering, individual, bureaucratic, and military. Lest there be any misunderstanding, it is important to recognise that the (largely Jewish) American and especially emigré nuclear scientists in the United States in 1939–41 had excellent reasons to flag the perils inherent in German nuclear science. Germany enjoyed a grand tradition in theoretical and experimental physics, had world-leading research and (potentially) industrial facilities, and – perhaps above all else – owned the loyalty of a nuclear theorist of the first rank in the person of the winner of the 1932 Nobel Prize for Physics, Werner Heisenberg. Imperial, Weimar, and even Nazi Germany was a cradle of modern physics, chemistry, and mathematics. It was in Germany that atomic fission was first achieved (January 1939); in Norway in April 1940 Germany acquired control over the world's only industrial plant supplying 'heavy water' (deuterium, the 'heavy' isotope of hydrogen, vital as an alternative to pure graphite, as the moderator for a sustained atomic chain reaction), and '[t]he German atomic bomb project [bureaucratically] was well begun' by the end of September 1939.[22] As late as 1939–40, nuclear physics was a transnational activity of the Republic of Science. German and Soviet scientists were members of that republic (though barely so in the Soviet case), and had fairly prompt professional access to the latest ideas and experimental data everywhere. Although the atomic bomb was an invention, in a crucial sense it was also a scientific discovery accessible to all competent nuclear scientists.

Science and politics met and fed on each other in the weaponisation of nuclear physics. The nuclear RMA expressed the answer to recognition of a political and military challenge which flowed logically from the promise of science. The RMA did not meet military needs after the fashion of the RMA of the First World War. The problem apparently shown, or prospectively alleviated, by the US (and British) atomic bomb was not a military conundrum of the moment, but rather the threat that would be posed were initially Germany, then the USSR, to secure symmetrically unmatched ownership of atomic weapons. It transpired that the Manhattan Project of 1942–45 was a US race against time to weaponise the science for relevance in the extant conflict. We now know, and in the German regard we knew by early 1945, that neither the Third Reich[23] nor the USSR had a bomb development programme worthy of the name during the Second World War. Stalin did not begin to transform Soviet research on bomb design (begun in 1943) into a crash programme to build the bomb until late August 1945.[24] Ironically, as the US programme went 'on-line' in 1942, the German government accepted the best (albeit, as we now know, incompetent) scientific advice available to it (i.e. from Heisenberg) and abandoned hope of building an atomic bomb.[25]

Notwithstanding the scientific, technological, and industrial costs and risks of an atomic weaponisation programme, many people have difficulty explaining the dismal German failure except with reference to *ex post facto* claims of a lack of enthusiasm by their leading scientists. In his sympathetic biography of Heisenberg, investigative journalist Thomas Powers is plausible, as to basic facts if not to inferred motives, when he argues that

> Germany's failure to build an atomic bomb was not inevitable. Scientists of the first rank, a huge industrial base, access to materials, and the interest of high-level military officers from the first day of war combined to give Germany a fast start. The United States, beginning in June 1942, took just over three years to do the job, and the Soviet Union succeeded in four [1945–49]. If a serious effort to develop a bomb had commenced in mid-1940, one might have been tested in 1943, well before the Allied bomber offensive had destroyed German industry. But despite the early interest of military officials – the six months' head start which worried Vannevar Bush [head of the US government's National Defence Research Council] so much – no serious effort to build a German bomb ever began. What happened to the early interest is not in dispute: it was deflated by German scientists who convinced officials the job was too big, would take too long and was too uncertain of success.[26]

Needless to say, perhaps, the Western Allies could not prudently approach the atomic issue by discounting the likelihood of success of German research. The theory that Werner Heisenberg deliberately killed the prospects for a serious atomic bomb programme seems increasingly unlikely as more and more evidence has revealed the critical errors that he made in his calculations, particularly concerning the quantity of fissile material necessary to achieve critical mass for a self-sustaining chain reaction. From the US 'Alsos' mission which in 1944–45 investigated the progress achieved in German atomic bomb research,[27] and particularly from the interrogation and 'bugging' of German nuclear scientists in Cambridge, England, in 1945, we know now that in its wartime isolation and the arrogant brilliance of Heisenberg, German nuclear science was on the wrong road for weaponisation. Nonetheless, it is easy to grasp why Allied scientists, soldiers, and officials in the Second World War had no practical option other than to assume a bad case about German progress towards the weaponisation of atomic physics. After all, Heisenberg was a genius, and the atomic bomb could be a war winner.

Parentage
Although the nuclear RMA plainly recorded its historical arrival in a definite 'strategic moment', such a moment does not necessarily a revolution make. The nuclear RMA was signalled by the three flashes of light in July–August 1945, but those explosive events were not synonymous with the revolution. The radical change(s) in the character or conduct of war heralded by the US and Soviet atomic tests in 1945 and 1949, respectively, and then by the hydrogen bomb tests of 1952 and 1955, again, respectively, required more than twenty years of sustained effort by four distinctive groups of people. The parents of the nuclear RMA, which is to say the people who consciously tried to effect a nuclear-keyed radical change in warfare, clustered as scientists, politicians and officials, military professionals, and strategic theorists.

The historical trajectory of the (US) nuclear RMA was as follows: (1) the scientists told the politicians and bureaucrats what might be achieved with patience, a great deal of money, and a huge industrial effort (1939–41); (2) the politicians and officials, after much delay and notwithstanding some initial scepticism, decided that the scientists' story had to be tested (1941–45); (3) the military sought to fashion a nuclear-armed long-range striking force which actually could express a radical change in the character and conduct of war (1948–54/55); (4) and finally a body of scholar–commentators appeared which tried to make strategic sense of the nuclear RMA that already was a well established fact (1954–57). Each of these four clusters of people shared parentage of the nuclear RMA. When we refer to the nuclear revolution we mean not just the military–technical epiphanies exploded in 1945, 1949, 1952, and 1955. In addition, we mean the military instrument(s) and the political, moral, strategic, and other contexts shaped by the radical change in warfare.

The nuclear RMA was not the product of one person's, or even one group's, vision of a strategically desirable (or unavoidable) future. The rapidly maturing nuclear RMA of the early 1960s bore no discernible relationship to the identifiable intentions of the scientists and politicians of the 1930s and 1940s. If, by the nuclear revolution, one refers to the arguably stable condition of super-power strategic standoff characteristic of the last 20 years of the Cold War, it is not obvious that any person or persons has persuasive claims to primacy in its parenthood. This is not, at least not quite, to retreat from named individuals into those barren wastes of 'structural history', wherein great impersonal forces move human beings as interchangeable pawns. Individuals matter and can change the course of history. As observed above, Germany's leading theoretical physicist, Werner Heisenberg, on one admittedly unper-suasive explanation, might personally have prevented Nazi Germany from transforming its nuclear research from laboratory hobby-shop activity into a bomb programme. It is one thing to cite the scientists, politicians, officials, and soldiers who collectively made the nuclear RMA in all senses, who brought research to technically satisfactory conclusions and then who shaped the growth of a military posture with operational nuclear weapons; it is quite another to assess the importance of particular individuals. The superior significance of the role that Heisenberg played stemmed directly from his national strategic context: he was working for a country which hindsight tells us had no route to strategic victory save the atomic one, of which Heisenberg in practice was the gatekeeper. As early as late summer 1942 Hitler almost certainly believed that Germany faced a long stalemated war of attrition. Plainly, a successful atomic bomb programme, such as should have been practicable between 1940 and 1945, could have changed the course of history.[28]

For the Allies a somewhat unhistorical long retrospective informs us that no candidate parent of the nuclear RMA could shift the course of strategic history in the early or mid-1940s. The Second World War in Europe was won without atomic assistance, while such assistance was a discretionary instrument even in the war against Japan. Such was the galaxy of scientific 'stars' available to serve the anti-German war effort; such was the synergistic benefit of Anglo-American cooperation; such in practice was the time available; and such was the geopolitical and ideological logic of world politics that even with different individuals in key positions it is hard to imagine a nuclear RMA not being made in the 1940s or 1950s, if not necessarily during the Second World War.

The nuclear RMA was a major military revolution in the sense that although particular people had to perform outstandingly at every step of the way, scientifically and militarily (from the discovery of fission to the shaping and management of a 'triad' of nuclear-armed forces after 1960), this was an RMA waiting to be made to happen. The basic reason why strategic history had to give birth to a nuclear RMA was because the transnational science was ever more ready for weaponisation, in a political context of competition and war wherein no very great power could with prudence dare eschew an atomic bomb programme. That fact renders the story of Hitler's non-bomb programme all the more extraordinary, though certainly understandable given Heisenberg's technical pessimism and the short-term focus and scarcity of resources of the Third Reich at war. In an historically executive sense, the parent of the nuclear RMA was President Roosevelt, who at a meeting on 9 October 1941 licensed Vannevar Bush, the head of the National Defense Research Committee/Council, to proceed to try and build an atomic bomb. The basis for that decision was Bush's ability to deploy a highly plausible technical argument from the July 1941 report of the British MAUD Committee of experts. That report, duly blessed by Winston Churchill, rested its case for the likelihood of success in bomb development upon a theoretical discovery in March 1940, by two German refugee scientists, Otto Frisch and Rudolf Peierls. They calculated that in theory, it should be possible and practicable to separate sufficient of the isotope U-235 from U-238 to achieve the critical mass for a self-sustaining chain reaction. The work of Frisch and Peierls rested, of course, on the whole transnational body of theory and experimentation that had preceded it, and has to be viewed in the light of later discoveries (e.g. the discovery of element 94 Plutonium (Pu) on 28 March 1941). From Ernest Rutherford's finding in 1911 that atoms have a nucleus, through the discovery of neutrons in 1932, to fission in 1939, through to the invention by Edward Teller and Stanislaw Ulam in 1952 of the radiation method of igniting the secondary (fusion) explosion of a true hydrogen bomb, and beyond, the scientific–technological 'parentage' of the nuclear RMA was diverse, partial, and sequential.

Notwithstanding the transfer of nuclear knowledge across frontiers, legally and illegally, there was always a great deal of near-parallel discovery in nuclear research and development. Happily, the great man of German nuclear physics, Werner Heisenberg, was not privy to the inspired calculation of Frisch and Peierls about the modest dimensions of the necessary critical mass, and his very eminence minimised the likelihood that anyone working in wartime Germany would dare challenge his erroneously large estimate. For example, although in 1945 Stalin insisted that his newly reinvigorated bomb programme copy slavishly the reliable 'Fat Man' Trinity–Hiroshima (Pu) implosion model, such a conservative approach probably saved the USSR only a year in lead-time. The Manhattan Project did not truly have a lock on atomic secrets or secrets which could be penetrated only by espionage. Such scientific parents of the research which resulted in the Soviet atomic bombs as Ioffe, Kapitsa, Khurchatov, Khariton, Flerov, Zel'dovic, Alikhanov, Leipunskii, and Sakharov, had little need of help from spies.[29] For example, the Teller–Ulam principle which enabled the true fusion weapon found its Soviet variant in 1954 in a like discovery by Sakharov (subsequently known as 'the father of the Soviet H-bomb'), Zel'dovic, and Khariton.[30]

Much as for the RMA of the First World War, we find that the nuclear RMA was made by a cast of hundreds of exceptionally talented and dedicated people. The twin atomic and hydrogen revolutions were ordered by the politicians, in historical sequence by Churchill, Roosevelt, Stalin, and Truman. Although their roles were vital, rather like Douglas Haig and even Erich Ludendorff in the First World War, their key function was to license and liberate effective people to organise and manage the revolution at issue. Although politicians uniquely could make things happen, by committing their countries to unusually expensive research programmes, their willingness to make that commitment typically rested upon the expert advice they received. Because Albert Speer was persuaded by Heisenberg that the atomic bomb, if feasible, was 'certainly no war-winning weapon in the near future',[31] he briefed the *Führer* on 23 June 1942 with such scant enthusiasm for nuclear research that Hitler in practical effect decided not to be the parent of a bomb programme. We turn now from parenthood of revolution to the revolution itself.

Enabling spark
Of the major RMAs discussed in this book, the nuclear was – indeed, remains – both the most sharply historically defined, and by far the most technological in character. The spark that enabled the nuclear revolution as an absolute *sine qua non*, for which quintessentially, and narrowly militarily, there could be no substitution across strategy's many dimensions, was the successful weaponisation of nuclear physics. The nuclear revolution was to find mature expression in large arsenals and dedicated forces with military doctrines tailored to the new military–technical context (though atavistic in the eyes of some critics).[32] But, that granted, the nuclear revolution has been all about learning to live with *the bomb*. The nuclear bomb, in its various technical guises, is to this RMA what Napoleon was to the RMA of the 1800s, what indirect artillery fire was to the RMA of the First World War, and what the computer was to the information-led RMA at the close of the twentieth century.

Strategic moment
Notwithstanding the awesome difference between the 14 kt 'Little Boy' dropped on Hiroshima on 6 August 1945 and the 10.4 mt of the thermonuclear 'Mike' device of 1952, the former is unchallengable by the latter for elevation as the strategic moment for this RMA. Hiroshima was to the nuclear RMA what, arguably, Italy in 1796, or Ulm–Austerliz in 1805, was to the Napoleonic RMA, what Cambrai was for the RMA of the First World War, and what the Gulf War was for the information-led RMA. In a 1959 book that despite its policy orientation still reads well today – no mean feat – Bernard Brodie wrote thus:

> People often speak of atomic explosives as the most portentous military invention 'since gunpowder'. But such a comparison inflates the importance of even so epoch-making an event as the introduction of gunpowder.[33]

He noted that '[f]ew people were unexcited or unimpressed by the first atomic weapons. That something tremendously important had happened was immediately understood by almost everyone'.[34] The military–technical fact that the leap from fission to fusion weapons in the mid 1950s was greater than that from conventional high explosives to fission, is really beside the point. While Hiroshima opened the gates of strategic imagination, speculation, and highly contingent planning, as well as technological possibility, actually it did more than that. A 'strategic moment' worthy of the title shows, or at the time was believed to provide, a tolerably accurate, if only partial, picture of the future. Such a moment cannot be a mere hypothesis, no matter how persuasive, rather it must demonstrate radical change beyond plausible argument.

For several years after Hiroshima, conservative commentators were sensibly sceptical of the claims for revolutionary strategic significance. The prudent scepticism rested upon the easily calculable facts of sharply defined atomic weapon effects, married to the assumption that nuclear bombs would long remain a scarce military resource. For once, at least, the golden mean in strategic analysis was simply wrong. The relevant values in predictable bomb damage assessment rose stratospherically with the thousand-fold increase in energy yield of fusion over fission weapons (after 1954), while the nuclear stockpile was emerging from scarcity as early as 1949–50. Much as the atomic revelation of 6 August 1945 quietened debate over claims for the decisiveness of strategic airpower (for nearly 50 years at least), so the advent of the 'super' device/weapon in 1952–54 settled definitively any residual argument over the destructive potential in nuclear warfare. It is probably worth noting that although retrospectively there were safety, logistical, and other military (e.g. missile targeting) rationales for the much smaller and lighter packages that were fusion weapons, the second, thermonuclear, step in this RMA was not taken to meet emerging military requirements.[35] The second step was taken for the same reason as the first in 1941–45. Each superpower feared coercion should the other proceed to develop the hydrogen bomb, and each rationally and correctly understood that the sheer momentum of technological invention could not be arrested.

Hiroshima was a strategic moment unique among its nominal peers in the other cases considered here. It revealed the secret that the weaponisation of nuclear physics worked in practice as well as in the theory which scientists had known for more than a decade. For a while this 'moment' did not accurately match contemporary military reality, but the expansion of the atomic arsenal,[36] and then the development of fusion weapons, promoted a wholly novel strategic context wherein 'the link between victory and self-preservation had been cut'.[37] Moreover, as the author of those words explains, '[a]t least the possibility had now to be taken into account that the greater the triumph gained over an opponent who was in possession of nuclear weapons, the greater the danger to the survival of the victor.'

Institutional agency

As in the quotation immediately above, it has long been commonplace to lay emphasis upon the interlocking of national fates which is a principal consequence of nuclear armed rivalry. *Mutual* assured destruction, *mutual* deterrence, *common* security, and in general a strategic stability which cannot be achieved unilaterally, have been the conceptual stocks-in-trade of nuclear theorists since the late 1950s.[38] The proposition, which became a virtual fact (if that is not an oxymoron), of a shared fate in victory and defeat was a central novelty of the nuclear era. However, for the particular purposes of this study it is more useful to explore the differences than the commonalities in nuclear matters between the superpowers. As usual with a major RMA – or MR (as explained in Chapter 2) – there is a sense in which those implementing the revolution have strictly limited policy discretion. We will focus upon the US and Soviet variants of the nuclear RMA as historical examples of strategic behaviour. This focus must not obscure the genuine, and important, superpower commonality of technological opportunity, of prudential military–strategy motivation, and eventually of the probable physical and political consequences in the event of nuclear war.

As in the previous cases, institutional agency refers to the principal organisations, operating concepts, and plans which propelled the RMA into operational life. For the nuclear, as also for the information-led, RMA, strategic theory assumes a relative significance absent from the Napoleonic and First World War cases. In those last two episodes the agents of military revolution tried to make effective use in wartime conditions of the military instrument which already was largely to hand. The nuclear (and information-led) RMA was not like that. Beyond the initially temporally sequential, then roughly parallel, exploitation of nuclear science, there appeared to be considerable scope for legitimate argument over how a state with nuclear arms should behave. In support of that claim I must point sceptics to the frequently intense debates over nuclear strategy, nuclear arms control, and the associated questions for conventional forces, which began in minor key in the late 1940s but which surged into animated life in 1954, and have continued irregularly to the present day.[39]

Appearances to the contrary notwithstanding, to mention the fact that *nuclear strategy* is an essentially contested concept – recall the words of Lawrence Freedman quoted at the beginning of this chapter – is not a digression in a discussion of institutional agency. The US and the Soviet institutional agents for the nuclear RMA sought rationally and responsibly to do that which most probably could not be done well.[40] Viewed in long retrospect, one can try to argue that both superpowers were guilty of treating a political weapon as a military weapon. John J. Weltman had a point when he wrote that '[t]he development of nuclear strategy represented an attempt at a Jominian solution to a problem that was essentially Clausewitzian in nature'.[41] His point, though powerful, nonetheless is unhelpfully idealistic and probably is misleading as to the proper scope of things strategic. Whether or not nuclear weapons would be strategically potent as a consequence of actual use, especially in large numbers, one can reasonably doubt. There is much less scope for such doubt, however, concerning the strategic potency of the threat of their use. Recent scholarship confirms Robert Jervis' claim that '[a]lthough *military* victory is impossible, victory is not: nuclear weapons can help reach many important political goals.'[42]

Virtually regardless of the strategic ideas favoured by statesmen, military institutions with military culture(s) will approach a weapon, any kind of weapon, in a military way.[43] As the executive agents of an RMA (inter alia), military planners and soldiers will intend and train to use the weapons available according to standard principles of military efficiency (which are different from civilian economic principles).[44] Scholars and politicians may believe, possibly correctly, that many of the details of nuclear weaponry and planning really do not matter for deterrence, and that nothing beyond (prewar) deterrence is of strategic interest. In practice, though, it is rarely practicable for governments to instruct their military instruments to be potent for deterrence, but not to strive to be militarily effective in war. This point could lead us far astray. Its significance here is that it translates unsurprisingly as meaning that the institutional agents of the nuclear RMA behaved very much according to their military institutional natures. If that fact is not understood, it can be difficult to comprehend how each superpower could field, at their respective stock-piling peaks, in excess of 30,000 nuclear weapons of all kinds. To narrow the question somewhat, how could the deeply expert and prudent professionals who directed the principal strategic nuclear institutions of the superpowers – for the United States, the Strategic Air Command (SAC) and the Navy's SSBN (ballistic missile submarine) force; for the USSR the Strategic Rocket Forces and Long Range Aviation – oversee the growth of grotesquely unusable forces?

Strategic historians, inevitably as usual looking backwards, know that by the mid-1960s at the latest both superpowers had acquired nuclear arsenals of such a size and character that in the event of war the only prospect of national survival reposed in the risky realm of reciprocated self restraint in weight and purpose of attack. Actual human historical agents in the 1940s, 1950s, and even the 1960s, did not know what historians now think they know with a sublime certainty. Despite the startling public impact of Hiroshima, the unarguable demonstration that with the atomic bomb something very different had just arrived, the nuclear era happened day by day, decision by decision, invention by invention, as had all previous eras. Gian P. Gentile was half-correct when he wrote as follows:

> In the aftermath of World War II planners did not see atomic weapons as revolutionary. They thought of strategic bombing, conventional and

atomic, as a method of attack against enemy war-making capacity that could lead to the breakdown of enemy will. This concept was based on war-winning, not war-deterring.[45]

Given half a chance, or less, any military institution will prepare for war with a view to conduct planning to do its best to achieve military victory. Deterrent effect is somewhat akin to love and happiness: it cannot be achieved directly.[46] The institutional agents of the nuclear RMA, as with other RMAs, have war as their trade. Military professionals, US and Soviet, did not need to be deeply read in Clausewitzian lore to know that war is an uncertain business. Armed forces cannot plan prudently with high confidence to deter. Instead, they plan to fight, and hope that putative enemy leaders anticipate combat loss of all kinds wholly disproportionate to the political stakes. Throughout the Cold War both sides hoped to deter, but their military institutions necessarily planned to make the best military use they could of the assets available to them.

The history of the nuclear RMA in its institutional agency is now reasonably well known, especially through the research, writing, and editing activities of David A. Rosenberg and Steven T. Ross.[47] The Soviet story is much less well established, but has begun to emerge in tolerably credible outline.[48] Military institutional context, culture, and history, are all hugely significant. SAC, *the* US institutional agent for execution of this RMA, was heir to faith in 'victory through air power'. The so-called 'strategic' nuclear forces, at least until the navy's first Polaris patrols in 1960, were shaped and controlled by the disciples of Giulio Douhet, Billy Mitchell, Hugh Trenchard, and the bomber barons of the Second World War.[49] We need to remember that the nuclear RMA was organised and led by some of the men who had waged the strategic air war over Europe and Japan from 1942 to 1945. It is worth recalling that the same man who was sent to rescue an obviously failing strategic bombing campaign against Japan in 1944–45, General Curtis LeMay, was moved on 19 October 1948 to save a visibly failing SAC.[50] LeMay, the ultimate unruly 'bomber baron', oversaw in the late 1940s and 1950s the creation of a vastly expanded SAC as a potential instrument of decision, and moved up to become Chief of Staff of the USAF in the early 1960s.

The US government under Truman was more than a little confused and undecided over its nuclear policy. LeMay's SAC suffered from neither malady. Its mission was to deter if possible, and win if it must. US nuclear strategy, which is to say what the executive agency of SAC actually intended to do in war, was a dynamic rational product of the matching of available assets to identified targets in a militarily efficient, that is, coherent, strike plan. SAC achieved control of the target list and of target classification and prioritisation; this was a vital bureaucratic victory because of the apparently logical connection between targets and force structure.[51] Much assisted by the growth in Soviet nuclear forces in the 1950s, and by the explosive potency of true fusion weapons after 1954, LeMay's SAC wrote the scenario for the final triumph of air power operating all but independently. Strategic air power – after 1958 imperially expanded by Air Force Chief of Staff Thomas D. White to 'aerospace' power – alone would deter, wage and decide the next great war. It should be unnecessary to add that a USAF dominated by strategic bomber barons and overseeing execution of by far the largest operational fraction of the nuclear RMA, was not overly enthusiastic about the promise in long-range ballistic missiles. Forty years on, the air force, though by then run by a 'fighter mafia' rather than by bomber barons, continued to express its dominant institutional culture by controlling military space development through co-operation licensed by that scientifically absurd, if politically convenient, concept of aerospace.[52]

As the American nuclear RMA was implemented and moulded primarily by the airman's view of the strategic world,[53] so the Soviet variant inevitably bore the stamp of continentalist culture and of the ground forces which had been the ultimate guardian of the geostrategic integrity of the Eurasian Soviet–Russian state. The Soviet style of nuclear RMA reflected in addition both the particular geopolitics of the East–West rivalry, and the fact that the United States had a long, indeed unassailable, lead in 'strategic' aviation. Soviet strategic behaviour in aid of the nuclear revolution was no less rational than was American. The initial strategic challenge to the USSR was not so much to discover how to exploit the nuclear RMA, rather was it to find effective ways to counter the American lead (in today's parlance, the USSR sought and found an asymmetric strategy). For the better part of 15 years, at least until the end of the 1950s, in a period of very considerable peril, the USSR had to try and protect its gains from the Second World War. In what one day may be labelled a classic case of successful asymmetrical strategy, the USSR responded to the American atomic menace by: (1) undertaking a crash programme in atomic, then thermonuclear, bomb research and development; (2) threatening western Europe with unmatchable ground and tactical air forces; (3) building a submarine force which could impose a third Battle of the Atlantic; (4) massively upgrading its air defence system; (5) acquiring some ability to strike North America with long-range atomic air power (initially strictly on one-way missions, of course); (6) acquiring a credible ability to deliver nuclear weapons to medium range around the 'periphery' of Eurasia (which were to contain staging refuelling bases for SAC aircraft);[54] and (7) racing to develop ballistic missiles of intercontinental range which either would, or would appear to, demote US long-range aviation to the status of 'yesterday's weapon'.

Three major points have to be registered concerning institutional agency for the Soviet nuclear RMA. First, in the words of David Holloway,

The development of long-range missiles was viewed very much as an extension of artillery, and the artillery chiefs took part in the formulation of the early missile development plans, as well as in the flight testing of the missiles [in the 1940s]. The first missile units were formed on the basis of the Guards mortar units, which had used the 'Katiusha' rocket artillery to great effect during the war.[55]

Second, from the 1960s to the 1980s the (nuclear-armed) missile orientation of the Soviet nuclear RMA was driven very largely by the political interests of the leading military–industrial barons from the Communist Party of the Soviet Union (CPSU).[56] While the Soviet nuclear RMA was an example of strategic behaviour, it was also political and bureaucratic behaviour which took virtually no account of a close analysis of military requirements from the eventual military operators. The 1930s-era 'merchants of death' literature,[57] which, updated to denounce an alleged 'military–industrial complex', enjoyed a generic revival in the United States in the 1960s and 1970s, is almost a joke when read in the context of the Soviet military–industrial–*party political* complex. This was not as clear to Western officials and scholars during the Cold War as subsequently. As always hindsight tends to score more bullseyes than did contemporary analysis. Today, it is reasonably obvious that in the later Cold War decades the US government greatly exaggerated the size of the Soviet gross national product (GNP), though it underestimated the percentage of GNP dedicated to defence functions, and it did not understand the military–industrial–political dynamic behind a great deal of Soviet military procurement.

Third, despite the sharp contrasts in institutional agency and strategic geography between the superpowers, the similarities in what today is known about their evolving operational responses to the nuclear RMA are far more impressive than the differences. Without abandoning the quest for military advantage in the nuclear arms competition – indeed, such abandonment would have been culturally and strategically impossible – both sides recognised that they had created a nuclear strategic instrument with almost no military utility if it was employed in action.

Instrument

In common with the major RMAs explored in Chapters 6 and 7, the nuclear revolution defeated itself with respect to unilateral military potency. As a result each of these RMAs eventually allowed competition between traditional and basic elements of strength and weakness to decide the course of history. The military instruments that were the physical expression of the nuclear RMA were enormously strategic significant. They cast a long shadow over much of world politics, and certainly over most aspects of the statecraft of East and West for the better part of 50 years. That granted, the strategic historical fact remains that the nuclear RMA, as with the RMAs of Napoleon and the First World War, and no matter how genuinely radical its meaning for the character and conduct of war, did not in practice yield an instrument of strategic, let alone military, decision. None of these truly major RMAs was exploited, or arguably were practicably exploitable, in ways adequate to secure decisive success. Recall that none of Napoleon's victories brought him the lasting European hegemony and dynastic security that he craved. Recall also that the superior methods of war generally well practised by the principal belligerents in 1918 tended to have offsetting consequences,[58] which meant that physically the stronger side was eventually certain to win (if its political will did not fail domestically). So too we find that even in the technologically awesome nuclear era, the RMA of the day delivered neither military victory nor, directly and unarguably, political victory. It is not implausible to argue that an important consequence of the nuclear revolution was the substantial elevation of the threshold of antagonism which generates decisions for war. This, however, is really the same point I have just made about 1918. If nuclear-armed forces helped keep war at bay, they thereby made space, bought time, for other factors (political, economic, cultural) to be effective.

None of what I have just written could prudently have provided much comfort to statesmen and soldiers from the late 1940s to the early 1980s. From the agreeable perspective of the early twenty-first century, one may be tempted to dismiss the great engines of nuclear destruction that East and West created as militarily absurd and hence not particularly interesting, certainly not very interesting in their technical and operational detail. The first corrective necessary to such a view is to note that even the rationally militarily unusable still might well have been used. The peaceful outcome to the Cold War was by no means a foregone conclusion. Furthermore, that peaceful outcome may yet come to be regarded by the balance of historians as inherently improbable, even though it happened. In other words, the human race may have been very lucky to avoid a third world war between 1945 and 1989. These thoughts should warn us against uncritically writing general RMA theory from an historian's point of view. History does indeed show yet again that a great RMA itself, directly, failed to deliver a crushing success. The social scientist as strategic theorist, however, nurtures the suspicion that 'victory', by some definition, might have been achieved with nuclear use at least from the later 1940s until the mid-1960s. Moreover, the responsible officials of East and West were obliged as a matter of basic prudence to treat the details of nuclear forces and doctrine as matters of great importance.

It is far easier to describe the evolution of military forces, even to describe the evolution of a 'balance' between rival forces, than it is to judge what those forces meant strategically. Rarely has the strategist's classic question 'so what?' been so pertinent as in relation to the highly competitive variant of the nuclear RMA developed by the superpowers during the Cold War. As in the earlier discussions of the Napoleonic and First World War RMAs, so here also the military instruments to execute the revolution varied greatly from period to period. However, unlike those previous cases, with the nuclear RMA there are at least some grounds for argument over whether much of the detail of evolution of the instrument was really of strategic significance. The Napoleonic and First World War RMAs were both tested repeatedly in action in the field. The competitive military instruments of the US and Soviet nuclear RMAs never underwent trial by battle. One can argue that the rival nuclear force postures were tested in the field of statecraft in both the crises that occurred and, and by inference, those that did not. Such virtual testing leaves ample room for endless argument. Virtual tests of rival military prowess can provide only virtual evidence, which is not really evidence at all. Scholars today are solemnly debating not only how well nuclear deterrence worked in the Cold War, but even whether it worked at all.[59]

The possible deficiencies of some standard RMA definitions are readily detected when the strategist's question 'so what?' is applied to the nuclear revolution. Andrew Krepinevich requires an RMA to produce 'a dramatic increase ... in the combat potential and military effectiveness of armed forces'.[60] Did the military instruments of the nuclear RMA meet this standard? If war were a unilateral exercise, perhaps. The problem, of course, would have been that even the securing of victory by the defeat of the enemy's armed forces could not guarantee strategic victory at tolerable cost. In other words, practicable military prowess came to be divorced from achievable political outcomes. At some risk of appearing egregiously politically incorrect, it is worth noting that all judgements on a Soviet–US nuclear war are, and must remain, strictly speculative.

As the Napoleonic and First World War RMAs were executed, as it were, against a moving target of an enemy, so also the nuclear RMAs of the West, then the East, developed their nuclear military instrument as the enemy changed shape. Given the character of the nuclear RMA in comprising essentially long-range independent bombardment, whereas the earlier RMAs discussed here entailed (more or less) firepower as an aid to manoeuvre, the story of the instrument is a tale of warheads for targets. As the kinds and numbers of the former expanded exponentially, so more and more enemy assets could be treated operationally as 'targets'. Similarly, as the enemy expanded the number and variety of its nuclear-armed forces, and constructed special facilities for the protection of key people and functions, so there were more and more enemy assets which nuclear forces were required to hold at risk. To select just one unusually important historical juncture, in 1961 the recently created US Joint Strategic Target Planning Staff identified no fewer than 80,000 potential targets for nuclear attack, among which 3,729 'were determined to be essential for attack'.[61] In practice this number of distinctive installations conflated to 1,060 aims points (DGZs, designated ground zeros). Between 1950 and 1960, the United States climbed out of its age of atomic scarcity into a new era of thermonuclear superabundance (from a stockpile totalling approximately 450 atomic bombs, to one pushing 18,500).

The military instruments of this RMA achieved full maturity in the 1960s, when both sides had proceeded to exploit the dawning of 'the missile age'. Notwithstanding the many alarms and excursions in nuclear policy, theory, and debate in the 1970s and 1980s, the nuclear RMA was comprehensively in place by the late 1960s. The US nuclear military instrument at the time of the beginning of the Berlin crisis in 1948 comprised close to 50 Mark III fission weapons which, once assembled (by 39 men taking two days for each bomb), could be delivered by 30 B-29s of the 509th Composite Bomb Group, based in Roswell, New Mexico.[62] To translate those numbers into an atomic campaign against the USSR would have been a task of a minimum of several weeks. A decade and a half later, the United States had a nuclear arsenal with some 32,000 weapons of all varieties and for all purposes, to be delivered by a cast of thousands of long-, medium-, and short-range aircraft, land and sea-based ballistic missiles, and artillery tubes. The Soviet story differs in detail, but not in kind. The Soviet armed forces received their first operational nuclear (atomic) weapons in late 1953, and – following the United States, technological–industrial possibilities, and military requirements – gradually achieved approximate parity (warheads and delivery means) and parity-plus (in the early 1970s) in total numbers of strategic warheads. The Soviet nuclear stockpile peaked in quantity in the mid-1980s, a generation later than that of the United States, probably at some 45,000 weapons of all kinds.[63] But what did all this mean strategically?

Execution and evolving maturity

The contrasts between our three principal RMA case studies are especially interesting at this stage of their life-cycle. All three eventually were dominated and defined in the scope of their specific historical opportunity by the dimensions of strategy writ large. The Napoleonic RMA was thwarted in good part by the 'enemy' dimension of strategy which produced countervailing RMA behaviour; by the poverty of Napoleon's statecraft (as contrasted with his personal generalship); and, as a direct consequence of that poor political leadership, by the inadequate quantity, and even quality, of French means to secure the boundless ends being sought. The RMA of the First World War, in some contrast, matured in its German and British (Allied) variants into the zone where its execution exposed, indeed accentuated, the material and moral limitations of the former, while serving to permit the latter to make good enough use of its superior assets.

The execution and evolution of the nuclear RMA had military and political consequences which apparently, though only apparently, were quite at odds. War and strategy's innately bilateral structure allowed, but could not guarantee, the enemies of Napoleon and of Wilhelmine Germany to do well enough in the RMA arena as to stay competitive and eventually triumph with larger numbers. In similar fashion, the rival endeavours of the nuclear-armed super-powers yielded a military condition, in this case of true stalemate,[64] which permitted non-military factors a cutting-edge role in the great Cold War. As Donald Kagan argues persuasively, American grand strategy in that war proved lethally effective.[65] Granted some luck and good-enough judgement in policy execution, the nuclear RMA allowed the West long-term political success because it was undergirded by a realistic policy vision, feasible grand strategic choices, and steady enough policy execution. US policy and strategy in the Cold War was almost everything that Napoleonic and Wilhelminian policy and strategy was not. Scholars have argued and will long argue about the responsibility of the nuclear revolution for this agreeable tale. The super-powers appeared to cope well enough with nuclear peril, though certainly there was an incalculable possibility of policy error, operational glitches, or technical military missteps (again incalculable) by either side.[66]

Two key US policy-oriented (we cannot quite say policy) documents, in 1946 and 1950, served to make policy sense of the nuclear revolution, even though the 1946 paper did not address nuclear issues directly. The documents in question were 'The Long Telegram', dispatched by George F. Kennan from the US Embassy in Moscow on 22 February 1946 (which became truly public property in 1947 when the core of its argument appeared as 'The Sources of Soviet Conduct' by 'Mr X' in *Foreign Affairs*), and the policy planning document, 'NSC-68' of 14 April 1950 on 'United States Objectives and Programs for National Security'.[67] The former was principally an analysis of broad Soviet vulnerabilities, while the latter expanded on that analysis, updated it for the crisis conditions of early 1950, and provided a plan of action for US statecraft. Both documents advocated a careful policy of long-term containment of the Soviet Union, with NSC-68 emphasising the need to cope with growing Soviet military power. In particular, NSC-68 looked to the period when the Soviet Union would acquire a nuclear arsenal, thereby in theory negating much of the US advantage in a nuclear-led deterrence.[68] The defining ideas in these two documents were to guide US policy for more than 40 years.

The technical details of the US and Soviet variants of the nuclear RMA are easily accessible in a whole library of specialist studies. If, however, we seek to take a historical overview in order to trace arguably strategically meaningful execution and evolving maturity, then we can readily identify three periods. The first was the period of US atomic monopoly which lasted technically for four years, though in militarily significant terms perhaps eight to nine (1945–49 or 1953–54). Next, there was a long period of clear US nuclear advantage which can be positioned between 1949 and, debatably, 1968–69. Whether or not there would have been any true operational advantage is, of course, highly scenario-dependent. Suffice it to say that for these two decades the United States enjoyed marked military advantages over the USSR in nuclear armed forces. It is not wholly implausible to suggest that in the 1950s and 1960s, if the United States could have secured a fast start (I will stop short of specifying a pre-emptive, let alone preventive, strike), Soviet long-range nuclear forces appeared vulnerable to a well co-ordinated counterforce strike resting upon (eventually) fairly good overhead and electronic intelligence. In their operational practices Soviet concern for internal security may have compromised the pre-launch survivability of their forces. It should be unnecessary to add that everything might well have gone hideously wrong for the United States 'on the night'.

The third period in superpower strategic nuclear relations was one of 'essential equivalence', or rough parity, on most (offsetting) quantitative measures of assay. This period can be dated between the onset of what became the SALT (Strategic Arms Limitation Talks) process in 1968–69 and, strategically functionally, either the close of the Cold War in 1989 or an open-ended condition which persists even today as the United States and the Russian Federation reach for a deep reductions regime. Readers relatively unschooled in strategic arcana should not imagine that just because the apparently most salient baskets of strategic-force metrics (raw numbers of missiles, missile launchers, missile throwweight, accuracy, for example) seemed to approach a fairly close comparability, there was less for officials and other experts to dispute. If anything, the dawn of the age of 'rough parity' rewarded ever finer grained analyses and the devising of more and more clever and technically stressful speculative scenarios of alarm.[69] This is not necessarily to criticise the responsible experts and officials. After all, it was their duty to worry about strategic nuclear peril to the national security.

The exact connections between the age of rough strategic nuclear parity (the SALT–START era) and on–off political détente, and then the demise of the great Cold War contest itself, are much debated but are likely to remain eternally uncertain. By a wide margin, in the judgement of this theorist, politics and the ideology that helps propel politics were in the driver's seat. The fact remains also, however, that rival, understandably self-serving, military analyses have to show a condition of 'balance' (or tolerably close imbalance) permitting at least broad agreement on technical matters. Experts, especially experts who read their Clausewitz carefully, know that the most vital elements in a strategic balance are not measurable;[70] there are no reliable figures to be counted and displayed graphically for the edification and overawing of a highly numerate audience of briefees in Moscow and Washington. The 'measures' that really count include the importance of national interests at stake in a conflict; the 'moral' character, judgement, and skill (and *perhaps*, but only perhaps, knowledge) of the chief executive; luck; quality, including timeliness, of information (especially, though not exclusively, about the putative enemy and its friends and allies); understanding of how well friendly and enemy forces are likely to perform 'on the night' (e.g. is the chain of command truly robustly reliable – under attack? are the tens of thousands of important and essential machines of all kinds, including the human ones, truly to be trusted when under the ultimate duress?).

None of the significant items just listed can be captured in strategic arms agreements. Some can be addressed indirectly, if not always with high assurance as to full compliance by a prudent and cunning foe. For example, one can agree to 'de-target' forces; to 'de-alert' them; with various degrees of rigour to disassemble them; and even – for the extreme case – to render them more or less 'virtual'.[71] These ideas provide rational expression of the sentiment that if one does not trust politicians, officials, soldiers, or even just the historical statistics of normal accident rates with extremely complex systems,[72] it is wise to remove some or all of the potential for damage to be done. In other words, place dangerous toys out of the reach of children. This argument–cum–proposal set is a precise characterisation of a large fraction of the nuclear debate in the United States of the mid-to-late 1990s.

Although the last 20 years of the Cold War witnessed a rough equivalence in superpower strategic forces, notwithstanding the traditionally distinctive weightings that each side gave to different legs of its 'triad', the quest for military advantage did not slacken. The Soviet Strategic Rocket Forces surpassed SAC's and the US Navy's deployed missile forces in crude numbers, size, throwweight, and almost certainly in robustness of physical protection in standards for launcher construction. But SAC responded – indeed, it was an anticipatory reaction as well as simply an example of the 'ripening plum' syndrome[73] – with multiple warheads per missile, with individual targeting for those warheads, with much higher accuracy, and with warhead and more general miniaturisation. In due course, initially in the tactical bomber realm (F-117), eventually with strategic bombers (the B-2), SAC challenged Soviet/Russian defensive prowess with the innovative development of 'stealth' technologies. Although public and much official attention was focused upon the familiar classes of strategic nuclear weapon systems, a literally vital cluster of effectiveness-enabling space systems was developed, deployed, and employed, to exploit the historic US lead in computers and in electronics generally. From long-haul communications, through intelligence gathering, strategic early warning, geodesy (for precise geophysical measurements for exact missile targeting), to navigation (especially when Francis X. Kane's idea of the Global Positioning System, or GPS,[74] became a reality in the 1980s and 1990s), the technical tide of strategic history was flowing ever faster in the US favour. This fact is as plain to us retrospectively as it was by the early 1980s to many Soviet officials and, eventually, political leaders.[75]

From 1968 until at least the mid-1980s, the USSR endeavoured, indeed largely was obliged by necessity, to seek strategic advantage the old-fashioned way, by linear improvement and by ever greater, if hopefully critical, mass. They did not slim down their strategic or general purpose forces as their technical quality improved; instead they just built more and more machines of like dimensions, though with better performance. To be fair, there was no slimming on the US/NATO side either. Both sides in the Cold War, for entirely comprehensible and even prudent reasons, had constructed impracticable military machines for strategic nuclear *and* (European) theatre warfare. This is a bold dual claim that requires explanation.

The Cold War was won by the West politically, socially, economically, and in terms of grand strategy. But both superpowers (not their allies, that is a different story) tried heroically, not least in the 1968–89 period, to position themselves to win a hot war. The USSR amassed a strategic nuclear arsenal absolutely so large and relatively so generous in its target coverage that it might well have triggered some variant (and who cares which?) of a global nuclear winter.[76] Somewhat reluctantly, necessarily tentatively and suspiciously, and inconclusively – even former Soviet officials are uncertain as to its true operational authority – Soviet strategic forces *might* have anticipated, or tried to mirror, notable political restraint (not quite limited nuclear options *à la* James C. Schlesinger) in targeting, or they might not![77] Overall, as Marshal Ogarkov, inter alia, appreciated by the early 1980s, the end result of the Soviet bid for nuclear advantage from 1945 was the creation of a militarily useless, politically suicidal death machine.[78] It is not less true to say that the United States, again for the most prudent of military reasons, and in the opinion of this author for the most praiseworthy of political and ethical ones, had achieved a like futile condition. Whereas the Soviet general staff hoped that more throwweight muscle, better accuracy, and greater numbers of weapons might somehow be able to deliver victory in classic fashion, US theorists and officials had long abandoned any such hope. Instead, the US nuclear theory focused on crisis-time coercion, a troublingly necessary reciprocation of self-restraint in targeting choices (exceedingly violent nuclear diplomacy),[79] and generally in waging only as little nuclear war as intra-war deterrence required. To be polite, neither side's theories could survive modest interrogation in a graduate seminar, let alone at the highest level of government looking at the possibility of Apocalypse very soon. After the fashion of the belligerents in the First World War, who in 1915–17 submitted to a self-defeating theory of victory through material abundance and mass (especially in artillery ammunition), so the Soviet Union impracticably sought a possibility of victory in war though nuclear firepower. If anything, Western fantasies of strategic advantage through escalation of dominance and control were even less credible.

In discussion of the RMA of the First World War the argument included the claim that although artillery was the most defining of elements, alone it could not deliver the military effectiveness necessary for strategic advantage. With like logic, the nuclear RMA was always linked umbilically to the military story about the defence of peninsular Europe from Soviet invasion. The geopolitics of the Cold War provided complex asymmetries. As the major stake in the conflict, continental Europe was nominally easily accessible to mobile Soviet land–air power. But the homeland of that Soviet land–air power was in its turn accessible from the United States-garrisoned European (and Asian) 'rimlands'.[80] Furthermore, although the distance separating the United States from NATO-Europe was a political–psychological and logistically geostrategic disadvantage, there were powerful offsetting realities. The geographical isolation of North America from Europe encouraged a more military logic about European defence in the minds of US planners than was typical of those who lived in the putative 'battlespace', and that 'battlespace' included (at least European) Russia. In addition, the intercontinental geography of US–Soviet strategic relations played throughout the Cold War decades to traditional US strengths in the conduct of long-range warfare. By way of historical precedents, consider the diversely impressive US successes in waging war over the huge distances involved in the Civil War and then in both world wars, but especially in the conduct simultaneously of war on the largest of scales in Europe and the western Pacific in 1942–45.[81]

By the close of the 1970s, and certainly by the very early 1980s, both superpowers effectively had despaired, and long despaired in the US case, of constructing a strategic nuclear arsenal that should be capable of winning a third world war. Neither mass nor quality, nor exceedingly cunning plans, carried any very convincing promise of likely victory, or even of notable strategic advantage. The superpowers devised operational, more strictly perhaps (multi-)theatre level, solutions to the undeniable strategic nuclear deadlock.[82] If escalation to and through the strategic nuclear zone had become desperately imprudent, then self-evidently any great war would have to be waged and won below that level.

Remember the geopolitically and geostrategically most basic relationship of the superpower conflict. The US ability to devastate the USSR directly with long-range atomic, then thermonuclear, weapons, was strategically variably (with issue and by period) offset by NATO's recognition of Soviet ability to conquer Western Europe. From the early 1970s until the close of the Cold War, the US Defense Department (DoD) decided that there could be realistic solutions to this politically paralysing persisting conundrum at both the technical–tactical and operational/theatre levels. Instead of trying to defeat a Soviet assault by forms of front-line attritional combat – definitely a losing proposition at the time – the DoD elected to explore a few potentially devastating, asymmetrical options.

Generically under the broad programme codename of 'Assault Breaker', weapons were to be developed which could rip the heart out of the dense mass of the Soviet Army's armoured and mechanised strengths. Norman Friedman usefully points out that 'Assault Breaker' was more promise than performance, but that '[to] an extent unappreciated in the United States in the 1970s, the Soviets believed that their American rivals were scientific magicians; what they said they could do, they could do. To the Soviets, Assault Breaker was a disaster. Once in place it would neutralise a major threat they could deploy against NATO, a conventional armoured attack.'[83] Using smarter technologies based on electronic miniaturisation (for sensing for all functions), weapons (including especially small, and it was hoped unit-item-cheap, sub-munitions) would be precisely deliverable by artillery tubes, by ballistic and cruise missiles, and of course by aircraft, literally to massacre deeply echeloned Warsaw Pact forces stacked up to pile-drive their way to the Channel in days or weeks. Assault Breaker was not the concept of a single magic 'silver bullet' device; rather, it was an intelligent commitment to compete with Soviet theatre-level military power in a tactically non-linear way for a prospectively operational-, even strategic-level consequence. Soviet military experts monitored this US policy and then (the set of) programmatic commitments, and were duly impressed. The computer revolution was well under way and Ogarkov and his colleagues knew that they were on the weaker side of this particular thrust of modern history.

At the operational, theatre, and even strategic, levels of military competition, as Samuel P. Huntington was to explain so brilliantly in a summary essay and notable period piece in1987,[84] the US government added to the longstanding Assault Breaker concept/programme the notion of a deep attack *into eastern Europe* under the rubric of Airland Battle (a US proposal that terrified many pusillanimous NATO-Europeans); the US Navy (and, somewhere in its wake, the British Royal Navy) crystallised many of its ancestral preferences in the boldly advertised Maritime Strategy,[85] which anticipated the posing of direct menace to the maritime flanks of Soviet power at home; and, most frightening of all for Moscow, President Ronald Reagan invented and then licensed actual bureaucratic/programmatic creation in 1983–84 of the Strategic Defense Initiative (Organisation) (SDI(O)).[86] In the President's mind, the SDI was designed to shift the principal burden of strategic deterrence from weapons that kill people to those that could protect them. In the minds of prudently conservative and notably sceptical Soviet (and many US academic) minds, the President was threatening to exploit the emerging information-led military-technical revolution (MTR) so as to augment deadly American nuclear swords with a strategically no less deadly shield.[87]

Although the Soviet Union of the very late Brezhnev, the interregnum, and then the early Gorbachev eras pursued the strategic competition in part by means of business as usual, with more of the same massive production of items of traditional military hardware, its more noteworthy intended competitive responses were rather different. In the 1970s, and ironically peaking in the mid-1980s (just as the political context at home was entering a terminal phase of no recovery under Gorbachev's misguided leadership), Soviet power elected to rediscover the master idea of operational manoeuvre on the largest scale for the conduct of deep battle far into the rear of the notional front line. This was Triandafillov in the 1920s, Tukhachevskii in the 1930s, and (arguably) it was Zhukov in 1943–45 (Stalin overruled his wish to effect a far deeper double enveloping Cannae with Operation Uranus in November 1942 against the German Sixth Army at Stalingrad).[88] In the later 1970s, recapitalised with new tanks and somewhat armoured troop carriers (BMPs), the Soviet Army reinvented the assault super-division, or Operational Manoeuvre Group (OMG).[89] The overriding purpose would be to race brutally and far into the NATO rear and disrupt the enemy's mobilising Aufmarsch and rather sclerotic plans for attritional resistance. In a grand (Soviet) demonstration of the truth in Colonel John Boyd's decision theory of the 'OODA loop',[90] the war (in continental Europe) would be decided before NATO could catch its breath and find time for its nuclear chains of command to respond with purpose and some possibility of worthwhile consequences.

There was much pessimism in the Soviet Army over the operational and strategic implications of nuclear employment, and deep disbelief in symbolic or demonstrative use of nuclear weapons. Nonetheless, Soviet/Warsaw Pact military planning documents seen by NATO analysts since the Cold War (especially those 'liberated' in the former East Germany) provide telling evidence supporting the long-standing suspicion that any Soviet bid for victory in Europe would have been immediately preceded and accompanied by an extensive pre-emptive laydown of theatre-nuclear and chemical weapons, in the (near-certain) event that NATO moves towards nuclear war were detected.[91] Such a practice, albeit only pre-emptive, obviously must have maximised the prospect of fairly swift escalation by the United States, France, and Britain against targets on Soviet territory. One is reminded of the cardinal strategic error committed on 7 December 1941, when the manner of Japan's initial military foray against US territory and assets in Hawaii ensured a potentially total US response. It is true that the USSR might have aspired to achieve intrawar deterrence via credible nuclear *threats* alone, but still one must observe that the initiation of a large nuclear war in Europe for the purpose of securing the swiftest of regionally decisive victories, had to carry an awesome risk of open-ended escalation.

Whether or not OMGs would have served up even a Pyrrhic victory we can never know. What we do know is that the more competent among Soviet military professionals became increasingly pessimistic about the ability of their economy, and hence of that economy's dependent military machines (illegal technological transfer notwithstanding), to compete effectively with the ever more electronically enabled, geographically multidimensional, threats posed by the computer-rich Western Alliance. The only practical solution was to abandon the struggle and make political peace. As history records, this is what happened in the late 1980s, even though military cause and political effect were not neatly correlated.

Strategically speaking, which of course is by no means the whole story of the Soviet implosive demise, the United States (with some help, and much resistance, from its allies) literally saw off the Soviet long-standing systemic advantage in land–(tactical) air power, and threatened to be able to exploit its technological long suits in maritime and strategic assets (and geopolitical location). The nuclear RMA matured into a true stalemate. That fact, recognised first by the West and then by the East, generated a strategic condition entirely familiar from the historical episodes of Napoleon and then of the First World War. Specifically, as an RMA becomes a more general achievement among competitors, its defining engine will be less and less capable of making a decisive military or strategic difference. The wonderful reorganisation of the French Army did not suffice to yield the kind of lasting benefit which could seal Europe's fate in France's favour for a generation; the (near) perfection of artillery technique, even when applied by an adequate mass of material, still had to be exploited by genuinely combined arms; and the competition in nuclear forces, expressing the RMA analysed here, may well have defined the military era for most of the years since 1945, but it did not unambiguously decide the admittedly only virtual strategic–military contest, let alone the course and outcome of the Cold War as a whole.

Feedback and adjustment

For many commentators, including politicians, journalists, and academics, 'feedback and adjustment' offers almost a perfect description of the heavily bilateral nuclear RMA of the decades of the Cold War. Indeed, the 'nuclear arms race' often was used as a phrase all but synonymous with the Cold War writ large. Given the prominence of weaponry, especially nuclear-related weaponry, in that conflict, and given the public salience of East–West discussion and periodic negotiation about that weaponry, the confusion was understandable if not excusable. Much as well-meaning but naïve observers persuaded themselves during the interwar decades that a malign functional coalition of amoral arms manufacturers, secret diplomacy, alliances, and adherence to the theory of the balance of power had brought on the catastrophe of 1914–18, so a supposedly mindless spiralling of competitive nuclear armaments became a popular villain in the 1960s and 1970s.

The general idea of a nuclear arms competition was sound enough. After all, East and West spent substantial fortunes on all kinds of intelligence gathering. The idea came unglued when it was permitted to transcend common-sense generic description and instead was elevated into a quasi-social scientific theory of actual, interlocking, state behaviour.[92] In particular, many American theorists and senior officials came to believe from the mid-1960s that there was a tight pattern of action and reaction locking the superpowers into a spiral of escalating futility.[93] The most potent fuel for action–reaction was held to be anxieties about the malign implications of strategic defensive weapons for the efficacy of strategic offensive weapons. The theory held that if strategic stability, the Holy Grail of safety in superpower Cold War relations,[94] requires that both sides be confident that their offensive nuclear weapons enjoy unrestricted access to the enemy's society, then the prospect of an effective defence (especially active missile defence) can be truly terrifying.[95] Strategic nuclear deterrence could cease to be mutual.

This is not the place to rehearse long-exposed scholarly arguments in praise or criticism of the notion of an arms race driven most potently by an all but extra-human and extra-political automatic action–reaction mechanism, save to say that the theory was demonstrably wrong.[96] The American and Soviet variants of the RMA shared many common features, above all else eventually effectively common access to the frontiers of science and technology. The political and military cultures of the two sides, expressing distinctive strategic geographies, ideologies, balances of political–bureaucratic coalitions of power, historical traditions, and sheer friction, among other factors, necessarily produced RMAs distinctive in detail. Of course, each superpower built its nuclear forces to fight the other, which meant necessarily that the forces were shaped to fit that enemy (as that enemy was understood). But the military professionals of each side did the best that they could with the actual resources available locally at the time, in the no less local climate of policy-making (despite irregular streams of locally filtered external stimuli), according to their understanding of the threat today and tomorrow. Scholars who look back over the arms competition of the Cold War would mistakenly subscribe to a Steven Spielberg-style view of modern strategic history if they expected to find a neat trail of timely feedback and adjustment. By way of a few suggestions why this has to be so: policy-makers would change their minds as foreign and domestic political events intruded (e.g. a threefold increase in the US defence budget triggered by the Korean War); many promising technologies either turn out not to be so (nuclear-powered aircraft, particle-beam ballistic missile defences, submarine wake detection, and so forth), or are overtaken by other technologies; and strategic ideas and doctrines shift. Overall, while granting the potency of estimation of foreign threat, the nuclear RMAs of both East and West were shaped very much by what broadly is best described as domestic processes, though domestic processes assuredly legitimised and fed by perception of events.[97] Although Americans and Russians did indeed regard the nuclear menace posed by the superpower foe with the utmost seriousness, those paralleling regards were held by distinctively American and Russian players.

The nuclear RMA of the Cold War had to occur. After all, the great enablers had been discovered on the frontiers of nuclear science in 1932 (the neutron), 1939 (fission), and 1940 (calculation of the necessary critical mass). Once US, British, and, pre-eminently, central European emigré scientists had demonstrated in 1945 that nuclear science really could be weaponised, the next political conflict between wealthy polities could not possibly eschew a nuclear (and missile) dimension(s) – the most modern of weapons. Given the persistence of the strategic dimension to human history, scientific and technological progress mandated the nuclear RMA. The engineering story of the nuclear RMA, including the succession of delivery vehicles for its eponymous centre-pieces, which is so beloved by the 'toy store' clutch of technical writers, really has been the generally unremarkable product of large, typically well-resourced, highly motivated and competent, military–industrial–political coalitions duly proceeding whither technological challenge took them. By and large, those weapons-developing coalitions produced what could be produced, unless service culture, prevailing official doctrine, lack of cash, or politics stopped them. Such was their nature. They varied in composition and functioning between the superpowers, but the core of their stories is identical.

Among our three historical case studies, only the nuclear RMA was not field-tested in actual combat. Errors in threat estimation, mistakes in tactical and operational experimentation, and faulty techniques were all exposed by poor military performance and defeat in the 1790s, 1800s, and 1910s, but not really from 1945 to 1989. In its direct military dimension between the super-powers, the nuclear RMA of the Cold War was a phoney or virtual conflict. How well did the USSR adjust to its shocking new post-1945 role as the severe nuclear laggard, in the context of total victory against the German foe? We know that the USSR survived four and a half decades of the Cold War. Although it is self-evident that every potential decision leading to a third world war that needed to be prevented was prevented, we lack access to definitive evidence which could show that offsetting nuclear weaponry actually functioned as the deterrent. It is impossible to prove a negative. The possibilities for Armageddon were so obvious that it is impossible not to be impressed by their non-actualisation in a moment of political miscalculation or insurmountable compounded 'friction'. But still we cannot be sure that our skill in monitoring feedback from the foe's behaviour, and then our consequent behavioural adjustments, literally were the most vital barrier against disaster. Perhaps we were all the underdeserving beneficiaries of a series of fortunate accidents.

Both sides proceeded a long way towards adjustment to the military realities of nuclear stalemate. Neither, however, could afford simply to assume compla-cently that strategic deadlock had been legislated by modern science. What if that assumption were wrong? Even with respect to the nuclear RMA, to assume the end of (strategic) history would be most imprudent, almost no matter how persuasive the available evidence of futility in the competition.

STRATEGIC BEHAVIOUR

For all its ultimate military indecisiveness (whose nuclear forces and doctrine best exploited this RMA?), every dimension of strategy all but begs for individual and especially coherent holistic analysis here. I chose to register that judgement more as evidence supportive of my general theory that RMAs must function strategically than as a compulsion to pursue every dimension, and many multi-dimensional nexuses, down every trail in sight. The commentary below, as with the corresponding entries in Chapters 6 and 7, must be selective. That commentary also must be notably debatable and frequently even ambiguous. The reasons are both that much of the evidence on the largely bilateral nuclear RMA of the Cold War is still not available (and in some key respects, especially on deterrence, will never be available), and that at least a couple of dimensions – such as theory and doctrine, and geography – betray both absolute strengths and weaknesses for each virtual belligerent.

Notwithstanding our emphasis upon the virtuality of the Cold War, it is probably important also to repeat the view that it was a war. Although there has to be an element of personal taste about the weight attached analytically to the all-important historical fact of non-war (to be less than daringly positivistic in this allegedly factless constructivist scholarly era), it can be all too easy for commentators today to forget that the real-time players could not know that outcome.

The observations offered here sometimes look contra-suggestive (ethics as a US weakness, economics and logistics as a defining Soviet strength? ... and so on and so forth) or at least somewhat odd. Complex analysis is like that. Nine linked items, some corresponding to individual dimensions, others comprising judgements which conflate several dimensions, will shed additional light on the superpower agents of the nuclear RMA in the Cold War.

The very complexity of strategy, with its many interacting dimensions, positively invites misunderstanding of why and how much relative strengths and weaknesses can matter. When, for example, Table 8.1 claims American society as a dimension of strategic affairs that is a source of weakness, it means weakness relative not to Soviet society but rather to some other American dimensions. The dominant reason for this approach is systemic to my understanding of how strategy works. Society does not fight society, technology does not joust with technology, and geography does not wage combat with geography over 'decisive points' and the like. Instead, each dimension plays blended with the totality of all US, or Soviet, dimensions, and each functions, perhaps variably, as relative weakness (perhaps poor leadership) in need of compensation, as an average performance that works just well enough, or as a source of strength itself providing compensation (perhaps organisation for policy- and strategy-making, perhaps technology).

First, although US politics, and even the politics of the global Western Alliance, often operated strongly as a source of net strength for quality of public and official debate over nuclear policy, the unique openness of American society could be an item of relative weakness.[98] A US political system with its jealously guarded separation of executive and legislative authority could command public explanation of unpersuasive-sounding assumptions and decisions. However, that system also framed a society and nurtured ethical nostrums which could press a would-be prudent government into hasty, ill-supported and unwise choices. This is not written as criticism, simply as an observation about a popular democracy. Claims concerning alleged bomber and missile 'gaps' are the stuff of democracy in a condition of dynamic arms competition (recall the Anglo-German dreadnought race – 'we want eight and we won't wait!').[99]

Table 8.1: The Nuclear RMA

Dimensions	United States	USSR
People		
Society	W	
Culture		
Politics	S	W
Ethics	W	
Economics and logistics	S	DS
Organisation	S	W
Military administration	S/W	S
Information and intelligence	W	
Theory and doctrine	DS/W	DS/W
Technology	DS	
Military operations		
Command		
Geography	S/W	S/W
Friction	W	W
Adversary	W	W
Time	S	W

Key: DS   Defining strength of this RMA
DS/W Both relative strength and weakness
S   Strength in this dimension
W   Weakness in this dimension

Of course, American society stayed, indeed gloriously outstayed, the course of the Cold War. The USSR did not have a civil society because its political system could not tolerate one. Eventually, that Soviet lack may have played a crucial role in the ethical weaknesses of an all but utterly cynical Soviet populace. Nonetheless, as a player in the strategic behaviour of the nuclear RMA, there is little doubt that American society and public and private ethics were more of a constraint upon, than an enabler of, prudent policy choice.

Second, not until the very late Brezhnev and beyond eras in Soviet Cold War history was economics a painfully limiting factor for Soviet strategic behaviour. Naturally, much of the European USSR of the later 1940s was a war-ravaged economic wasteland. But a comprehensively ruthless political command system, the opportunity to plunder occupied territories, the wartime legacy of Western aid, and the temporary lack of interest of new foes in energetic competition, all combined to help the USSR pass through its lengthy period of nominally appalling weakness. By way of immediate compensation, the USSR had very large, fairly combat-ready armies in the field in central–eastern Europe, and was in a position to offset any small US atomic offensive with a fast run to the Pyrenees and beyond, or even to the Channel. Despite the high competitive economic promise of Soviet natural resources, a generally first-rate technical educational system, and a sustained dedication to frontier science and technology, a series of abominable central planning decisions, an arthritic political–industrial complex, and the fundamental economic strengths of the whole maritime West had to mean that Moscow could not succeed in long-term strategic competition. The 'absolute' quality of nuclear weapons did, of course, tend to blind many people to the political implications of this deeper reality.[100] If those weapons deter existentially, and if such deterrence is all but thoroughly reliable,[101] then surely the West could aspire politically to nothing more ambitious than détente and encouraging the USSR to become a more responsible world citizen; such at least it seemed before Ronald Reagan dared call the 'evil empire' what it was.

Third, the higher organisation for policy- and especially strategy-making in the United States is probably flattered by the mark accorded it in Table 8.1. Nonetheless, when contrasted with the succeeding and overlapping Soviet periods of unduly personal, manifestly physically incompetent, and overwhelmingly Party-bureaucratic experience, the US record attracts a favourable notice. In some senses the Cold War was contested between, on the one hand, a Soviet superpower that was an overcentralised, cultural–party-political 'cause' rather than what is normally perceived to be a great power,[102] and, on the other, the distinctly feudal monarchy that is the United States, with its overmighty bureaucratic and legislative barons. A great deal of the two variants of nuclear RMA must be explained by reference to the sharp differences in policy-making structures and cultures.

On balance – though it is only on balance – the US model of higher policy and strategy organisation must be judged to have outperformed its Soviet rival. More to the point, perhaps, despite irregularly renewed efforts and demands for radical reform in the US policy-making process – including the wholesale rewriting of such key items of legislation as the National Security Act of 1947 – nothing terribly significant ever seems to change. Much the same could be said for vital aspects of Soviet performance. The most potent explanation is not hard to locate. Countries, even 'causes' and rather 'feudal polities' like the Cold War superstates, are not really at liberty to reform radically the way in which they make policy and strategy. They are what they are. The USSR could not perform in policy and strategy in other than a deeply flawed Soviet/Russian manner. That manner, be it noted, was (barely) good enough, acting with the rest of the Soviet value on strategy's many dimensions, to defeat the Nazi hordes. In strategy usually it is sufficient just to win; elegantly if feasible, uglily if need be, though not at crippling cost. It is a perennial and well-founded complaint that the United States malperforms in strategic policy. Its scale of resources, geography, cultural appeal (divine blessing?), or whatever, has permitted the American strategic experience generally to be successful.[103] That point does require some amendment to reflect the experience of the Southern states and, more recently, Vietnam. However, when you are as powerful relative to all others as the United States typically has been, victory has shown itself forgiving of (typically temporary) limitations in the quality of military performance.

Fourth, despite the purple prose of 'jointness', the armed services of the United States continue, as always has been the case, to be raised, administered, equipped, and trained largely in isolation from each other. Paradoxically perhaps, we register military administration as a strength as well as a weakness, because the separate service stories by and large are stories of high competence and eventual war-fighting success. It is true that those armed forces have paid a price for unduly 'stovepipe' isolation, but there is a lot of military ruin in a country as large as the United States. Certainly no war, or substantial expedition, has been lost because of US service parochialism. American military operations tend to be the reverse of seamless between the services, but the reality generally is an expensive redundancy which is the consequence pre-eminently of abundant resources. The Soviet case does not parallel the American, because its continental geopolitical fixation necessarily accorded the army a superiority of status and therefore influence which no American service has been able to match, though the newly created USAF came close in the 1950s.

We cannot know really how well administered, how expert at military operations, or how well commanded, were the rival nuclear forces in this RMA. But what we do know is deeply impressive. If the political and technological peace needed to be kept by would-be nuclear deterrents, then it was kept.[104] For nearly 40 years both superpowers, in detail according to the shaping elements of their distinctive local contexts, with stimuli from abroad (the political and arms competition of the Cold War), invented, developed, tested, administered, and operated, and planned to command in combat, many largely novel weapons of frightening potency, and they did so while avoiding both war-lethal accidents and mistakes or a failure of deterrence. There is much to criticise about the administration of the superpower nuclear war machines, a broad subject the pathology of which attracted a small tribe of quite expert investigators in the West.[105] I do not disdain a literature that points to apparently excessive procurement, overly mighty military barons, unduly cosy congressional–industrial and CPSU–industrial coalitions and the like. But, how high on our Richter scale of discontent should such notice be allowed, given the apparently monumental achievement in non-war which the contending nuclear RMAs probably facilitated? For decade after decade the nuclear arsenals had to be ready for war, but not too ready. To maintain alertness with safety was little short of a persisting bilateral superpower managerial triumph. Even though the instrumental purpose of armed forces is to be able to fight – we administer them strictly, ultimately, only for that purpose – nothing authoritative can ever be said or written about how well the superpowers would have commanded and conducted a great nuclear war. Happily, unlike our two previous case studies, this third illustration of historical RMA must forever remain a story without a military, though not a strategic, conclusion.

Fifth, the respective strengths and weaknesses of the superpowers in the murky realm of information and intelligence defy neat overall judgement. What can be claimed with confidence, as here in Table 8.1, is that US performance on this particular dimension of strategy typically was not a bright spot.[106] In fact, in the 1950s the United States was almost wholly bereft of reliable intelligence on Soviet nuclear missile and space programmes. Even aside from its lack of technical assets to aid intelligence assessment, as a geopolitically isolated superstate, recently victorious in two world wars (Europe and Asia), under-standably hubristic, overly attached to technological solutions to national security, and quintessentially culturally and ideologically self-confident, the United States of the early Cold War decades was not well equipped to perceive the USSR except through the lens of a perilously distorting mirror.[107] Scant comfort should be drawn from the fact that the malign effect of Soviet cultural, political, and traditional bureaucratic blinkers could be at least as misdirecting in their effect as were their American counterparts. Because the coalition leaders in the Cold War constituted an ill-matched pair of open and closed societies, one side obviously enjoyed at least nominally a systemic advantage in the intelligence zone. That advantage was enhanced on the individual human side by the disloyalty issue for the West occasioned by the communist sympathies entertained by some intellectuals with powerful minds but puerile political judgement who never outgrew a foolish view of the 1930s and early 1940s.

Notwithstanding the fundamental correctness of the underlying US intelligence understanding of the Cold War – the soundness of a militarised version of containment, deep confidence in US values and institutions, satisfaction with the national and coalition resources base – the Soviet enemy periodically was seriously misassessed. For a few telling examples:

1. The probable pace of Soviet atomic progress first was underestimated, then was overestimated.
2. Genuine Soviet economic optimism in the 1950s, 1960s, and early 1970s over their ability to compete with the United States was taken far too much on trust in the West.
3. The apparent distinctiveness of Soviet military doctrine and science, especially as it was applied to the nuclear revolution, was discounted hubristically as

evidence of Soviet backwardness (an assumption which contained only an element of truth).[108]

4. The true strain on the Soviet economy imposed by decades of political misrule, 'imperial overstretch', purposeful American strategic competition (particularly in the later 1970s and the 1980s), and an indifferent Soviet workforce, was systematically underappreciated in the United States.

Those who find comfort in such offsetting thoughts should be warmed by the points that the USSR of the early and mid-1970s no more predicted the return under President Ronald Reagan, and then the rise and yet further rise, of the US rival from the morass of post-Vietnam-era politics, than many Americans dared anticipate the near-term fall of the Soviet imperium. At a lower level of focus, it was quite commonplace in Washington in the early 1980s for 'experts' to claim that because the USSR/Russia had never lost a counterinsurgency campaign (total ruthlessness does work),[109] it would be immoral for the US government to support the anti-Soviet resistance in Afghanistan. The President and his CIA director disagreed, with consequences which, however mixed for that sad country, were to be noticeably destabilising inside the USSR.

Much that each nuclear-arming superpower should have benefited from knowing about the other was protected by the distorting effect of alien culture, while much else was hidden by deceptive practices. Again, we can only marvel that despite the obvious relevance of these disturbing thoughts, somehow the nuclear peace was kept for nearly 45 years.

Sixth, to those among us introduced seriously to strategic studies in the 1960s and even the 1970s, Western, especially American, achievements in nuclear-related theory and doctrine all too readily could appear as a transcendent intellectual, if ethically highly contestable, triumph of the modern age. Yes, the nuclear revolution was potentially petrifying, but rational thought had mastered it, had it not? If not, what else was the conflated grand theory of strategic stability, with its triad of stable mutual deterrence, limited war, and arms control, all about?[110] Ironically, albeit culturally predictably, when the dominant theory for nuclear policy came to be challenged by other Americans, that counterculture (e.g. on alleged arms race dynamics and arms control and strategic defence) presented its rational wares with all the self-confidence that had marked the consolidation of the erstwhile market-leading nostrums. With no nuclear battles punctuating those decades, we can never know which American school of thought had devised the more useful, as contrasted with rationally elegant, theory for nuclear doctrine, nor whether that really would have mattered in the face of probable Soviet determination to do its best to win the war. Even the most rational of wise-seeming nuclear theories and doctrines could fall victim to the lethal implications of Clausewitz's friction, or simply to political and military incompetence.[111]

Seventh, the USSR did not (quite) lose the Cold War because of its industrial inability to compete technologically in the emerging era of information, but the evident approach of that period did pose political challenges that the country could not reform itself to meet. The United States did not win the Cold War, and particularly not the nuclear RMA narrowly, because it built or might build superior machines. Rather, success occurred because the military technological frustration of the USSR set the stage for, and advanced, systemic, Western strategic advantage. The USSR was always coming up from behind in the nuclear RMA, a competitive position pregnant with both opportunity and risk. The opportunity was to compete intelligently and economically against a foe that had shown its hand (e.g. the Soviet Union could try to rush to be first in the space and 'missile age', given the traditional US strength in manned aircraft). The risk lay in the prospect one day of confronting a true technical shortfall, as happened for technological and political reasons over electronics in the 1970s and 1980s.

The USSR lost the Cold War primarily for reasons of its deep-seated political noncompetitiveness, but there is no doubt that technology was the defining strength of its US rival. Economically, the USSR simply was outclassed, and that was a condition that in practice the CPSU was structurally and culturally unable to reverse. Norman Friedman saw the matter plainly when he wrote:

> The Western economic system had been flexible enough to support the military comeback of the Reagan years. Gorbachev's attempt to redress the military would sink the Soviet system. He failed not because Reagan outspent the Soviets, but because what he was buying involved a revolution in military technology.[112]

Eighth, notwithstanding the defining significance of high technology for its origins, occurrence, and course, the nuclear RMA reaffirms the persisting importance of geography for strategic behaviour. Even though the nuclear arms competition appeared at times to be in command of the political framework of the superpower contest,[113] that conflict was always shaped by geopolitical parameters. Friends and allies may have contributed relatively little to the real strength of the superpowers, but their territory provided or denied battlespace, or access to battlespace, around the rimlands of Eurasia. Reciprocal geostrategic problems of military access beset the Cold War principals with especial difficulties both early and late in the struggle. Early, which is to say in the 1940s and the 1950s, both sides had to overcome notable challenges to military reach. In its class-leading US form, the nuclear RMA had to be based or staged forward, if it were to menace Soviet power in the heartland of Eurasia. Lacking allies in North or Central America prior to the 1960s (when Cuba discovered some common cause with Moscow), the USSR was obliged to express its nuclear RMA logistically via the posing of both nuclear and conventional threats to areas closer to home than the continental United States.

Although neither side's nuclear RMA had noteworthy problems of intercontinental reach by the 1970s and 1980s, those decades recorded characteristically geopolitical shadows over strategic behaviour. Because of the great military–technical success of both superpowers' long-range nuclear forces, that technological and logistical triumph could not prudently be employed operationally. Both superstates sought practical alternatives to the conduct of nuclear war. The practical US solution, along with 'Assault Breaker' as a generic challenge to the Soviet ground forces, was to try to fine-tune its nuclear doctrine (declared and operational also) in an attempt to offset the negative impact on credibility of commitment feared to flow from a great distance and only measured political interest. Intellectually, and to an important degree politically and militarily also, the armed forces of the US nuclear RMA spent most of the Cold War years, certainly those after 1945–55, endeavouring to offset any negative strategic implications of the geopolitical fact that the United States was a power in Europe, but not a European power. As the Soviet nuclear RMA matured, in the context of the posing of a continuing fairly credible threat to be able to overrun western Europe, American strategic thinkers were more and more exercised with the difficulty of maintaining nuclear credibility for extended deterrence. If the armed forces of the two RMAs cancelled each other out, as most American officials and theorists claimed to be desirable in reflection of a benign condition of mutual nuclear deterrence (even mutual assured destruction, MAD),[114] what positive strategic role might those weapons play, and what should our nuclear strategy be (declaratory and operational?)? For example, are limited nuclear options (LNOs) more credible, and therefore strategically stabilising, than the contingent threat of massive strikes? What if the Soviet chain of command should prove unresponsive to American LNOs?

A conundrum such as that just posed was very much the product of strategic geography. The USSR and the United States' most important allies were generally adjacent in Eurasia, but the United States was not. As we noted earlier, it seems probable that the US-led military–technical answer to the dilemmas of geostrategy which most powerfully captured the Soviet strategic imagination was the not incredible threat to be able to use smart emerging technologies to defeat an invasion. The principal Soviet solutions to their return to the geostrategic problem of the 1940s–50s (which then had been the logistical inability credibly to reach targets in North America) comprised the combination cited above of thrusts by OMG super-divisions, to be greatly assisted by nuclear and chemical operations and operations by special forces deep in NATO's rear.

It is worth re-emphasising the almost bizarre juxtaposition of classic enduring geopolitical realities with the latest in high technology. The Cold War was about the containment of the contemporary heartland power, so that it could not secure access through the rimlands of Eurasia to the wider maritime world.[115] Moreover, the most potent strategic behaviour both conducted and contemplated during the late 1970s and the 1980s had little to do with near-term deployments of the artefacts of the rival nuclear RMAs. Instead, the strategic behavioural action was focused on the US-led destabilisation of the then ever-more extensive Soviet imperium (e.g. in Afghanistan and as Americans perceived to be the case in Nicaragua); upon the global exploitation of Western maritime ascendancy; and upon the prospective ability to menace Soviet military geography deep in east-central Europe.

Ninth, analysis of the nuclear RMA of the Cold War must acknowledge the high significance of strategy's temporal dimension. Militarily, both RMA leaders were granted the time to develop succeeding generations of new weapons, and they had ample opportunity, even if it was not always taken, to learn from events, from themselves, and from the foe. The contrast with 1914–18 could hardly be sharper. Of course, the stakes absolutely were higher from 1945 to 1989. Whereas the misuse of time in 1917–18 might produce a lost battle, campaign, or even the war at hand, such misuse in the 1950s or later could have produced truly a 'war to end all wars'. Although the superpowers were accorded, or bought, the time to learn how to behave responsibly as nuclear powers, good fortune may have contributed as much as did sound habits and useful new technologies (especially for intelligence-gathering from space, for command and control, and for safety in weapon design and handling). Moreover, there were limits to the uses that could be made of additional time. Did either side really learn how to deter the other reliably? Most expert commentators came to believe so, but probably they were wrong.[116]

Time is identified as a dimension of relative strength for the United States and of weakness for the USSR, because the constructivist view of world affairs is fatally flawed. For most of the Cold War years Soviet leaders, armed with the authoritative theory of positive historical change, were more or less convinced that although the dynamics of progress required a helping hand, the force of the future was with them. This belief was as sincere as it was to prove incorrect. Wishful thinking (a characteristic constructivist weakness), no matter how genuine in the minds of the leaders of the CPSU, could not transform the USSR of the later Cold War decades into a highly productive international competitor, hugely friendly to the dawning of the alleged information age.[117] The United States employed the time granted by the protracted non-war outcome to the great contest by transforming advantageously its objective economic and strategic bases. The longer the Cold War, indeed the rival nuclear RMAs of that struggle, persisted, the greater the objectively founded, relative US superiority. The truth in this claim is attested in the fact that, by the early to mid-1990s, the new Russian Federation was barely a great power, let alone a superstate, by some key measures of comparative standing.

Strategy, including strategy for chaos, is not infinitely forgiving. There may be potent protection for strategic effectiveness lurking in the sheer multi-dimensionality of strategy, but that protection has important limits. Narrowly regarded, the examples of modern RMA examined in this book arguably all failed to deliver strategic victory. Even the Allied success in 1918 notably was achieved less through exploitation of the 'modern style of warfare', essential though that certainly was, and rather more because of progressive German human and material enervation. The unmistakable story of the 1800s, 1910s, and 1950s–70s is that military method and quantity need to be good enough to stand against the RMA leader of the day. But strategy's holistic qualities, in the context of the competitive nature of strategic history, must ever imperil what an RMAed military machine can achieve. The nuclear RMA was not so much sidelined in the 1980s, as treated as a realm of essential stalemate so as to drive the contestants into ancillary fields of struggle (wherein systemic advantage lay with the West). With historically specific detailing, the identical argument applies to the Napoleonic and First World War RMAs also.

From the case studies of Chapters 6–8 we now proceed expeditiously towards the close of our investigation. The concluding chapter develops the Clausewitzian premise that strategy is a duel, and adds the proposition long familiar through the body of this discussion, that historical RMAs function strategically.

NOTES

1. Lawrence Freedman, *The Evolution of Nuclear Strategy*, 2nd edn (New York: St Martin's Press, 1989), p. 433.
2. Ibid., pp. 432–3.
3. Schelling wrote about 'the threat that leaves something to chance' in his dazzling and pathbreaking collection of essays, *The Strategy of Conflict* (Cambridge, MA: Harvard University Press, 1960), pp. 187–203.
4. Norman Friedman, *The Fifty-Year War: Conflict and Strategy in the Cold War* (Annapolis, MD: Naval Institute Press, 2000), p. xi.
5. When Michael Mandelbaum wrote about two revolutions, he referred to expectations of technical and then of political change: *The Nuclear Revolution: International Politics before and after Hiroshima* (Cambridge: Cambridge University Press, 1981), esp. pp. 1–4. The thesis of the nuclear revolution is probed succinctly and most intelligently in Ernest R. May, 'Introduction', to John Lewis Gaddis *et al.* (eds), *Cold War Statesmen Confront the Bomb* (Oxford: Oxford University Press, 1999), pp. 1–11.
6. John Lewis Gaddis, 'Conclusion', to Gaddis *et al.*, *Cold War Statesmen Confront the Bomb*, p. 263
7. On 1 November 1952 the United States tested a thermonuclear device. Deliverable H-bombs were not tested until 1954. On 12 August 1953 the Soviet Union tested a boosted-fission device, which it misadvertised as a true H-bomb. The first Soviet H-bomb was tested on 22 November 1955: Friedman, *Fifty-Year War*, p. 146.
8. By 1959 the leading strategic thinker in the United States was in no doubt that 'between the use and non-use of atomic weapons there is a vast watershed of difference and distinction, one that ought not be cavalierly thrown away, as we appear to be throwing it away, if we are serious about trying to limit war': Bernard Brodie, *Strategy in the Missile Age* (Princeton, NJ: Princeton University Press, 1959), p. 327.

9. Stephen I. Schwartz (ed.), *Atomic Audit: The Costs and Consequences of US Nuclear Weapons since 1940* (Washington, DC: Brookings Institution Press, 1998), pp. 58–9.
10. See Richard Rhodes, *The Making of the Atomic Bomb* (New York: Touchstone, 1988), pp. 164–5.
11. Ibid., p. 260.
12. Guy Hartcup, *The Effect of Science on the Second World War* (London: Macmillan, 2000), pp. 171–4, is attractively succinct.
13. Thomas Powers, *Heisenberg's War: The Secret History of the German Bomb* (Cambridge, MA: Da Capo Press, 2000), reads well in its defence of Werner Heisenberg, but ultimately is thoroughly unconvincing. Mark Walker, *German National Socialism and the Quest for Nuclear Power, 1939–1949* (Cambridge: Cambridge University Press, 1989), is far more persuasive.
14. The Soviet story is told superbly in David Holloway, *Stalin and the Bomb* (New Haven, CT: Yale University Press, 1994).
15. See Williamson Murray and Allan R. Millett, *A War To Be Won: Fighting the Second World War* (Cambridge, MA: Harvard University Press, 2000), ch. 2.
16. From a large literature see Neville Jones, *The Origins of Strategic Bombing: A Study of the Development of British Air Strategic Thought and Practice up to 1918* (London: William Kimber, 1973); Lee Kennett, *A History of Strategic Bombing* (New York: Charles Scribner's Sons, 1982), ch. 2; idem, *The First Air War, 1914–1918* (New York: Free Press, 1991), ch. 3; and C. M. White, *The Gotha Summer: The German daytime air raids on England, May to August 1917* (London: Robert Hale, 1986). For the whole of the air war in considerable detail, see John H. Morrow, Jr, *The Great War in the Air: Military Aviation from 1909 to 1921* (Washington, DC: Smithsonian Institution Press, 1993).
17. Uri Bialer, *The Shadow of the Bomber: The Fear of Air Attack and British Politics, 1932–1939* (London: Royal Historical Society, 1980), ch. 1.
18. See Kenneth P. Werrell, *Blankets of Fire: US Bombers over Japan during World War II* (Washington, DC: Smithsonian Institution Press, 1996).
19. Hew Strachan, *The First World War, Vol. I: To Arms* (Oxford: Oxford University Press, 2001), ch. 1; and Gary Sheffield, *Forgotten Victory: The First World War: Myths and Realities* (London: Headline Book Publishing, 2001), ch. 2, are fair and persuasive.
20. A German historian has written: 'Hitler's long-range aim, fixed in the 1920s, of erecting a German Eastern imperium on the ruins of the Soviet Union was not simply a vision emulating from an abstract wish. In the eastern sphere established in 1918, this goal had a concrete point of departure. The German Eastern Imperium had already been – if only for a short time – a reality': Andreas Hilgruber, *Germany and the Two World Wars* (Cambridge, MA: Harvard University Press, 1981), p. 47.
21. See David Alan Rosenberg, 'American Atomic Strategy and the Hydrogen Bomb Decision', *Journal of American History,* 66 (June 1979), pp. 62–87; Melvyn P. Leffler, *A Preponderance of Power: National Security, the Truman Administration, and the Cold War* (Stanford, CA: Stanford University Press, 1992), pp. 327–33; and Richard Rhodes, *Dark Sun: The Making of the Hydrogen Bomb* (New York: Simon & Schuster, 1995).
22. Rhodes, *Making of the Atomic Bomb*, pp. 311–12, 346.
23. See Walker, *German National Socialism and the Quest for Nuclear Power*, ch. 5.
24. Holloway, *Stalin and the Bomb,* pp. 130–3.
25. Walker, *German National Socialism and the Quest for Nuclear Power*, esp. p. 78.
26. Powers, *Heisenberg's War*, p. 478.
27. Walker, *German National Socialism and the Quest for Nuclear Power*, ch. 5.
28. Ian Kershaw, *Hitler, 1936–45: Nemesis* (London: Penguin, 2000), pp. 731–2, is sensible on Germany's decision not to engage in a crash programme for the atomic bomb.
29. See Holloway, *Stalin and the Bomb,* p. 97, and especially the biographical details on pp. 447–52.

30. Friedman, *Fifty-Year War*, p. 146.
31. Powers, *Heisenberg's War*, pp. 150–1.
32. For thought-provoking analysis by a leading critic, see Robert Jervis: *The Illogic of American Nuclear Strategy* (Ithaca, NY: Cornell University Press, 1984); and *The Meaning of the Nuclear Revolution: Statecraft and the Prospect of Armageddon* (Ithaca, NY: Cornell University Press, 1989).
33. Brodie, *Strategy in the Missile Age*, p. 147.
34. Ibid., p. 150.
35. Thomas B. Cochran, William M. Arkin, and Milton M. Hoenig, *Nuclear Weapons Databook: Vol. 1, US Nuclear Forces and Capabilities* (Cambridge, MA: Ballinger Publishing Company, 1984), p. 34.
36. See David Alan Rosenberg, 'US Nuclear Stockpile, 1945–1950', *Bulletin of the Atomic Scientists*, 38, 5 (May 1982), pp. 25–30; and Cochrane, Arkin, and Hoenig, *Nuclear Weapons Databook, Vol. 1*, p. 15. Cochrane and his colleagues record an expansion from 2 to 450 atomic warheads between 1945 and 1950.
37. Martin van Creveld, 'Through a Glass, Darkly: Some Reflections on the Future of War', *Naval War College Review*, 53, 4 (Autumn 2000), p. 28.
38. Schelling's 1960 book, *Strategy of Conflict*, was extraordinarily influential. The alleged commonality of security values came to dominate scholarship in the 1990s. Superior period pieces include Barry Buzan, *People, States and Fear: An Agenda for International Security Studies in the Post-Cold War Era* (Boulder, CO: Lynne Reinner Publishers, 1991); Godfried van Benthem van den Bergh, *The Nuclear Revolution and the end of the Cold War: Forced Restraint* (London: Macmillan, 1992); Andrew Butfoy, *Common Security and Strategic Reform: A Critical Analysis* (London: Macmillan, 1997); Keith Krause and Michael C. Williams (eds), *Critical Security Studies: Concepts and Cases* (London: UCL Press, 1997); and Barry Buzan, Ole Waever, and Jacop de Wilde, *Security: A New Framework for Analysis* (Boulder, CO: Lynne Rienner Publishers, 1998).
39. Colin S. Gray, *Strategic Studies and Public Policy: The American Experience* (Lexington: University Press of Kentucky, 1982); Freedman, *Evolution of Nuclear Strategy*; Marc Trachtenberg, *History and Strategy* (Princeton, NJ: Princeton University Press, 1991); and John S. Duffield, *Power Rules: The Evolution of NATO's Conventional Force Posture* (Stanford, CA: Stanford University Press, 1995). John Lewis Gaddis, *We Now Know: Rethinking Cold War History* (Oxford: Clarendon Press, 1997), overpromises, as does David Miller's distinctly pedestrian work, *The Cold War: A Military History* (London: John Murray, 1998). Friedman, *Fifty-Year War*, is brilliant but (understandably) frequently overreaches on the evidence.
40. An argument I advance and defend in my *Modern Strategy* (Oxford: Oxford University Press, 1999), ch. 11.
41. John J. Weltman, *World Politics and the Evolution of War* (Baltimore, MD: Johns Hopkins University Press, 1995), p. 152.
42. Jervis, *Meaning of the Nuclear Revolution*, p. 22 (emphasis in original).
43. Moreover, they will approach a new weapon through the filter of an appreciation of institutional interests. Different military organisations grow distinctive cultures. See Williamson Murray: 'Does Military Culture Matter?', *Orbis*, 43, 1 (Winter 1999), pp. 27–42, and 'Military Culture Does Matter', *Strategic Review*, 27, 2 (Spring 1999), pp. 32–40. The most powerful study of military culture is Andrew Gordon, *The Rules of the Game: Jutland and British Naval Command* (London: John Murray, 1996).
44. The classic treatment is Edward N. Luttwak, *The Pentagon and the Art of War: The Question of Military Reform* (New York: Simon & Schuster, 1984), ch. 5, 'The Materialist Bias: Why We Need More "Fraud, Waste, and Mismanagement"'.
45. Gian P. Gentile, 'Planning for Preventive War, 1945–1950', *Joint Force Quarterly*, 24 (Spring 2000), p. 68.

46. Keith B. Payne, *The Fallacies of Cold War Deterrence and a New Direction* (Lexington: University Press of Kentucky, 2001), is essential reading.

47. David Alan Rosenberg, 'The Origins of Overkill: Nuclear Weapons and American Strategy, 1945–1960', *International Security*, 7, 4 (Spring 1983), pp. 3–71; and Steven T. Ross, *American War Plans, 1945–1950* (London: Frank Cass, 1996). See also Harry R. Borowski, *A Hollow Threat: Strategic Air Power and Containment before Korea* (Westport, CT: Greenwood Press, 1982); Cochrane, Arkin and Hoenig, *Nuclear Weapons Databook, Vol. I*; William S. Borgiasz, *The Strategic Air Command: Evolution and Consolidation of Nuclear Forces, 1945–1955* (Westport, CT: Praeger Publishers, 1996); and Schwartz, *Atomic Audit*.

48. For an unusually eclectic set of sources see William T. Lee, 'Soviet Nuclear Targeting Strategy', in Desmond Ball and Jeffrey Richelson (eds), *Strategic Nuclear Targeting* (Ithaca, NY: Cornell University Press, 1986), pp. 84–108; Thomas B. Cochrane and others, *Nuclear Weapons Databook: Vol. IV, Soviet Nuclear Weapons* (New York: Harper & Row, 1989); Holloway, *Stalin and the Bomb*; John G. Hines, *Soviet Intentions, 1965–1985: Vol. II, Soviet Post-Cold War Testimonial Evidence* (McLean, VA: BDM Federal, 22 September 1995); Andrei A. Kokoshin, *Soviet Strategic Thought, 1917–91* (Cambridge, MA: MIT Press, 1998); and Nikolai Sokov, *Russian Strategic Modernisation: The Past and Future* (Lanham, MD: Rowman & Littlefield Publishers, 2000).

49. Eugene M. Emme (ed.), *The Impact of Air Power: National Security and World Politics* (Princeton, NJ: D. van Nostrand, 1959); and Phillip S. Meilinger (ed.), *The Paths of Heaven: The Evolution of Airpower Theory* (Maxwell AFB, AL: Air University Press, 1997), are the outstanding collections of extracts and analyses on air power theory and history.

50. Borowski, *Hollow Threat*, chs 7, 8.

51. Rosenberg, 'Origins of Overkill'.

52. Lest anyone had missed their point, in the 1990s the USAF changed the title of the official organ of its Air University from the *Airpower Journal* to the *Aerospace Journal*.

53. See J. C Wylie, *Military Strategy: A General Theory of Power Control*, ed. John B. Hattendorf (Annapolis, MD: Naval Institute Press, 1989 [1967]), pp. 36–41.

54. A. J. Wohlstetter and others, *Selection and Use of Strategic Air Bases*, R-266 (Santa Monica, CA: RAND, April 1954).

55. Holloway, *Stalin and the Bomb*, p. 247 (emphasis added).

56. Hines, *Soviet Intentions, 1965–1985*, I, II.

57. Philip Noel-Baker, *The Private Manufacture of Armaments* (New York: Oxford University Press, 1937), is a classic.

58. Not only were Germany's new infantry tactics self-defeating, but the so-called Hindenburg programme of industrial mobilisation for total war scored several 'own goals' of a debilitating kind. For example, the Germans invested too heavily in new factories, at the expense of what those factories might produce; the national railway, the *Reichsbahn*, was run down with inadequate maintenance; and scarce effort was wasted on the mass production of U-boats, inter alia. I am grateful to Trevor Wilson and Robin Prior for these persuasive examples: 'Conflict, Technology, and the Impact of Industrialisation: The Great War, 1914–18', *Journal of Strategic Studies*, 24, 3 (September 2001), esp. p. 154.

59. See Richard Ned Lebow and Janice Gross Stein, *We All Lost the Cold War* (Princeton, NJ: Princeton University Press, 1994); Fred Charles Ikle, 'The Second Coming of the Nuclear Age', *Foreign Affairs*, 75, 1 (January/February 1996), pp. 119–28; Keith B. Payne, *Deterrence in the Second Nuclear Age* (Lexington: University Press of Kentucky, 1996); idem, *Fallacies of Cold War Deterrence*; and for a useful overview, the collection

of essays in T. V. Paul, Richard J. Harknett, and James J. Wirtz (eds), *The Absolute Weapon Revisited: Nuclear Arms and the Emerging International Order* (Ann Arbor: University of Michigan Press, 1998).

60. Andrew F. Krepinevich, 'Cavalry to Computer: The Pattern of Military Revolutions', *The National Interest*, 37 (Fall 1994), p. 30.

61. Schwartz, *Atomic Audit*, p. 201 n. 11.

62. On the state of SAC in 1948, see Borowski, *Hollow Threat*, ch. 6.

63. For stockpile estimates, see Cochrane *et al.*, *Nuclear Weapons Databook*, Vol. IV, p. 25, table 2.1.

64. For a statement of the undeniable see Neville Brown, *Nuclear War: The Impending Strategic Deadlock* (New York: Praeger, 1965).

65. Donald Kagan, 'The End of Wars as the Basis for a Lasting Peace', *Naval War College Review*, 53, 4 (Autumn 2000), pp. 11–24, is magnificent.

66. Those of a nervous disposition might lose sleep reading Bruce G. Blair, *The Logic of Accidental Nuclear War* (Washington, DC: Brookings Institution Press, 1991); Peter Douglas Feaver, *Guarding the Guardians: Civilian Control of Nuclear Weapons in the United States* (Ithaca, NY: Cornell University Press, 1992); Scott D. Sagan, *The Limits of Safety: Organizations, Accidents, and Nuclear Weapons* (Princeton, NJ: Princeton University Press, 1993); and Peter Vincent Pry, *War Scare: Russia and America on the Nuclear Brink* (Westport, CT: Praeger, 1999).

67. The two documents are readily accessible, for example in Thomas H. Etzold and John Lewis Gaddis (eds), *Containment: Documents on American Policy and Strategy, 1945–1950* (New York: Columbia University Press, 1978). 'The Long Telegram' is reprinted on pp. 50–63, and 'NSC-68' on pp. 383–442. See also 'Mr X' [George F. Kennan], 'The Sources of Soviet Conduct', *Foreign Affairs*, 25, 4 (July 1947), pp. 566–82.

68. See Trachtenberg, *History and Strategy*, ch. 3.

69. There is some lasting merit in Warner R. Schilling's irreverently titled article, 'US Strategic Nuclear Concepts in the 1970s: The Search for Sufficiently Equivalent Countervailing Parity', *International Security*, 6, 2 (Fall 1981), pp. 48–79.

70. The great man advises: 'If you want to overcome your enemy you must make your effort against his power of resistance, which can be expressed as the product of two inseparable factors, viz. *The total means at his disposal* and *the strength of his will*. The extent of the means at his disposal is a matter – though not exclusively – of figures, and should be measurable. But the strength of his will is much less easy to determine and can only be gauged approximately by the strength of the motive animating it': Carl von Clausewitz, *On War*, trans. Michael Howard and Peter Paret (Princeton, NJ: Princeton University Press, 1976 [1832]), p. 77 (emphasis in original).

71. These ideas are discussed in Michael J. Mazarr (ed.), *Nuclear Weapons in a Transformed World: The Challenge of Virtual Nuclear Arsenals* (London: Macmillan, 1997); Jonathon Schell, *The Gift of Time: The Case for Abolishing Nuclear Weapons Now* (London: Granta, 1998); and Harold A. Feiverson (ed.), *The Nuclear Turning Point: A Blueprint for Deep Cuts and De-Alerting of Nuclear Weapons* (Washington, DC: Brookings Institution Press, 1999).

72. Sagan, *Limits of Safety*.

73. 'Arms race' practices comprise deeply contested theoretical territory. See Colin S. Gray, *The Soviet–American Arms Race* (Farnborough: Saxon House, 1976); Patrick Glynn, *Closing Pandora's Box: Arms Races, Arms Control, and the History of the Cold War* (New York: Basic Books, 1992); and Grant T. Hammond, *Plowshares into Swords: Arms Races in International Politics, 1840–1991* (Columbia: University of South Carolina Press, 1993).

74. Personal communication.

75. Friedman, *Fifty-Year War*, chs 36, 38.

76. See US Congress, House of Representatives, Subcommittee on Natural Resources, Agriculture Research and Environment of the Committee on Science and Technology, and the Subcommittee on Energy and the Environment of the Committee on Insular Affairs, *Nuclear Winter, Joint Hearing*, 99th Cong., 1st sess. (Washington, DC: US Government Printing Office, 14 March 1985).

77. The testimonies deployed and analysed in Hines, *Soviet Intentions, 1965–1985*, are not conclusive on this question of possible restraint in nuclear targeting. Readers inclined to favour the argument that is optimistic about the prospect for Soviet restraint may be sobered by the deeply expert analysis in William E. Odom, *The Collapse of the Soviet Military* (New Haven, CT: Yale University Press, 1998). See Lynn Etheridge Davis, *Limited Nuclear Options: Deterrence and the New American Doctrine*, Adelphi Papers 121 (London: IISS, Winter 1975–76); Benjamin S. Lambeth, *Selective Nuclear Options in American and Soviet Strategic Policy*, R-7034-DDRE (Santa Monica, CA: RAND, December 1976). I discuss Secretary of Defence James R. Schlesinger's ideas on limited nuclear options in historical context in my *Strategic Studies and Public Policy*, ch. 10 (esp. pp. 149–51), and in strategic–intellectual and policy contexts in my *Nuclear Strategy and National Style* (Lanham, MD: Hamilton Press, 1986), ch. 9 (esp. pp. 277–80).

78. Nikolay Vasil'yevich Ogarkov, *Always in Readiness to Defend the Homeland*, trans. Foreign Broadcast Information Service, JPRSL/10412, 25 March 1982 (Moscow: Voyenizdat, 1982).

79. If Thomas C. Schelling's *Arms and Influence* (New Haven, CT: Yale University Press, 1966), captures superbly the spirit of the mainstream American (civilian) approach to nuclear operations, Benjamin Lambeth's article, 'On Thresholds in Soviet Military Thought', *Washington Quarterly*, 7, 2 (Spring 1984), pp. 69–76, probably was closer to the mark for Soviet operational intentions.

80. For the 'rimland' concept see Nicholas J. Spykman, *The Geography of the Peace* (New York: Harcourt, Brace, 1944), pp. 37–8, 40–1.

81. See Herman Hattaway and Arthur Jones, *How the North Won: A Military History of the Civil War* (Urbana: University of Illinois Press, 1983), pp. 58, 485–7, 685. We are told that 'all three branches of the art of war – logistics, strategy, and tactics – played crucial and interrelated roles in the Civil War, but more or less their relative importance was in that order' (p. 720). See also Thomas M. Kane, *Military Logistics and Strategic Performance* (London: Frank Cass, 2001), ch. 3.

82. For a discussion of the (nominal) architecture of choice conducted with great sensitivity to levels-of-analysis issues, see Edward N. Luttwak, *Strategy: The Logic of War and Peace* (Cambridge, MA: Harvard University Press, 1987).

83. Friedman, *Fifty-Year War*, p. 448.

84. Samuel P. Huntington, 'US Defense Strategy: The Strategic Innovations of the Reagan Years', in Joseph Kruzel (ed.), *American Defense Annual, 1987–1988* (Lexington, MA: Lexington Books, 1987), pp. 23–43.

85. See James D. Watkins and others, *The Maritime Strategy*, Special Supplement to US Naval Institute *Proceedings* (January 1986); US Congress, House of Representatives, Seapower and Strategic and Critical Materials Subcommittee of the Committee on Armed Services, *The 600-Ship Navy and the Maritime Strategy*, Hearings, 99th Cong., 1st sess. (Washington, DC: US Government Printing Office, June and September 1985); Norman Friedman, *The US Maritime Strategy* (London: Jane's, 1988); and Steven E. Miller and Stephen Van Evera (eds), *Naval Strategy and National Security: An 'International Security' Reader* (Princeton, NJ: Princeton University Press, 1988).

86. Helpful sources include Zbigniew Brezinski (ed.), *Promise or Peril: The Strategic Defense Initiative* (Washington, DC: Ethics and Public Policy Center, 1986); Craig Snyder (ed.), *The Strategic Defense Debate: Can 'Star Wars' Make us Safe?* (Philadelphia: University

of Pennyslvania Press, 1986); Donald R. Baucom, *The Origins of SDI, 1944–1983* (Lawrence: University Press of Kansas, 1992); and Edward Reiss, *The Strategic Defense Initiative* (Cambridge: Cambridge University Press, 1992).

87. On the relationship between offence and defence (and ancillary matters) see Fred S. Hoffman, Albert Wohlstetter, and David S. Yost, *Swords and Shields: NATO, the USSR, and New Choices for Long-Range Offense and Defense* (Lexington, MA: Lexington Books, 1987); Colin S. Gray, *Weapons Don't Make War: Policy, Strategy, and Military Technology* (Lawrence: University Press of Kansas, 1993), esp. chs 1–2; and Sean M. Lynn-Jones, 'Offense–Defense Theory and Its Critics', *Security Studies*, 4, 4 (Summer 1995), pp. 660–91.

88. See V. K. Triandafillov, *The Nature of the Operations of Modern Armies*, trans. William A. Burhans (London: Frank Cass, 1994); and Kokoshin, *Soviet Strategic Thought, 1917–91*, pp. 160–3.

89. See the excellent discussion in Odom, *Collapse of the Soviet Military*, pp. 72–82.

90. 'Observation, orientation, decision, action': John R. Boyd, 'A Discourse on Winning and Losing', unpub. ms. (August 1987). Colonel Boyd has one intellectual biographer to date: Grant T. Hammond, *The Mind of War: John Boyd and American Security* (Washington, DC: Smithsonian Institution Press, 2001), which, fortunately, is first-rate.

91. Beatrice Heuser, 'Warsaw Pact Military Doctrines in the 1970s and 1980s: Findings in the East German Archives', *Comparative Strategy*, 12, 4 (Winter 1994), pp. 437–57.

92. As, for example, in George W. Rathjens, 'The Dynamics of the Arms Race', *Scientific American*, 220, 4 (April 1969), pp. 15–25. For a critique, see Gray, *Soviet-American Arms Race*. Readers may find merit in Barry Buzan and Eric Herring, *The Arms Dynamic in World Politics* (Boulder, CO: Lynne Rienner Publishers, 1998).

93. Paul C. Warnke, 'Apes on a Treadmill', *Foreign Policy*, 18 (Spring 1975), pp. 12–29.

94. For a contemporary critique of American theories of strategic stability, see Gray, *Nuclear Strategy and National Style*, ch. 5.

95. Jereme H. Kahan, *Security in the Nuclear Age: Developing US Strategic Arms Policy* (Washington, DC: Brookings Institution, 1975), is a canonical text for this strategic perspective.

96. Even Buzan and Herring do not endorse it: *Arms Dynamic in World Politics*, ch. 6.

97. Ibid., ch. 7.

98. Henry Kissinger, *Diplomacy* (New York: Simon & Schuster, 1994), provides a fair historical overview.

99. The clearest explanation of the British anxiety over the rate of German dreadnought construction, in the context of the debate over the Naval Estimates in 1909, is to be found in E. L. Woodward, *Great Britain and the German Navy* (1935; London: Frank Cass, 1964), chs 9–11.

100. Bernard Brodie (ed.), *The Absolute Weapon: Atomic Power and World Order* (New York: Harcourt Brace, 1946); Paul, Harknett, and Wirtz (eds), *Absolute Weapon Revisited*.

101. See McGeorge Bundy, 'Existential Deterrence and Its Consequences', in Douglas MacLean (ed.), *The Security Gamble: Deterrence Dilemmas in the Nuclear Age* (Totowa, NJ: Rowman and Allanheld, 1984), pp. 3–13. Bundy's views had not changed since his 'To Cap the Volcano', *Foreign Affairs*, 48, 1 (October 1969), pp. 1–20, in which he endorsed an exceedingly minimalist view of the requirements of minimum nuclear deterrence. A leading trouble with the proposition that nuclear weapons deter simply by virtue of their existence (presumably assembled in the arsenal), is that it is not a responsible policy position for a superpower which has extended deterrent duties on behalf of distant friends and allies.

102. Henry Kissinger offers this valuable insight into the nature of nineteenth-century Russia: 'Unlike the states of Western Europe, which Russia simultaneously admired,

despised, and envied, Russia perceived itself not as a nation but as a cause, beyond geopolitics, impelled by faith, and held together by arms': *Diplomacy*, p. 143.

103. See Colin S. Gray, 'Strategy in the Nuclear Age: The United States, 1945–1991', in Williamson Murray, MacGregor Knox, and Alvin Bernstein (eds), *The Making of Strategy: Rulers, States, and War* (Cambridge: Cambridge University Press, 1994), esp. pp. 589–98.

104. The term 'technological peace' is deployed usefully in Kenneth Booth, 'Teaching Strategy: An Introductory Questionnaire', *Survival*, 16, 2 (March/April 1974), p. 82.

105. For example, see Blair, *Logic of Accidental Nuclear War*; and Sagan, *Limits of Safety*. On the operational management, or mismanagement, of nuclear forces, see Paul Bracken, *Command and Control of Nuclear Forces* (New Haven, CT: Yale University Press, 1983); Bruce G. Blair, *Strategic Command and Control: Redefining the Nuclear Threat* (Washington, DC: Brookings Institution, 1985); Ashton B. Carter, John D. Steinbruner, and Charles A. Zraket (eds), *Managing Nuclear Operations* (Washington, DC: Brookings Institution, 1987); Kurt Gottfried and Bruce G. Blair (eds), *Crisis Stability and Nuclear War* (New York: Oxford University Press, 1988); and Paul B. Stares, *Command Performance: The Neglected Dimension of European Security* (Washington, DC: Brookings Institution, 1991).

106. See Lawrence Freedman, *US Intelligence and the Soviet Strategic Threat* (London: Macmillan, 1977).

107. Robert B. Bathurst, *Intelligence and the Mirror: On Creating an Enemy* (London: SAGE Publications, 1993), is exceptionally perceptive.

108. Fritz Ermath, 'Contrasts in American and Soviet Strategic Thought', *International Security*, 3, 2 (Fall 1978), pp. 138–55, was a landmark publication.

109. Edward N. Luttwak proved spectacularly erroneous in his judgement about the likely course of a current conflict, this time over Afghanistan. Luttwak wrote in 1984 of a 'leisurely [Soviet] imperial pacification': *Pentagon and the Art of War*, p. 111. Even brilliant strategic theorists are fallible.

110. See Booth, 'Teaching Strategy', and Gray, *Strategic Studies and Public Policy*.

111. Scholars of nuclear matters would do well to read Eliot A. Cohen and John Gooch, *Military Misfortunes: The Anatomy of Failure in War* (New York: Free Press, 1990).

112. Friedman, *Fifty-Year War*, p. 468.

113. Some of us who were deeply sceptical of the notion that there was an effectively autonomous nuclear arms race, were also troubled by what often appeared to be an American endeavour to evade political differences via an arms control process. I stated, indeed probably overstated, this view in my book, *House of Cards: Why Arms Control Must Fail* (Ithaca, NY: Cornell University Press, 1992). Albert Wohlstetter and others, *Legends of the Arms Race*, USSI Report 75–1 (Washington, DC: United States Strategic Institute, 1975), does a powerful demolition job on the mainstream theory of arms racing.

114. See Wolfgang K. H. Panofsky, 'The Mutual Hostage Relationship Between America and Russia', *Foreign Affairs*, 52, 1 (October 1973), pp. 109–18. The classic argument against mutual assured destruction was advanced in Donald G. Brennan, 'The Case for Missile Defense', *Foreign Affairs*, 43, 3 (April 1969), pp. 633–48.

115. Colin S. Gray: *The Geopolitics of the Nuclear Era: Heartland, Rimlands, and the Technological Revolution* (New York: National Strategy Information Center, 1977); and *Maritime Strategy, Geopolitics, and the Defense of the West* (New York: Ramapo Press, 1986).

116. See Payne, *Fallacies of Cold War Deterrence*.

117. Friedman, *Fifty-Year War*, ch. 36, is persuasive.

9

Strategy as a Duel: RMA Meets the Enemy

To the disappointment of some, though probably for the reassurance of many others, the more important conclusions to this lengthy and complex forensic examination of strategy and the theory and practice of RMA are clear and unambiguous. Notwithstanding the rich variety of detail among the three historical case studies, those candidate examples of RMA lend themselves persuasively to a common framework of strategic explanation. Indeed, I will venture the thought that were the multi-faceted mechanisation revolution of the 1920s and 1930s explored as above in this text, it would serve only to confirm what the other three cases already reveal.[1]

RMA theory, in truth theories, can be neither correct not incorrect. It could provide a way of helping us understand the process of change, if it does not mislead more than it assists, and it might even aid the purposive agents of such change, though one should be more than a little sceptical on that score. Self-styled revolutionaries are to be trusted neither to select ideas with prudence nor to cope adequately with the full, holistic scope of the context within which they aim to be effective. If that sounds unduly cynical, perhaps just pessimistic, we should recall the merit in humility, because, historically speaking, at best serendipity frequently triumphs. In fact, although this discussion is deeply unimpressed by most of the specific promises of RMA theory, our argument is strategically optimistic. Strategy can and does serve high policy. Effective strategic behaviour need not be random or chaotically unpredictable.

Some readers may find diversion on the farther shores of chaos theory, or with the intriguing 'what ifs ...' of the new virtual history,[2] but the accessible modern stories of RMA experience reveal a notable ordinariness of key explanation that is almost banal. Specifically, for reasons exposed already and discussed below, what we may cite as 'the bigger battalions' eventually won each of the great contests that provided the political contexts for the case studies. Napoleonic France, imperial Germany, and the USSR were each in due course massively overmatched by their enemies. The RMA connection to that repeated political outcome was by and large negative in kind. It is impressive to record what RMA executives could not achieve with a radically modernised (in absolute, rather than relative terms) military machine. These historically based reflections should alert us to the probable fragility of some of the more exciting claims advanced today in support of the notion of an information-led RMA.

POLITICS AND RMAs

The conclusion to our analysis clusters conveniently, if deceptively simply, under seven banners. What follows summarises and knits together the theoretical and the historical parts of the enquiry.

1. *Politics rule.* Unless RMA as a process is reduced merely to the administration of innovation, the primacy of politics must be acknowledged. An RMA is not an event-sequence apart from its political context. None of the three great RMAs considered in detail in Chapters 6–8 make sense save with direct reference to their political placement in strategic history. Of course, to a degree each was waiting to happen. Military thought and practice in the mid- to late eighteenth century anticipated much of what the French Republic and Empire was to implement. The RMA of the First World War was constructed of many techniques and tactics long known in principle, if typically not actually executed. The nuclear revolution, in its turn, naturally was built upon the edifice of many decades of theoretical and experimental science. One can argue that strategic history was ready for the new ways in warfare of the three cases, and that the political propulsion for the RMAs certainly would have been provided by some political agents, if not those who actually played the historical roles that they did. I find this line of argument persuasive in terms of detail, but unhelpful in broad terms.

Great RMAs are made by people with powerful and generally quite specifically political motives, even if the process of innovation includes a lengthy period of gestation, experiment, and evaluation in peacetime. It may be a sad commentary upon the human race, but still it seems to be true that strategically we perform better when we have a particular enemy in mind. In that connection, much of the recent literature on an information-led American RMA has yet to step up to the still emerging reality of China as the next worthy foe ('global terrorism' probably is too difficult, too asymmetrically challenging, to win election to 'principal enemy'). The concept of 'peer competitor' has been popular, but it should be retired promptly.[3] The phrase implies an approximate symmetry which is likely to prove strategically misleading.

For an RMA to succeed, both narrowly as a military–technical (inter alia) enterprise, and strategically as an agent for enhanced effectiveness, it has to translate into politically defined goals. The political nexus to the RMA process is pervasive and utterly inescapable. Napoleon, imperial Germany, and the

USSR, *and their respective RMAs,* were each defeated by political contexts of their own malign creation that they could not evade. In some ways, the more glittering the military achievements of the Napoleonic, German First World War, and Soviet nuclear RMAs, the more thorough the eventual political demise was likely to be. Success in military innovation could only postpone defeat, it could not point to an alternative, apolitical route to success. American RMA theorists today, rendered hubristic by the dazzle of computer-shaped warfare, need to remember that battle and war, like tactics and strategy, are very different. Tactically superior armies do not always win wars. In the Second Punic War, Hannibal's mercenary veterans were invincible in combat (until the very end, at Zama), just as he himself could not be worsted operationally by anyone available to Rome for more than a decade. Unfortunately for the premier army and general of the day, however, the Romans declined to offer themselves up to destruction in the open field.[4] A superior way in warfare can function as such only if, as the Royal Navy's toast has it, one enjoys 'a willing foe and sea room'.

2. *Strategy (and war) is a duel.* Robert H. Scales Jr claims usefully that 'Western militaries have proven to be "complex adaptive systems".[5] He is probably correct in asserting that

> The history of warfare suggests a martial corollary to Newton's fundamental law of physics: every successful technical or tactical innovation that provides a dominant military advantage eventually yields to a countervailing response that shifts the advantage to the opposing force.[6]

Why should this be so? Because in war, and for strategy, there is always an enemy motivated, if only variably competent, to find ways to beat us. There is no law of strategic history requiring a particular foe to be successfully adaptive at a particular time. Nonetheless, the passage of time is likely to yield usable strategic opportunity to some would-be enemy to discover means and methods to effect our humiliation (if we are, or appear to aspire to be, the contemporary hegemon – local, regional, or global). We need look no further than to Clausewitz to explain the nature of our topic.

> War is nothing but a duel on a larger scale. Countless duels go to make up war, but a picture of it as a whole can be formed by imagining a pair of wrestlers. Each tries through physical force to compel the other to do his will; his *immediate* aim is to *throw* his opponent in order to make him incapable of further resistance.

> War, however, is not the action of a living force upon a lifeless mass (total non-resistance would be no war at all) but always the collision of two living forces. The ultimate aim of waging war, as formulated here, must be taken as applying to both sides. Once again, there is interaction. So

long as I have not overthrown my opponent I am bound to fear he may overthrow me. Thus I am not in control: he dictates to me as much as I dictate to him.[7]

It is surprising how often the attractions of what can amount to enemy-independent analysis are allowed by clever people to overrule lessons of historical experience and even just common prudence. The enemy(ies) of the day may warrant disdain, but what might they learn by the day after tomorrow? The Soviet Red Army was a fairly pitiful monster in 1940–41, but by 1943–45 it had acquired sufficient skills, in large enough quantity, to be second to none in the operational conduct of war.[8] The Austrians, Prussians, Russians, and even the British, were never in the same class as the Grande Armée *with Napoleon* in its glory years. But, by the 1810s, the emperor was aging rapidly, his enemies were improving, and France was tiring. An RMA leader can hardly help but teach its enemies the trade of modern war through painful first-hand experience. When belligerents adapt in the duel that is a strategic relationship, they are not required to adapt systematically, let alone elegantly. France's enemies learned that the French way in warfare was markedly more lethal when it was commanded personally by the emperor. Ergo, it was a sound principle to try to fight those French armies, or detached corps, that were not directed personally by the great man.[9] For a similar thought, quite early in the Soviet–German war of 1941–45 the Red Army discovered that it was far more competitive with the Östheer when it contested urban areas, than when it tried to manoeuvre in open terrain with mechanised forces.

It may be unnecessary to say that strategy can be approached as a duel only because 'war does not consist of a single short blow'.[10] Clausewitz explains further that 'If war consisted of one decisive act, or a set of simultaneous decisions, preparation would tend toward totality, for no omission could ever be rectified.' Only in the nuclear case among the three RMAs examined above might military action effectively have 'consisted of one decisive act', which, by definition, would have precluded adaptive strategic behaviour. In practice, even the nuclear RMA of the Cold War did not reduce to a final move. Quite the contrary occurred. During four and a half decades, the superpowers conducted virtual combat, in prominent part through the agency of an arms competition.[11] Considered as a duel, that competition was executed in exceedingly slow motion and often maladaptively. In this case, at least, constructivism has much to recommend it as a guide to understanding. Each superpower duelled according to its own distinct notion of what would constitute effective strategic behaviour. Given that neither side could secure a tight empirical grasp upon the other's strategic force posture five to ten years in the future, invention (guesswork, intelligence) was king.

The different political contexts of our three RMAs – wartime (Napoleonic, First World War) and peacetime competition (nuclear) – obviously drive the

273

character of the strategic duelling behaviour; they did not, however, determine its nature. Strategy and strategic behaviour inherently imply a foe, and that foe implicitly must be assumed to be motivated and able to conduct its affairs adaptively.

3. *RMAs are strategic behaviour.* Because there is a unity to strategic behaviour across time, technology, and adversaries,[12] and because RMAs must be considered to be expressions of that behaviour, it has to follow that strategically RMAs comprise but a single class of historical events. As noted already, the nature, purpose, and working of RMAs essentially are unchanging across the centuries. The detail of each RMA narrative will be unique, but they have in common the nature and structure of strategy that we explained in Chapters 4–5. The theory of strategy is the toolbox necessary to reveal secrets about the occurrence, course, and outcome of any particular RMA. Once strategy's multidimensionality and holistic functioning for total effect on behalf of policy (wise or foolish) are clearly understood, then a great deal of what otherwise would be mysterious can be opened for scrutiny.

In strategic affairs generally, contenders seek, and sometimes find, relative strengths to offset relative weaknesses. As a subset of strategic phenomena, the same judgement applies to the conduct of an RMA. In 1813 and 1814 Napoleon's operational genius and personal leadership frequently, but far from reliably, could offset the inexperience and numerical shortage of his troops. Ultimately, thinking of the entire 1812–15 period, strategy's political, ethical, logistical, and geographical dimensions, along with militarily better educated foes and the net effect of the sheer ravages of time, shaped a strategic context fatally nonpermissive of the emperor's many errors. He might survive his own failing health for a while, and possibly (again for a while) the political enervation of his French patrimony, but his cause was unlikely to endure when, incredibly, he placed Marshal Ney in battlefield command at Waterloo.[13] Now, had the Prussians not been closing to renew contact at Waterloo, having declined to retreat away from Wellington's coalition army after defeat at Ligny, had the emperor been physically fit, and had Wellington not been a superb battlefield general, then even Marshal Ney might not have succeeded in ruining the French Army. But strategy, we insist, is both multidimensional and historically is played out only once in circumstances unique to time and place.

When considering the strategic historical course of a particular RMA – say, the Napoleonic – scholars can have difficulty distinguishing the contingent from the structural and hence allegedly probable. The detail of Napoleon's rise and fall is rich in 'accidents', up to a point. However, the political context of France in the 1790s was a land ripe for exploitation by ambitious military talent. Similarly, it was not inevitable that Napoleon's career must yield to the outcome of decisive battles in June 1815. *It was always* strongly probable, though, that the emperor's reach eventually would exceed his grasp in circumstances from which there could be no recovery. A proclivity to overreach was built in to the Napoleonic RMA on its human and command dimensions. This eponymous revolution would always be asked to deliver more strategic effect than was achievable, simply because that was the character of its imperial director. No matter how often he could scramble to victory against the odds, he was certain to roll the iron dice once too often.

Failure to register the point that RMAs are strategic behaviour, and need to be assessed as such, is akin to confusing battles and even campaigns with war. For an RMA massively to enhance net military effectiveness, let alone the kind of strategic effectiveness of which political success is made, it has to work well enough across the board of strategy's dimensions. The Napoleonic operational instrument can appear glittering, the infantry- or artillery-led agency of 1917–18 will impress, and the military–technical accomplishments of nuclear-missile technology inspire awe. But the structural fact of an adversary, the likelihood that it will have time it can use, and the inconvenient fact that an RMA is embedded in a prospective or actual conflict, have to mean that narrow focus on what RMAs can offer is sure to mislead. Theorists and officials forearmed with the cannon lore that RMAs are examples of strategy in action should avoid the grievous error of (strategic) context-free analysis. The full context for that analysis must include such strategic dimensions as, inter alia, the human, the political, the ethical, the geopolitical, and the temporal.

4. *Strategy need not be chaotic.* Many an insight becomes a fallacy if pushed too far. Of recent years, the proposition that it is the nature of war to be chaotic is an example of just such an insightful fallacy. A misreading of Clausewitz on the importance of friction, chance, risk, and uncertainty in war,[14] combined with an appreciation of the chaotic conditions of actual combat, has encouraged a newly orthodox view that chaos rules in war and, in reality, over strategy. This view is mistaken, though it does rest upon the valid points that war (and strategy) is complex, is often really or apparently nonlinear, and betrays chaotic features. Undetectable (perhaps because one was not looking) changes in initial conditions may lead to thoroughly unpredictable consequences well downstream.

Without denying the possibility of the occurrence of a genuinely chaotic course of events, this study has not found the ideas of nonlinearity and chaos powerfully helpful as aids to strategic historical explanation. Even the notion of complexity, though objectively true of the structure of strategy and the conduct of war, has sharp limits as a tool for understanding. Certainly, in principle, complexity in the form of strategy's many dimensions suggests fungibility.[15] For example, a belligerent disadvantaged in generalship or strategic geography may seek compensation in the fighting quality of well-trained troops, in new weapons technologies, or in superior machinery and processes for policy- or strategy-making. But our case studies did reveal that there are dimensional deficits for which adequate compensation cannot be found, at least it was not found in the reality of the historical record ('virtual' historians can always invent 'what ifs …').

Strategy posits a purposeful relationship between means and political ends. If strategic history truly were nonlinear and chaotic, then chance would rule. While chance plays a role, most assuredly it does not rule, and it may not even often reign, in the world of strategic behaviour. Napoleonic France, Wilhelmine Germany, and the USSR – the three great losers in the case studies developed earlier – were none of them in any serious sense unlucky to be defeated. The details of June 1815, November 1918, and November 1989, were not predicted or predictable. But, with substantial, if less than total, hindsight–foresight, we can readily identify systemic causes for the shortage in overall strategic effect that translated as eventual defeat. All three of our 'losers' were riding for the fall that they experienced. No single chance-driven event, or even a clutch of them, produced their demise. In each case, enduring weaknesses on the political dimension of strategy meant that the eventual loser, notwithstanding some period of relative advantage, always would find itself seriously physically disadvantaged. Also, it should be noted that in all three cases, notwithstanding the differences in technological context between the 1810s, the 1910s, and 1980s, it was the European *continental* protagonist that lost. The belligerent that was significantly a maritime coalition was the victor in 1815, 1918, and 1989 (not to mention 1945). Geostrategically regarded, imperial France, imperial Germany, and the USSR could none of them employ the RMAs of their day to such comprehensive and persisting benefit in coercion or war on contiguous land as to offset sufficiently the advantages of insularity to their leading foes.[16] We noted that even in the technologically rarified case of the nuclear RMAs of the Cold War, the old-fashioned-seeming geographical dimension of strategy played vital roles, including that of shaper of nuclear strategy itself (the dilemmas of extending deterrence).

It is no great challenge to find a plausible explanation why what occurred in 1792–1815, 1914–1918, and 1945–1989 was always likely to happen. Balance-of-power and coalition theory provide all the explanation one really needs. France, Germany, and then the USSR invited the (accurate) perception that they were in hegemonic pursuit of a universal imperium. While some small states would bandwagon with the apparently rising hegemon, and a large polity or two temporarily would do likewise for tactical reasons, in the long run the greater powers would be obliged to form, and if needs be re-form, a coalition to oppose the hegemonic menace of the day. It was not predictable that Napoleonic France would last until 1814, and then re-emerge in 1815, or Wilhelmine Germany until 1918, or the USSR until 1991. It was predictable, however, that each of these polities would lose the grand competition upon which it was embarked. This is not to pretend that the fall of the USSR was widely predicted; it is to claim, though, that it has to be admitted that when viewed in retrospect the decline and demise of the Soviet empire was hardly 'chaotic'.

War and strategy may be a 'gamble', as Clausewitz affirms,[17] but it is not a gamble in which the odds are the same for all principal possible outcomes.

The coalitions that eventually beat Napoleonic France, imperial Germany, and the USSR, outperformed their enemies strategically, which is to say in net total strategic effect. Strategically speaking, Napoleonic France, Wilhelmine Germany, and the USSR deserved to lose. We cannot permit complexity–nonlinearity–chaos theory to obscure the fundamental point that the outcomes to the three great conflicts in our case studies were each the intended consequence of effort purposefully applied across all of strategy's dimensions. In the old Soviet-era phrase, 'it was no accident ...' that 1815, 1918, and 1989 (–91) recorded the strategic verdicts that they did. Strategic history humours chaos, but it is not pervasively chaotic. If, oxymoronically, 'chaos rules', strategy is impossible.

5. *Military performance only has to be good enough.* Military effectiveness is a relational variable; even performances notably flawed in absolute, and even some relative, terms, still may prove good enough. For the most obvious of examples from among our cases, consider the much-chequered history of the British Army from 1914 to 1918. From being far too small and ill-equipped for large-scale continental warfare in 1914–15, the BEF evolved by mid- to late 1918 into the most effective instrument of land warfare extant. The learning curve was long, bloody, and materially and financially hugely expensive. It is not surprising that few historians of the Great War are able to resist the temptation to grade negatively the generalship displayed and possibly the fighting power of the troops. With such an exercise authors inadvertently perform serious disservice to their readers. It is all too easy to forget that the flawed BEF of, say, 1916, 1917, and 1918, was not required to pass some test whose standard for a good grade was near perfection. Rather did the BEF of those years have to perform effectively – which is to say, in practice, through attritional combat – against a flawed German Army. The adaptive enemies who duel, or wrestle, are each apt to commit blunders and to be harassed by what collectively is termed friction. Although the BEF of 1918 was a very good army by an (irrelevant) absolute standard, there is no doubt that its campaign performance from August to November was much flattered by the fact that the enemy frequently could offer only a shadow of its former military effectiveness.

Strategic performance, even if good enough to secure victory, cannot really be judged 'good enough' if the success secured is Pyrrhic in character. Many people soon after the grim event, as well as today, were less impressed by the skill with which Sir Douglas Haig's BEF discovered and practised the RMA of the First World War, than they were by the human, political, social, and economic costs of the victory achieved. More recently, the accusation of putative Pyrrhic victory always lurked, explicitly or implicitly, close to the subject of nuclear strategy. Regardless of the degree of optimism in the operational assumptions, no-one ever invented a nuclear strategy in the Cold War that reliably would have avoided casualties on such a scale as to delegitimise victory. For reasons of the believed need to enhance credibility for extended deterrence, idea after idea was pursued in the United Stated for the ever more constrained employment of nuclear weapons.[18] Both the course of contemporary public debate and sombre reflection many years on point to the merit in the judgement that nuclear use on anything beyond a truly token scale most probably would have been a self-defeating enterprise. This author is not at all content with that logic for the nuclear RMA of the Cold War. Unfortunately, perhaps, if nuclear weapons were to help keep the peace after 1945, foreign and military policy required operationally sensible-seeming, responsible strategies for the actual use of those weapons.[19] Similarly, Pyrrhic victory or not for European civilisation, I judge that the Great War waged to deny European hegemony to imperial Germany was a necessary conflict.[20]

The first of our RMA case studies recorded distinctly imperfect military performances by Allied forces, a fact happily overborne by the yet more flawed military (inter alia) performance of the French. The final coalition's military power, inelegant though some of it remained in relation to the highest standards of the day, certainly was good enough in its strategic coercive effect to enforce and then police a generally tolerable new international order.[21] The same cannot be said of the military performances in our second case study. It may seem unjust to blame the soldiers of 1914–18 rather than the somewhat miscast statesmen of 1919 and after for the course and consequences of the interwar period. Nonetheless, the events of the 1920s and 1930s were very much the product of the way in which the war had been conducted and the manner in which it was concluded. The RMAed Allied forces of 1917–18 that proved good enough to defeat the RMAed German Army of those years, were only able to do so at a human cost that all but disarmed those who must strive to police a post-war order. Neither side in the Great War was good enough in the field to be able to win at a price that would not mortgage the long-term prospect for peace with security. In the Cold War, the strategic performance of the West proved good enough because its nuclear plans were never brought to operational trial.[22] The paradox was, and remains, that to be politically effective nuclear weapons require an operationally plausible rationale.[23]

6. *Continuity in strategic history.* It may seem contradictory, or at least paradoxical, to suggest that a proper grasp of change in strategic history can rest only upon the firm foundation of an understanding of history's continuities. The bedrock of that understanding lies in the comprehension of strategy's unchanging nature, purpose and dimensions. As we can attempt to assess the character, role, and performance of a Scipio Africanus or an Alexander of Macedon, as well as a Douglas Haig or a Winston Churchill, because they were all human, so we can examine conflicts in all periods with a single, common, toolbox of strategic ideas and analysis. The theory of strategy presented in this book applies to all periods, all rivals, and all technologies. It is a principal merit of this general theory that it does not permit the scholar or prophet-advocate of RMA to focus unwisely strictly upon the dimensions of strategy

278

wherein large discontinuities are projected. Our theory of strategy includes the proposition that every dimension always is in play, though the relative importance of, say, geography, ethics, or technology, must vary with historical context.

The three great RMAs, transformations perhaps, examined in detail in Chapters 6–8 collectively impress at least as much for the continuities they reveal in strategic history as for their measure of radical change. Each RMA was the servant of high policy, whether or not the agents of revolution kept that inalienable fact clearly in sight and whether or not they performed well. A miserable political record proved the undoing of Napoleonic France, as it was also of imperial Germany and the Soviet Union. Neglect of the whole story of strategy, with its historically continuous themes (dimensions or elements), encourages the view that a particular realm of advantage (e.g. technology, ethics, genius in command, alleged incompetence of the enemy) will be decisive. Our case studies demonstrate that none of strategy's dimensions can be ignored safely. Let us consider just one class of example, the ethical.

The victors in all three case studies benefited in practical ways from what can be called a moral advantage. This is not to offer canonical judgement, but rather simply to claim that the foes of the French Empire, the German Empire, and the Soviet Union all succeeded in seizing and holding the moral high ground. Each of these three great losers, over a period of two centuries, was portrayed plausibly by its enemies as posing an intolerable menace to right (enough) conduct. Napoleon was not trusted to abide by any agreement. Imperial Germany was believed to pose a hegemonic threat to the security of other polities. The USSR lent itself to American (inter alia) description, though some said caricature, as an evil empire. Whether or not such hostile portraiture was fully deserved, it was certainly strategically damaging. From the Truman Doctrine to the Reagan Doctrine, the leading edge of the US competitive drive against Soviet imperialism was expressed as *Moralpolitik*, not *Realpolitik*.[24] Scholars of RMAs who focus heavily upon operational or technical issues can easily miss the political significance of a state's failure to compete effectively on the ethical dimension of strategy. The point is not that right conduct wins because it is right. First, judgement as to what conduct is 'right' often is legitimately subject to contention, while, second, the concern here is not with the rightness or otherwise of state behaviour, but rather with its strategic effectiveness. Our claim is that it is one of history's continuities that states suffer strategic disadvantage if they affront persistently and unduly egregiously the values, and therefore broadly the interests, of other polities and peoples. It is rarely wise carelessly to help the enemy mobilise its will to fight.

The history developed above shows clearly the limited value of advanced technology as a source of strategic effectiveness.[25] One hesitates to praise Stalin's distinctly self-excusing concept of war's 'permanently operating factors', but the idea does have merit.[26] Provided belligerents are militarily approximately of the same generation, military advantages and disadvantages will tend to even out over a period, leaving the contest to be decided by the issue of quantity rather than quality. Moreover, the issue of relative quantity (who had the bigger battalions?) is likely to be driven by political and moral (or ideological) matters. Technology is important to strategy, but then so also is everything else. Poor policy and ethical affronts have doomed more bids for empire and hegemony than has inadequate military technology.

7. *Déjà-vu all over again: an information-led RMA.* As usual, the immortal words of Yogi Berra hit the spot. Whether or not an American I-led RMA currently is under way, we know that whatever it is that is happening on the technological frontier of military power is subject to the complex, but still decipherable, workings of strategy. To risk giving gratuitous offence, authors of some of the more technically committed RMA advocacy literature can be likened to monkeys making chess moves and parrots repeating clever phrases. The monkeys and parrots may well perform accurately, but they will not understand the meaning of what they are doing. In his book, *Lifting the Fog of War*, which combines arguable history with a great deal of technical enthusiasm, Admiral Bill Owens nonetheless says many sensible things about the importance of sound policy, suitable organisation, rigorous training, proper doctrine, and so forth. The problem is that he, and others who share his quintessentially technical view of military affairs, fail to convince even when they strive carefully to present the whole picture. For example, Owens follows a paragraph which has expounded wisely on the proposition that '[t]echnology alone is not enough ...', with the claim that 'the technological base of the Revolution in Military Affairs remains the central component of a transformed twenty-first-century American fighting force and the best hope for the United States to keep its armed forces superior to any other nation's'.[27] Owens' difficulty is that he does not seem to understand how strategy works, or fails to work. Should he ever read this book he would learn that strategy has many dimensions, none of which strictly, ever, can be labelled 'the central component', save perhaps the political – which provides meaning for the whole enterprise. His claim that 'the technological base of the Revolution in Military Affairs' is such a component would be more plausible were it applied to the nuclear RMA, but even in that extreme case a focus on the technological competition would risk missing a great deal of the plot. The action that matters most in strategic history, to repeat an all too familiar refrain, is the political and the human. It is wise to deny the status of 'central component' to any of strategy's dimensions, lest inadvertently one slips into commission of the reductionist fallacy (better, even 'decisive', weapons win wars, 'the longer purse wins', and so forth). Strategy does not reduce to control by any single element. Even a nuclear arsenal cannot deter existentially. An intended deterree first must decide that it is deterred. There is no evasion

of the human dimension, with its literally incalculable political and cultural content.[28]

The proposition that an I-led RMA is under way is neither true nor false, but is likely to mislead and to educate in roughly equal measure. If recent strategic history records a seismic shift it is more in the realm of geopolitics than the character, let alone the nature, of war. This fact has contributed to the apolitical and astrategic bias evident in the great RMA debate of the 1990s. Not for the first time in the twentieth century, American commentators confused an interregnum, or interwar period, with the end of seriously strategic history.[29] The most active years of the RMA debate in the United States postdated the end of the Soviet imperium, yet predate any general willingness to acknowledge the rise of China as the basis for the world's next grand geostrategic struggle.[30] (To repeat, although terrorism, even terrorism with weapons of mass destruction (WMD), is the fashionable 'threat of the day', it is an aside to strategic history, not the main event.) As Williamson Murray and MacGregor Knox conclude in the summative essay to a superb collection of historical studies, an RMA requires belief in a particular real enemy as a strategic challenge; in addition, they advise that history reveals the need an RMA for intellectual coherence.[31]

Thus far, at least, the proclaimed American RMA has lacked convincing targets and has betrayed anything but intellectual coherence. Those debating RMA have not agreed on what it is they are arguing about – recall the discussion in Chapter 2 about revolutions in military affairs, military revolutions, and military–technological revolutions, to cite only the leading categories – or on whether, absurdly, the nature as well as the character of war is at issue. Because form usually follows function, the absence of clear vision in the 1990s about future strategic function(s) translated into open season for technocrats. Unencumbered by strategic guidance worthy of the name, the US defence community rallied gladly around the flag of RMA as the *Big Idea* of the day. Naturally enough, the services rallied to protect their most valued force structure and preferred major platforms from potentially menacing interpretations of the implications of an I-led RMA. Overall, however, the American RMA debate was sustained by officials and theorists more than content to limit their attention to second-order military–technical topics.[32]

A defence community lacking meaningful policy guidance is likely to think and behave as culturally comes naturally to it.[33] In the American case, the national history shows an unmistakable preference for technical over political solutions and problems. Indeed, many of those who happily debated RMA matters in the 1990s seemed blissfully unaware that they were discussing answers to unposed questions. This is not surprising. Even when American officials and scholars broadly knew what they were about and why, they still sought in the Cold War to reduce political and strategic issues to terms susceptible to technical, even calculable, answer. Modern deterrence and arms control theory, and some attempted US practice thereof, was all but bereft of political and human content.[34] The relational variable of strategic stability literally was calculated with reference to the estimated ability of each side to inflict unacceptable damage upon the other, even after it had suffered a first strike. 'Vulnerability analysis' was the name of the strategic nuclear stability game, at least it was if one adhered to the intellectually dominant RAND school of US defence analysis from the 1950s to the 1990s.[35] Because the frozen politics of East–West relations rendered significant political accommodation impossible in the 1960s and 1970s, arms control was pursued zealously as an attempt at a functional substitute. Inevitably, the outcome was a disappointment. Arms control is about politics, regardless of the apparent elegance of American technocratic theory which infers the contrary. The technocrats flourished similarly in the 1990s in their fascination with the concept of RMA. Again, as in the 1960s and 1970s, there was no active official political or strategic agenda obliging them to address broader matters. In the earlier decades, the great questions of policy and strategy were already settled, while in the 1990s they were undefined and absent from the stage. When people and organisations are not required to think about difficult topics (in this case, policy assumptions and strategy), they will choose to focus on more congenial topics (e.g. a technically defined RMA).

Necessarily, a sense of *déjà vu* pervaded the recent RMA debate. Much of the loudly trumpeted content of this RMA has proceeded by generally evolutionary steps for at least forty years.[36] In addition, as noted immediately above, many Americans have debated their latest 'big organising concept' in an unsurprisingly distinctively American way. They have discussed an I-led RMA as if it could provide military–technical answers to (unasked) political and strategic questions; they have neglected strategy's adversarial dimension until very recently, when, with characteristic enthusiasm, enemies guided by 'asymmetric strategy' have become intellectually fashionable;[37] but they have not recognised convincingly the continuing harm that is self-inflicted by the interservice competition, which reveals hugely separate military cultures. Of no country's military establishment can it be said more truthfully than of the American that it scarcely needs foreign enemies, so bitter are the domestic rivalries. Finally, the pervasive sense of *déjà vu* stems healthily from the appreciation that computer-assisted information-led warfare – expressing an alleged I-led RMA – must work strategically, as did previous RMAs. The theory of strategy developed above cannot be employed directly to provide prediction about the effectiveness of I-led RMAed forces. However, it can be used to educate for holistic understanding of the sources, and hindrances, to that net effectiveness. As has been common throughout the analysis, this last point is thoroughly Clausewitzian.[38]

ENVOI: STRATEGY AND HISTORY

My narrative trajectory, or 'story arc' as they say in Hollywood, has been perilous, embracing a social-scientific concern for theory together with respectful deployment of three historical case studies useful to help test the ideas of general explanation from the theory. Many contestable matters threatened the unity of my vision and grand design. The discussion has related the recent, arguably still unresolved, largely American debate over RMAs (Chapters 2–3), to ideas about complexity, nonlinearity, and chaos (Chapter 4), which fed into consideration of the general theory of strategy (Chapter 5); while all of that was employed lightly as a set of educational aids to help improve comprehension of three candidate historical RMAs (Chapters 6–8). The above comprised an ambitious agenda. By far the most sensible way to approach alleged RMAs is as expressions of strategic behaviour. Because that behaviour is timeless in its fundamental purposes, nature, and structure, possible RMAs from different periods can be explored with a common methodology so that cumulative understanding may be gained.

Two powerful sources of potential mischief for sound analysis require additional comment. First, in his masterly revisionist history of *The Seven Years' War*, Fred Anderson warns us of the need to 'resist the subtler [than seeing this war as a precursor to the main event for Americans in the mid-1770s] tyranny of a hindsight that suggests the creation of the American Republic was somehow foreordained'.[39] In a full explanation of this 'tyranny', or historians' fallacy, as I termed it earlier, Anderson advises that

> Virtually all modern accounts of the [American] Revolution begin in 1763 with the Peace of Paris, the great treaty that concluded the Seven Years' War. Opening the story there, however, makes the imperial events and conflicts that followed the war – the controversy over the Sugar Act and the Stamp Act crisis – into precursors of the Revolution. No matter how strenuous their other disagreements, most modern historians have looked at the years after 1763 not as contemporary Americans and Britons saw them – as a postwar era vexed by unanticipated problems in relations between colonies and metropolis – but as what we *in retrospect* know those years to have been, a pre-Revolutionary period. By sneaking glances, in effect at what was coming next, historians robbed their accounts of contingency and suggested, less by design than inadvertence, that the independence and nationhood of the United States were somehow inevitable.[40]

Because RMA and associated acronyms refer to conceptual conceits rather than actual historical events, they offer prodigious scope to erect theoretical castles on soft sand. Although it is plausible to label Napoleonic, First World War (in 1917–18), and, putatively, nuclear-era *nuclear* warfare 'revolutionary', such can only be a matter of intellectual discretion. Save for 1917–18, the strategic behaviour referred to is not generally contestable in many respects. But whether or not those sequences of behaviour should lend themselves analytically to dissection as datable historical event sequences, notably distinctive from what preceded and postdated them, is a question that cannot be settled definitely by future study.[41] It is a matter of choice.

A second source of political mischief lies in the temptations of endless contingency. Far from being an abstruse academic point, this caveat penetrates to the heart of strategy and to a central intention behind this book. One should not be seduced by the intriguing recognition that just because the future has not happened, and therefore anything is possible, that every possibility is equally likely to occur. It can be difficult to give the ideas, and realities, of friction, complexity, nonlinearity, and even chaos, their proper historical due, without unintentionally overstating their significance. Provided one pays attention to all the elements that contribute to strategic performance, no matter how many dimensions one elects to employ analytically, it is practicable to seek strategic advantage. Of course, friction and chance may upset the schemes of clever strategists and can undo the best efforts of highly competent armies. Nonetheless, strategic competition and war itself are not realms of pure chance, despite the ease with which Clausewitz can be misread (or more probably, mis-skimmed) to that effect. The playing field of conflict is not level for all players and the differences rarely can be attributed simply to bad luck. For example, armies that do not train hard are not likely to fight well, almost regardless of the quality of their weapons or the operational skills of their generals. Small and relatively elite armies need to win rapidly, or hastily change their recruitment and training practices, before larger foes raise their game sufficiently and win by attrition.

The temptations of contingency are not confined to the realms of friction and chance. Historians can spin alternative narratives with the potent formula of 'what if ...', almost as speedily as advocates and critics of new ideas for ballistic missile defence can outline plausible-looking graphics and claims in 'PowerPoint' presentation. Too often, historians who indulge in virtual history forget that in the very potency of their initial premise lie the roots of the folly of the whole enterprise. The hypothesised contingency that has dramatically alternative, linear or apparently nonlinear, consequences could not have happened in isolation. Virtual history is of practical necessity only a highly selective virtuality; its scholarly perpetrator cannot know what else ought to be altered or what the holistic consequences of those required changes would have been. In other words, the 'what ifs ...' of virtual history are self-indulgent nonsense by people who should know better.

The professionals at the 'what if ...' game are those scholars and officials who must look to the future. Senior defence persons delight in referring to 'the foreseeable future', but the truth is that, although we know how to weight the odds against our being seriously strategically disadvantaged, there is no way in which the future can be foreseen. Visions of the strategic future typically are not in short supply. Unassisted by the press of bloody events, actual or believed imminent, however, those visions at best will appear materially as evolutionary innovation much as usual. The several geographically specialised mechanisations of the 1920s and 1930s, though notching up impressive material, conceptual, and organisational achievements in different countries, all required combat validation in war (by some polity) and financial support on a new scale if they were to be realised. The event sequences examined here were each, in a vital sense, waiting to occur in a form that attracts the label RMA. Those caveats granted, still there were many and powerful reasons, principally pertaining to rapidly evolving political and strategic contexts, why these three RMAs should explode into life when, where, and in the manner that they did. To challenge the historical probability of the RMAs of the 1790s–1800s, 1914–18, and 1945–89, it would not suffice simply to alter a contingency here and a contingency there. Historical actors frequently, perhaps usually, fail to predict at all accurately the consequences of action and inaction, when indeed they even attempt so to do, but that fact does not deny the authority of strategy. Much about strategy is predictable, always barring the occurrence of some quite 'out of the box' happening. Chance, friction, genuinely chaotic sequences of events which upset rational *and reasonable* expectations, can happen, but by definition they do not happen regularly and the evidence tells us that strategic history does not produce truly random outcomes.

The historical dialogue between the influence of underlying persisting trends and the power of contingency has nowhere been expressed so poignantly in recent scholarship as in the book by Fred Anderson quoted above. The Seven Years' War emerged on a political and strategic stage that had been set for more than a century by three previous major wars and countless raids and skirmishes. Accidents of human character and events in 1754 bearing upon the Ohio Country produced the war, but that is not the whole story. A common dilemma besets the social scientist who seeks theory, a logic of general explanation, from events – in this instance, what have been termed RMAs – and the historian who tries to understand the uniqueness of those events. Should one emphasise origins and causes, or triggers? The hunt for origins is potentially a journey without authoritative end, while the quest for triggers, or fingers on triggers, deprives analysis of strategic historical context and meaning. Unless one studies allegedly pre- and post-RMA eras, how can one know that an RMA warrants the revolutionary title? Anderson obliges his readers to take a bold look back before the Revolutionary War in ways empathetic to the actors in the 1760s. Those people were not self-consciously the agents of anything more radical than endeavour by some measured acts of rebellion to prevent new disadvantages in the terms of imperial membership.

Anderson highlights in a historically concrete manner much of the subject area of complexity–nonlinearity–chaos which has been of interest here. Undoubtedly, his words lend themselves to different interpretations. I read them as useful recognition of the potency of contingency, especially on strategy's human dimension, and as being in no way challenging to the theory of strategy.

> There could hardly be a clearer example of a historical moment when events vastly incommensurate with human intention begin to follow from the efforts of an individual to cope with a situation than this otherwise ordinary Wednesday morning in May 1754 [when wounded French prisoners were massacred by George Washington's Indian allies]. Nothing could have been further from Washington's mind, or more alien to the designs of the men who had entrusted him with troops and ordered him to the Ohio Valley, than beginning a war. Neither he nor his masters imagined that they were setting in train events that would destroy the American Empire of France. Much less could they have foreseen that a stunning Anglo-American victory would lead to yet another war, one that would destroy Britain's empire and raise in its ruins the American republic that Washington himself would lead.
>
> So extraordinary indeed were the events that followed from this callow officer's acts and hesitations that we must begin by shaking off the impression that some awesome destiny shaped occurrences in the Ohio Valley during the 1750s. For in fact the presence of French troops and forts in the region, the determination of Virginia's colonial governor to remove them, and the decisions of the French and British governments to use military force to back up the manoeuvring of the colonists deep in the American interior all resulted from the unusually powerful coincidence of some very ordinary human factors: ambition and avarice, fear and misunderstanding, miscalculation and mischance. How such a combination could produce a backwoods massacre is not, perhaps, hard to imagine. How that particular butchery gave rise to the greatest war of the eighteenth century, however, is less easy to explain.[42]

But explain it he does. Easily or not, plausibly or not, and certainly in different ways, historians and social scientists can explain anything and everything. In earlier chapters we have explained how the French Royal Army (with some volunteer assistance) at Valmy in 1792 was transformed into the temporarily peerless Grande Armée of 1805–6; how the foot, horse, and guns of 1914 became the genuinely combined-arms, firepower-heavy, instrument of 1918; and how an age of atomic plenty saw a global audit of literally a handful of American nuclear weapons grow into a thoroughly operationally unusable all-country total inventory well in excess of 50,000 weapons (of all sizes and yields, for all purposes) by the mid-1980s. In each of these cases of RMA it can be argued that the military context came to dominate the political.

The French Army of the Revolution and Empire needed war both to pay for past wars and to satisfy the personal needs of its soldiers (and leaders). By 1917–18, the cost of the Great War had become so enormous that its military demands at least appeared to demote the political context to that of a function supporting the belligerency. As for the nuclear RMA of the Cold War, the rival superpowers constructed and operated competing nuclear arsenals for eminently rational motives which yet appeared for a long period to have scant connection with their political context. As we have noted, the modern theory of arms control was invented and practised by the United States, though not by the USSR, precisely as an intended alternative to an unattainable political accommodation.

Writers who seek dramatic contingency are not usually disappointed. Not implausibly, the Napoleonic RMA can be attributed in large part to a necessarily unique genius. The RMA of the First World War, by a more indirect logic of contingent triggering, might just be attributed significantly to that weakness of character of Kaiser Wilhelm II which permitted the July crisis of 1914 to unfold as it did. The RMA of the Cold War could be traced to the scientific contingency of Otto Frisch and Rudolf Peierls' calculation in February 1940 of the encouragingly modest mass of fissile material required for achievement of criticality to produce a self-sustaining chain reaction for an atomic bomb. The subsequent discovery of plutonium (as a practical alternative to enriched uranium) as an artificial element similarly was a significant triggering event. All of these examples are, of course, grossly reductionist and wholly inadequate in different ways as stand-alone keys to reveal the mysteries of strategic history.

Undue focus on RMAs leads to reductionism, while overmuch contextuality sees the nominal RMA subject disappear into the general warp and woof of the course of history as usual. The tight Clausewitzian definition of strategy, and the provision of a clear general theory of strategy, as maintained here, should suffice to reconcile the need for focus in historical comparisons with the necessity for context. The message of our case studies, as it is of the recent debate over a possible I-led RMA, is that they derive their meaning from and in terms of strategy, for their net contribution to the strategic effectiveness which is intended to forward the ends of high policy.

The US defence community is distinctly prone to prefer to debate military instruments themselves rather than their possible strategic utility. We conclude this long journey on the positive note of an encouraging comment from a spokesman for the Department of Defense of the second Bush administration. Referring to the general eagerness to know what changes to current and near future defence budgets would be requested, he advised that 'Everyone wants to get the numbers, but you have to do the strategy first, so you have the philosophical underpinning before you start spending money.'[43] The value of an RMA can be assessed, and is tested, ultimately only according to strategic criteria, and those criteria all relate to success or otherwise in the support of policy. Policy and strategy are difficult to do well and very few people formally are charged to attempt to do them. It follows that almost everyone in a defence community is encouraged by self-interest and other natural inclinations to focus narrowly on the means of strategy rather than its ends. The RMA debate of the 1990s is recent proof of the validity of this judgement. Here I have sought to stimulate a broader discussion on whether, why, when, how, and with what consequences, RMAs happen.

NOTES

1. See Williamson Murray and Allan R. Millett (eds), *Military Innovation in the Interwar Period* (Cambridge: Cambridge University Press, 1996); Williamson Murray and Allan R. Millett, *A War To Be Won: Fighting the Second World War* (Cambridge, MA: Harvard University Press, 2000), ch. 1; and, yet again, Williamson Murray, 'May 1940: Contingency and Fragility of the German RMA', in McGregor Knox and Murray (eds), *The Dynamics of Military Revolution, 1300–2050* (Cambridge: Cambridge University Press, 2001), pp. 154–74. Anyone in peril of being overimpressed by claims for RMA in the interwar years should be duly sobered by J. P. Harris, 'The Myth of Blitzkrieg', *War in History*, 2, 3 (November 1995), pp. 335–52; and Stephen Biddle, 'The Past as Prologue: Assessing Theories of Future Warfare', *Security Studies*, 8, 1 (Autumn 1998), pp. 1–74.
2. For example, as developed in Harold Deutsch and Dennis Showalter (eds), *What If? Strategic Alternatives of WWII* (Chicago, IL: Emperor's Press, 1997); Niall Ferguson (ed.), *Virtual History: Alternatives and Counterfactuals* (London: Picador, 1997); and Robert Cowley (ed.), *What If?* (London: Macmillan, 2000).
3. Donald Kagan and Fredrick W. Kagan, *While America Sleeps: Self-Delusion, Military Weakness, and the Threat to Peace Today* (New York: St Martin's Press, 2000), pp. 2, 20–1, is usefully sceptical of the concept of the peer competitor.
4. See J. F. Lazenby, *Hannibal's War: A Military History of the Second Punic War* (Warminister: Aris & Phillips, 1978); Alvin Bernstein, 'The Strategy of a Warrior–State: Rome and the Wars Against Carthage, 264–201 BC', in Williamson Murray, MacGregor Knox, and Bernstein (eds), *The Making of Strategy: Rulers, States, and War* (Cambridge: Cambridge University Press, 1994), esp. pp. 76–83; and Nigel Bagnall, *The Punic Wars: Rome, Carthage and the Struggle for the Mediterranean* (London: Pimlico, 1999), pt 4.
5. Robert H. Scales, Jr, *Future Warfare Anthology* (Carlisle, PA: US Army War College, n.d.), p. 36.
6. Ibid.
7. Carl von Clausewitz, *On War*, trans. Michael Howard and Peter Paret (Princeton, NJ: Princeton University Press, 1976 [1832]), pp. 75 (emphasis in original), 77.
8. David M. Glantz and Jonathan House, *When Titans Clashed: How the Red Army Stopped Hitler* (Lawrence: University Press of Kansas, 1995); and Horst Boog and others, *Germany and the Second World War: Vol. IV, The Attack on the Soviet Union* (Oxford: Oxford University Press, 1998). In *A War to Be Won*, Murray and Millett offer unstinting praise of the Soviet way in war by 1944. They conclude persuasively that 'the Soviets displayed the greatest abilities at the operational level of war. From [operation] Bagration, which took out virtually all of Army Group Center in Summer 1944, to the operations that destroyed German forces in East Prussia and Poland in winter 1945, Soviet commanders exhibited outstanding capabilities in deception, planning, and the conduct of

operations. Their victories were far superior to anything the Germans had achieved early in the war' (p. 683).

9. The fragility of Napoleon's command system is emphasised repeatedly in David Chandler, *The Campaigns of Napoleon* (London: Weidenfeld & Nicolson, 1967), e.g. pp. 504, 860, 939.

10. Clausewitz, *On War*, p. 79.

11. It is far too soon for reliable histories of the East–West Cold War to be written, but the following appear to have merit: Richard Crockatt, *The Fifty Years War: The United States and the Soviet Union in World Politics, 1941–1991* (London: Routledge, 1995); John Lewis Gaddis, *We Now Know: Rethinking Cold War History* (Oxford: Clarendon Press, 1997); and Norman Friedman, *The Fifty-Year War: Conflict and Strategy in the Cold War* (Annapolis, MD: Naval Institute Press, 2000).

12. A proposition argued, perhaps a truth revealed, throughout Colin S. Gray, *Modern Strategy* (Oxford: Oxford University Press, 1999).

13. See Chandler, *Campaigns of Napoleon*, pp. 1022, 1068.

14. See Ch. 4 above.

15. Biddle assigns a key significance to the management of complexity in explaining successful military performance in the twentieth century. He promotes that managerial competence to a controlling importance in historical explanation. His argument against the validity of RMA theories for the past hundred years points instead to the thesis of 'essential continuity', keyed to the vital role of managing the ever increasing complexity of modern warfare: 'Past as Prologue'.

16. The structure of asymmetrical struggle between land powers and sea powers is the central thread to Colin S. Gray, *The Leverage of Sea Power: The Strategic Advantage of Navies in War* (New York: Free Press, 1992). For other examinations in this realm see James Cable, *The Political Influence of Naval Force in History* (London: Macmillan, 1998); Raja Menon, *Maritime Strategy and Continental Wars* (London: Frank Cass, 1998); and Norman Friedman, *Seapower As Strategy: Navies and National Interests* (Annapolis, MD: Naval Institute Press, 2001).

17. Clausewitz, *On War*, p. 85.

18. See Desmond Ball and Jeffrey Richelson (eds), *Strategic Nuclear Targeting* (Ithaca, NY: Cornell University Press, 1986); William C. Martel and Paul L. Savage, *Strategic Nuclear War: What the Superpowers Target and Why* (Westport, CT: Greenwood Press, 1986); Lawrence Freedman, *The Evolution of Nuclear Strategy*, 2nd edn (New York: St Martin's Press, 1989); Janne E. Nolan, *Guardians of the Arsenal: The Politics of Nuclear Strategy* (New York: Basic Books, 1989); and Scott D. Sagan, *Moving Targets: Nuclear Strategy and National Security* (Princeton, NJ: Princeton University Press, 1989). Alas, ideas about nuclear targeting had little operational relevance save in the contexts, first, of command and control, and second, of the enemy's military strategy. On the first, selected from a large literature, see Bruce G. Blair, *Strategic Command and Control: Redefining the Nuclear Threat* (Washington, DC: Brookings Institution, 1989); on the second, see John G. Hines, *Soviet Intentions, 1965–1985: Vol. I, An Analytical Comparison of US–Soviet Assessments During the Cold War*, and *Vol. II, Soviet Post-Cold War Testimonial Evidence* (McLean, VA: BDM Federal, 22 September 1995); and William E. Odom, *The Collapse of the Soviet Union Military* (New Haven, CT: Yale University Press, 1998), ch. 5.

19. The logic of this argument is developed and explained impeccably in Michael Quinlan, *Thinking about Nuclear Weapons* (London: Royal United Services Institute for Defence Studies, 1997), esp. p. 15.

20. 'Those of the generation that won the war, at least in Britain, may have emerged weary and disillusioned, but they had no doubt that the war had to be fought, and that the victory was worthwhile. It is not for us to say that they were wrong': Michael Howard, 'The Great War: Mystery or Error?', *The National Interest*, 64 (Summer 2001), p. 84.

21. The literature on world order(s) has begun to grow of recent years. For examples, see Andrew Williams, *Failed Imagination? New World Orders of the Twentieth Century* (Manchester: Manchester University Press, 1998); and Ian Clark, *The Post-Cold War Order: The Spoils of Peace* (Oxford: Oxford University Press, 2001).

22. Martin van Creveld has had this to say about the long-time search for a 'credible' employment strategy for nuclear weapons: 'Of the numerous theories they [very large numbers of analysts in government, the military, and various think tanks] proposed, not a single one ever showed the slightest promise of achieving its goal': 'Through a Glass, Darkly: Some Reflections on the Future of War', *Naval War College Review*, 53, 4 (Autumn 2000), p. 31. Van Creveld's opinion closely follows that offered by Lawrence Freedman. 'No operational nuclear strategy had yet [to 1981] been devised that did not carry an enormous risk of degenerating into a bloody contest of resolve or a furious exchange of devastating and crippling blows against the political and economic centres of the industrialised world': *Evolution of Nuclear Strategy*, p. 395. Unsurprisingly, Freedman's judgement on US strategy in the 1980s was no more upbeat than was his view of the earlier decades (pp. 432–3).

23. Freedman does not so much deny, as sidestep, this point. 'The standard question, "What do we do if deterrence fails?" is largely beside the point not because failure is inconceivable, but because it is extremely unlikely under current political circumstances': *Evolution of Nuclear Strategy*, p. 432. Well, probably so, but just as many defence analysts are prone to flee to the sanctuary of narrow technical issues, so academic strategic thinkers can be guilty of seeking undue shelter beneath political cover. The plain fact is that the United States required a nuclear strategy and the war plans to give expression to it. It is not especially damning of such strategy and plans to judge them – insofar as they are accessible to outsiders – exceedingly high-risk in character, or even in nature. One might ask how plans for general nuclear war could be otherwise.

24. An argument advanced strongly in Henry Kissinger, *Diplomacy* (New York: Simon & Schuster, 1994), ch. 18. See also Melvyn P. Leffler, *A Preponderance of Power: National Security, the Truman Administration, and the Cold War* (Stanford, CA: Stanford University Press, 1992); and Michael J. Hogan, *A Cross of Iron: Harry S. Truman and the Origins of the National Security State, 1945–1954* (Cambridge: Cambridge University Press, 1998).

25. An argument developed in Colin S. Gray, *Weapons for Strategic Effect: How Important is Technology?* Occasional Paper 21 (Maxwell AFB, AL: Centre for Strategy and Technology, Air War College, January 2001).

26. If the course and outcome of war is driven by 'permanently operating factors', then the negative effect of surprise, as in June 1941, should prove ephemeral. According to Stalin the factors were: '(1) the stability of the rear, (2) the morale of the army; (3) the quantity and quality of divisions; (4) the armaments of the army; (5) the organizational ability of command personnel': David M. Glantz, *The Military Strategy of the Soviet Union: A History* (London: Frank Cass, 1992), p. 174.

27. Bill Owens, *Lifting the Fog of War* (New York: Farrar, Straus, & Giroux, 2000) p. 97.

28. This logic is developed and explained with unequalled clarity in Keith B. Payne, *The Fallacies of Cold War Deterrence and a New Direction* (Lexington: University Press of Kentucky, 2001).

29. See George W. Baer, *One Hundred Years of Sea Power: The US Navy, 1890–1990* (Stanford, CA: Stanford University Press, 1994), ch. 6, 'Treaty Navy, 1922–1930'; and Colin S. Gray, 'Clausewitz Rules, OK? The Future is the Past – with GPS', in Michael Cox, Ken Booth, and Tim Dunne (eds), *The Interregnum: Controversies in World Politics, 1989–1999* (Cambridge: Cambridge University Press, 1999), pp. 161–82.

30. A controversial book by Richard Bernstein and Ross H. Munro remains the strongest extended analysis extant: *The Coming Conflict with China* (New York: Alfred A. Knopf,

1997). Two essays by Aaron L. Friedberg expose the structure of the issue extremely well: 'Will Europe's Past be Asia's Future? *Survival*, 42, 3 (Autumn 2000), pp. 147–59; and 'The Struggle for Mastery in Asia', *Commentary Magazine*, November 2000, <www.commentarymagazine.com/0011/friedberg.html>.

31. Williamson Murray and MacGregor Knox, 'Conclusion: The Future Behind Us', in Knox and Murray, *Dynamics of Military Revolution, 1300–2050*, pp. 192–3.

32. A somewhat parallel point is made by Baer when he discusses the US Navy's problems with War Plan Orange (against Japan) in the 1930s. 'Operations received the main attention because, lacking an answer to the primary question of all strategic thinking – namely, What is the political goal of the military action? – that was all there was for the Navy to think about': *One Hundred Years of Sea Power*, p. 120.

33. This general judgement owes much to the superior analysis in Robert B. Bathhurst, *Intelligence and the Mirror: On Creating an Enemy* (London: SAGE Publications, 1993).

34. A claim well sustained by Keith B. Payne: *Deterrence in the Second Nuclear Age* (Lexington: University Press of Kentucky, 1996); and *Fallacies of Cold War Deterrence and a New Direction*.

35. See Edward S. Quade (ed.), *Analysis for Military Decisions: The RAND Lectures on Systems Analysis* (Chicago: Rand McNally, 1964); Charles J. Hitch, *Decision-Making for Defense* (Berkeley: University of California Press, 1965); Charles J. Hitch and Roland N. McKean, *The Economics of Defense in the Nuclear Age* (New York: Atheneum, 1966); and E. S. Quade and W. I. Boucher (eds), *Systems Analysis and Policy Planning: Applications in Defense* (New York: American Elsevier, 1968).

36. This thought places a fairly fundamental question mark over all RMA theory. A cognate point also has impressed Stephen Biddle: 'To argue, however, that an RMA has not yet been realised but can be achieved by ordinary, gradualist, incremental adaptation is to render moot the RMA thesis as a current-day policy concern. If the policy implications of RMA and non-RMA are the same – gradual incremental adaptation to continuously changing technology – then why does it matter whether we declare the late twentieth-century a "revolution" or not? The importance of the RMA debate lies in its policy consequences; if these are defined away, the distinction degenerates to mere semantics': 'Past as Prologue', p. 51 n124.

37. The most enlightening introduction to this naturally opaque subject is Steven Metz and Douglas V. Johnson II, *Asymmetry and US Military Strategy: Definition, Background, and Strategic Concepts* (Carlisle, PA: Strategic Studies Institute, US Army War College, January 2001).

38. '[A] theory need not be a positive doctrine, a sort of *manual* for action … theory then becomes a guide to anyone who wants to learn about war from books; it will light his way, ease his progress, train his judgement, and help to avoid pitfalls': Clausewitz, *On War*, p. 141 (emphasis in original).

39. Fred Anderson, *Crucible of War: The Seven Years' War and the Fate of Empire in British North America, 1754–1766* (London: Faber & Faber, 2000), p. xxiii.

40. Ibid., pp. xvii–iii (emphasis added).

41. Biddle probably would disagree: 'Past as Prologue'.

42. Anderson, *Crucible of War*, p. 7.

43. Quoted in Thomas E. Ricks and Walter Pincus, 'Pentagon to Abandon Two-War Strategy', *International Herald Tribune*, 8 May 2000, pp. 1, 4.

Select Bibliography

This bibliography is confined to a distinctly short list of those works that were most useful for the book. The listing below is sub-divided into eight subject areas: strategy; chaos, friction, and complexity theory; RMA theory and strategic history; the French Revolution and Empire; the First World War; the nuclear age; information-led warfare; and others.

STRATEGY

Beaufre, André, *An Introduction to Strategy*, trans. R. H. Barry (London: Faber & Faber, 1965).
Betts, Richard K., 'Should Strategic Studies Survive?', *World Politics*, 50, 1 (October 1997), pp. 7–33.
——, 'Is Strategy an Illusion?', *International Security*, 25, 2 (Fall 2000), pp. 5–50.
Booth, Ken, *Strategy and Ethnocentrism* (London: Croom Helm, 1979).
Brodie, Bernard, *War and Politics* (New York: Macmillan, 1973).
Buchan, Alastair (ed.), *Problems of Modern Strategy* (London: Chatto & Windus, 1970).
Clausewitz, Carl von, *On War*, trans. Michael Howard and Peter Paret (Princeton, NJ: Princeton University Press, 1976 [1832]).
Gray, Colin S., *Explorations in Strategy* (Westport, CT: Praeger, 1998).
——, 'Why Strategy is Difficult', *Joint Force Quarterly*, 22 (Summer 1999), pp. 6–12.
——, *Modern Strategy* (Oxford: Oxford University Press, 1999).
Handel, Michael I., *Who is Afraid of Carl von Clausewitz? A Guide to the Perplexed*, 8th edn (Newport, RI: Department of Strategy and Policy, US Naval War College, Summer 1999).
——, *Masters of War: Classical Strategic Thought*, 3rd edn (London: Frank Cass, 2001).
Howard, Michael, 'The Forgotten Dimensions of Strategy', *Foreign Affairs*, 57, 5 (Summer 1979), pp. 975–86.

Jablonsky, David, 'Why Is Strategy Difficult?', in Gary L. Guertner (ed.), *The Search for Strategy: Politics and Strategic Vision* (Westport, CT: Greenwood Press, 1993), pp. 3–45.

Jomini, Antoine Henri de, *The Art of War* (London: Greenhill Books, 1992 [1862]).

Liddell Hart, B. H., *Strategy: The Indirect Approach* (London: Faber & Faber, 1967).

Luttwak, Edward N., *Strategy: The Logic of War and Peace* (Cambridge, MA: Harvard University Press, 1987).

Murray, Williamson, MacGregor Knox, and Alvin Bernstein (eds), *The Making of Strategy: Rulers, States, and War* (Cambridge: Cambridge University Press, 1994).

Paret, Peter (ed.), *Makers of Modern Strategy: From Machiavelli to the Nuclear Age* (Princeton, NJ: Princeton University Press, 1986).

Sun Tzu, *The Art of War*, trans. Ralph D. Sawyer (Boulder, CO: Westview Press, 1994).

Wylie, J. C., *Military Strategy: A General Theory of Power Control*, ed. John B. Hattendorf (Annapolis, MD: Naval Institute Press, 1989 [1967]).

CHAOS, FRICTION, AND COMPLEXITY THEORY

Beaumont, Roger, *War, Chaos, and History* (Westport, CT: Praeger, 1994).

Beyerchen, Alan, 'Clausewitz, Nonlinearity, and the Unpredictability of War', *International Security*, 17, 3 (Winter 1992/93), pp. 59–90.

Cimbala, Stephen J., *Clausewitz and Chaos: Friction in War and Military Policy* (Westport, CT: Praeger, 2001).

Coveney, Peter, and Roger Highfield, *Frontiers of Complexity: The Search for Order in a Chaotic World* (London: Faber & Faber, 1995).

Gleick, James, *Chaos: Making a New Science* (London: Penguin, 1988).

James, Glenn A., *Chaos Theory: The Essentials for Military Application*, Newport Papers 10 (Newport, RI: Center for Naval Warfare Studies, US Naval War College, October 1996).

Kellert, Stephen L., *In the Wake of Chaos: Unpredictable Order in Dynamical Systems* (Chicago, IL: University of Chicago Press, 1993).

Mann, Stephen R., 'Chaos Theory and Strategic Thought', *Parameters*, 22, 3 (Autumn 1992), pp. 54–68.

Nicholls, David, and Tudor D. Tagarev, 'What does Chaos Theory Mean for Warfare?', *Airpower Journal*, 8, 3 (Fall 1994), pp. 48–57.

Ruelle, David, *Chance and Chaos* (London: Penguin, 1993).

Waldrop, M. Mitchell, *Complexity: The Emerging Science at the Edge of Order and Chaos* (London: Penguin, 1994).

Watts, Barry D., *Clausewitzian Friction and Future War*, McNair Paper 52 (Washington, DC: Institute for National Strategic Studies, National Defense University, October 1996).

RMA THEORY AND STRATEGIC HISTORY

Biddle, Stephen, 'The Past as Prologue: Assessing Theories of Future Warfare', *Security Studies*, 8, 1 (Autumn 1998), pp. 1–74.

Black, Jeremy, *A Military Revolution? Military Change and European Society, 1550–1800* (London: Macmillan, 1991).

——, 'Eighteenth-century Warfare Reconsidered', *War in History*, 1, 2 (July 1994), pp. 215–32.

——, 'Revolutionary and Napoleonic Warfare', in Black (ed.), *European Warfare, 1453–1815* (London: Macmillan, 1999), pp. 224–46.

Boemke, Manfred F., Roger Chickering, and Stig Förster (eds), *Anticipating Total War: The German and American Experiences, 1871–1914* (Cambridge: Cambridge University Press, 1999).

Buzan, Barry, and Eric Herring, *The Arms Dynamic in World Politics* (Boulder, CO: Lynne Rienner Publishers, 1998).

Colin, J., *The Transformations of War*, trans. L. H. R. Pope-Hennessy (London: Hugh Rees, 1912).

Corum, James S., *The Roots of Blitzkrieg: Hans von Seeckt and German Military Reform* (Lawrence: University Press of Kansas, 1992).

Creveld, Martin van, *The Transformation of War* (New York: Free Press, 1991).

Downing, Brian M., *The Military Revolution and Political Change: Origins of Democracy and Autocracy in Early Modern Europe* (Princeton, NJ: Princeton University Press, 1992).

Duffy, Michael (ed.), *The Military Revolution and the State, 1500–1800*, Exeter Studies in History 1 (Exeter: University of Exeter, 1980).

Falls, Cyril, *A Hundred Years of War* (London: Gerald Duckworth, 1953).

Freedman, Lawrence, *The Revolution in Strategic Affairs*, Adelphi Paper 318 (London: International Institute for Strategic Studies, 1998).

Fuller, J. F. C., *Armament and History* (London: Eyre & Spottiswoode, 1946).

Gray, Colin S., *Weapons for Strategic Effect: How Important is Technology?* Occasional Paper 21 (Maxwell AFB, AL: Center for Strategy and Technology, Air War College, January 2001).

Hanson, Victor Davis, *The Wars of the Ancient Greeks and Their Invention of Western Military Culture* (London: Cassell, 1999).

Knox, MacGregor, and Williamson Murray (eds), *The Dynamics of Military Revolution, 1300–2050* (Cambridge: Cambridge University Press, 2001).

Krepinevich, Andrew F., 'Cavalry to Computer: The Pattern of Military Revolutions', *The National Interest*, 37 (Fall 1994), pp. 30–42.

Latham, Andrew, 'Re-imagining Warfare: The "Revolution in Military Affairs"', in Craig A. Snyder (ed.), *Contemporary Security and Strategy* (London: Macmillan, 1999), pp. 210–35.

Liddell Hart, B. H., *The Revolution in Warfare* (London: Faber & Faber, 1946).

MacKenzie, S. P., *Revolutionary Armies in the Modern Era: A Revisionist Approach* (London: Routledge, 1997).

Metz, Steven, and James Kievit, *Strategy and the Revolution in Military Affairs: From Theory to Policy* (Carlisle, PA: Strategic Studies Institute, US Army War College, 27 June 1995).

Millett, Allan R., and Williamson Murray (eds), *Military Effectiveness*, 3 vols (Boston, MA: Allen & Unwin, 1988).

Murray, Williamson, 'Thinking About Revolutions in Military Affairs', *Joint Force Quarterly*, 16 (Summer 1997), pp. 69–76.

Murray, Williamson, and Allan R. Millett (eds), *Military Innovation in the Interwar Period* (Cambridge: Cambridge University Press, 1996).

——*A War to be Won: Fighting the Second World War, 1937–1945* (Cambridge, MA: Harvard University Press, 2000).

Paret, Peter, 'Revolutions in Warfare: An Earlier Generation of Interpreters', in Bernard Brodie, Michael D. Intriligator, and Roman Kolkowicz (eds), *National Security and International Stability* (Cambridge, MA: Oelgeschlager, Gunn & Hain, 1983), pp. 157–69.

Parker, Geoffrey, *The Military Revolution: Military Innovation and the Rise of the West, 1500–1800* (Cambridge: Cambridge University Press, 1988).

Reynolds, Clark G., *Command of the Sea: The History and Strategy of Maritime Empires*, 2 vols (Malabar, FL: Robert E. Krieger Publishing, 1983).

Rogers, Clifford J. (ed.), *The Military Revolution Debate: Readings on the Military Transformation of Early Modern Europe* (Boulder, CO: Westview Press, 1995).

Rosen, Stephen Peter, *Winning the Next War: Innovation and the Modern Military* (Ithaca, NY: Cornell University Press, 1994).

Scales, Robert H., Jr, *Future Warfare Anthology* (Carlisle, PA: US Army War College, n.d.).

Wawro, Geoffrey, *Warfare and Society in Europe, 1792–1914* (London: Routledge, 2000).

THE FRENCH REVOLUTION AND EMPIRE

Chandler, David G., *The Campaigns of Napoleon* (London: Weidenfeld & Nicolson, 1967).

Connelly, Owen, *Blundering to Glory: Napoleon's Military Campaigns*, rev. edn (Wilmington, DE: Scholarly Resources, 1999).

Corrigan, Gordon, *Wellington: A Military Life* (London: Hambledon & London, 2001).

Elting, John R., *Swords Around a Throne: Napoleon's Grande Armée* (New York: Free Press, 1988).

Epstein, Robert M., *Napoleon's Last Victory and the Emergence of Modern War* (Lawrence: University Press of Kansas, 1994).

Esdaile, Charles J., *The Wars of Napoleon* (London: Longman, 1995).

Esposito, Vincent J., and John R. Elting, *A Military History and Atlas of the Napoleonic Wars*, 2nd edn (London: Greenhill Books, 1999).

Griffith, Paddy, *The Art of War of Revolutionary France, 1789–1802* (London: Greenhill Books, 1998).

Luvaas, Jay (ed.), *Napoleon on the Art of War* (New York: Free Press, 1999).

Lynn, John A., *The Bayonets of the Republic: Motivation and Tactics in the Army of Revolutionary France, 1791–94* (Urbana: University of Illinois Press, 1984).

Muir, Rory, *Britain and the Defeat of Napoleon, 1807–1815* (New Haven, CT: Yale University Press, 1996).

Paret, Peter, *Yorck and the Era of Prussian Reform, 1807–1815* (Princeton, NJ: Princeton University Press, 1966).

——, *Understanding War: Essays on Clausewitz and the History of Military Power* (Princeton, NJ: Princeton University Press, 1992).

Rothenberg, Gunther E., *The Art of Warfare in the Age of Napoleon* (Bloomington: Indiana University Press, 1980).

Schroeder, Paul W., 'Napoleon's Foreign Policy: A Criminal Enterprise', *Journal of Military History*, 54, 2 (April 1990), pp. 147–61.

Weller, Jac, *Wellington in the Peninsula, 1808–1814* (London: Greenhill Books, 1992).

Wilkinson, Spenser, *The French Army Before Napoleon* (Aldershot: Gregg Revivals, 1991 [1915]).

——, *The Rise of General Bonaparte* (Aldershot: Gregg Revivals, 1991 [1930]).

THE FIRST WORLD WAR

Bailey, J. B. A., *Field Artillery and Firepower* (Oxford: Military Press, 1987).

——, *The First World War and the Birth of the Modern Style of Warfare*, Occasional Paper 22 (Camberley: Strategic and Combat Studies Institute, Staff College, 1996).

Bidwell, Shelford, and Dominick Graham, *Fire-Power: British Army Weapons and Theories of War, 1904–1945* (London: George Allen & Unwin, 1982).

Bond, Brian (ed.), *The First World War and British Military History* (Oxford: Clarendon Press, 1991).

——, and Nigel Cave (eds), *Haig: A Reappraisal 70 Years On* (London: Leo Cooper, 1999).

Brown, Ian Malcolm, *British Logistics on the Western Front, 1914–19* (Westport, CT: Praeger, 1998).

Chickering, Roger, and Stig Förster (eds), *Great War, Total War: Combat and Mobilization on the Western Front, 1914–1918* (Cambridge: Cambridge University Press, 2000).

Falls, Cyril, *The Great War, 1914–1918* (New York: Perigee, 1959).

Ferguson, Niall, *The Pity of War* (London: Allen Lane, 1998).

French, David, *British Strategy and War Aims, 1914–1916* (London: Allen & Unwin, 1986).

Griffith, Paddy, *Battle Tactics of the Western Front: The British Army's Art of Attack, 1916–18* (New Haven, CT: Yale University Press, 1994).

—— (ed.), *British Fighting Methods in the Great War* (London: Frank Cass, 1996).

Gudmundsson, Bruce I., *Stormtroop Tactics: Innovation in the German Army, 1914–1918* (New York: Praeger, 1989).

Harris, J. P., *Amiens to the Armistice: The BEF in the Hundred Days' Campaign, 8 August–11 November 1918* (London: Brassey's, 1998).

Herwig, Holger H., *The First World War: Germany and Austria–Hungary, 1914–1918* (London: Arnold, 1997).

Lupfer, Timothy T., *The Dynamics of Doctrine: The Changes in German Tactical Doctrine During the First World War*, Leavenworth Papers 4 (Fort Leavenworth, KS: Combat Studies Institute, US Army Command and General Staff College, July 1981).

Palazzo, Albert P., 'The British Army's Counter-Battery Staff Office and Control of the Enemy in World War I', *Journal of Military History*, 63, 1 (January 1999), pp. 55–74.

Prior, Robin, and Trevor Wilson, *Command on the Western Front: The Military Career of Sir Henry Rawlinson, 1914–18* (Oxford: Blackwell, 1992).

——, *Passchendaele: The Untold Story* (New Haven, CT: Yale University Press, 1996).

Sheffield, Gary, *Forgotten Victory: The First World War: Myths and Realities* (London: Headline, 2001).

Strachan, Hew, *The First World War, Vol. 1: To Arms* (Oxford: Oxford University Press, 2001).

Terraine, John, *Douglas Haig: The Educated Soldier* (London: Hutchinson, 1963).

Travers, Timothy, *The Killing Ground: The British Army, the Western Front and the Emergence of Modern Warfare, 1900–1918* (London: Allen & Unwin, 1987).

——, *How the War Was Won: Command and Technology in The British Army on the Western Front, 1917–1918* (London: Routledge, 1992).

Tucker, Spencer C., *The Great War, 1914–18* (London: UCL Press, 1998).

Wilson, Trevor, and Robin Prior, 'Conflict, Technology, and the Impact of Industrialization: The Great War, 1914–18', *Journal of Strategic Studies*, 24, 3 (September 2001), pp. 128–57.

Zabecki, David T., *Steel Wind: Colonel Georg Bruchmüller and the Birth of Modern Artillery* (Westport, CT: Praeger, 1994).

Zuber, Terence, 'The Schlieffen Plan Reconsidered', *War in History*, 6, 3 (July 1999), pp. 262–305.

THE NUCLEAR AGE

Ball, Desmond, and Jeffrey Richelson (eds), *Strategic Nuclear Targeting* (Ithaca, NY: Cornell University Press, 1986).

Blair, Bruce G., *The Logic of Accidental Nuclear War* (Washington, DC: Brookings Institution Press, 1993).

Bobbitt, Philip, Lawrence Freedman, and Gregory F. Treverton (eds), *US Nuclear Strategy: A Reader* (New York: New York University Press, 1989).

Borden, William Liscum, *There Will Be No Time: The Revolution in Strategy* (New York: Macmillan, 1946).

Borgiasz, William S., *The Strategic Air Command: Evolution and Consolidation of Nuclear Forces, 1945–1955* (Westport, CT: Praeger, 1996).

Borowski, Harry R., *A Hollow Threat: Strategic Air Power and Containment Before Korea* (Westport, CT: Greenwood Press, 1982).

Brodie, Bernard, (ed.), *The Absolute Weapon: Atomic Power and World Order* (New York: Harcourt, Brace, 1946).

——, *Strategy in the Missile Age* (Princeton, NJ: Princeton University Press, 1959).

Brzezinski, Zbigniew (ed.), *Promise or Peril: The Strategic Defense Initiative* (Washington, DC: Ethics and Public Policy Center, 1986).

Bundy, McGeorge, *Danger and Survival: Choices About the Bomb in the First Fifty Years* (New York: Random House, 1988).

Carter, Ashton B., John D. Steinbruner, and Charles A. Zraket (eds), *Managing Nuclear Operations* (Washington, DC: Brookings Institution Press, 1987).

Cochrane, Thomas B., William M. Arkin, and Milton M. Hoenig, *Nuclear Weapons Databook: Vol. 1, US Nuclear Forces and Capabilities* (Cambridge, MA: Ballinger, 1984).

Cochrane, Thomas B., and others, *Nuclear Weapons Databook: Vol. IV, Soviet Nuclear Weapons* (New York: Harper & Row, 1989).

Ermath, Fritz, 'Contrasts in American and Soviet Strategic Thought', *International Security*, 3, 2 (Fall 1978), pp. 138–55.

Etzold, Thomas H., and John Lewis Gaddis (eds), *Containment: Documents on American Policy and Strategy, 1945–1950* (New York: Columbia University Press, 1978).

Freedman, Lawrence, *The Evolution of Nuclear Strategy*, 2nd edn (New York: St Martin's Press, 1989).

Friedman, Norman, *The Fifty-Year War: Conflict and Strategy in the Cold War* (Annapolis, MD: Naval Institute Press, 2000).

Gaddis, John Lewis, *We Now Know: Rethinking Cold War History* (Oxford: Clarendon Press, 1997).

——, and others (eds), *Cold War Statesmen Confront the Bomb* (Oxford: Oxford University Press, 1999).

Gray, Colin S., *Strategic Studies and Public Policy: The American Experience* (Lexington: University Press of Kentucky, 1982).

——, *Nuclear Strategy and National Style* (Lanham, MD: Hamilton Press, 1986).

Heuser, Beatrice, 'Warsaw Pact Military Doctrines in the 1970s and 1980s: Findings in the East German Archives', *Comparative Strategy*, 12, 4 (Winter 1994), pp. 437–57.

Hines, John G., *Soviet Intentions, 1965–1985*, 2 vols (McLean, VA: BDM Federal, 22 September 1995).

Holloway, David, *Stalin and the Bomb: The Soviet Union and Atomic Energy, 1939–1956* (New Haven, CT: Yale University Press, 1994).

Jervis, Robert, *The Meaning of the Nuclear Revolution: Statecraft and the Prospect of Armageddon* (Ithaca, NY: Cornell University Press, 1989).

Kaplan, Fred, *The Wizards of Armageddon* (New York: Simon & Schuster, 1983).

Lambeth, Benjamin S., *Selective Nuclear Options in American and Soviet Strategic Policy*, R-2034-DDRE (Santa Monica, CA: RAND, December 1976).

Lebow, Richard Ned, and Janice Gross Stein, *We All Lost the Cold War* (Princeton, NJ: Princeton University Press, 1994).

Odom, William E., *The Collapse of the Soviet Military* (New Haven, CT: Yale University Press, 1998).

Payne, Keith B., *The Fallacies of Cold War Deterrence and a New Direction* (Lexington: University Press of Kentucky, 2001).

Powers, Thomas, *Heisenberg's War: The Secret History of the German Bomb* (Cambridge, MA: Da Capo Press, 2000).

Pry, Peter Vincent, *War Scares: Russia and America on the Nuclear Brink* (Westport, CT: Praeger, 1999).

Rhodes, Richard, *The Making of the Atomic Bomb* (New York: Simon & Schuster, 1986).

——, *Dark Sun: The Making of the Hydrogen Bomb* (New York: Simon & Schuster, 1995).

Rosenberg, David Alan, 'The Origins of Overkill: Nuclear Weapons and American Strategy, 1945–1960', *International Security*, 7, 4 (Spring 1983), pp. 3–71.

Ross, Steven T., *American War Plans, 1945–1950* (London: Frank Cass, 1996).

Sagan, Scott D., *The Limits of Safety: Organizations, Accidents, and Nuclear Weapons* (Princeton, NJ: Princeton University Press, 1993).

Schelling, Thomas C., *The Strategy of Conflict* (Cambridge, MA: Harvard University Press, 1960).

——, *Arms and Influence* (New Haven, CT: Yale University Press, 1966).

Schwartz, Stephen I. (ed.), *Atomic Audit: The Costs and Consequences of US Nuclear Weapons since 1940* (Washington, DC: Brookings Institution Press, 1998).

Trachtenberg, Marc, *History and Strategy* (Princeton, NJ: Princeton University Press, 1991).

Walker, Mark, *German National Socialism and the Quest for Nuclear Power, 1939–1949* (Cambridge: Cambridge University Press, 1989).

Williamson, Samuel R., Jr, and Steven l. Rearden, *The Origins of US Nuclear Strategy, 1945–1953* (New York: St Martin's Press, 1993).

INFORMATION-LED WARFARE

Arquilla, John, and David Ronfeldt, 'Cyberwar is Coming!', *Comparative Strategy*, 12, 2 (April–June 1993), pp. 141–65.

——, *The Advent of Netwar*, MR-789-OSD (Santa Monica, CA: National Defense Research Institute, RAND, 1996).

——, (eds), *In Athena's Camp: Preparing for Conflict in the Information Age*, MR-880-OSD/RC (Santa Monica, CA: RAND, 1997).

Biddle, Stephen, 'Victory Misunderstood: What the Gulf War Tells Us About the Future of Conflict', *International Security*, 21, 2 (Fall 1996), pp. 139–79.

Blaker, James R., *Understanding the Revolution in Military Affairs: A Guide to America's 21st Century Defense*, Defense Working Paper 3 (Washington, DC: Progressive Policy Institute, January 1997).

Campen, Alan D. (ed.), *The First Information War: The Story of Communications, Computers and Intelligence Systems in the Persian Gulf War* (Fairfax, VA: AFCEA International Press, October 1992).

Cebrowski, Arthur K., and John J. Garstka, 'Network-Centric Warfare: Its Origins and Future', US Naval Institute *Proceedings*, 124, 1 (January 1998), pp. 28–35.

Cohen, Eliot A. (Director), *Gulf War Air Power Survey*, 5 vols and Summary (Washington, DC: US Government Printing Office, 1993).

Cooper, Jeffrey R., *Another View of the Revolution in Military Affairs* (Carlisle, PA: Strategic Studies Institute, US Army War College, 15 July 1994).

Gray, Colin S., *The American Revolution in Military Affairs: An Interim Assessment*, Occasional Paper 28 (Camberley: Strategic and Combat Studies Institute, Joint Services Command and Staff College, 1997).

Johnson, Stuart E., and Martin C. Libicki (eds), *Dominant Battlespace Knowledge*

(Washington, DC: Institute for National Strategic Studies, National Defense University, April 1996).

Joint Chiefs of Staff (US), '"Joint Vision 2010": America's Military – Preparing for Tomorrow', *Joint Force Quarterly*, 12 (Summer 1996), pp. 34–49.

Joint Chiefs of Staff (US), *Joint Vision 2020* (Washington, DC: US Government Printing Office, June 2000).

Khalizad, Zalmay, and John White (eds), *Strategic Appraisal: The Changing Role of Information in Warfare* (Santa Monica, CA: RAND, 1999).

Lambeth, Benjamin S., 'The Technology Revolution in Air Warfare', *Survival*, 39, 1 (Spring 1997), pp. 65–83.

Libicki, Martin, *What Is Information Warfare?* (Washington, DC: Institute for National Strategic Studies, National Defense University, August 1995).

——, *The Mesh and the Net: Speculations on Armed Conflict in a Time of Free Silicon* (Washington, DC: Institute for National Strategic Studies, National Defense University, August 1995).

——, 'The Emerging Primacy of Information', *Orbis*, 40, 2 (Spring 1996), pp. 261–74.

Molander, Roger C., Andrew S. Riddile, and Peter A. Wilson, *Strategic Information Warfare: A New Face of War*, MR-661-OSD (Santa Monica, CA: RAND, 1996).

Murray, Williamson, 'Clausewitz Out, Computer In: Military Culture and Technological Hubris', *The National Interest*, 48 (Summer 1997), pp. 57–64.

National Defense Panel, *Transforming Defense: National Security in the 21st Century, Report* (Washington, DC: Department of Defense, December 1997).

Nye, Joseph S., Jr, and William A. Owens, 'America's Information Edge', *Foreign Affairs*, 75, 2 (March/April 1996), pp. 20–36.

O'Hanlon, Michael, *Technological Change and the Future of Warfare* (Washington, DC: Brookings Institution Press, 2000).

Owens, William A., 'The Emerging System of Systems', US Naval Institute *Proceedings*, 121, 5 (May 1995), pp. 35–9.

——, 'The American Revolution in Military Affairs', *Joint Force Quarterly*, 10 (Winter 1995–96), pp. 37–8.

——, *Lifting the Fog of War* (New York: Farrar, Straus, & Giroux, 2000).

Pfaltzgraff, Robert L., Jr, and Richard H. Shultz Jr, (eds), *War in the Information Age: New Challenges for US Security Policy* (Washington, DC: Brassey's, 1997).

Sullivan, Brian R., 'The Future Nature of Conflict: A Critique of the "The American Revolution in Military Affairs" in the Era of Jointery', *Defense Analysis*, 14, 2 (August 1998), pp. 91–100.

Thomas, Keith (ed.), *The Revolution in Military Affairs: Warfare in the Information Age* (Canberra: Australian Defence Studies Centre, 1997).

Toffler, Alvin, and Heidi Toffler, *War and Anti-War: Survival at the Dawn of the 21st Century* (Boston, MA: Little, Brown, 1993).

OTHERS

Anderson, Fred, *Crucible of War: The Seven Years' War and the Fate of Empire in British North America, 1754–1766* (London: Faber & Faber, 2000).

Avant, Deborah D., *Political Institutions and Military Change: Lessons from Peripheral Wars* (Ithaca, NY: Cornell University Press, 1994).

Cohen, Eliot A., and John Gooch, *Military Misfortunes: The Anatomy of Failure in War* (New York: Free Press, 1990).

Creveld, Martin van, *Supplying War: Logistics from Wallenstein to Patton* (Cambridge: Cambridge University Press, 1977).

——, *Fighting Power: German and US Army Performance, 1939–1945* (Westport, CT: Greenwood Press, 1982).

——, *Command in War* (Cambridge, MA: Harvard University Press, 1985).

——, *The Rise and Decline of the State* (Cambridge: Cambridge University Press, 1999).

France, John, *Western Warfare in the Age of the Crusades, 1000–1300* (Ithaca, NY: Cornell University Press, 1999).

Gallagher, Gary W., *The Confederate War* (Cambridge, MA: Harvard University Press, 1997).

Glantz, David M., and Jonathan House, *When Titans Clashed: How the Red Army Stopped Hitler* (Lawrence: University Press of Kansas, 1995).

Gray, Colin S., and Geoffrey Sloan (eds), *Geopolitics, Geography and Strategy* (London: Frank Cass, 1999).

Jones, Archer, *The Art of War in the Western World* (Urbana: University of Illinois Press, 1987).

Keegan, John, *A History of Warfare* (London: Hutchinson, 1993).

Lawrence, T. E., *Seven Pillars of Wisdom: A Triumph* (New York: Anchor, 1991 [1935]).

Peters, Ralph, *Fighting for the Future: Will America Triumph?* (Mechanicsburg, PA: Stackpole Books, 1999).

Wavell, Archibald, *Generals and Generalship* (New York: Macmillan, 1943).

Weigley, Russell F., *The Age of Battles: The Quest for Decisive Warfare from Breitenfeld to Waterloo* (Bloomington: Indiana University Press, 1991).

Weltman, John J., *World Politics and the Evolution of War* (Baltimore, MD: Johns Hopkins University Press, 1995).

Index

An environmentally friendly book printed and bound in England by www.printondemand-worldwide.com